Unmasking Lucy Letby

Unmasking Lucy Letby

The Untold Story of the Killer Nurse

JONATHAN COFFEY
&
JUDITH MORITZ

SEVEN DIALS

First published in Great Britain in 2024 by Seven Dials
An imprint of The Orion Publishing Group Ltd
Carmelite House, 50 Victoria Embankment
London EC4Y 0DZ

An Hachette UK Company

1 3 5 7 9 10 8 6 4 2

A CIP catalogue record for this book is
available from the British Library.

ISBN HB 978 1 3996 2516 6
ISBN TPB 978 1 3996 2517 3
ISBN eBook 978 1 3996 2519 7
ISBN Audio 978 1 3996 2520 3

Typeset by Input Data Services Ltd, Bridgwater, Somerset

Printed in Great Britain by Clays Ltd, Elcograf, S.p.A.

MIX
Paper | Supporting
responsible forestry
FSC® C104740

www.orionbooks.co.uk

Contents

Authors' Note

All of the babies in the Lucy Letby case have been given legal anonymity, as have their families, and some of the doctors and nurses who worked with Letby. It means we can't reveal their identities. In our reporting of Letby's trial, we referred to each of the babies in the case using letters – Baby A, Baby B, Baby C, and so on. We adopt the same approach in the narrative that follows.

In the course of our research, we have been shown a range of documents that shed new light on the Lucy Letby story. Where these documents are cited, they are done so in the public interest and in a manner that protects confidential sources.

Introduction

For seven months, as words of accusation and incrimination swirled all around her, Lucy Letby stayed mute. Though she was the epicentre of all the arguments in one of the biggest murder trials in British legal history, she had no speaking role in it. She sat at a remove from the fireworks of the legal benches, contained behind the screen of the dock. It had the effect of reducing her status to that of an observer, but how could she remain unobserved? She might have wished for that, but there was no chance of it. The glass-fronted dock took on the quality of a zoo enclosure. There sat Letby, flanked by her keepers. We reporters craned to see, fascinated by minutiae. Was that a frown? A smirk? Hard to tell.

We craved colour and pounced on each detail. She's writing a note! She asked for a tissue! Everyday trivialities rendered dramatic. But she stayed silent. Thus far, her invitation to the spectacle wasn't a participatory one.

The trial had begun in the autumn and ground on through the winter months – judge, jurors and journalists trudging their way through Mancunian sleet to the courtroom. Letby, operating under a different regime, was up long before dawn each day for the prison van drive over the Pennines from Yorkshire. The year turned, and the mornings lightened. The evidence kept coming. Winter gave way to spring and Letby stayed silent.

The prosecution case ended after twenty-six weeks. It had been carefully constructed. Charge upon charge, stacked one on top of another, its full weight now sitting on the nurse's shoulders.

The air was heavy with expectation. The drama needed its protagonist to perform, but there was no guarantee that she would.

Rumours and counter-rumours echoed along the court corridors. 'She's going to appear.' 'Not a chance, she's staying quiet.'

Courtroom seven crackled with energy, and then in early May, Letby finally broke the fourth wall and emerged from behind the glass.

Her new position in the witness box was at the heart of the arena, almost touching distance from where we were sitting. She must have played this moment over and over in her mind. What impression to create? Which note to strike? Mousy hair ironed straight. Prim polyester bank-teller suit. Respectful. Dull. It was a guise that screamed 'Don't look at me!' But there wasn't a spare seat in the public gallery and all eyes were trained on her. Keenly aware of the attention, the nurse chose a point in the mid-distance to focus on. She looked straight ahead at the jury but avoided making eye contact.

Name?

We all knew it, of course. All of us inside the courtroom, and by now, millions outside it too.

'Lucy Letby.'

Date of birth?

'January fourth, 1990. I'm thirty-three.'

It was humdrum territory, but no less interesting for it. Just hearing Letby speak after so long was gripping. Was that an accent? Possible traces of the West Country, perhaps. Her tone was polite, clipped, careful. After all, she'd had months to prepare, and this was the shallow end, questions-wise.

Where did you grow up?

'Hereford.'

Who did you grow up with?

'My mum and dad.'

She sounded confident. But this was primary-school stuff, and the inquisitor was her own barrister, Ben Myers KC, who seemed to be treating the exercise as a courtroom edition of *This Is Your Life*. He asked her when she first knew that she wanted to become a nurse.

'I always knew I wanted to work with children,' was the response.

They settled into a routine, the nurse and her defender. Easy question, easy answer.

'Did you have to go to university to study nursing?'

'Yes, I was the first person in my family to go.'

'Where did you do your nursing degree?'

'The University of Chester.'

'Did you ever want to hurt any baby?'

That's what we all wanted to know. It was the reason she was standing trial after all. During the course of her evidence hundreds of questions were put to her. But this was what they all boiled down to. Ben Myers looked at his client. He'd asked the question casually, as though it carried no more weight than any other. Letby paused.

'No,' she said. 'That's completely against what being a nurse is. I only wanted to help and care.'

It was a textbook answer. How could she possibly say anything else? And yet there was no passion – no sign of indignation or anguish in her voice. Her tone was flat. She didn't seem to be railing against being wrongly accused or outraged at the suggestion of such heinous criminality.

Myers moved on. An experienced defence lawyer, he was perhaps conscious that Letby was in danger of appearing unfeeling. He asked her how she felt when she first learned that she was accused of attacking babies on her unit. 'It was sickening,' she said calmly. 'It was devastating.'

The babies' parents were listening closely. They tensed. Hard to be there at all. Harder still to witness the nurse's composure and listen to the smooth words of denial coming from her mouth. The police had left them in no doubt that this woman had killed their babies.

Ben Myers made another attempt at provoking some emotion.

'How hard had you worked to become a nurse?' he asked.

'Very hard,' Letby replied.

'And how did it feel to have it taken away and to be made responsible for the death of babies?'

Bingo. Letby began to cry. 'My job was my life,' she sniffed. 'My whole world was stopped.'

She'd been in the witness box for twenty minutes, and now the tears came. It had been hard to cope, she said. Her arrest was traumatising. She needed medication to sleep. There had been times when she didn't want to live.

Letby reached for the tissues. Myers paused and asked if she was OK to continue. She was, she said.

Her agitation was evident. But it was hard not to notice that it had been prompted by thoughts of her own misfortune.

A couple of rows back, Sue and John Letby were watching their only daughter begin to unravel. He was brooding and stoic. She was red-eyed and disbelieving. A handwritten note seized by police from the nurse's house seemed to anticipate this day. 'I don't deserve mum and dad,' she'd scrawled. Whether that was true or not, it was hard not to feel for them, and wonder at the extent to which their loyalty was being tested.

Earlier in the trial Letby's handwritten notes had been produced with a flourish by the prosecution, and her defence team knew that there was no getting away from them. 'I AM EVIL I DID THIS,' screamed one. 'I killed them on purpose because I'm not good enough,' she'd scribbled.

Ben Myers asked for the notes to be displayed on the screens around the courtroom. Scrappy bits of paper covered in tessellated scrawl now glowed in enlarged high definition.

'Why did you write that?' he asked.

It can't have been an unexpected question, and Letby had her response ready.

'I felt at the time that if I had done something wrong, then I must be an evil, awful person,' she ventured.

The prosecution had presented this note as a confession, arguing that there was no other way to interpret 'I killed them on purpose because I'm not good enough'. The defence tried to debunk that.

'Did that mean you did something intentionally to kill them?' Myers asked.

'No,' replied Letby. 'It meant that I didn't think I'd been good enough . . . and had somehow failed in my duties.'

The tears had stopped. The nurse regained her composure. Her barrister explained that he was about to start the process of asking her about each of the babies in the case. His questions would have to cover harrowing territory. Letby shifted in her seat. She was ready.

Court seven was an unassuming stage for such high drama. No theatrical splendour here. No royal box, or proscenium arch. Nor any oak panelling, stone filigree or green leather, as per the kind of courtrooms you see on TV dramas. Of course, this was no soap opera. But there are plenty of real-life trials of equal prominence which have taken place in more memorable surroundings.

The Moors Murderers Ian Brady and Myra Hindley were tried at Chester Assizes Court – a nineteenth-century Grade One listed pile, fronted by a Doric-columned portico. Harold Shipman's trial took place in the imposing Edwardian baroque surrounds of the Preston Sessions House. Lucy Letby's case was being played out in the absence of any such grandeur.

Manchester Crown Court is a study in morose brutalist concrete, reached via an umbrella-challenging wind tunnel. Its grey solidity seems to act as a bulwark against the showier neon and glass of the city's nearby Spinningfields district. Its neighbours are legal offices, pricey coffee chains and fancy restaurants. But there's no such hospitality inside the court precinct. The canteen closed years ago. Its replacement, a Klix vending machine, has also been removed.

Pushing through the double doors, you walk through metal detectors into an atmosphere of immediate distrust, under a pergola of knife arches and into the arms of security staff who operate a friendly-but-firm regime, searching bags and frisking every visitor with an electronic wand. No one is exempt. Over the course of ten months, the faces of those turning up for the Letby trial became familiar. A recognisable cast list of lawyers, families and police officers, and a secondary circuit of reporters and court 'watchers' destined for the public gallery. As the weeks passed, the guards warmed up. Nods turned to smiles which became chat and then banter. But all were subject to the same scrutiny. It always felt slightly uncomfortable queuing up next to Lucy Letby's parents as they patiently waited for their turn. What to say to them? Hard to know.

The screening process over, you're left to your own devices inside the court building. For those unsure of where to go, the day's cases and defendants' names are displayed on TV screens, like station departure boards for the legal community. Up the stairs then, towards the courts.

There's no respite from the functional civic architecture. Long corridors, with small courtrooms off to each side. Like a cinema multiplex which only shows tragedies, each room promises a miserable day out. In courtroom one, a gangland shooting gone wrong. In number two, rape. In courtroom three, fraud. Keep going, past robbery, drugs conspiracy and GBH. Finally, here's courtroom seven. Multiple child murder. The Letby case. Room reserved for as long as it might take.

It's an underwhelming space. Beige carpet, magnolia walls, flip-up seats and beechwood desks. Even before it fills up, there's a cloying atmosphere that isn't helped by the windowless design and malfunctioning air-conditioning system. For a trial of such magnitude it felt unremarkable.

But there was electricity in the air. The gravity of the charges levelled against Lucy Letby always marked her trial out as high profile. Visitors involved in other cases would walk past the door and whisper, 'That's the Letby court.' There was so much interest that a second courtroom was set aside so that members of the public could come along and watch on video link, and a third was made available for reporters who couldn't fit into the main courtroom.

Why the fascination? What was it about this case that struck such a nerve? Serial killers have always captured the public imagination, perhaps because they occupy a space somewhere between reality and chimera. The consequences of their crimes are acute and real. Their savagery prompts a visceral response, leaving a trail of devastation, distress and raw grief. But they operate at the fringes of humanity, beyond the realms of everyone else's normality. Most of us dare not imagine how such depravity might be possible. Is that why we gaze upon such extreme examples of human behaviour?

We treat them like characters from horror movies, mythologising them, trivialising them, removing them from everything familiar and banal. The Yorkshire Ripper. The Crossbow Cannibal. The Suffolk Strangler. The Teacup Poisoner. The Moors Murderers. Somehow these monikers keep them at some sort of fictional distance. We know that they've moved among us in the real world – but nearly all of us have the luxury of knowing that they never came anywhere near us. We read about their crimes without ever really having to confront them.

And what of those whose surname alone is enough to chill the blood? The likes of Shipman whose name was left unembellished in popular culture. No need. It was his very ordinariness that made him so frightening and his story so spellbinding. We feel sympathy for the vulnerable upon whom he preyed and tense up at the thought of something similar happening to those we love. For some, there's voyeuristic titillation to be had from stories of terrible crimes – and an industry of newspapers, podcasts and docu-dramas to provide it. But it's someone else's horror. We gawp for a few moments and then flick over to another channel for the football. How lucky we are, we think.

Why are we so interested? Shouldn't our disgust make us turn away? And what is it about women who murder that seems to occupy a special place of morbid fascination? Such cases are rare, and female serial killers even rarer. Mary Bell, Myra Hindley, Rose West, Beverley Allitt – as we watched Letby's trial unfold, these names entered our minds once again. Was this mousy young nurse in the dock about to join the ranks of Britain's most notorious female killers? Looking over at her, so meek in the dock, it seemed fanciful. But then what are such women supposed to look like? Of course, there's no answer to that.

Those were the stakes that gave the trial its profile, but this was a case which was ultimately defined by the extreme vulnerability of its victims. For the prosecution, this was a story of vulnerable, tiny babies in a hospital neonatal unit, clinging on to life only to have it taken away by a killer posing as a saviour.

These were longed-for babies, nurtured through pregnancy and coaxed into life. Their loving parents sat by their temperature-controlled incubators, relieved that they were being given the best chance of survival, and grateful for the medical advances which afforded such precision protection from the outside world. None of them suspected that the greatest threat to their children was loitering alongside them in medical scrubs.

The prosecution told the story of a nurse who subverted her role and everything it stood for, using her position to prey on society's most defenceless, snuffing out their chances before they'd got a foothold on childhood. Conviction would make her one of the most reviled serial killers of all time.

We all know how this story ends. Letby is guilty. At least that's what the jury finally concluded. Were they right? That's a subject for later chapters. But this is a case full of hard questions. What about the other nurses sharing shifts with Letby? Didn't they suspect anything? Why would they? What about the doctors and hospital managers? Where were they? How could a nurse become a killer? Why would she do it? Who was this woman, accused of the most heinous of crimes? Was she guilty at all?

All eyes trained on courtroom seven, hoping for answers. But they weren't as easy to come by as the questions.

The prosecution was constructed carefully – charge by charge, baby by baby. Technical terminology flew around, unfamiliar at first, but used with increasing fluency as the weeks went by. One of the prosecutors referred to a 'constellation' of evidence – medical notes, charts, graphs and data. But at times it felt like a teetering pack of cards. There were plenty of unanswered questions too. Almost nothing was said about Lucy Letby's character, psychology or motive. We all craved it, but no real information was forthcoming from the prosecution about what on earth could have possessed her to commit such crimes. The evidence was laid out in almost every direction bar one. Letby remained a complete enigma.

The lawyers who'd spent years building the case against the nurse, and who now filled the prosecution benches in court, had made the decision that there was no need to get into matters of motive or personality. They reasoned that the jury had to be persuaded of her criminal intent and needed to be convinced of the solidity of the medical evidence, but that they didn't need to understand her mindset to convict her. They felt it would take the court into realms of speculation, and away from the rational, empirical approach they'd adopted. In other words, they didn't feel that they needed to prove the case by answering the question 'Why?'

But on the press benches and in the public gallery it didn't stop us wondering, and as the case rolled on, the elephant in the room grew ever larger. We caught glimpses of Letby's personality, in text messages which she sent to friends, in her scribbled notes, and most of all during her time in the witness box. But the jurors weren't shown any psychiatric reports or told about her likely state of mind. Brief details were given about her family and childhood, but there was no deep dive into her background or likely influences. The lawyers may have decided it was an unnecessary factor, but for plenty of onlookers, Lucy Letby's psyche was an unresolved issue which lay heavily over the case.

For some of those observers who found themselves vacillating between the arguments for Letby's guilt and innocence, the verdicts, when they came, offered finality and surety. The case was proven, and a legal line drawn. But the itch to understand the young nurse had not been fully scratched, and as the newspapers filled their pages with damning coverage, and Letby's face filled TV news screens, the need to understand her only grew larger. What had caused her to commit these murders? What had caused such evil to incubate in someone so seemingly benign? Why would an ambitious young nurse throw away her promising career for a life behind bars? Was it even possible for this young woman to be capable of such evil?

Some believed it wasn't. Even before the end of the trial, talk of a miscarriage of justice was gathering momentum. Online forums hummed with talk of the nurse's innocence. Crowdfunding sites sprang up to raise money for an appeal. For the best part of a year, such discussion was largely confined to the fringes of the internet but in recent months, mainstream newspapers, magazines, and documentaries have joined in, questioning whether Lucy Letby really is guilty. For Letby's most committed supporters, the search for answers – for an explanation of her crimes – is a futile endeavour for one simple reason: they believe she's innocent.

As BBC journalists, we had invested the best part of a year in the case, following it at close quarters to make a *Panorama* documentary, 'Lucy Letby: The Nurse Who Killed'. We spent months researching and filming for the hour-long programme, immersing ourselves in the evidence and speaking to those most closely involved in the saga.

As the debate raged online, many of those who were personally caught up in the case ran a mile from the media. Most of the nurses who worked with Letby have refused to speak. All but two of the babies' families have preferred to avoid public interviews. And virtually no one within Letby's network of family and friends has put their head above the parapet.

We spent time with some of the parents, grappling with the life-changing trauma of what happened to their babies. For months, they sat quietly in court just metres away from the woman accused of murdering or attempting to murder them.

We spent hours talking to the consultants at the Countess of Chester Hospital – each of whom has made a long and painful journey to the point of believing that one of their colleagues was a baby killer. In the days and weeks after Letby's conviction, they were celebrated as heroes for stopping the deaths and forcing their hospital bosses to call in the police.

We spoke to one of Letby's oldest friends, Dawn. Dawn believes her friend is innocent and carries the pain of believing that someone she loves and believes in has been wrongly jailed and demonised. When we first spoke to Dawn, she was a lonely voice. She isn't now.

Today, social media and the internet are abuzz with commentary and opinion on the Letby case. But virtually no one in this commentariat was there when Letby gave evidence in court. She spent fourteen days in the witness box and Judith was there throughout.

In many ways, the nurse's performance in the witness box sealed her fate. We explain how and why.

And yet despite our immersion in the case, Letby's trial raised more questions than it answered. Who was this woman? Where had she come from? What was her home life like? What was she like at university? Were there hidden secrets in her background that might make her official status as one of Britain's most prolific serial killers easier to accept?

What about the hospital where she worked? What really happened and how did suspicion come to fall on Lucy Letby? Our conversations with the consultants at the Countess of Chester Hospital pointed to a much bigger story than the one which was presented in court. For months, a desperate battle over the truth played out between the consultants – convinced that Letby was harming babies – and some of Letby's nursing colleagues, equally convinced that their colleague was being scapegoated. Senior managers at the hospital sided with Letby. History is still being written on this dramatic clash of personalities and convictions.

If we accept the jury was right to find Letby guilty, it is natural to wonder whether the murders in her trial were the tip of something bigger. The case focused only on a neatly boxed-off period between June 2015 and almost exactly the same time a year later. And yet we knew that Letby had worked at the hospital for a much longer period. Had her behaviour suddenly changed overnight or were there other victims whose stories hadn't been told?

And what of the question some are now asking: is Lucy Letby really guilty? For the parents in the case, even entertaining the idea is an affront, after the pain they have gone through and the years they've waited for Letby's convictions. The consultants are also aggrieved by this question. They too have suffered an ordeal – all too visible when you meet them.

And yet a young woman is destined to die in prison while growing numbers of experts and commentators believe she has been wrongly convicted. Ignoring this question is not an option – and we don't.

This book deals head on with the questions that have been raised since the verdicts, including the science which was so instrumental to Letby's convictions. We've spoken to the experts involved in the case – both the prosecution's star witnesses and the medical consultant who advised Letby's defence. We try to answer some of the biggest outstanding questions: why did Letby have no expert witnesses testifying for her and was the science in the trial solid? How sure can we be that she actually did it?

We haven't been afraid to confront the areas of hottest dispute. How was the nurse convicted, despite no forensic evidence? How well does the science support the allegations? How can we be sure that she was to blame when things went wrong? How could she have duped her friends and family? What are the chances that she's been wrongfully convicted? What are the chances that she hasn't?

The 'unmasking' of Lucy Letby is still a work in progress. We've followed a trail of breadcrumbs – the written notes which offer a window into her mind; the text messages which give a glimpse of her friendships; the testimony of those who know her. They're all legitimate pieces of the jigsaw, and yet the whole picture isn't fully formed yet. The nurse is content to remain an enigma. We know that she was aware of the *Panorama* programme, and has been told about this book, but she has taken no part in either.

During the many months when the lead neonatal consultant Dr Steve Brearey tried to get his managers to listen to his concerns, he emailed the ward manager to say, 'We still need to talk about Lucy.' Several years have passed since then, and hours of airtime have been filled with the nurse's story, and yet the doctor's words continue to hold true.

There are some who say that the name Lucy Letby should never be uttered again. Others have vowed to keep her case in the spotlight until it has been declared a miscarriage of justice.

Only Lucy Letby knows the truth of what happened at the Countess of Chester Hospital between June 2015 and June 2016. This book is an effort to get as close to that truth as possible.

The Lucy Letby story is unlike any other – in its complexity and the strength of feeling that it arouses. This book will offend some because of the questions it asks and some of the answers it gives, but for those who come to the subject with an open mind, we hope it will reveal much more about this fascinating and horrifying case.

Chapter 1

An Ordinary Girl

Before the summer of 2018, no one had heard of Lucy Letby. She was just an ordinary twenty-eight-year-old nurse, working shifts at the Countess of Chester Hospital. Nothing about her stood out. She wore the same blue scrubs as all the other junior nurses. She turned up on time and seemed to be good at her job – working with sick babies in the hospital's neonatal unit. She watched the same TV programmes as the other nurses and laughed at the same jokes. She read about famous people, from pop stars to criminals, the way the rest of us do – never imagining that one day she might be the headline. Or at least, that's the impression she gave.

But on 3 July 2018, all of that changed. Just after 6 a.m., detectives from Cheshire Police knocked on Lucy Letby's door, a mile and a half away from the hospital where she worked.

It's hard to tell from the police bodycam footage what was going through Letby's head when she opened the door that morning. Was she shocked to see those suited police officers on her front step? Or, as one of the officers later told us, had she always known that this moment was coming?

Minutes later, Letby was led outside in handcuffs to a waiting police car. There were no hysterics. No struggle or tears. Just a look of quiet dread on the young nurse's face as the police bodycam followed her to the car. Much as she would later be in court, the Lucy Letby in this grainy police video was inscrutable. Even the hoodie she was wearing – faded blue with girly pink writing on the front – seemed designed to keep us wondering and scratching our heads: could this woman really be a child serial killer?

By the time journalists got wind of Letby's arrest, she was already in custody. But swarms of officers had now begun combing

1

her house for evidence and it wasn't long before Letby's street was a media circus. Much like Letby herself, the house was unassuming and ordinary – a seventies semi-detached, halfway up a quiet sub-urban street. All the other houses on the street looked much the same. But number 41 was now a crime scene, cordoned off with blue-and-white tape.

We could only guess what was going on inside. Officers dressed in black from head to toe carried bags and crates from the house to a blue tent erected on the driveway. Outside, more officers appeared to be scouring the exterior of the property, inch by inch. Some had shovels. Others perched on ladders, poking around in the drains and the guttering for who knows what.

A few of the neighbours came out to watch the police operation. But most did their best to hide away from hard-pressed reporters – all jostling for a quote or a soundbite before their next deadline. One of the chattier neighbours suggested Letby had owned a silver Suzuki, which had been moved from her driveway to make room for the police tent. Another said the woman in number 41 had moved in about two years previously. For journalists, even the most trivial scraps of information seemed like mini-breakthroughs.

The cops weren't saying much. A 'healthcare professional', they said, had been arrested on suspicion of murdering eight babies and attempting to kill six others. Police had been investigating seven-teen baby deaths and fifteen non-fatal collapses at the Countess of Chester Hospital between March 2015 and July 2016. The focus of the investigation was the hospital's neonatal unit.[1]

We all recognised the magnitude of the story. Not since the case of Rosemary West had a British woman been accused of being a mass killer of children. Overnight, Lucy Letby had gone from perfect obscurity to national infamy. Innocent until proven guilty? Sure. But it's hard to look innocent when police are crawling all over your home.

We identified the 'healthcare professional' as Lucy Letby long before her name was confirmed officially. A smattering of other details soon trickled out – like the fact that she was a nurse; she was twenty-eight years old and her birthday was 4 January 1990.

She'd studied nursing at the University of Chester before going on to work at the Countess of Chester Hospital. But the question we all wanted to answer was: who was this Lucy Letby? Where had she come from? What was her background?

Although Letby lived and worked in Chester, her roots were a hundred miles away in Hereford – a cathedral city with the feel of a modest little market town. Her parents, John and Sue, still lived there. Sue was fifty-eight. Initial reports described her as an accounts clerk who'd been married once already before she met John and gave birth to Lucy. John was much older – seventy-three at the time of his daughter's arrest. He'd been a manager in a furniture shop – one of those old-fashioned family businesses staffed by well-mannered men dressed in suits.

The Letbys weren't hard to locate. As police searched their daughter's home in Chester, officers were busy searching the family home in Hereford too.

This was another postcard of English ordinariness – a cul-de-sac of uniform semi-detached houses with a green and a little round-about at the bottom. The Letbys lived at that end of the street – tucked away, safe from the world – until now.

The houses had nice big back gardens. You could imagine the kids on the street having great summers. But there was nothing fancy about the place. The people here were neither rich nor poor. This was the heartland of decent, hard-working England.

Following their daughter's arrest, the Letbys' address was splashed online. It wasn't long before the nation's media descended and set up camp outside. But the couple had already gone to ground. The curtains remained closed. Any journalists who made it as far as the front door were met by the police.

Some of the neighbours were less shy. 'Lucy was just a quiet girl. Nothing strange about her,' one told *The Times*. 'She was just a normal, lovely girl. The family must be in bits over this.'[2] 'She was a good little girl. She was a delight,' recalled another neighbour.[3] 'We're still reeling from it, to be honest,' said one family friend, according to the *Mail*. 'Even after sleeping on it, I think everybody around here is still in a state of shock and disbelief. Lucy was doing the job she dreamed of doing and appeared nothing but dedicated and professional. You can't imagine her hurting a fly let alone defenceless babies.'[4]

Everyone on the street seemed to feel the same way. The sweet little girl they'd seen growing up just didn't fit with what they were now hearing on the news. 'Her parents have been my neighbours for at least twenty-five years, so I watched Lucy grow up,' said one neighbour. 'Lucy lives away but visits them frequently as any good daughter would. They adored her. I just truly can't believe it.'[5]

There wasn't much detail to go on, but everything these neighbours said about Letby and her parents conjured a picture of wholesomeness, love and contentment. She was an only child – and the apple of her parents' eye. The three of them had apparently just spent a week in Torquay together, and Lucy had been to stay with her parents in Hereford only a couple of days before her arrest.

But was there another side to Lucy Letby's background? We've all heard about the troubled childhoods suffered by many serial killers. Fred West grew up in a house where incest and sexual abuse were the norm, while his wife Rose suffered repeated sexual abuse at the hands of her paranoid schizophrenic father. Some killers *appeared* to have ordinary childhoods, while secretly cultivating an inner demon. The teenage killers of Brianna Ghey, convicted in 2023, are one such case. To the outside world, they were normal kids, but in private they fuelled a mutual obsession with torture and murder. So was there a dark side to Lucy Letby's childhood in Hereford?

Letby's friends weren't as talkative as some of her neighbours. *The Times* managed to track down an ex-boyfriend of a girl who knew Letby growing up. 'She was quite awkward and geeky,' he recalled. 'But [she] seemed like a kind-hearted person.'[6] Another friend described her as 'an amazing person'. But that was pretty much it. No one who knew Letby well was saying anything.[7]

Social media was more revealing. Like so many others, Letby charted her life on Facebook. Her Facebook photos were a virtual scrapbook going right back to her childhood. For journalists trying to understand Lucy Letby, this was the first window into her social world. But anyone hoping to see early signs of a future killer or a damaged personality was disappointed. The Lucy Letby on Facebook was a smiling, happy-looking girl with the kind of friends that any parent would want for their child.

Every photo was a freeze-frame of innocent, wholesome fun. Like the one of young Lucy with her friends, lying in a star-like formation on a green – everyone beaming at the camera. Or the one of Lucy and her little gang of girlfriends laughing while they try to balance on one leg. There were lots of pictures of Letby and her friends pulling funny faces and striking silly poses. In some, Letby was just smiling while giving the camera a boisterous thumbs up.

Then there were the pictures of more grown-up Lucy – still a teenager but now old enough to go to the pub. Here again, Letby and her little gang look happy and smiling. There's no hint of teenage angst. Just more funny faces and poses, only this time with pint glasses and cocktails in hand. In one photo, we see Letby indulging in some girlish high jinks draping herself around a pole in a pub. In another, she's in someone's car, literally bursting with laughter – as if the photographer has just told her the world's funniest joke. It's hard to look at these photos, knowing how Letby's story would end. How could the smiling girl sitting on her bed, surrounded by her friends and holding a teddy bear, have become a serial killer? Was it even possible? We both wrestled with these questions when we saw these pictures for the first time. Judith captured what we were both thinking: 'I don't know what Britain's most prolific child killer should look like. I'm pretty sure it's not this though.'

But despite the rich scattering of photos on Facebook, Lucy Letby's childhood was still unknown. Where had she gone to school? What was she like at school? Was she popular? What did she do for fun and what were her friends like? And what about her home life and her relationship with her parents? Were there any hints of a troubled childhood – despite the happy impression given on Facebook? Did Lucy Letby show signs of having a dark side? And what about boyfriends – or girlfriends?

By the time Letby's trial began in October 2022, none of these questions had been answered. It's remarkable when you think about it. Four years had passed since Letby had first been arrested. Throughout this time, her name and the grim accusations against her had been swirling around. If the accusations were true, Lucy Letby would officially be Britain's most prolific child killer. And yet no one had really managed to unearth anything significant about her. We weren't even sure which school Letby had gone to or whether she had any siblings or ex-boyfriends. The young woman accused of being a serial killer of babies was a ghost.

We'd managed to figure out who some of her childhood friends were. Although Letby's own Facebook account had long been taken down, her friends' Facebook pages told at least part of the story. But none of them would speak to us. One girl told us she'd been at primary school with Letby – St James's Church of England School in Hereford – but that was it. Even the local journalists in Hereford seemed to have hit a brick wall.

What about Letby's parents? Would they not want to give their account of their only child? Although the family home was in Hereford, John and Sue Letby relocated to Manchester to attend their daughter's trial. Every day without fail, they came to Manchester Crown Court – on foot. Each morning, they'd turn off Bridge Street and make their way down the narrow little road where the entrance to the court was located. It was all so ordinary and banal. You'd never have guessed that they were the parents of a suspected baby killer, but their downcast expressions were a clue.

John's a tall man with broad shoulders and a strong jawline. He wore unfashionable steel glasses and always seemed to be smoking. He walked with a bit of a limp, but he looked like he had been fit and strong in his younger years. His wife Sue on the other hand – although fifteen years younger than her husband – looked frail, stooped and permanently shell-shocked. She still dyed her hair, but her face was aged with worry.

One morning, before court began, we approached them on the street to see if they might talk to us. They were both wary – John more so than Sue – but they didn't hurry off or tell us to get lost. You could tell they were both desperate for a lifeline – Sue especially. Anything to save their daughter.

'There's a lot that we could say after what we've been put through over the last few years,' Sue said, clearly wanting to unburden herself. So would they talk to us? John straightened up and took a deep drag on his cigarette. 'What good would it do?' he said, while his wife stared into the middle distance.

Had we said we could help their cause at that moment, who knows – they might have done an interview there and then. But no sane journalist would give such an undertaking. It's against the law to try to affect or influence a live trial. And in any case, we had no idea whether Lucy Letby was innocent or guilty. We, like everyone else, had to wait until the trial was over before airing our take on the story. Unfortunately for the Letbys, that was too late.

'What's the point if by then my daughter has been convicted?' John asked pitifully. We made the best case that we could, but there was no convincing them.

It was impossible not to feel sorry for the Letbys. They looked like regular, honest people. They'd probably never been in a courtroom before all of this. Now, their world had been turned upside down. They looked broken and incredibly lonely.

Every day, for ten long months, they trudged faithfully into court. Occasionally they said hello to us and even ventured the odd comment about how the trial was progressing. But as the months went by, their wariness of the media hardened. As far as they were concerned, the media, the police and the courts were all part of the same system that, as they saw it, was perpetrating a great injustice against their daughter.

Still, no one who knew Letby would speak. Even the Letbys' neighbours in Hereford had by now become hostile towards the media. There was, however, one person who we knew was close to Letby and might – just might – be persuaded to talk to us. Dawn and Letby had grown up together in Hereford. We'd seen tons of pictures of the two of them together on Facebook.

We'd also heard through the grapevine that Dawn might want to talk. Dawn was terrified of the media and the danger of being misrepresented – everyone in this story was. But she believed her friend was innocent.

One of our researchers managed to find a mobile number. Dawn was cagey at first, but she confirmed she was friends with Letby, and by the end of the call she was open to the idea of a meeting – no strings and in confidence. She had a family and a busy job so it might be a few weeks before she could find the time.

Another two months passed without word. Perhaps Dawn had changed her mind. But in January 2023, she texted to say that she was ready to meet. Dawn was clear about her motivation. She'd known Lucy since they were twelve. She was certain that Lucy was innocent and she wanted to get her message out there without her words being twisted by the media.

Dawn is well spoken, serious and intelligent. She comes across as decent, principled – possibly a little old-fashioned – certainly a good person with a strong moral compass. Could someone like Dawn really be best friends with a serial killer? It was clear that Dawn was a gateway into Letby's childhood world in Hereford. As far as Dawn was concerned, she knew Letby in a way that hardly anyone else did. They even exchanged letters while Letby was in prison awaiting trial.

Two more months passed before Dawn finally agreed to be interviewed on camera. She no longer lives in Hereford but she agreed to meet us there and show us around.

Hereford is a humble little place near the Welsh border, surrounded by countryside of stunning beauty. It's England at its most traditional and understated. The city centre is basically a couple of streets – a few old hotels and the odd wonky Tudor house, a market square, the usual high street shops, and a cathedral with well-kept greens on all sides. The composer Edward Elgar had lived here. There's even a statue of this most English of composers leaning against his bicycle outside the cathedral.

'We'd walk into town, have meals along this strip, and hang out on the cathedral green,' Dawn reminisced as we drove by. 'Lucy and I and all of our friends would hang out in the summer, just sitting on the grass having picnics and chatting.'

Dawn and Letby met in Aylestone School – the local secondary. 'I think it was the second year, queuing up to go to an RE lesson,'

Dawn recalled. 'We just got chatting, and at that age you were just trying to make friends and find your place.' We drove past the school – a comforting old red-brick building at the bottom of a tree-lined suburban street. Dawn pointed to the geography block where she and Letby and their little gang used to hang out at lunchtimes playing Uno.

According to Dawn, neither she nor Letby were in the popular crowd at school. 'We sort of formed our own little group, Lucy, me and our friends,' Dawn recalled. 'We were probably considered the geeky ones, to be fair – the ones that were very focused and studious. Our studies sort of came first for us. We were the ones who weren't very popular at school.'

But even though she wasn't one of the cool kids, Letby had her own little gang of in-betweeners, and they all seemed to have fun. 'Outside of our group she would present as shy, reserved, serious, you know, level-headed,' Dawn reflected. 'But inside the safety of our group, she sort of lets her hair down a bit more and is goofy and makes us all laugh.'

Most school kids have no idea what they want to do for a living when they're older. But Letby did. '[Nursing] was the only career that I ever remember her saying that she wanted to go and do,' Dawn recalled. According to Dawn, Letby had personal reasons for being so focused on nursing. Early in their friendship, Letby had confided to Dawn that she had had a difficult birth herself. 'She was very grateful for being alive to the nurses that would've helped save her life,' Dawn said, almost appearing to relive the conversation with her old friend. 'I feel like everything that she did was geared towards that ultimate goal of becoming a nurse.'

After secondary school, Dawn and Lucy moved to the nearby Hereford Sixth Form College to do their A-levels. Letby knew what subjects to pick – whatever it took to study nursing at university. According to Dawn, everything in her friend's school life seemed directed to becoming a nurse. And not just any nurse. A neonatal nurse. In any other life story, this would probably be impressive and endearing. But in Letby's case, could it possibly have been an early warning sign? Was there perhaps something slightly weird

9

– sinister or not quite right – about this lifelong obsession with newborn babies?

We drove from the secondary school to the sixth form college to take a look. It was a Sunday so the car park was empty. Dawn pointed to a strip of flower beds and benches where she and Letby used to spend time when they weren't in class. Letby always brought a packed lunch to school, Dawn recalled. Her parents were much more organised than Dawn's. Dawn laughed as she reminisced, but it was an uneasy laughter. You could tell this was difficult for her.

So what about the allegations against her friend? Could Lucy Letby have murdered babies in her care? Dawn's allegiance to Letby was unshakeable. Lucy, she said – always 'Lucy' – was the kindest person she'd ever known. 'Think of your most kind, gentle, soft friend,' she said imploringly. 'And think that they're being accused of harming babies. She would only ever want to help people. To say that she could have harmed any baby – it's just not in her nature.'

'Have all of Lucy's friends stood by her?' we asked. 'Yes,' replied Dawn earnestly. There was no nervous laughter now. 'We know she couldn't have done anything that she's accused of, so without a doubt we stand by her.'

It was fascinating talking to Dawn, but also unnerving. Everything she told us only seemed to make the allegations against Letby even more incomprehensible. The person Dawn described was geeky, plain – a goody-goody. Was it possible for one person to be all these things and yet be incubating a future murderer at the same time?

Of course, it was always possible that Dawn was giving us a selective account – a sanitised version of her friend. Until now, no one else from Letby's circle has spoken publicly. But after months of trying, we managed to persuade some of Letby's other school friends to speak to us anonymously. One recalled Letby getting a part-time job in the local WH Smith when she was sixteen. It was a good fit. In previous years, she liked to visit the shop on Saturday mornings where she'd leaf through biographies of people with tales of struggle or triumph over adversity.

At school, Letby wasn't a high-flyer. She had to work hard to get the grades she needed, but she was diligent and conscientious. One classmate recalls her being a teacher's pet. Maths wasn't her forte. History and English were much more comfortable for her. When she was fourteen, she went on a school trip to France to visit some of the battle sites from the First World War. Either the history or the food didn't agree with her. One friend who found herself sleeping in the same dormitory as Letby recalls her throwing up after a day's sightseeing.

But the one subject in which Letby truly excelled was geography. She got top marks at GCSE and went on to do geography A-level. There isn't an obvious connection between geography and nursing, but it was probably Letby's attention to detail that accounted for her aptitude for both. One classmate recalls Letby's meticulous note-taking on field trips. 'She was so good and accurate and careful and considered.' Even outside of school hours, Letby threw herself into geography projects and after-school clubs. In her early teens, she took part in a national weather-monitoring exercise. Not surprisingly, her geography teacher, a woman called Catherine Close, liked her immensely and gave her plenty of validation and affirmation for her efforts. In later years, when Letby's world started to implode, she scribbled the name Catherine Close on random bits of paper. Even the thought of her old geography teacher, many years on, was a comfort.

Was Letby passionate about her schoolwork? One of her former classmates put it this way: 'I would say she was more passionate about being good at the things than she was actually passionate about the subjects themselves.' What about mistakes? Was she prone to blunders – practical or otherwise? No, the former classmate told us. 'This is somebody who does not tend to make mistakes.'

It was impossible not to read into these recollections about the young Lucy Letby. During her trial, a jury would be asked to consider why so many babies had died while Letby was present. Inaccuracies and omissions in Letby's medical notes would also feature in the case. It was all bad luck and innocent error, according to her defenders, but it didn't sound like the young Lucy Letby we'd been told about – the fastidious note-taker who never made mistakes.

Socially, the adolescent Letby appeared unremarkable. 'She was one of the boffin group who always did really well at school and always had their shirt tucked in and their tie done up,' according to one recollection. 'She was boring if anything.' 'She didn't exude much personality,' another classmate recalled. 'She was almost invisible.'

We managed to speak to the former principal of Letby's sixth form college but he didn't remember her. The fact she wasn't on his radar indicated that she was neither exceptional nor troubled or in need of support. She was, he assumed, a normal, well-adjusted student. No one among the staff ever raised any concerns about her. Nothing in her schooling pointed to the grim denouement of Letby's story. So what, if anything, could have turned an ordinary girl from Hereford into a serial killer? The former headmaster's guess is as good as almost anyone's: 'Some physiological problem or issue – a short circuit in her mentality – resulted in her behaving in that way.'

The impression of Lucy Letby as a bland, almost invisible, character is hard to resist. But she wasn't so invisible that she and her circle escaped the attention of the school bullies. The rowdier kids thought she was strait-laced, and Letby and her circle were all too aware that they weren't part of the popular crowd. But to most of her school peers, Letby was barely noticeable.

It didn't help that she was socially reserved around people she didn't know. According to one recollection, she could appear 'stony and cold'. Even Letby's long-suffering friend Dawn admitted as much.

But Dawn had told us about a less reserved side of Letby – a more outgoing, funny, 'goofy' side that she revealed to those she knew and trusted. Another school friend echoed this. Sure, Letby was quiet, but she was also funny. 'She had quite an acerbic wit,' the friend recalled. 'Like you wouldn't expect it sometimes because she was so quiet, and then she'd just come out with something really witty, and you'd be like, "Oh, I can remember you're funny."'

Other people who knew Letby at school described a plain but good-natured girl. 'She was sweet and kind,' recalled one. She seemed to look out for her friends too. One classmate recalls her writing two copies of geography notes – one for herself and one for a friend who kept missing classes. In later years, Letby would become godmother to the children of one of her school friends. If Letby was fooling people about her true nature, it was the people who believed they knew her best whom she managed to fool most easily. Or maybe Letby's innocence hadn't yet been corrupted. Of course, Letby's supporters argue it never was.

Outside of school, Letby's pastimes were basic: pizza, cinema and her pet dog, a Yorkshire terrier called Whiskey. One classmate from primary school recalls Letby walking little Whiskey to school with her mum. 'She absolutely loved her dog,' they told us. 'She was obsessed with him. She took great care of him.' In later years, when Letby was feeling the heat of her colleagues' suspicions at the hospital, she scribbled Whiskey's name on bits of paper next to phrases like 'please help me' and the names of Letby's few remaining allies. In a story where Letby's future actions seem completely disconnected from the world of her childhood, Whiskey was somehow a thread of continuity or constancy.

By all accounts, there wasn't a huge amount to do growing up in Hereford in the early 2000s. But there was always Castle Green beside the cathedral – the centre of the universe for the city's youth. When Letby and her friends finished their A-levels, that's where they went to celebrate. But with so few opportunities and outlets, anywhere seemed like fun – even the local church hall. One of Lucy's crowd was a devout Christian, and Lucy and the rest of the boffins seemed happy to take her up on social invitations at her local church.

Like her social life, life at home for Lucy Letby was simple but contented. 'Her mum idolised her,' one observer told us. 'She did everything for her. They were very close.' Inside the family home, pictures of Letby adorned the walls.

In many ways, she was a model daughter. She had no appetite for transgression or rule-breaking. She was 'by the book'. While some of the naughtier kids at school were pushing the boundaries, Lucy was hosting sleepovers for her girlfriends. *The X Factor* was on the telly and she and her friends were hooked. Letby's mum

Sue would cook for them – always the same thing. And there'd be a bottle of lemonade to wash it down.

Friends recall seeing less of Letby's dad John. One friend recalls he always seemed to be wearing a suit. He was traditional – like his furniture business. But John was no less devoted to his daughter than Sue. He sometimes collected Lucy from school, and in later years he would become her staunchest defender.

What about boys? Did Letby show any interest in that direction while she was at school? There was at least one boy among Letby's close-knit group of friends. But there were no boyfriends. No one we spoke to recalls her ever talking about boys, boyfriends or love interests. In fact, one fellow student speculated that Letby seemed to disapprove when some of her friends started seeing boys. Perhaps she was jealous. She didn't say. But there's little doubt that Letby wanted a family some day. 'We'd have the "what would you wear on your wedding day?" chats,' one of Letby's school friends recalled. In years to come, when Letby's life began to fall apart, she wrote a note to herself bemoaning the fact that she would never be able to have a family of her own. But the obstacle to her finding love – whatever it was – seemed to be something deeper and something she carried from her schooldays right up until the day she was arrested.

One possible explanation for her failure to find love is that she never quite grew up. When she was sixteen, Letby moved from secondary school to the local sixth form college. It was supposed to bridge the gap between school and university, and students generally used the more relaxed, grown-up college atmosphere to spread their wings. But Letby and her small circle of five or six friends seemed less interested in broadening their horizons. Letby and her gang were perfectly happy sitting chatting in the school library. Maybe that's why they called themselves the 'miss-match family'. But if Letby didn't quite grow up – if she remained the girl who liked sleepovers with lemonade and *The X Factor* – her future crimes are all the more incomprehensible. Everyone we spoke to from Letby's Hereford days seemed to agree with Dawn. 'There is not a single one of us that can wrap our minds around the Lucy that we knew [killing babies],' said one girl. To the wider world, Letby was strait-laced and bland. But a killer? No way – according to those who knew Letby growing up.

'She had enough friends. She had fun when she wanted to,' observed one former friend.

'There's nothing in that entire period that you saw or heard about that looked like a dark spot on her character?' we asked.

'No. Never, no.'

14 August 2008. A-level results day.

For as long as she could remember, Letby had set her sights on becoming a neonatal nurse. She'd worked hard to get the grades she needed and finally it had paid off. At last, she was on her way to university to pursue the career she'd always dreamed of.

Her parents John and Sue were proud as punch. Neither of them had been to university. Letby was the first in the family to go.

For all its charms, Hereford wasn't exactly bursting with career opportunities for young people. Anyone who wanted to go to university and pursue a career had to move away.

Some in Letby's year headed to the big cities, but Letby chose the quieter, more genteel city of Chester – just south of Liverpool and about a hundred miles away from her parents' home in Hereford. She enrolled there at the University of Chester. Her chosen course: Child Nursing – what else?

Like Hereford, Chester is small, picturesque and steeped in history. One survey described it as the most beautiful city in the world. A little over the top, perhaps, but it's easy to see the city's appeal. Tourists visit regularly to see the remains of old Roman walls and what is still the largest Roman amphitheatre in Britain. The city's most eye-catching features, however, are the black-and-white Tudor-style buildings that line the main streets, as well as the cathedral in the city centre with its stunning medieval choir stalls and mosaics.

It's hard not to notice the architectural parallels with Hereford. Letby may have flown the nest, but her new world was in some ways just a different version of the one she had left.

Despite this, she struggled with the change of environment and became homesick. She returned to Hereford whenever she could – meeting up with her old pals for reunions and cocktails. The old Hereford gang had gone their separate ways, but when they were together, it was just like old times. A video filmed just before Letby was due to begin her second year at university shows her and her old friend Dawn after a boozy night out – arm in arm, staggering around and collapsing in fits of laughter.[8] 'A night of terror' was the caption for the video on Facebook. Terror indeed. This was Letby at her most unguarded.

But eventually, she found her feet in Chester. She found a new little band of friends too, and they looked every bit as wholesome as the old Hereford gang. They had the same self-conscious awkwardness. Photos from the time show Letby in fancy dress – an angel no less – enjoying herself or pulling more of her trademark faces.

But at heart, Letby was no party girl. In Hereford, she had been one of the goody-goodies, the 'boffins' – studious, shirt tucked in, and so on – and that's how she was at university too. She was known as one of the 'geeky girls'.[9] Peers recalled that she was always the first one home after a night out.[10] One recalled a plain girl who avoided the mischief and excesses often associated with university life. 'There is not very much to say about her. She was never one of the rowdy ones and never came to university hung-over – as many others did. She came in, did her work and went home.'

It's hardly surprising. For Letby, university – like school – was a means to an end: it was all about becoming a nurse.

As a student, Letby was competent but not exceptional. As in Hereford, whatever she achieved academically was hard won. One person from her course recalled: 'She wasn't a First Class Honours student. I can't remember if she got a 2:1 or a 2:2.'

Naturally enough, some of Letby's new friends found boyfriends. But romantic love was elusive for Letby. It seemed unfair. She wasn't any more awkward or any less pretty than any of her friends. If it hurt, she didn't show it. Even to her closest friends, she appeared to be good-natured to her core.

We'd heard about one girl from Letby's nursing course that she'd become particularly friendly with. According to one person from the time, the pair were inseparable – 'sellotaped together'. We wanted to learn more so we reached out to Letby's old friend on LinkedIn. She didn't want to talk, but she confirmed our understanding was correct. She also gave us her take on the claims that her friend was a murderer:

'Whoever spoke to you was correct, Lucy was my closest friend at uni. She was a wonderful student nurse and I firmly believe she is innocent of all the charges against her.'

Another person we spoke to from Letby's course was similarly sceptical. 'My gut instinct is rarely wrong. I am a reasonable judge of people and I can't believe it – based on my experience,' they told us. 'I can't believe she's a murderer based on my experience of her.'

Like most students, Letby attended lectures and seminars. But nursing is hands-on, and for a student nurse, that means getting real-life hospital experience. Fortunately for Letby, Chester had its own hospital with a neonatal unit and a welcoming attitude to student nurses.

Chester is on the small side, compared to some of the major hospitals in the North West of England. You can see the modesty of the place as soon as you drive in. Some hospitals are sprawling campuses with countless buildings and miles of polished walkways and corridors. Chester, by contrast, feels not much larger than a big secondary school. You could miss the main entrance if you blinked.

The neonatal unit wasn't especially large either. Most women going into hospital to give birth – if everything goes well – probably won't see a neonatal unit. These units are where sick and premature babies are taken to be looked after and nursed so they can eventually go home like other babies.

The neonatal unit at Chester was essentially four rooms – called nurseries – each containing incubators, ventilators, screens and other equipment for looking after vulnerable babies.

The biggest of the nurseries could accommodate four babies at any one time. The others had room for two each. So – all in all, fairly small. Not the kind of place where stuff goes unnoticed – you would have thought.

All neonatal units have their tragedies. It goes with the territory. But most stories in Chester had a happy outcome. The unit was what medics call a 'Level 2' unit. That means it wasn't set up to deal with the sickest babies. The really acute cases were directed elsewhere – to 'tertiary' units like Arrowe Park or Liverpool Women's Hospital.

When Lucy Letby first entered the Countess of Chester neonatal unit, there were about twenty-five to thirty nurses on the rota and a further fifteen junior nurses. A little daunting for any trainee nurse – even if it was one of the smaller units. But she was well supported. The unit gave her a mentor – an older senior nurse who'd been on the unit for years. She and Letby would eventually become close friends. Like many on the unit, her mentor would struggle to come to terms with the idea that the nurse she had helped train was a baby killer.

While at university, Letby did two stints at the Countess of Chester neonatal unit. If she managed to graduate with the results she needed to be a nurse, it would be the ideal place to get a job – familiar, local, not too large, and friendly.

On 4 January 2011, Letby turned twenty-one. In the run-up to the big day, a birthday message appeared in the local newspaper:[11] 'Happy 21st Birthday. Lots of love from Thomas and Matthew. xx'. In the course of our conversations with former friends of Letby's we were told that Thomas and Matthew are her godchildren. Beside the message was a picture of an angelic Letby as a young child – smiling cheekily, perched upright, with long golden hair topped with a black bow. It's hard to look at this picture of undaunted innocence, knowing how Letby's life would turn out.

September 2011 was another landmark month. Letby finally qualified as a nurse after finishing her degree – a BSc in Child Nursing. Back home in Hereford, her parents were over the moon. Now it was their turn to place a notice in the local newspaper to mark their daughter's achievement: a photo of Letby from gradua-tion day – complete with mortar board and gown – and a message for everyone in Hereford to see: 'We are so proud of you after all your hard work. Love Mum and Dad'.[12]

Things seemed to be working out as Letby had always planned. Her training placements at the Countess of Chester Hospital had gone well and as soon as she graduated, she was offered a job in the hospital's neonatal unit. It was a seamless transition from university to working life. By now, Letby knew the Countess of Chester Hospital and the staff and they knew her. It also helped that one of her fellow students from her nursing degree course had also landed a job in the same unit.

Melanie Taylor had also studied Child Nursing at the University of Chester, and after graduating she too got a job in the Countess of Chester's neonatal unit. Over the next four years, Letby and Mel would work closely together. Little did Mel know that she'd end up in a courtroom – testifying against her old university peer in one of the biggest murder trials in British legal history.

The senior nurses at the hospital seemed to like Letby. The doctors, on the other hand, were somewhat indifferent. 'She was very nice,' recalled one doctor. 'The worst you could have said about her is that she was a bit bland.' Another recalled conversations with Letby as 'bland and superficial'. 'There was nothing really exciting at all about her. She was vanilla.'

The most senior doctor on the unit, Dr Steve Brearey, was more diplomatic: 'She didn't strike me as too different to most nurses on the unit at the time, to be honest,' he recalled. 'She didn't strike me as being overly extrovert or overly introvert. She just appeared to be a normal band 5 neonatal nurse.'

Bland, inoffensive – a bit boring – seemed to be the general view from the doctors. The rank-and-file nurses were more varied in their opinions of Letby. To this day, Letby's former nursing colleagues are reluctant to speak about her publicly. Many of them have been deeply affected by being told that they were working alongside a killer. But one agreed to talk to us as long as we didn't reveal her name.

Her impressions of Letby sound familiar. 'She seemed quite timid,' the nurse told us.

'Really quite shy, very quiet.' But there was also a hint of some-thing else in Letby's reserve.

'I found her a little bit – I can't put my finger on it really. I just found her a little bit odd – odd in personality.'

As she had been at school, Letby was something of an in-betweener – socially speaking. She wasn't especially outgoing or popular. But she had a close group of nursing friends on the unit. Some would remain loyal to her right until the bitter end.

'They were a mixture really of younger and older nurses,' her former colleague told us. 'They seemed to see each other as a group out of work.'

Social media photos from the time show Letby smiling happily on nights out with her little posse of work pals. The more raucous 'goofy' antics of earlier years are absent from these pictures. The vibe is mumsy and sensible. Some in her group looked old enough to be her mother. But they all looked happy – Letby included.

On paper, Letby had friends and an active social life. She went to hen-dos, Christmas drinks, the gym and hula-hoop practice. She also started salsa lessons with another nurse from her unit. Letby had always liked dancing, but some of those who knew her have speculated that the salsa lessons might have been Letby's way of looking for a boyfriend. If that was her aim, she was unsuccessful. Letby remained single.

Most of the older nurses on the unit were already married with families. And as the months and years went by, the younger nurses started pairing off too. Some had kids. But Letby didn't. She'd been living in hospital accommodation until April 2014, at which point she moved into a rented house in the city. But in June 2015, she moved back into hospital accommodation – the very same month when babies on her unit started to die.[13]

Letby's parents remained as supportive and devoted to their daughter as they had been when she was in Hereford, and she leaned on them when things got difficult. She texted them most days and the family home in Hereford was a safe space when-ever she needed it. The trio even went on regular holidays to Torquay together. They'd been doing it since Letby was a child.

Their last stay in Torquay was just days before Letby's arrest in 2018.

But although she and her parents appeared to adore one another, at times Letby felt smothered. She confided to a friend that her parents hated the fact that she'd moved so far away from Hereford. It seems they hoped she'd come back after her degree. The fact that she'd stayed was a sore point. It didn't help that they worried constantly about her. 'My parents worry massively about anything & everything,' she wrote in a text exchange with one of her colleagues.

How trivial these everyday worries would look later on. Letby's parents would be unwavering in their loyalty to their daughter, but what of Letby's treatment of her parents? By the end of her trial, they would be broken people. If Letby is everything she was accused of being, her parents are certainly to be counted among her victims.

As a nurse, there was nothing exceptional about Lucy Letby. As she had been at school and university, she was competent and conscientious. No one on the neonatal unit had any worries about her abilities.

One thing did mark her out, however. She was always calm under pressure – unusually so. 'I saw a lot of instances where she was the one calling for help – being this very calm, collected person in a very stressful situation,' recalled one colleague. 'And then being there with families following those horrible situations where thankfully babies survived. She was incredibly effective and competent in a way that a lot of her peers in that smaller unit were not.'

Another colleague who had seen plenty of emergency situations in other hospitals reported a resuscitation in which Letby had been 'unbelievably calm – quite matter-of-fact'. Was this a testament to Letby's skill as a nurse whose job it was to look after vulnerable babies? Or could it have been a glimpse of something else – a coldness or even a sense of well-being in situations where babies were at risk of dying?

Letby's experience of looking after vulnerable babies wasn't confined to the Countess of Chester Hospital. In early 2012, she did six weeks' training at Liverpool Women's Hospital – about forty-five minutes' drive from Chester. It was a routine induction. All new neonatal nurses in the region had to do it. It was a way of ensuring they were all trained according to the same standards and procedures.

Unlike the Countess of Chester Hospital though, Liverpool Women's Hospital was a 'Level 3' unit, which meant it was officially equipped to care for the sickest babies. For Letby, this was a draw. According to Steve Brearey, who ran the neonatal unit in Chester, Letby had a preference for working in the intensive care environment with the sicker babies. In the case of any other nurse, this wouldn't have been a cause for alarm or suspicion. It was quite normal for nurses starting out to want to be where the action was. But what were Letby's motivations?

Whatever they were, Letby returned to Liverpool Women's Hospital for a further five weeks of training in 2015. This time, the training was more specialised – aimed at preparing her to care for the sickest babies in the unit back in Chester.

In the years to come, investigators would pore over Letby's two stints at Liverpool Women's Hospital. Were there any suspicious incidents while Letby was there? Had she harmed or attempted to harm babies during her training? Were there any signs of what was to follow at the Countess of Chester Hospital? But at the time, her colleagues in Liverpool noticed nothing amiss. Letby passed through the system as she had done at school and university. Senior staff there don't even remember her.

But managers at the Countess of Chester Hospital clearly liked Letby. She was the new girl, and for a while she even became the public face of her unit as part of an effort to get badly needed new facilities. When Letby started working there back in 2011, the unit was already on its last legs. The building – a drab 1970s structure – was shabby, pushing the limits of its lifespan. The fabric was outdated and its décor tired. There was hardly any space either. Cots and incubators were stored in the corridor, and there wasn't enough room for exhausted new mothers when they wanted to breastfeed their babies. Temporary screens had to be rolled in to afford them some privacy. Hospital executive Susan Gilby would later describe the place as 'dark, dingy and cramped'.[14] There were no external windows to let natural light in, the ceiling tiles were stained, and despite the best efforts of staff, who decorated the walls with cartoon animals, it was hardly the sort of soothing environment needed for the tender care of fragile families. Nor did it lend itself to the fast-changing hi-tech demands of such a challenging area of medicine, with equipment crammed into small storerooms and wheeled out on demand.

A new unit was badly needed, but NHS funds wouldn't cover the cost, and so the hospital had to find its own cash. In 2012, the hospital launched a public fundraising drive to raise the £3 million needed for the job. The local newspaper, the *Chester Standard*, jumped on board with splash coverage of the launch and vowed to bring readers weekly updates about the campaign.[15] It was called the Babygrow Appeal – and Letby was the poster girl.

In 2012, a photograph of Letby in her uniform smiling as she held a newborn baby appeared alongside a story about a donation to the appeal.[16] That same photograph would later appear on every newspaper front page below headlines about Britain's most prolific child serial killer.

In 2013, Letby was back in the local press – representing the Countess of Chester Hospital and the ongoing Babygrow Appeal. This time, she had her own profile piece about her life as a neonatal nurse.[17]

'What would a typical day in the neonatal unit involve?' she was asked.

My role involves caring for a wide range of babies requiring various levels of support. Some are here for a few days, others for many months and I enjoy seeing them progress and supporting their families. I am currently undergoing extra training in order to develop and enhance my knowledge and skills within the Intensive Care area and have recently completed a placement at Liverpool Women's Hospital.

'What will having a bigger neonatal unit mean to you?'

I hope the new unit will provide a greater degree of privacy and space for parents and siblings.

All very much on-message. So much so that hospital bosses gave the nurse top billing again and she featured in a full-page photograph in the Trust's annual report for 2012/13.[18] Back home in Hereford, Mr and Mrs Letby had plenty to stick in their cuttings book.

By 2015 there was another photo to add to the collection.[19] After endless coffee mornings, skydives and marathons, the fundraising drive had hit its halfway target. The paper celebrated with a bumper article, and a photograph of a small group of staff holding up signs to indicate the £1.5 million raised. Letby stands left of shot, smiling broadly and holding a large pound sign. Beside her was one of the hospital consultants. Years later, he would be one of many medics from Letby's unit whose court testimony would help send her to jail.

Chapter 2

Babies Begin to Die

Around one in thirteen babies born in the UK every year is premature[1] and many of those spend their earliest days in a hospital neonatal unit. It's not uncommon. But even so, ending up in a neonatal unit is never the plan of any expectant parent. In the afterglow of a positive pregnancy test, excited mums-and-dads-to-be may discuss baby names, talk about nursery colour schemes, or start researching buggies and high chairs. Seldom do they let their minds contemplate another possibility: that the start of their baby's life might involve incubators and nasal feeding tubes.

It would certainly have felt far-fetched to one loved-up couple on holiday at the end of 2014. Thoughts of babies weren't on their minds. That was, until an unexpected positive pregnancy test which was to change their lives forever.[2] They were thrilled, and the excitement ramped up even further when a scan later provided a second surprise, revealing that twins were on the way. '2015 was going to be the best year of our lives,' they reflected. We were going to become parents of a little boy and a little girl!'[3] The future looked wonderful as they got ready to become a family.

There was only one thing that put a possible dampener on the celebrations. The mum-to-be had an autoimmune blood disorder, and she was worried about the impact it could have on the pregnancy. Although the couple lived in the catchment area for the Countess of Chester Hospital, the mother was under the care of a professor in London and wanted to have the babies there by elective Caesarean section, with specialist support. The couple decided to stay at home in the North West of England until close to the end of the pregnancy, and then move to the capital in time to have the babies.[4]

But it wasn't to be. With just a week to go before they were due to relocate, the twins' mother started suffering from symptoms which doctors suspected could be pre-eclampsia – a potentially serious condition which causes high blood pressure during pregnancy. She was declared unfit to travel. The local hospital would have to suffice. Less than a month later, with her blood pressure rising, she was taken down to theatre for an emergency Caesarean section, and the babies were born just under nine weeks early.[5]

The twin girl arrived first, weighing 3lb 11oz, and her brother emerged one minute later weighing just one ounce more than his sister. It should have been a moment of celebration for both parents, but there was no chance for them to enjoy their first moment as a family, for soft words of hello, or baby cuddles. The twins were checked and taken straight to the intensive care section of the neonatal unit, and their mother was moved to the high-dependency recovery area. For medical reasons she'd had to give birth under general anaesthetic and although the twins' dad was able to visit them overnight, it wasn't until the following day – more than fifteen hours after giving birth – that their mum was put into a wheelchair and taken round to meet her babies.[6]

The twins were still in the intensive care room, known as Nursery One. It was an overwhelming place to host such a tender first meeting. The room rang to the sound of alarms and machines pulsing with metronomic bleeps. Monitors flashed with line charts and constantly refreshing data. There was apparatus everywhere, and although staff had made efforts to soften the décor with painted cartoons and animal friezes, the childish pictures were somewhat lost amidst a forest of screens, plugs and gas ports.

The twins' parents longed to hold their son and daughter and start to bond with them, but the babies were both in incubators and they weren't able to pick them up yet. The two cots were at ninety degrees to each other in a corner of the nursery,[7] and they peered through the plastic sides at their children who seemed so tiny and fragile. The baby girl couldn't breathe by herself and she was hooked up to a ventilator. Her brother was doing a little better, and was coping without extra oxygen, but his parents' eyes were drawn to his belly button, which was attached to a catheter tube.[8] It was terrifying, but they felt better when they were told that the babies were stable and doing well.[9] This was the nurses' normality, and they bustled around, reassuring the couple that things were OK.

Lucy Letby was on duty that night. All the babies in the unit had their own 'designated nurse' and she was assigned to the boy twin, which was good news as far as her manager was concerned. Letby was thought of as a model nurse – conscientious, calm under pressure, and good with parents – the ideal carer for a baby needing intensive care.

The parents of the twins had spent an hour gazing at their son and daughter before the nurses told the twins' mum that she really needed to rest, and they went to the maternity ward. It was hard to sleep though, and as evening drew in they decided to go and watch TV in a side room with the twins' grandmother, who'd arrived to meet the new arrivals. It was a chance to relax after the intensity of the last twenty-four hours. But suddenly there was a commotion. A male nurse ran in shouting, 'You need to come quickly, there's something wrong with twin two!'

They raced back to find a crowd of people surrounding the baby boy's cot. 'It felt like hundreds of people were standing there, trying to resuscitate him,' his mum recalled later. 'A nurse asked if I was religious, and if I wanted them to say a prayer.' A consultant and a registrar were working on the boy, giving him shots of adrenaline to stimulate his heart, and trying everything that would normally work to bring a baby back from the brink of death. It was fruitless, and his grandmother knew it. Years later she recounted the events of that harrowing evening. 'The minute I went into that room and saw him, I knew he was gone. He was blue.'[10] But the twins' mum couldn't bring herself to let them stop. Crying uncontrollably, she sobbed, 'Please don't let my baby die! Please don't let my baby die!'[11]

Letby was there among the throng. She'd been on duty for less than half an hour when the emergency started, but she was known to be good in a crisis and if she was panicking, she certainly didn't show it. The other medics knew what they were doing too. But this emergency had caught all of them by surprise. For some reason, the little boy had stopped breathing. No one could work out why, or why they couldn't get his heart to restart. There were also strange fleeting patches of pink and blue which seemed to appear and disappear on the baby's chest. It was like nothing they'd ever seen before.[12] Lost in surreal trauma, his helpless family could only watch, plead and pray. They were in this limbo for twenty minutes,[13] but it felt like an eternity, and even now the memory is still so painful they say they've blanked much of it out.[14]

The baby's father was rooted to the floor in shock, unable to take in what he was witnessing. He couldn't bring himself to speak, but through the haze of his disbelief he became aware that the doctors were telling them that they'd tried all they could, and his son would have brain damage and other complications if he survived. They'd now been striving to save the infant for half an hour. Doctors felt the kindest thing to do would be to stop,[15] but they needed the couple's permission.

The mother was hysterical and pleaded for them to carry on with the chest compressions, but her partner somehow found the words to tell her, 'We have to let him go, he's not there any more.' He later described it as one of the most difficult things he'd ever had to do.[16] Eventually the baby boy's mother relented and nodded. Almost exactly twenty-four hours after he was born, the baby was pronounced dead. The family was poleaxed.[17]

The medics were upset too. Babies rarely collapsed without warning, and when they did it was usually possible to revive them. It was one of the first deaths that paediatric registrar David Harkness had experienced. 'This was a completely stable, well baby, who had no reason to suddenly deteriorate,' he recalled.[18] Years later, neonatal nurse assistant Lisa Walker said she could still recall the 'sadness in the atmosphere' on the unit that evening; she remembers thinking, 'What on earth is happening?'[19]

After the boy's death, Lucy Letby tried to comfort the grieving parents. She took hand and footprints of the baby, photographed him, and snipped a lock of his hair.[20] She later wrote in her nursing notes that she did it with the couple's blessing, for a memory box, but the parents were too distressed to accept.

One of the nurses asked the couple if they wanted to hold their son. They said they did, and so Lucy Letby brought him to them. They sat quietly with the baby in their arms, saying loving goodbyes to their boy, whose life had ended just one day after it began.[21] As they struggled to comprehend their loss, they realised that they'd never even had the chance to cuddle their boy while he was alive. 'By the time I was brought to him, he was gone,' his mother recalled bitterly.[22]

Just a few feet away, the boy's surviving twin sister was sleeping quietly in her incubator. She was too fragile to be held for long, but the nurse told her parents it was safe to take her out for short periods. The new mum took her little girl in her arms. Was it possible to feel joy and grief at the same time? After everything that had happened, this moment had both.[23] For the babies' dad, it was too much. 'She was so small I said no as I didn't want to hurt her,' he recalled.[24]

As the medics tried to make sense of what had just happened, an emergency post-mortem examination was ordered to ascertain why the baby boy had died. But it was inconclusive – the cause of death was ultimately recorded as 'unascertained'.[25]

After the shock of what had just happened, doctors were now worried that the surviving twin could also be at risk of a sudden deterioration. They managed to rule out the mother's blood condition as a potential concern, but stress levels on the unit were running high.

At 8 a.m. on 9 June 2015, Lucy Letby and the rest of the night staff finished their shift. They were all reeling. Back at home, Letby searched for the twins' mother on Facebook. Knowing how Letby's story would turn out, it seems weird and unsettling. It wouldn't be the first time Lucy Letby would search for grieving parents online.

The next evening, Letby was back on duty for another night shift and she appeared to be apprehensive. She texted two colleagues to say that she didn't want to encounter the twins' parents or look after the surviving baby:[26]

I think we all did everything we possibly could under very difficult & sad circumstances. Haven't slept much, don't really want to see parents tonight but it's got to be done.[27]

Dad was on the floor crying Saying please don't take our baby away when I took him to the mortuary, it's just heart-breaking . . . It was the hardest thing I've ever had to do.[28]

Her colleagues were sympathetic. 'You did amazing,' one messaged. 'So proud of you. Hope that doesn't sound patronising. It's genuine. You did fab. Xxxx'[29] The unit's deputy manager[30] Yvonne Griffiths texted to see how Letby was coping, and gushed, 'I'm sure the girls were glad you were there xxx.'[31]

Nurses look out for each other and Letby's colleagues sensed she was feeling shaken. She'd said she couldn't face seeing the family again so soon, so she was given responsibility for two babies in a different part of the unit.[32] But that didn't mean she stayed away from the surviving twin sister, who was still in the intensive care room. During the evening, Letby helped with the baby girl's feeds and took a reading of her blood gas.

Then, just after midnight, the baby's monitors sounded their alarms. Her oxygen levels had suddenly plummeted and she wasn't breathing. Letby was quick to the scene after one of the nurses called for help. She had done specialist training for moments like this and her skills were now needed. An emergency 'crash' call was put out and medics came running, just as they had for the baby's brother the night before.[33]

Though the twins' parents had kept vigil by their daughter's cot-side ever since their son's death, they hadn't eaten and had been told to get some rest. Their mum was back on the maternity ward when she had the worst of all déjà vu experiences. For the second time in just over twenty-four hours she was told there was something wrong, and she had to rush to her child. She remembers feeling – 'Not my baby. Not again!' – as she hurried to the neonatal unit.[34] It seemed particularly shocking as she thought the girl was doing well. She'd even been able to cuddle her earlier that afternoon, when the baby was well enough to spend two hours without breathing support, and as she'd held her to her skin, the infant had made signs of rooting for milk.[35]

But now she too needed resuscitation. The nurse who began the effort to save the baby noticed that her skin was changing colour rapidly and was covered in unusual purple and white blotches. Her heart rate was dropping and a tube was put down her tiny throat so she could be given oxygen through a ventilator.

This time, after forty minutes, the medics' efforts worked.[36] They managed to resuscitate the baby girl, her heart rate increased, and her breathing restarted. She even became lively, and by the time the on-call consultant arrived to respond to the emergency, the little girl's skin was no longer as discoloured,[37] though it was still noticeable, and it surprised the doctor who said she'd never seen it before.[38] She hadn't been on shift the previous night.

Mercifully, the baby made a full recovery.[39] But her parents were forever changed by the experience of nearly losing her too, a day after losing her brother.

'From that moment on I became frantic about it. I wouldn't leave her side,' the mother said later. The baby's father was similarly affected: 'We both became, and still are, extremely protective of our daughter.'[40]

For the nurses on the neonatal unit, the events of the past two nights were a shock. Letby seemed as shaken as anyone. On 10 June, she messaged a couple of her fellow nurses from the comfort of her sofa to ask how the baby girl was doing: 'I think we all need answers,' she wrote.[41] But there was room for small talk too. *An Hour to Save Your Life* was on TV – a documentary about doctors and midwives battling with neonatal emergencies and fighting to keep babies alive. It was an odd choice of viewing, given what had just happened. But Letby was glued. One of the nurses texted back in surprise, 'I don't really watch things like that. Get enough in work . . . I just like chill out stuff.' Letby replied: 'Yeah true. I just find it interesting to see how our work is portrayed to the public. X'[42]

On average, there were just two or three deaths a year on the neonatal unit at the Countess of Chester Hospital. But 2015 was different. The month of June alone would see two more baby deaths – and in each case, staff couldn't figure out why.

Three days after the death of the twin on 8 June, Lucy Letby was at home and at a loose end. She wanted to be back at work so she texted the deputy unit manager Yvonne Griffiths: 'Hi Yvonne, are you OK for staffing over next few days? I don't have anything on if need any extra or need to change my nights X'. It was classic Lucy – always keen and available to work. As it happened, the rota for the next few days was already well staffed.

But Letby didn't just want to be back at work. She wanted to be where the action was. 'Think I need to throw myself back in on Sat X', she texted her manager. 'Think from a confidence point of view I need to take an ITU [intensive therapy unit] baby soon X'.[43]

Nursery One was where the high-dependency babies were looked after. It's where the twin had just died. But when Letby returned to work on 13 June, she found herself relegated to Nursery Three – one of the rooms for neonates with fewer vulnerabilities.[44]

It clearly annoyed her. Shortly after the night shift began, she texted an off-duty nursing colleague and friend: 'I just keep thinking about Monday,' she wrote, referring to the death of the twin boy earlier that week. 'Feel like I need to be in [nursery] 1 to overcome it.'[45]

For some reason, Letby needed to process the experience of seeing a baby die by returning to the very spot on the ward where the tragedy had happened. Or at least that's what she said. Even Letby's friend found this a bit strange. 'I agree with [the shift manager],' she texted back. 'Don't think it will help. You need a break from full on ITU . . . It sounds very odd and I would be complete opposite.' But Letby was insistent, arguing that it was how they'd done things at Liverpool Women's Hospital during her work placement there. 'I lost a baby one day and few hours later was given another dying baby just born in the same cot space,' she wrote. 'Girls there said it was important to overcome the image.'

Lucy Letby was frustrated. Being frozen out of Nursery One was eating her up. She didn't seem particularly happy with her on-duty colleagues that night either. There wasn't much 'team spirit', she complained. Even her friend Jenny Jones-Key got the brunt of her frustration.

'Forget it,' she texted Jenny tetchily. 'I can only talk about it properly with those who knew him . . . I'll overcome it myself.'

She was talking about the twin boy who had died almost a week earlier. Whatever was going through Letby's head, she was clearly still brooding on the death.

'That's a bit mean isn't it,' replied Jenny. 'Don't have to know him to understand – we've all been there.'

'Forget it,' Letby repeated. 'I'm obviously making more of it than I should X.'

Six minutes after Lucy Letby's text exchange with her friend finished, crisis struck again. A young nurse called Sophie Ellis was on duty that evening. Sophie was fairly new to the job, but the shift leader had given her a baby in Nursery One to look after – the room where Letby wanted to be. At 11.15 p.m., Sophie had left the nursery for a few minutes when the alarms on the baby's incubator sounded. She ran back in a panic.

Letby was already there when she got back. The baby's heart rate and oxygen levels had dropped. A few minutes later, the baby's monitors sounded again, and this time Nurse Sophie put out a crash call for the doctors to attend. But by now the baby boy was fighting for his life. Lucy Letby seemed to read exactly what was happening. 'He's going,' she said. And she was right.[46]

Sophie did chest compressions while one of the other nurses went to wake up the boy's mother, who was asleep on the post-natal ward. The baby's heart rate had nosedived and he'd suddenly stopped breathing.[47] No one could understand it. Earlier that day he'd been well enough to be taken out of the incubator. His mother had held him on her chest and cuddled him 'skin-to-skin'.[48] Now he was dying.

When the baby's mother arrived, she was distraught as she watched the medics fighting to save her son. Nothing they were doing seemed to be working. It was all too much for the baby's nurse, Sophie. 'Do you want me to take over?' Letby asked her. 'Yes,' said Sophie.

For forty minutes, the medics did everything they could to save the baby. But his vocal cords were swollen, and they struggled to get a breathing tube into position. Despite multiple attempts to resuscitate him, the baby failed to respond.

Eventually one of the nurses asked the boy's parents if they wanted a priest to be called. What a gut-wrenching question to put to a new mother. Was her baby going to die? she asked. 'Yes, I think so,' came the response. And so the priest came and the baby boy was baptised. 'It was a way in which we were able to validate that he had been here,' his mother reflected later. 'We wouldn't have had anything else.'[49]

A consultant asked the parents if they wanted CPR to continue. Scans showed that the baby's brain had been badly damaged from lack of oxygen, and they decided not to carry on. 'I just wanted us to be together,' the mother said.

The boy's short life had all but ended, but as his mother held him, she could still feel him breathing.[50]

With nurse Sophie Ellis recovering from the shock of what had just happened, Lucy Letby took on the role of helping the baby's grieving parents. It seemed to be something she wanted – or needed – to do. Perhaps she was trying to prove something. Whatever it was, there was something awkward or misjudged about her manner. After the resuscitation efforts had stopped, Letby helped take the baby, his parents and grandparents to a family room. The little boy's father remembers that, as they sat with him, one of the nurses – who he thought could have been Letby – brought a ventilator basket in and said, 'You've said your goodbyes; do you want me to put him in here?' It was a jarring question. The awful decision to stop the resuscitation had been taken. The parents knew their baby boy was going to die. But for now, there was still life in his tiny body and his family weren't ready to part with him.[51]

Nor, it seems, was Lucy Letby. She had embraced the role of family comforter, but her shift leader that night wasn't impressed. Reflecting later on the events of that evening, the senior nurse recalled asking Letby several times to give the parents space. To Letby's colleagues, her behaviour probably looked like an excess of sympathy and wanting to help. But was there a darker compulsion that was pushing her towards these grieving parents and their pain? Was this the same compulsion that had left her fretting at being excluded from Nursery One?

By now, two babies had died within the space of a week. After the second death, Letby texted her friend Jenny Jones-Key, picking up from the tense conversation they'd been having six minutes before the baby collapsed:

Sorry if I was off just wasn't a great start to shift but sadly it got worse. X[52]

I was struggling to accept what happened to [the first boy who had died six days earlier]. Now we've lost [another boy] overnight & It's all a bit much. X

Jenny was as shocked as everyone else. But Letby seemed philosophical about the latest baby to die: '[It was] the little 800g baby, went off very suddenly. Sophie was looking after him . . . We worked really well . . . Think we all supported each other brilliantly.' She ended the text with a brisk, 'anyway it's happened . . . have to carry on.'

'Hoping you're going to be OK,' Jenny replied. 'This isn't like you. Sending you biggest hugs. Xx'

Letby seemed glad of the sympathy. 'No one should have to see & do the things we do,' she replied immediately. 'It's heartbreaking. But it's not about me. We learn to deal with it.'

'It's not about me or anyone else, it's those poor parents who have to walk away without their baby. It's so unbelievably sad.'

Letby texted her mum back home in Hereford too.

'We lost a little one overnight,' she wrote. 'Very unexpected & sad . . . Sophie the new girl was looking after him, she's devastated.' Sue Letby sent sympathy back, with some added encouragement – 'we r so proud of you. Love u xxx'.[53]

Nurses and medics are a special breed. They have to be kind and soft and compassionate. But they also have to be tough. They see the full range of human emotions, from joy and elation to abject pain and suffering. Occasionally, a bit of old-fashioned gallows humour helps lighten the darkest moments. That's where the term 'shit magnet' comes from. A 'shit magnet' is a nurse or medic who experiences an especially bad run of luck, and to her colleagues, that's what Letby was.

On 22 June, a fourth baby on the neonatal unit collapsed unexpectedly. The baby girl was just two days old. Fresh horror for another set of unsuspecting parents. The birth hadn't been smooth, and the hospital hadn't helped. The baby's mother recalled being sent away when she was almost ready to give birth and maternity staff failed to give her much-needed antibiotics to stave off possible infection.[54] But by the time the baby girl reached the neonatal unit, her parents believed the worst was behind them.

The doctors and nurses did too. Although the little girl had pneumonia, medics thought it was under control and the baby was on the mend. But at around 1.30 in the morning of 22 June 2015, nurses noticed a change in her appearance. The infant appeared stiff and parts of her skin had turned brown and black.[55]

The baby's mum, who was still exhausted from major surgery, was asleep back on the postnatal ward. The next thing she knew, she was being woken up in the early hours by one of the nurses who seemed to be in a panic. There was no time to lose, she said. Her daughter was dangerously ill. They raced to the neonatal unit to find a doctor trying desperately to resuscitate the baby. As he worked on her, Lucy Letby held a phone to his ear so he could take instructions.

This was the third time that night that the baby girl had needed resuscitating. Twice before, the on-call registrar had managed to save her, but there was little more that he could do now. Five doses of adrenaline within ten minutes and half an hour of CPR weren't enough.[56] The doctors realised that their efforts were futile and after a discussion with the parents, the decision was taken to stop. Four minutes after treatment was withdrawn the little girl died.[57] Her parents were inconsolable. No one had told them this could happen. That night still haunts them. 'I was never given the impression that [our daughter's] condition was life-threatening,' the dad reflected. 'And it didn't even cross my mind that she was in danger of dying. When she died, we just were not prepared for it.'[58]

Something didn't add up. After the baby girl's death, the broken couple contacted a solicitor to see if they could get any answers. But there were none to be found. No one had done anything wrong. 'This isn't a criminal matter,' the solicitor assured them.[59]

Everyone was baffled. The unit had just seen as many deaths in two weeks as they would normally expect to see in a year. Everyone felt sorry for Lucy too. She'd been on duty for all three deaths. For any normal nurse, it would be devastating. 'I can't believe you were on again,' one of her nursing pals texted her. 'You having such a tough time . . . Oh Hun. You need a break . . . you've had it all recently.'[60]

'We have the shittiest [job] in the world at times. And the best,' the nurse added.

Letby agreed. It seemed it was what she needed to hear. But still – why? Why so many deaths in such a short space of time? Letby herself appeared to be wrestling with this same question:

[O]n a day to day basis it's an incredible job with so many positives. But then sometimes I think, how do such sick babies get through & others just die so suddenly & unexpectedly? Guess it's how it's meant to be . . . I think there is an element of fate involved. There is a reason for everything

Letby's nursing pal was less philosophical. 'There's something odd about that night and the other 3 that went so suddenly,' she wrote in a text exchange with Letby a week later.

But Letby had ready answers to explain her run of bad luck. One baby was tiny and compromised *in utero*, another was septic, she said. It was the twin boy who was a puzzle, she suggested: 'I can't get my head around [him].'

By now, the senior medics on the unit were concerned too. Post-mortems into the three deaths were done quickly. Pneumonia with acute lung injury was the official explanation for one of the deaths. Another was blamed on heart damage caused by lung disease, while the first of the three deaths was recorded as 'unascertained'.[61] But these post-mortem reports took months to complete, and, in any event, they left the big questions unanswered. What was the root cause of these deaths and why had no one seen them coming? That was a particular red flag – medical staff on these units are trained to anticipate, and they usually spot warning signs early. One unexpected death is abnormal. Three in the space of two weeks was a shock.

On 2 July 2015, the unit's lead paediatric consultant Steve Brearey met with two hospital bosses and the unit manager, a plain-speaking Welshwoman called Eirian Powell.[62] Powell managed the nurses and seemed to have their trust. The meeting was calm and rational, with systematic examination of the quality of medical care given to each baby.

'We tried to be as thorough as possible,' Dr Brearey recalled later. 'We looked at microbiology, ventilator places, incubator spaces.'[63]

But no one could find a common medical link between the deaths. No one at the meeting was looking for scapegoats, but, naturally enough, the question of staffing was raised – in particular, which staff had been on duty when the babies died. All three times, it had been during the night. Different teams of regular nurses had been on duty, and while some had been there for one or two of the deaths, only one had been present for all three.

'A staffing analysis was done,' Brearey recalled. 'And that analysis did identify that Lucy Letby was on shift for those three episodes.'[64]

But no one had any reason to be suspicious. Lucy Letby had been working on the unit for four years. She was good at her job and she was trusted by her colleagues. Three deaths in a single month was shocking, certainly. But statistical blips do happen. 'I can remember saying, it can't be Lucy. Not nice Lucy,' Brearey recalled. He spoke for everyone at the meeting. No one had entertained the idea Letby was in some way at fault.

The meeting ended without any firm conclusions. But, although no one was blaming Letby, her name was now on the radar of senior staff – and not just the hands-on medical staff. Alison Kelly – the head of nursing and one of the most senior bosses in the hospital – had been at the meeting with Brearey and the others. She'd heard Letby's name come up and she'd clearly clocked it. 'Keep an eye on it,' she said.

That same month, Letby went on holiday – one of her habitual trips to Torquay with her parents. But by August 2015, she was back on night shifts. A new set of twins had arrived on the unit. The two boys had been born during the previous week, delivered eleven weeks early because of an issue with their mum's placenta. She was supposed to have had them at Liverpool Women's Hospital but there were no beds available, and she was told that she could end up as far away from home as Sheffield or Cardiff. So, even though she and her husband had never heard of the Countess of Chester Hospital they were relieved when they were told that's where she was going to be sent, as it wasn't too far for friends and family to come and visit.[65]

The birth went smoothly, and because of the twins' prematurity there was a team ready to take them to the neonatal unit. When their parents went to visit them together a few hours later they were told that the boys were in great condition. The older one was doing exceptionally well and was already breathing by himself. The younger baby needed a bit more help, but it all looked positive, and the new parents were absolutely thrilled.[66] It was just hard to believe that they were here at the beginning of August, when they hadn't been due until October. Years later, their mother told us, 'I didn't believe they were mine. I just looked at them and said, "They're too small, they're not mine!" but then thought, "Absolutely yes, they're my children. They look exactly like my husband . . . just a really small, tiny version of him."'

The twins had been born on a Wednesday, and though they were too small to be breastfed yet, their mum started expressing milk to be fed to them by tube. By the weekend, she was in her stride with her routine. At night she'd set an alarm to wake herself up at three-hourly intervals, express the milk, and walk down to the unit to drop it off.

She'd then take a look at the boys before going back to bed. Everything seemed good. The boys were thriving too. The younger twin was still being given some moderate breathing support, but the older one was much more self-sufficient. His mum says 'he was exceeding everybody's expectations . . . He was just absolutely brilliant.'

For a while, the neonatal unit was home for the new mother. She got to know the staff and the nurses – including Lucy Letby. She and Letby chatted about everything from houses to love lives. 'She told me about her life, we told her about our life,' the mother told us. 'She told me that she was single and she was quite happy being single, and just general chit-chat like that.' What about her personality? What was Letby like? 'Lucy was respectful,' the mother told us. 'She was always very softly spoken and she seemed quite timid. And that was her whole demeanour.'

By 3 August 2016, the boys were strong enough to spend much of the day having 'skin-to-skin' cuddles with their parents, and that evening their dad thought he'd better go home to start getting the house ready for when they were eventually ready to be discharged.

Letby was the designated nurse for both twins that night. They were the only babies in Nursery One, and she was in her favourite room on the unit with no one to disturb her. But at around 9 p.m., the twins' mother popped down from the maternity ward to deliver expressed milk for her boys. As she walked along the corridor towards the unit, the mother heard a horrifying sound – a scream from the room where her two boys were lying. 'It was a sound that shouldn't have come from a tiny baby,' she recalled later. 'It felt like more than crying . . . I've never heard anything like it since . . . and I thought, "My word, somebody's baby is really upset."' She went into the room and saw that it was her boy – the older and stronger of the twins. 'He was screaming,' she remembers, 'and I thought, "What's the matter with him? . . . What on earth is happening? I literally left an hour and a half ago. How have we gone from that to this?"'[67]

Lucy Letby was in the room, but she didn't seem to be reacting. '[Her behaviour] was almost dismissive,' the mother recalls. 'She made no eye contact with me . . . You know when it feels like someone wants to look busy but they're not actually doing anything? It felt like that. She was moving things around, and just didn't seem bothered.'

The little boy's mother went over to his incubator and saw that he had dark blood all around his mouth. It hadn't dried and was still tacky. She felt in her gut that there was something badly wrong, but Lucy Letby was calm and reassured the boy's mother there was nothing to worry about. 'She was very softly spoken and said, "Oh, don't worry. It's his feed tube rubbing the back of his throat. I've contacted the registrar and he's going to be here soon." She almost made it sound like it happens all the time.' The distressed mother took Letby at her word. She had no reason not to. 'She told me to go back to the ward, and if there was a problem she'd contact me.'

The twins' mum obeyed, but her instinct told her that her boy was in trouble so she raced back to the maternity ward to get her phone and call her husband. 'Although I'd had a (Caesarean) section I literally felt like I levitated up the stairs,' she recalled. 'I needed to ring my husband. I knew something wasn't right.'

Her husband tried to reassure her. The medics knew what they were doing, he reasoned. But back on the neonatal unit, the baby boy was deteriorating. Shortly after 10 p.m. he vomited fresh blood. The same thing happened again less than an hour later. By now, medics were concerned about the amount of blood that the boy was losing. The on-call consultant had been called, but by the time she got to the unit, the situation had escalated.

Just before 11 p.m., one of the midwives told the boy's mother to come down to the unit. Through the window of the intensive care room she could see a crowd around her baby's incubator. She watched the frenetic scene for about ten minutes, and then somebody came out from the room into the corridor and asked the baby's mum if she wanted to have him christened. It was too much to process. 'Even at that point it never dawned on me that he would die. My husband arrived and we were taken in and told to talk to him and hold his hand. And then he was christened, and there were still lots of people around, and he just seemed so small.'

The doctors had been battling for more than forty-five minutes, with two rounds of CPR and five shots of adrenaline. It was hopeless. Even the distressed young mother could see that now. 'The consultant said, "We're going to stop, it's no good. We've been working on him and it's not helping, and we want him to die in your arms rather than being worked on." So we said OK, and they passed him to us, and he died.'

Years later, the events of that night would be dissected in police interview rooms, lawyers' offices, and in a public courtroom for all to see and hear. Witnesses would be questioned about every minute of that evening. But the search for answers would be a frustrating one. The consultant on duty that night could see how distressed the parents were. They could barely think straight or process what was happening. She offered them the option of a post-mortem examination, but she decided not to push for it. She believed that the baby had died as a result of a bowel condition, and she told them so. The baby's mother later said, 'She mentioned a post-mortem, and I think my husband asked what it would tell us, and she said, "It won't really tell you anything apart from what I've told you." So we said, "OK, we won't have one," because we wanted to get him back home. To be honest, we wanted our other son out of there.' No post-mortem was carried out. It would be the first of several missed opportunities to figure out why so many babies were dying unexpectedly.[68]

Once again, Lucy Letby was hands-on with the grieving parents. 'She took control of the situation,' the mother recalled. 'She asked if I wanted to bathe him, and I said I couldn't. I just couldn't. I'd gone from having a healthy, albeit small, baby in my arms a few hours earlier – almost without a care in the world, thrilled to bits – to having my baby die in my arms. I just couldn't understand what had happened. I was shocked at how quickly it had all played out. So she asked me if I would like her to bathe him in front of me, and I said yes. I was sitting there with my husband, and she bathed him, and dressed him in a little woollen gown, and gave him back to us. I just remember being thankful because we had no clothes for him because he was so little.'[69]

They held their son for a little while longer, and then the nurse put him back in his incubator. Later, Letby took photographs of the baby. She hadn't asked the parents. Perhaps she thought they wouldn't mind.

Here was another couple mourning the death of one of their twins while the other twin slept peacefully in the same room – a surreal and cruel déjà vu.

The next morning when the couple arrived to see their younger twin, they found their deceased son's body lying in the adjacent incubator. It utterly devastated them. The mother told us, 'I got a real shock because he was just lying in that woollen gown in his incubator and I said, "Why is he still here?"'

The previous night, Lucy Letby had spoken to her dismissively. Now her voice was back to being sing-song soft. 'He's still going to be here,' explained Letby. 'Until you ask us to take him away, he'll stay there.'

The mother believes it was Lucy Letby who led the after-death process, and kept the baby in the room. She told us, 'It shouldn't have been for me to say when I was ready for him to go, because I didn't know. I remember feeling horrified that he was just lying in the incubator. We weren't given the opportunity to go and be with him in one of the family rooms. We weren't given the opportunity to grieve as a family in private. Everything was in full view.'[70]

For the young couple, Nursery One was now a place of death and grief, so they had their surviving twin moved to another of the four nurseries on the unit. They stayed with him all day, until it was time to leave him some milk and say goodnight.

At about half past one in the morning, there was a knock on the door. It was a nurse. The couple's second twin had suddenly become very unwell, and his heart rate was soaring. The baby's mum recalled that awful moment with haunting clarity. 'It was almost exactly twenty-four hours since our other son had died, and I thought it was happening again. I said to my husband, "Please, not again. We can't do this again. What on earth is happening? What's going on?"'

They raced to their son's side and although they thought he looked OK, his monitors said otherwise. The baby's heart rate was off the scale, and it was terrifying to watch. 'It was absolutely through the roof,' his mother told us. 'And I sat in the chair all night just focusing on watching the monitor and looking at him, and looking back at the screen, and listening to the bleeps all night, and almost trying to will the machine to bring his heart rate down and make it OK.'

An unexpected drop in blood sugar had caused the little boy's heart to surge. No one knew why. All they knew was that if they didn't keep pumping him with dextrose and glucose, the boy might die. For sixteen hours, medics fought to stabilise him. They changed his nutrition bags and checked his blood, and by the evening of 5 August, he was far more stable and seemed to be returning to normal.[71]

The boy survived and a few days later arrangements were made to move him to another hospital. Lucy Letby was there to say good-bye to the couple. Afterwards, she WhatsApp'd another off-duty nurse: 'They both cried & hugged me saying that they will never be able to thank me for the love & care I gave to (the older twin) & for the precious memories I've given them. It's heartbreaking.'[72]

'It is heartbreaking,' her colleague texted back, 'but you've done your job to the highest standard with compassion and profession-alism . . . You should feel very proud of yourself Xxxx'

The family had made an impression on Letby. Over the coming months, she searched for them online. She'd already started looking at the couple's social media profiles before they left the hospital, and she made multiple further searches in the days and months that followed – even on Christmas Day.

To staff on the neonatal unit, the near-death of the second twin was another inexplicable event. But it shouldn't have been. A week after that terrifying day of plummeting blood sugar levels, the nearby lab in Liverpool got in touch with the neonatal unit at the Countess of Chester Hospital. They'd been asked to run a test on the boy's blood and found high levels of insulin. According to the lab results, the insulin wasn't natural and the boy hadn't been prescribed any at the time. So why was it there?

We've seen medical records from the time. They record one of the doctors on the unit telling a senior consultant about the results of the blood test – the same consultant who hadn't ordered a post-mortem after the death of the first twin. To trained medical eyes, the insulin blood results for the second twin should have been an instant red flag. But nobody seemed to realise the seriousness of the situation. There was no crisis moment and no investigation into why a baby had apparently been poisoned with insulin. Why? We spoke with the consultant concerned. Here's what they told us:

> The blood results were very confusing as Child F had not been prescribed insulin and we checked and no other baby on NNU had been prescribed insulin that day, making accidental administration unlikely. Neonatal blood samples are very small and difficult to obtain. As a result, it is relatively common for samples to give inaccurate results as the blood cells are broken down (haemolysis) or clotted together. It happens most commonly with urea and electrolyte tests or full blood count tests. I felt that the most likely explanation for the results was some sort of inaccuracy with the test and I would have liked to repeat them, but Child F had no further periods of hypoglycaemia and was transferred back to his local unit. It is our usual practice to repeat neonatal bloods that do not fit with the expected clinical picture. I did consider that insulin could have been delivered deliberately but this seemed absurd and ridiculously unlikely so the tests being wrong seemed the only possible explanation.[73]

It's a very human reaction. What doctor would think that a colleague was poisoning babies? But it was also a deeply unfortunate oversight. It's painful to think of the heartache that might have been avoided had that blood insulin result from the lab been properly assessed at the time. And there would be more baby deaths and collapses before medics on the unit arrived at an explanation for what was going wrong.

Chapter 3

A Hospital in Crisis

By August 2015, four babies had died in just three months – all while Letby was on duty. But the overwhelming feeling from Letby's colleagues was sympathy rather than blame.

'Poor you. You're having a shit time of it,' one of her friends texted her. 'I really feel for his parents, but for you too. You've had some really tough times recently.'

'We're on a terrible run at the moment,' wrote another. 'You need a break from it being on your shift.'

'It's the luck of [the] drawer [*sic*] isn't it, unfortunately,' replied Letby.

'You seem to be having some very bad luck though,' came the response.

'Not a lot I can do really,' she retorted. 'He had massive haemorrhage – could have happened to any baby x'[1]

The following month, another baby on the unit died while Lucy Letby was on duty, and there were more unexpected collapses too. With such fragility of life on the unit, it was no wonder that, when babies hit significant milestones, there was extra reason to make a fuss. And 7 September 2015 was one such special day. One of the babies had defied the odds and reached her one hundred days birthday. Doctors had given the baby a 5 per cent chance of survival.[2] When she was born, she weighed just 1lb 2oz[3] and was no bigger than her father's hand. 'We had something like five discussions with doctors about her not making it,' her mother recalled. 'But she showed the doctors that she was a fighter.'[4]

To mark her hundred days birthday, one of the nurses brought in a cake, and a group of them worked together at the main desk to craft a banner, which they hung with balloons around her cot.[5]

It was real cause for celebration, and the team was determined to make it a special occasion. It was a landmark day for the parents too – now their daughter was one hundred days old, she'd reached the equivalent of thirty-seven weeks' gestation,[6] and could be classed as a full-term baby. After so many months of hoping and praying for her survival, they could now dare to start planning for the day they'd take her home.[7]

That night, however, the baby girl suddenly deteriorated. Shortly after 2 a.m., she vomited violently – with such force that it sprayed over the cot canopy, the floor, and on to a chair several feet away. It didn't take a trained medic to know that something was badly wrong. Why was there so much milk in her stomach? She was being fed through a tube, but extremely gently and slowly. Her nurse had checked her stomach just beforehand, and she confirmed it was empty. Even more bizarrely, when the baby's tummy was checked again after she was sick, there was still the same volume of milk in it as she had been fed, despite the amount of vomit that she'd just produced. What had gone wrong? Just hours earlier, staff were celebrating how well the baby was doing. Now this.

Lucy Letby was one of the nurses on duty that night. It was her first night shift in a month. 'Thank goodness Lucy's on!' her nursing colleagues probably thought. 'Lucy's great in a crisis.' The baby's nurse was on her break when the incident occurred. When she got back, Letby and one of the other nurses were already there, helping to get the situation under control. That was Lucy – always there saving the day.

Later that afternoon, Letby texted one of her nursing pals. She'd finished her shift and her friend had now taken over.

'How are parents?' she asked.

'Devastated but determined she'll get through "as always". Thought that if she got to 100 then they could feel confident she'd be fine.'

'Awful isn't it,' Letby commiserated. 'We'd all been sat at desk at start of night making banner . . . Any idea what's caused it?'

'Nope. Just seems to be a circulation collapse. Chest sounds clear.'

'Hmm,' wrote Letby. 'What can cause that?'[8]

Two weeks later, the same baby girl suffered another unexpected and violent vomit. It sounds unremarkable compared to the baby deaths in June and August. But whatever had caused the baby girl to vomit so violently also damaged her brain – damage that she and her family still live with today. Once again, Lucy Letby was on duty.

With hindsight, viewed through the prism of Letby's trial, it looks suspicious. But no one on the unit had gone there in their minds. The lead consultant Steve Brearey and Letby's nursing manager Eirian Powell had spotted the association between Letby and the three deaths back in June, and by the end of September tongues had started wagging among some of the staff. Some were beginning to question Letby's competence. But her managers had no such doubts. At the end of September, after a run of unexpected baby collapses, the deputy manager of the neonatal unit sent Letby this message of support: 'I just want to commend you for all [your] hard work these last few nights. You composed yourself very well during a stressful situation. It's nice to see your confidence grow as you advance through your career x'.[9]

Letby was appreciative: 'Thank you. That's really nice to hear as I gather you are aware of some of the not so positive comments that have been made recently regarding my role which I have found quite upsetting. Our job is a pleasure to do & just hope I do the best for the babies & their family.'

There was also reassurance from one of the registrars: 'Try to think of all the babies you've saved and have gone home happily with their parents. You're a fab nurse.'

That same weekend, one of the older nurses on the unit also got in touch with a message of support. 'You're a star. [You've] done yourself proud,' she texted. It was a nice touch – a morale boost for a wounded pal. The older nurse had mentored Letby since her earliest days on the unit and the two had become friends. 'Always a pleasure to work with you even if we're a "shit magnet" team,' the older nurse added wryly.

There were more warm words back and forth. Then this from

Letby: 'It's all just so rubbish lately isn't it. And always seems to happen at night when less people.'[10]

Despite the low-level sniping, Letby still had the respect of most of her colleagues. For many of the nurses, the Countess of Chester Hospital had bigger problems than one member of staff. On the neonatal unit, 2015 and 2016 were exceptionally busy years. In fact, they were manic. The unit did care for high-dependency babies, but during those years, there were more and more babies arriving with ever more complex needs. There weren't enough staff either. It was a perfect recipe for mistakes to be made. And mistakes were made. At the end of September, one baby was left with a needle in her chest. There were delays in her treatment too and a tube for emptying fluid and air from her chest was put in the wrong place.[11]

We managed to speak to one of the nurses who worked on the unit at the time alongside Letby. She'd been there for decades, but 2015–16 was like nothing she'd seen or experienced before. The nurse doesn't want to be identified, but she agreed to speak to us about her memories of the Letby years:

> 2015 and 2016 were horrendously busy years working on the unit. They were probably the worst years I can remember in more than twenty years. On average we had twelve to sixteen or eighteen babies every week each day, but then suddenly there was a big influx but there weren't any more staff to look after those extra babies. Everybody was absolutely stretched to the limit, working twelve-hour days, twelve-hour nights. Some were asked to do extra shifts. You didn't get hardly any drinks. You didn't get hardly any breaks. You were expected to look after the maximum number that you could – sometimes over the number that you should. And the way I see it, we were just run ragged.

The nurse went as far as to warn the unit manager that safety was being compromised. 'I remember saying to her this is just so, so busy and such a stressful time for everybody. The team was so stretched, and I remember saying to her: something awful is going to happen here because we can't carry on like this.' The unit manager needed no persuading. She'd been telling senior management about the unit's staffing problems and 'banging her head against the wall' over the issue, according to the nurse we spoke to.

But not everything that went wrong could be blamed on poor staffing and pressures on the unit. Often the most unexpected and troubling incidents happened in the dead of night when the unit was quiet. Tuesday, 13 October 2015 was one such quiet night. Lucy Letby was on shift with her more junior colleague Ashleigh Hudson. Letby was in Nursery One, while Hudson was looking after a baby girl in Nursery Two. The baby was just over two months old. Her growth rate had been poor, and she'd also had a worrying collapse two weeks previously while Letby was looking after her. But doctors seemed happy with her progress and her parents were planning for her to go home in a couple of weeks.

At three in the morning, Nurse Hudson left the room where the baby was resting. Shortly after she returned, she saw Lucy Letby in the doorway. Letby commented that the baby looked pale – and she was right. When Hudson went over to check on her, the baby was gasping for breath. She looked like she was about to die. Without Letby's warning, the baby probably would have died. But how did Letby know she was pale? It was after midnight, the lights were low, and the baby was covered. Letby was standing by the doorway, several feet away.[12]

The baby recovered, but ten days later, she suffered another serious collapse. Once again, it was at night. At around midnight, the baby let out a loud cry. 'It was relentless, almost constant,' Ashleigh Hudson recalled later. 'There was no stopping or starting, no fluctuating and it was constantly very loud.' It was like nothing Hudson had heard before.[13]

She shouted for help and Letby came immediately. The two nurses then paged the on-call doctors. When they arrived, the baby's skin had turned a strange colour. Blue 'mottling' was how one of the consultants described it. An X-ray revealed a large 'bubble' in the baby's stomach. The baby was successfully resuscitated, but just over an hour later she collapsed again.

Ashleigh Hudson was out of the room this time when the baby's alarm sounded. She raced back. Lucy Letby was already there, with her hands in the incubator offering the baby a dummy. Hudson was distressed: 'She's going to do it again! It's the same cry!' she said.[14]

This time the baby wasn't so lucky. Her heart rate and blood oxygen levels had started to drop. By the time the baby's parents arrived at the hospital, CPR was already well under way. Doctors had been trying for twenty minutes but it was a losing battle. 'Every time they pumped her, her stats would go up and then she'd flatline,' the baby's mother recalled. 'I said, "You can't keep doing this to her." My partner couldn't watch.'

Medics spent an hour trying to save the little girl. But there was nothing they could do. Not even eight shots of adrenaline were enough to bring her back from the brink. Another baby had been lost, and for another set of parents, the world imploded. 'When they eventually stopped working on her they passed her to me,' the baby's mother remembered later. 'It was about 2 a.m. or 3 a.m. when she actually went. After she passed away we were left alone. All the other babies were moved, and we were left alone.'[15]

The nursing staff were devastated too. They'd spent two months on and off nursing the little girl and getting to know her. One described her as 'quite a character herself. We were all fond of her and had high hopes for her. It was gut-wrenching for the nurses as a group.'[16] Another nurse recalled the resuscitation. You'd think medics are pretty hardened to these things, but the sight of the baby's helpless parents was overwhelming. She said, 'I remember them walking in [during the resuscitation], and standing there not really knowing what to do, and myself not knowing what to say . . . Right at the end the doctor decided to call it and said we should stop. I'd been looking at the baby and the monitor thinking she was going to come out of it. My heart just dropped. When he said "stop" I was just devastated, especially when I looked at the parents.'[17]

Lucy Letby was on hand for the aftermath. The baby's mother later recalled the scene: 'Ashleigh [Hudson] and Lucy asked if I wanted to bathe her. My partner initially said no, but I didn't want to look back later and regret not doing it, so I said yes. Lucy brought the bath in and said I could get ready. She said she'd take some pictures which we could keep.'[18]

But there was something slightly off about Letby's manner as the parents began to process what had just happened. This is the recollection of the baby's mother:

> When [my partner] and I were bathing her, Lucy came back in smiling and kept going on about how she'd been present at [our daughter's] first bath and how much she'd loved it. I wished she would just stop talking. Eventually I think she realised and stopped. It wasn't something we wanted to hear at that point. We just wished she and Ashleigh would go and swap with the night shift. I remember it was Lucy who packaged up our baby's belongings for us to take home.

It wasn't the last they were to hear from Lucy Letby. The following month, several members of staff went to the baby's funeral. Letby didn't go to the service – she'd just come off a night shift that morning. But she wrote a sympathy card for the parents and snapped an image of it to keep on her phone. 'There are no words to make this time any easier,' she wrote.

> It was a real priviledge [sic] to care for [the baby] + and get to know you as a family – a family who always put [her] first + did everything possible for her.
>
> She will always be a part of your lives + we will never forget her.
>
> Thinking of you today + always – sorry I cannot be there to say goodbye.
>
> Lots of love
> Lucy x[19]

When news of the baby's death reached lead consultant Steve

Brearey, he was troubled. Brearey emailed the unit manager Eirian Powell. A discussion with Letby's manager was now needed with full information about which staff had been on duty for each of the baby deaths on the unit since June. Powell emailed back with a staffing list confirming that Lucy Letby was the only common presence. We understand that Powell dutifully passed the information up the managerial chain to the hospital's head of nursing, Alison Kelly. Kelly and others in senior management remained silent.

Powell herself was reluctant to consider the possibility that there might be a link between Letby and the deaths. She was protective of her staff and Letby was a good nurse. But Dr Brearey was uneasy. In an email to Brearey, she wrote:

> [I]t is unfortunate that she [Letby] was on – however each cause of death was different, some were poorly prior to their arrival on the unit and the others were ?NEC [necrotising enterocolitis] or gastric bleeding/congenital abnormalities.[20]

Steve Brearey, however, was starting to see things very differently. From where he was standing, babies who had seemed well were collapsing unexpectedly. Some had spent time in other hospitals without incident, only to deteriorate and die after coming to Chester. And Lucy Letby was a common link.

What exactly was Brearey thinking about Letby at this point – in October 2015? Had he begun to suspect the worst? Did he think Lucy Letby was killing babies? We spoke to Dr Brearey and asked him these very questions – among many others. His answers were always sober – measured. There were no histrionics or signs of exaggeration. He'd spotted the coincidence between Letby and the deaths, and it worried him. But murder? Brearey hadn't gone there yet in his mind. The thought was just so crazy: a nursing colleague at a small hospital in genteel Chester – secretly killing babies. Who would entertain such a notion?

Nonetheless, the death in October 2015 and the differing reactions of Steve Brearey and Eirian Powell marked the beginning of a rift that would leave the neonatal unit at the Countess of

Chester Hospital painfully divided. And it wasn't just the deaths that were causing alarm. Other babies were suffering unexpected deteriorations or collapses. Some almost died. August, September and October had all seen babies collapse in unexpected circumstances while Letby was on duty. And there would be further incidents like these in November and December.[21]

The Christmas holidays couldn't come soon enough. Lucy Letby worked until Christmas Eve and then went to Hereford to spend the holidays with her parents. There she had the chance to catch up with her old school friends. But there were no New Year's Eve parties. By 31 December she was back on the night shift in Chester, ringing in 2016 with her fellow nurses, all of whom were doubtless hoping for a much smoother year ahead.

It didn't take long for their hopes to be dashed. On 8 January, another baby on the unit died. You'd think so many unexpected baby deaths in a small neonatal unit would have begun to ring alarm bells among the hospital's senior management. But still, from where the consultants were standing, there was silence. The doctors and nurses on the unit were on their own.

In early February 2016, Steve Brearey and other medical staff from the unit, including Eirian Powell, met to review each of the baby deaths to see if there were any common 'themes' that might help to explain them. The meeting raised more questions than it answered.

The known medical issues were different for each baby. A report of the meeting noted one of the babies had 'severe HIE' – or hypoxic-ischaemic encephalopathy – a medical term for brain damage. Another baby was noted to have had 'severe multiple congenital abnormalities with a very poor prognosis'. In lay terms, the baby had been born with abnormalities. One baby had 'significant congenital heart disease and probable sepsis', while two or three babies were believed to have died of 'sepsis despite timely antibiotic treatment'. In two or three cases, the cause of death was 'uncertain'.

One person at the meeting brought up Ranitidine – a medicine used to reduce stomach acid reflux and heartburn. There was a suggestion that Ranitidine brings an increased risk of death for premature babies and two of the babies who had died had been given the drug. Ranitidine is no longer in use, but it was being used in many neonatal units at the time, and its use at the Countess of Chester Hospital couldn't explain why seven babies had died in the space of just seven months.

Other aspects of the care and treatment given to the babies on the unit were also discussed. Someone mentioned 'cord clamping' – the procedure for cutting of the umbilical cord after birth. Three of the babies who had died on the unit had had the clamping of their cords delayed – a deliberate and established practice that allows babies to benefit from being attached to the placenta for longer. However, the process of delayed cord clamping is more complicated for premature babies because of the other demands associated with their prematurity that also need to be attended to. No one at the meeting suggested that delayed cord clamping had caused any babies to die, but it was confirmed that there should be no delayed cord clamping for premature newborns. It was a measure of the desperation felt by Brearey and his colleagues for answers.

Other areas of possible improvement were also identified – like the fitting of tubes called Umbilical Venous Catheters – or UVCs. But there was nothing that anyone could see in the care by medical staff that could explain the deaths. A senior consultant from a neighbouring hospital who had agreed to attend the meeting noted 'a clear and strong governance culture' within the hospital. The fact that so many post-mortems had been undertaken was another indication of the quality of the unit and 'a willingness to learn and improve'. Everything – from the use of Ranitidine and delayed cord clamping to the fitting of UVCs and unit management practices – was pored over. But Brearey and his colleagues were clutching at straws. In reality, no one had a clue why so many babies had died.

It's clear from the write-up of the meeting that even at this stage – February 2016 – nobody was officially talking about foul play. The search for innocent explanations was still the priority. The report did, however, make two more general observations that would later interest the police, as well as the lawyers in the Crown Prosecution Service, whose job it would be to prosecute Lucy Letby.

Some of the babies deteriorated 'suddenly and unexpectedly' with 'no clear cause for the deterioration/death identified at [post-mortem]'. For non-medics, this might seem unremarkable, but for doctors and nurses on a neonatal unit, sudden and un-explained deaths are highly unusual. One former hospital insider told us, 'There were deaths and near deaths which could not be explained and were unexpected – and that just does not happen on a neonatal unit.'

Then there was the timing of the incidents. Nine cases were reviewed. In six of these cases, babies were found to have suffered 'arrests' between midnight and 4 a.m. No one was thinking it yet, but if there was a murderer on the neonatal unit, the small hours of the morning were the perfect time to strike. Beyond these observations though, there was no further comment or speculation in the report about why so many incidents might have occurred in the dead of night. It was just another fact left hanging for readers of the report to pick up on – or ignore.

As the February meeting drew to a close, Dr Brearey mentioned something else: Lucy Letby and the fact that she had been on duty for all of the deaths. No one was ready to think the unthinkable. Brearey recalls his observation was met with something like a collective shrug and Lucy Letby's name was left out of the report.

After the meeting, Brearey says he emailed a copy of the Feb-ruary report to the hospital's head of nursing Alison Kelly and the hospital's medical director Ian Harvey. He knew the subject of Letby's association with the deaths would require careful hand-ling, so as well as sending his report, he says he asked Kelly and Harvey for an urgent meeting. As far as we know, Letby wasn't mentioned – that was the point of having a meeting. But another three months – and more unexpected baby collapses – would go by before any meeting took place.

By now, Brearey was beginning to feel isolated. His concerns about Letby were growing, and yet senior management was silent. In mid-February 2016, shortly after Brearey and his colleagues had completed their thematic report on the baby deaths, a team from the Care Quality Commission visited the Countess of Chester

Hospital. The CQC is one of those faceless bureaucratic organisations tasked with inspecting public services. The CQC's visit to the Countess of Chester Hospital in February 2016 was a routine inspection – every hospital has them. But this visit would be unusual.

As they worked their way round the hospital, the team from the CQC met with some of the consultants from the neonatal unit. None of the consultants mentioned Lucy Letby by name, but one of them made it clear to the CQC team that the consultants were worried. 'We have serious patient safety concerns that aren't being listened to,' she said.

You'd think that might have caused alarm. But, like the senior management of the hospital, the CQC seemed uncurious. 'We'll come to that at the end of the meeting,' said one member of the CQC team. And that was the final word on the matter. The meeting ended with no further discussion of the consultants' concerns. In its report, the CQC noted that 'nurse staffing levels on the neonatal unit did not meet standards recommended by the British Association of Perinatal Medicine'. It continued: 'Between January 2015 and January 2016, 11 incidents were recorded that related to the acuity of patients and staffing breaching BAPM [British Association of Perinatal Medicine] standards and on seven occasions in that period the neonatal unit had been closed to admissions.'[22] To a casual reader, it looked like the unit had significant failings. Inadequate storage facilities were also flagged. But the tenor of the CQC's report was 'requires improvement' rather than 'unit in crisis'. The CQC report noted breezily: 'Between January 2015 and January 2016, 254 incidents were recorded by the children's unit, neonatal unit and paediatric outpatients' clinic. Of these, 252 were reported as low or no harm.' There were warm words about the unit's high hygiene standards and the fact that mothers with babies on the neonatal unit were encouraged to express milk for their babies. Incredibly, there was no mention of concerns about the spike in unexplained deaths and collapses, nor was there any mention that one of the consultants on the unit had expressed concern about patient safety.

The report also suggested that the hospital – and in particular the hospital's medical director Ian Harvey – had good processes in place for monitoring and responding to patient deaths within the hospital: 'Multidisciplinary mortality and morbidity reviews were held on a monthly basis, which was chaired by the medical director. All cases were reviewed through this process to identify key learning and to identify any actions if appropriate.'[23] No one reading the CQC report would see any cause for concern about neonatal deaths at the Countess of Chester Hospital.

'Perinatal and neonatal mortality and morbidity meetings were held separately to allow time for discussion,' the report noted. 'Key messages and learning points were then given to staff.'[24]

But on the floor of the neonatal unit, consultants other than Steve Brearey were also becoming concerned about Lucy Letby. According to Brearey's colleague Dr Ravi Jayaram, the evening of 17 February 2016 was when his concerns about Letby really ratcheted up. It was shortly after 2 a.m. and a young mother had just given birth. The baby was fifteen weeks premature – too premature to stay at the Countess of Chester Hospital – so arrangements were made to have her moved to a more specialist hospital. In the meantime, she was moved to the unit's Nursery One. She was in good hands. Her designated nurse, Joanne Williams, knew what she was doing. Ravi Jayaram was on hand too. He'd been present for the baby's birth and was keeping an eye on things in the unit while transport arrangements for the little girl were being made.

At 3.30 in the morning, Nurse Williams checked the baby was stable before leaving the unit to go and speak to the infant's mother, who was convalescing in the maternity ward. Lucy Letby was now on her own in the nursery with the baby girl. It should have been reassuring to know that another nurse was there. But Dr Jayaram says he felt uneasy. He too had noticed the coincidence between Letby's presence and unexpected deaths on the unit. So he went into the nursery to check that everything was OK. When he got there, he says he saw Letby standing over the baby girl's incubator. The baby's oxygen levels were dropping, but strangely her alarm wasn't sounding. Lucy Letby wasn't calling for help either. 'She's just started deteriorating now,' Letby said, according to Dr Jayaram

On closer examination, Dr Jayaram discovered that the baby's chest had stopped moving and her breathing tube had been dislodged – the same breathing tube that the baby's designated nurse had checked just minutes earlier. He gave her manual breathing support to revive her, but a few hours later, something similar happened again. The baby's breathing tube mysteriously slipped down her throat.

At lunchtime, the transport team finally arrived and the baby was transferred to another, more specialist hospital. Tragically, she passed away two days later. Ravi Jayaram told the story of that night in an emotional TV interview, broadcast in August 2023. 'That is a night that is etched on my memory and will be in my nightmares forever,' he said heavily. In court, Dr Jarayam would be questioned about that night. How suspicious was he of Letby? If he was suspicious, why didn't he call the police? The consultant says it wasn't that straightforward. Meanwhile, Letby was still well regarded by her nursing colleagues, and no one had actually seen her doing anything wrong. But among the consultants – particularly Steve Brearey – concerns were now acute. One consultant recalled Brearey coming into her office with a worried expression. 'I think Lucy's doing something,' he told her. At last, the unthinkable had been said. Lucy Letby was now a marked woman.

In early March 2016, Brearey emailed Letby's boss Eirian Powell. 'I think we still need to talk about Lucy,' he wrote. '[M]aybe when you are back and free [we] can meet to talk about it?' Four days later, another baby died while Letby was on duty.

The correlation between Letby's presence and the baby deaths was undeniable. On 17 March, Letby's manager Eirian Powell emailed Alison Kelly, the hospital's head of nursing, to request a meeting to discuss the deaths. Powell's email mentioned 'a particular nurse' as a common factor. She also noted that a doctor was identified as 'a common theme however not [for as many events] as the nurse.' 'Despite reviewing these cases,' Powell continued, 'there was nothing obvious that we were able to identify – therefore your input would be valued.'

This was another email that should have worried management. Alison Kelly had been at the meeting with Brearey and Powell back in July 2015 – just after the first three baby deaths. Letby's name had come up then. Her name had also been flagged to Alison Kelly in October 2015 after another unexpected baby death. So by March 2016, an email about more baby deaths and an apparent commonality with the same nurse should have been a cause for managerial concern and intervention. But Kelly's response was matter-of-fact. She asked for a copy of February's thematic review into the baby deaths to be sent to her and Ian Harvey – something Steve Brearey said had already been done a month earlier. '[O]nce we have reviewed this, I think it would be good for me, you, Ian and Steve/Ravi to meet to discuss,' Kelly wrote. Another two months would go by before any such meeting took place.

Of course, the consultants didn't really know Lucy Letby – not well anyway. They didn't socialise with her. In fact, they didn't know much at all about her private life. But did that matter? Did they need to know her in order to suspect her? Many may wonder how well anyone really knew Lucy Letby. As far as her friends could tell, though, her life was looking rosy. She was young – twenty-six – and doing the job she loved. And she'd just bought her first home, a neat 1970s semi on a quiet road near the hospital, for £179,000.[25] It was near enough to the neonatal unit for her to be able to walk to work, and on 5 April she moved out of the nurses' accommodation where she'd been living for the previous year and into the prim three-bed house, with its privet-hedged driveway and neat garden. The house move was hectic, but Letby didn't take any time off work to settle in.

'Unpacking! Stuff everywhere lol. May do extra shift over weekend. X' she texted one friend.[26]

'How's the house pal? Xxx,' asked another.

'Hey, it feels a bit weird having a whole house but it's good thanks,' she replied. She'd worked every day since the move and was planning to work overtime at the weekend too. 'Few more pennies,' she explained.

But back at the hospital, Lucy Letby's nursing manager Eirian

Powell knew that she couldn't ignore the consultants' concerns – even if she did think they were unfounded. Although no one was yet talking about murder, the fact that so many deaths had occurred during Letby's night shifts couldn't go without some sort of practical response. So in early April, Powell agreed to move Letby to day shifts. It was a concession to the consultants, but Powell was careful to play it down. A month later, she wrote: 'In order to support this particular practitioner [i.e. Letby], I have brought her into days to ensure she is well supported.' But even that didn't put a stop to the crises.

Saturday, 9 April 2016 was Grand National day and spring was in the air. Letby had come to work to begin a day shift, but although she was assigned to look after two babies in the intensive care room, her mind was also on the race. She texted a workmate who'd gone to Aintree, and then messaged her mum, Sue, back in Hereford: 'Is dad betting on grand national? If so can he see which are Greys and put a bet on for me please x'[27]

Her mum replied straight away. Dad had already gone to the bookies. He'd put £2 each way on three horses including one called 'Rule The World' – a reference to the Take That song. It was a good bet. Later that afternoon, Letby's phone pinged again. 'You've won rule the world :-D xxx. You'll get £125.'

Letby was excited about her new house too. 'You can come to mine if you want to,' she texted two of her nursing pals. 'Just need to unpack first! Haven't got a spare bed yet tho so can't stay unfortunately . . . Looking forward to a catch up! . . . Got magnum prosecco and vodka woop. No disco ball but sure we can manage. X'.

Someone suggested an unpacking party. Letby was game: 'Unpacking party sounds good to me with my flavoured vodka haha. Just won the grand national!! £135 🐎'

To her friends and family, it seemed that Lucy Letby was having a quiet shift, and rather a sociable Saturday afternoon. They may have been surprised to learn that she was replying to their texts while in the midst of a highly fraught day in the neonatal unit. Crisis had struck again – an emergency involving another pair of twins, who prosecutors would later allege Letby had attempted to murder.

They were one-day-old twin boys. One suffered a dramatic drop in blood sugar – hypoglycaemia in medical parlance. The other suffered an unexpected collapse with a sudden drop in heart rate and breathing.[28] Medics found it so difficult to resuscitate the second twin that they were at the point of withdrawing treatment when the baby miraculously improved. No one knew why the twins had collapsed. A blood test from the first baby was sent to the lab for analysis and came back a week later. The results were terrifying. They showed high levels of insulin in the baby's blood – insulin that he couldn't have produced himself. It looked like a repeat of what had happened eight months earlier in August 2015. This time, it seems that it was a junior doctor who missed the significance of what the lab had found.[29] Should the lab have done more to flag it? The truth is, everyone involved – the lab and the doctors – should have sounded the alarm. But no one did. Another possible opportunity to stop the carnage had been missed.[30]

Even without knowledge of the insulin test results, Steve Brearey was getting more and more worried. With every passing incident on the unit, his concerns about Lucy Letby grew. But although Letby's association with the deaths and unexpected collapses was undeniable, senior nursing staff were still resistant to the idea that their colleague was up to no good. At a meeting on 5 May, Letby's manager Eirian Powell met with the hospital's lead nurse for urgent care, Karen Rees.

Karen Rees would later claim that she had little knowledge of Lucy Letby before the end of June 2016. She would also claim to have been unaware of any complaints that had been made about Letby by Steve Brearey and his fellow consultants before 24 June 2016.[31] But straight after the 5 May meeting, Eirian Powell emailed Karen Rees, including an attachment entitled 'Lucy's shifts'. It's evidence that Letby and concerns about her association with baby deaths was on the radar of another senior hospital manager.

A week later, Dr Brearey finally got the urgent meeting with the senior bosses that he'd requested three months previously. On 11

May 2016, he sat down with unit manager Eirian Powell, head of nursing Alison Kelly, and the number two in the entire hospital, medical director Ian Harvey. At long last, the time had come to talk about Lucy.

Views were now as polarised as they'd ever been. For Brearey, Letby's association with the deaths was incontrovertible and deeply alarming. Eirian Powell, on the other hand, believed a good nursing colleague was being unfairly maligned and that it was up to her – Eirian Powell – to defend her colleague.

Powell took the bull by the horns and came to the meeting armed with an 'assurance document' outlining why in her view the association between Letby and the deaths was innocent. According to the document, there was 'no evidence whatsoever against LL other than coincidence'. Because of her specialist qualifications, Letby was likely to be looking after the sickest babies on the unit. Letby also worked extra shifts when staffing was stretched or the unit was under strain. Powell's assessment of Letby could not have been more glowing: 'I have found LL to be diligent and have excellent standards within clinical care.'

But what about the spike in baby deaths? Why had there been so many deaths on the unit in such a short period of time? Back in February 2016, Brearey, Powell and other senior medics had met to discuss the baby deaths and try to identify common themes. One of the conclusions had been that the medical issues for each baby who had died – to the extent that they were known – were different in each case. Now, three months on, Powell's view was firm: the babies had died of different causes – none of them due to Lucy Letby.

According to Powell's 'assurance document', four of the babies had 'congenital abnormalities', and two of the post-mortems had identified 'Congenital Pneumonia'. Another two babies had NEC – a potentially fatal intestinal condition – and one had 'overwhelming sepsis'. 'Some of the issues were related to midwifery problems', as well as issues at another hospital where one of the babies had spent time.

Most interestingly of all, Powell's assurance document did address the question of foul play head on. 'Of all the post-mortem results,' she noted, 'there was no evidence of foul play.' It's a remarkable line. It shows just how frank discussions had become. The question was now being asked out loud: was Lucy Letby harming babies?

But Powell was resolute. Such was her belief in Letby that her document even named two doctors who she said had also '[appeared] to be involved in many of the mortalities'. The implication was clear. Suggestions of foul play based on who was on duty when babies died could also potentially implicate doctors. It was almost as if Powell was telling Brearey: 'You doctors aren't beyond suspicion either – if that's the game you want to play.'

Some will criticise Eirian Powell for defending Lucy Letby so vigorously. But it's not so difficult to understand when you think about Powell's position and her relationship with Letby. Powell was Letby's boss.[32] Good bosses stick up for their staff – and Letby seemed easy to stick up for. She was polite and diligent, and no one doubted that she was a capable nurse. Nurses like Eirian Powell probably thought they were better placed to judge Letby than the consultants. The consultants may have been at the top of the medical pecking order, but they weren't around all the time. They didn't get to know all of the nurses properly. The nurses, not the consultants, were the real eyes and ears of the unit. In other words, the consultants weren't seeing the full picture.

Everyday workplace politics might have been a factor too. There's always been a bit of professional tension between nurses and the better-paid, more senior doctors, and it's possible that this was somewhere in the mix too. Whatever the motivations, there was now little common ground between Powell and Brearey.

What about the hospital's senior managers – the highly paid executives who sat above both Brearey and Powell in the chain of command? Where were they while Brearey and Powell were wrestling over the truth? It would be easy to forget that two of these senior managers – head of nursing Alison Kelly and medical director Ian Harvey – were in the room for the meeting with Brearey and Powell on 11 May. In fact, Powell's 'assurance document' had been prepared at least in part for their benefit.

Alison Kelly was an NHS high-flyer. But she'd put the years in. She'd become a nurse in 1988 and spent nearly three decades learning the system. By all accounts, she'd been an excellent nurse. But being a boss on a generous salary brought different demands. As head of nursing at the Countess of Chester Hospital, her job was not only to manage the nurses, but also to make sure that patients were safe and properly looked after. Whether she chose to face it or not, the Lucy Letby question was squarely her concern – or should have been.

Ian Harvey had had a different path to senior management. He'd had a successful career as a surgeon and – according to his critics at least – had airs of intellectual superiority. Consultants from the neonatal unit found him arrogant and condescending. Whether or not that's fair, the months that followed would show him to have a steely belief in his own judgement and antipathy to the views of the senior medics who worked for him.

Strangely though, the input from Alison Kelly and Ian Harvey at the May 2016 meeting with Steve Brearey and Eirian Powell was limited. They remained passive – preferring to act like school-teachers defusing a childish argument between Brearey and Powell rather than grapple with the substance of what was being said. That passivity from senior managers would soon harden into resistance.

Brearey already faced resistance from another senior manager too. At the top of Powell's assurance document, a second name was scribbled alongside Powell's: Karen Rees – the hospital's lead nurse for urgent care. According to Brearey, Rees had helped Powell put the document together. If true, Karen Rees had clearly picked a side. Despite her claims later on, it appeared that Rees had entered the fray and decided that Eirian Powell was right: Letby had done nothing wrong.

Dr Brearey and his fellow consultants were now facing a struggle on two fronts: on one side nursing colleagues who believed Letby had done nothing wrong, and on the other senior managers like Ian Harvey and Alison Kelly, who, as far as Brearey was concerned, didn't appreciate the seriousness of the situation on the neonatal unit.

The consultants' point of view is clear. But what were the senior managers thinking? Why had it taken three months for Ian Harvey and Alison Kelly to meet with Dr Brearey? And why did they appear to be so passive in the face of what for the consultants was clearly a crisis?

None of the senior managers has spoken publicly, but Ian Harvey did write to us to give his version of events. He told us that he didn't recall any communication from the consultants in February 2016 requesting a meeting:

> It is surprising, given the level of concern that some of the paediatricians professed having had at the time, that there was no follow up to chase a response, either with my secretary, or directly with me. As Medical Director I had an open door policy . . . At no time prior to May 2016 did a consultant paediatrician come to my office to express or discuss their concerns.

He also blamed the consultants for not spotting the fact that two babies in their care had been poisoned with insulin, as indicated by the lab tests on the babies' blood samples. Harvey said:

> These serious medication errors were never brought to my attention either directly, or through the [hospital] Trust's Datix incident reporting system, or subsequently in June 2016, when Dr John Gibbs, consultant paediatrician – together with a senior neonatal nurse – carried out a review of babies who had collapsed . . . These blood test results were potentially the only concrete evidence that we could have had that accidental or malicious acts had harmed babies. Had I been told about them at or before the meeting in May 2016 I would have recommended meeting with the police immediately.

Harvey added that Ravi Jayaram later conceded that, had incidents been recorded in the hospital's incident reporting system, the investigative process culminating in Lucy Letby's trial would have happened sooner.[33]

Despite the growing tensions, Brearey, his fellow consultants, Eirian Powell and the bosses managed to keep their arguments under wraps. We spoke to one junior doctor on the unit who told us the first time he'd heard about the extent of the consultants' concerns about Lucy Letby was during her trial in 2023.

Many of the nurses were similarly oblivious. We spoke to one who told us: 'I don't think anybody suspected anything for the majority of that year. You wouldn't have expected it to have been one of the nursing staff that was harming the babies. People were saying, "Gosh, poor Lucy! Was Lucy on? Why has this happened to Lucy again? Poor girl, it must be awful." That sort of thing. But we didn't even know that these consultants were becoming suspicious of Lucy. It was all kept very quiet.'

It meant that life for Lucy Letby, despite what the consultants were thinking and saying, continued to look and feel pretty normal. Outside of work, she still went to salsa class and the gym. She watched the same mainstream TV shows. She had a June holiday to Ibiza planned too. Inside work, the pressures on the unit and the staff were huge, but it was the same for everyone. Apart from that, it was like any other hospital unit. There was even time for some workplace flirtation.

In early June 2016, a message popped up on Letby's Facebook feed. It was one of the junior doctors on the unit: a married guy.[34]

Dr ██: Hi Lucy, are you working Sunday or next week? I need a favour – more like an opinion on something and wondered if you'd mind? No problem if you can't!

Letby didn't really have any male friends in Chester. And there was certainly no love interest. She was intrigued.

Letby: Im on nights at the moment, on days next Wed, Fri, Sat if that helps? Hope I can help!

That evening, Letby texted one of her nursing pals. The message from the doctor was playing on her mind.

Letby: Had strange message from [Dr ▮▮▮] earlier . . .

Friend: Did u? Saying what? Go commando? 😂

Letby: 😂😂😂😂 Asking when I was working next week as wants to talk to me about something, has a favour to ask . . . ?

Friend: Think he likes u too
Hmm did u not ask what it was?

Letby: No just said when I was working and he said wants my opinion on something Hmm . . . 🤔

Friend: Hmm

Letby: Do you think he's being odd?

Friend: Thought as flirty as u

Letby: Shut up!

Friend: What?!

Letby: I don't flirt with him!

Friend: OK

Letby: Certainly don't fancy him haha just nice guy

Friend: OK

The next day, Letby was back in work, and another baby collapsed.

Mercifully he survived, and the veneer of normality on the unit continued for a little while longer.

In the days that followed, Letby's rapport with the doctor developed quickly. They'd become text pals, sometimes texting late into the night. We don't know what 'opinion' he had wanted Letby to give him. Maybe Letby's friend was right – maybe he fancied her and the 'favour' line was just a pretext. It was new territory for Letby, but she was clearly enjoying it – even if he was married.

On 14 June, Letby was looking after the little baby who'd collapsed the day after her mysterious Facebook message from the doctor. The boy had deteriorated over the course of the day and his problems worsened overnight. Letby would later be accused of 'sabotaging' the little boy before finishing her day shift,[35] but her messages that evening suggest she had other things on her mind.

At 9.17 p.m. – another Facebook message from the doctor:

Dr ▆: Am I right in thinking you'll have done 6 long days in the last 8? No wonder you're tired.[36]

He was on the overnight shift that night, but he seemed keen to be distracted.

Letby: Yep, 6 in 8. My own doing though as holiday is during days off rather than AL [annual leave] . . . I'm having some problems with my thyroid which doesn't help. Just having some cereal & watching Corrie!

Dr ▆: Bonus that you didn't use any AL for your break. Are you going to Torbay again this year? Let me know if I can do anything endocrine to help – as well as coffee, cake and computers I know my way round (thyroid blood tests) if you need any help.

Letby: Thanks – a man of many talents!! We are off to Torquay 2nd July – my parents go 3 times a year.

The next morning, Letby woke early to another message:

Dr ■■■: What a chaotic 7 hours! . . .

Letby: What have you been doing?! Is it mad? Hope you've
had plenty of ☕☕!

Dr ■■■: We haven't had any time to stop so far. Hopefully it
will be calmer when you come in. 😱

Letby went into work early that day – nearly fifty minutes early.
Was it to see the doctor before he finished his night shift at eight?
The night team had worked hard to stabilise the baby boy whom
Letby had been looking after the previous day, but just minutes
after her arrival on the unit, the baby's oxygen level dropped. Letby
was the one who spotted it, but strangely the boy's alarm had failed
to sound. The married doctor came to have a look.[37] The boy's
throat had swollen and there was fresh blood in his throat too. The
baby was haemophiliac, so he could be prone to bleeding. Again,
the child survived, and Letby and the doctor had helped saved
the day. And yet, something about the incident had left Letby
unnerved. Later that day, she messaged the doctor:

Letby: Sorry if I was off during intubation. Bernie (one of the
other nurses) winds me up faffing etc, I like things to be
tidy and calm (Well, as much as possible!)

Dr ■■■: No, you were perfectly fine with me. I couldn't tell
who you were annoyed with, but the look on your face
when taking wrappers off the top of the intubation trolley
was priceless 😊!

Letby: oh Well I have got my hair in a bun today, it's only
fitting that I was 'serious Lucy'!!

Dr ▮▮▮▮: It sounds like 'Serious Lucy' did well to keep calm –
I don't like faffing when there's a job to do either 😳

Had the story stopped then, had the unexpected baby collapses and deaths ended there, we still might never have heard about Lucy Letby or the Countess of Chester Hospital. The official post-mortem results identifying natural causes might have remained unquestioned. The insulin test results might never have been discovered. Parents of babies who had died might still be thinking that their babies had died of natural causes.

But events at the end of June 2016 changed everything. Letby went on holiday to Ibiza with one of the other nurses. It was a girls' trip – plenty of sangria and fun on the beach. They let their hair down on an inflatable pulled by a speedboat, and the nurse couldn't wait to tell her doctor-crush all about it, texting from her sunlounger, 'You get flung up in the air & all sorts on the inflatable, caught my elbow on the handle & left some of it behind!'

While the nurse was enjoying herself on holiday, there was a feeling of festivity on the unit too – for a quite different reason. The hospital was celebrating the unusual arrival of naturally conceived identical triplets, and there was extra relief and delight that the three babies were all healthy.[38] It was big news, and Lucy Letby's phone pinged by the pool, as her doctor friend texted to update her. One of the nursery nurses, Jennifer Jones-Key also messaged: 'The triplets have delivered . . . when are you back in?' As it happened, Letby's holiday was almost over. She replied to say that she'd be on shift the very next day. 'Probably be back in with a bang lol,' she typed.[39]

Letby had no sooner returned than chaos hit. Just two days after sending her text about being 'back in with a bang,' two more babies would be dead.[40]

On 23 June, Nurse Letby clocked on for her day shift at 7.30 a.m. and was allocated responsibility for two of the three triplet boys, who were both doing well in Nursery 2 – the third triplet was still in the intensive care room under the supervision of a different nurse.[41]

Letby had plenty to keep her occupied, with a third – unrelated – baby also requiring attention, but she felt relaxed enough to spend the first three hours of the shift attached to her phone, sending a stream of messages on Facebook and WhatsApp.

The two triplets were breathing normally by themselves and feeding well too. Their parents and grandparents were bursting with pride over the three boys who'd each been born a minute apart at thirty-three weeks' gestation, weighing around 4lb. They snapped some mobile phone photos.[42] 'They'd been given their names and were identical in every way,' their grandmother later recalled. You couldn't tell them apart, apart from the hospital tags.'[43]

The family spent the morning in and out of both rooms housing the triplets. They were reassured that everything was fine, and their mum – who was recovering from the effects of delivering three babies by Caesarean section – went to the postnatal ward to rest.

At one point, the shift leader Melanie Taylor considered moving the middle-born triplet back into Nursery One to be safe, because she had a gut instinct that he looked less well than he had earlier,[44] but Lucy Letby disagreed.[45] According to Nurse Taylor '[Lucy] said no quite plainly. She felt he was OK and wanted to keep him in Nursery Two. It's a joint care decision. Lucy was the one looking after him and knew him inside and out. When I look back, I think maybe I should have been firmer. Hindsight is a wonderful thing.'[46]

Under Letby's care the triplet went downhill fast. He vomited suddenly and had several emergencies with his heart rate and oxygen levels. The nurse called for help each time, and the married doctor came running.

A nurse went up to the postnatal ward to fetch the triplets' parents, simply telling them to go downstairs because there was something going on. When they got there it was pandemonium.[47] The baby was now in intensive care. 'It was a scene of chaos,' his mother recounted years later. 'Lucy was there all the time. I sat outside Nursery One in my wheelchair and Lucy was rushing around helping the doctors and going in and out of the room marked "sterile". The staff seemed to be in a state of panic and didn't seem to be controlled. I just sat outside and couldn't bring myself to go any closer.'[48]

The triplets' father did venture nearer and could see that his son's swollen body kept changing colour. 'You could see his veins were all bright blue,' he recalled. 'All of them were different colours. It looked like he had really bad prickly heat. You could see something through his veins. There was something wrong with his temperature. They put a plastic bag over him, like a sheet, to try and regulate it in some way. I can remember lines being put in and all kinds of drugs . . . I swear to God, at one point it was like they were trying anything . . . His stomach looked like [the film character] ET's stomach. It was mad.'[49]

At 4.15 p.m. the baby boy had another cardiac arrest and it was suggested to the family that they might want to have the baby christened. The triplets' grandmother arrived during the baptism and remembers, '[The parents] were hysterical and at a loss about what had happened . . . and I knew things weren't good. Lucy Letby was there – she was very softly spoken when speaking to the family.'[50]

The ordeal continued for an hour and a half, with four doctors trying to save the baby until it became clear that, despite their expertise, there was nothing more that could be done, and they withdrew. The middle triplet died just before six o'clock in the evening and was given to his mum to cradle. 'The whole episode came like a bolt out of the blue,' she said as she recounted the events of that night years later. 'On the face of it everything had been going so well. It was never explained to us how it happened. As a family we were naturally devastated.'[51]

The babies' father remembers that one of the consultants offered her condolences. 'She said she didn't have any explanation for us, no reason why he'd passed away. She was quite upset and apologetic and said there was nothing more they could do, but "we're going to get to the bottom of this".'[52]

Letby put her coat on and headed for home. She pulled out her phone to text one of the other nurses who was on holiday, telling her: 'Lost a triplet today, been shit x'.

'Fuckin hell, what happened?' was the startled reply.

'Blew up abdomen, think it's sepsis,' typed Letby. 'Had big

tummy overnight but just ballooned after lunch and went from there.'

The other nurse was puzzled. All three triplets had been stable. 'Jesus . . . Big hugs,' she wrote. 'Bet you don't want to go in tomoz 🙁'

'I do and I don't, think it's good to go back and talk about it,' said Letby. 'Hard when parents still on unit,' she added.[53]

At home in Hereford Sue Letby thought she'd see how her daughter's day had been. She got in touch to ask but got short shrift in response. 'Off to bed. Sorry, not very chatty just tired. All OK. Ni night x', she told her mum.

'No worries I understand. Down to earth with a bump after lovely holiday xxx', replied Mrs Letby, adding a frown emoji for good measure.

'Yep, it's just as well I love my job!! X,' Letby said.

It was late – now after 10 p.m. – but despite telling her mother she was too tired to chat, Letby seemed to be in need of company. She spent the next three and a half hours in an intimate message chat with the friendly registrar.

'Not the first day back you were expecting. I was glad you were there. Everything felt safe – thank you for looking out for me,' he wrote.

'No but it happens. Don't need to thank me,' she gushed. 'I'm pleased you were there, think we work well together.'

The next day, as Lucy Letby clocked back on to shift, the unit was still reeling from the death of the first triplet. But there was fresh horror to come. Nurse Letby was allocated responsibility for the two remaining brothers. 'I'll be watching them both like a hawk,' she texted the married doctor.[54]

The triplets' parents were getting breakfast on the maternity ward when they were told that another of their sons was in trouble. With rising panic, they raced to see their boys, and were met with a scene which was a carbon copy of what they'd experienced the previous day. The mother says, 'It was like déjà vu. Everyone was running around again.' Her partner adds, 'It was absolutely mental. It was worse than the day before – there were more people on hand and more people coming down.'[55]

It was the eldest triplet. He was put on a ventilator, but then deteriorated again.[56] He was given adrenaline, and his circulation was restored, but then one of his lungs collapsed.[57] The medics were perplexed[58] and it was agony for his parents, who spent long periods sitting outside the room while their son was given CPR.

Lucy Letby picked up her phone to text her friend – the nurse who was on holiday. 'Another triplet collapsed,' she reported. 'I've got him. Everyone involved.'[59] She turned to the consultant who was supervising the baby's treatment, and said, 'He's not leaving here alive, is he?' The consultant was shocked. She felt the baby may recover. Talk of him dying was inappropriate and the consultant was quick to rebuke Letby. 'Don't say that.'[60] But the nurse's remark would turn out to be prophetic.[61]

Efforts to resuscitate the baby were getting the doctors nowhere, and eventually it was decided that it was time to stop. The eldest triplet died at four o'clock that afternoon – less than twenty-four hours after his middle brother. The whole team was stunned and had no idea what to say to the obviously inconsolable family. The parents were lost in their own distress, but amidst their grief they became aware that one of the staff members seemed particularly affected. The children's mother says, 'Lucy was extremely upset, emotional and in pieces. She seemed almost as upset as we were. She brought the babies to see us . . . she was in floods of tears.' The father remembers, 'Lucy Letby wheeled the two boys down to us in the cold box – a frozen box for them to lie on. She brought them down, and said how sorry she was, and dressed them for us . . . She did the memory boxes for us and got us a (camera) card to take pictures.'[62]

Though she was busy with the family, Nurse Letby picked up her mobile to text her doctor friend. Despite being visibly upset on the ward, she now seemed much more controlled.

'Just going to dress him & take footprints,' she told him, adding that she was OK. 'Not sure it's really hit me yet.'[63]

Two deaths in two days. No one could deny that this was now a crisis. The triplets' parents begged for their third son to be moved to another hospital. The baby's father said, 'There's no way he's staying at this hospital. If you don't take him, we'll take him ourselves.'[64]

After the death of the second triplet, a debrief was held for the resuscitation staff. Steve Brearey went along too. Having lost two healthy babies in two days, the team was badly shaken. Most of them needed comfort and moral support. But if Lucy Letby was troubled she didn't show it.

'She was sitting next to me,' Steve Brearey recalls. 'And I spoke to her towards the end of the meeting and said how tired and upset she must be after two days of this and hoped that she was going to have a restful weekend. And she turned to me and said, "Um, no I'm back on shift tomorrow."' It wasn't just Letby's readiness to return to work that struck Brearey. At that moment, her demeanour was calm and untroubled. 'The other staff were very traumatised by all of this,' he says. 'Crumbling before your eyes almost, and [Letby] was quite happy and confident to come into work [the next day].'

Was Brearey reading Letby correctly? Hours earlier, she'd been in floods of tears. Might she simply have been putting on a brave face or hiding her feelings in front of the consultants? Brearey is firm in his recollection. For him, Letby's behaviour at the meeting only reinforced his worst fears. That evening, he called Karen Rees, who was the hospital's most senior executive on duty.

'I phoned the duty executive on call, Karen Rees, senior nurse in the urgent care division. She was familiar with our concerns already. I explained what had happened and said I didn't want Nurse Letby to come back to work the following day or until this was all investigated properly.' But according to Brearey, Karen Rees was having none of it. 'Karen Rees said no to that, and that there was no evidence. I put it to her was she happy to take responsibility for this decision in view of the fact that myself and my consultant colleagues all wouldn't be happy with Nurse Letby going to work the following day. She responded she was happy to take that responsibility.'[65]

Since Letby's trial, Karen Rees has kept her head down. But after the verdicts, she released a statement through her lawyer disputing Brearey's account of events. She concedes that Brearey did ask her to take Letby off duty after the death of the second triplet. But she claims Brearey offered no reasons or evidence in support of his request. Meanwhile, Letby still enjoyed the support of her unit manager Eirian Powell. 'I asked [Powell] whether she had any concerns about any nurses on the unit,' Rees recounts. 'She said that she did not. I then asked her specifically whether she had any clinical concerns about Lucy Letby. She said she had no concerns. She mentioned nothing about any concerns raised by any consultants.' As for Brearey's claim that he asked Rees whether she was prepared to take responsibility for any more incidents involving babies while Letby was on duty – 'That is completely untrue, and an outrageous allegation to make,' Rees said defiantly.[66]

No one, other than the two people involved, can say for sure what was or wasn't said in that phone call between Steve Brearey and Karen Rees on 24 June 2016. But Brearey's fears about what might happen if Letby came back to work as normal were confirmed. On 25 June 2016 – the day after the death of the second triplet and the phone call with Karen Rees – another baby under Lucy Letby's care collapsed. The baby survived,[67] but for Dr Brearey and his colleagues, it was the final straw. Even Letby's manager Eirian Powell now agreed that Letby had to be taken off duty.

On 27 June 2016, Steve Brearey called the hospital's medical director Ian Harvey to brief him on what had happened. Harvey promised a review into the deaths by the Royal College of Paediatrics and Child Health, but for Brearey that wasn't enough.

'I spoke to Ian Harvey,' Brearey recalls. 'I said, "We need to be safe. We would like Lucy Letby to be removed from the neonatal unit."' Eventually, Harvey agreed. That evening, Eirian Powell phoned Lucy Letby and told her not to come in for her scheduled night shift. Remarkably, Letby worked a further three more shifts before finally being removed from the unit. For the staff on the neonatal unit at the Countess of Chester Hospital, it had been a year like no other: thirteen baby deaths, several without any obvious explanation – and Lucy Letby on duty every time crisis struck.

Outwardly, Letby was devastated. She couldn't deny her association with the baby deaths and collapses over the past thirteen months. But she maintained the countenance of a diligent nurse battered by bad luck, unfair insinuation, and systemic failings on the unit. And even now, she still had the support of most of her nursing colleagues. Despite the number of deaths and Letby's presence for them, the nursing staff hadn't entertained the thought that one of their colleagues had been harming babies. The thought was so contrary to every instinct of a neonatal nurse, it was impossible to comprehend. There had to be another explanation – even if it hadn't yet been found.

What about Eirian Powell – Letby's manager and supporter through those long and painful months? Had she finally begun to doubt her support for her long-time colleague? We tried calling and emailing Powell, but she didn't want to talk to us. We can only wonder what she must be thinking now. Does she still think what happened between June 2015 and June 2016 was a series of unfortunate coincidences, or has she now made the painful journey to seeing Lucy Letby, the former colleague she regarded so highly, as a baby killer?

Chapter 4

The Bosses Side with Letby

Lucy Letby's removal from the neonatal unit in July 2016 bought time – for Brearey and the consultants, for the hospital bosses, and for Letby's nursing colleagues. But it resolved nothing. The question of what to do next was yet to be answered. Many will argue that the answer was glaringly obvious. Senior doctors at the hospital suspected that one of their colleagues was a serial killer. Surely it was time to call the police. And yet it would take almost a year before the consultants' concerns reached detectives. Why?

The moral history of this story – the designation of villains and heroes – is still being written. No doubt it will be rewritten many times over. But the facts are unchanging. So too is the terrible wrangle at the heart of the saga. The consultants feared that Lucy Letby was a cruel and devious serial killer, and took her off duty. Her most loyal nursing colleagues felt she was the pitiful victim of an institutional witch hunt. Some still feel like that. Both sets of people can't be right.

The contrast between these alternative truths is like nothing in everyday life. It is as disturbing and extreme as anything in Greek tragedy – all the more surreal because of its setting: the drab, brown-bricked enclosure of a regional seventies hospital.

We always knew there was a story to be uncovered about how the police finally became involved – and why it took so long. One of the medics on the unit had told us as much right at the beginning of the trial – when we were just getting going with our *Panorama* research. But we were given no details, and with the trial under way, everyone with any connection to the Countess of Chester Hospital seemed too afraid to speak. Our emails went unanswered or met with frosty responses. Doors were closed in our faces. In some cases, our numbers were blocked.

The fear among the medical staff was understandable. The Letby trial was one of the biggest murder trials in British legal history. An ill-judged comment to an unscrupulous journalist could comprom- ise the whole process.

Right from the beginning, it was clear that Steve Brearey was important. He was, after all, the lead consultant for the neonatal unit where Letby worked. His response to our initial approach was polite but frustrating:

'I'm happy to talk to you after the trial. In the meantime, you'll understand that I can't talk about anything related to the trial. Please do not contact me until the trial is over.'

But it wasn't until five months into Letby's trial that we began to realise just how important in the case Steve Brearey was – and how significant his personal story might be. Like many of his colleagues, Brearey testified in court. But his testimony pointed to wider issues in the hospital, beyond the question of whether or not Lucy Letby was guilty. He hinted at missed opportunities, information that was ignored, unheeded warnings, and failings by hospital managers. It was clear he had a story to tell. But when – and to whom?

He'd told us not to contact him until the trial was over. Another email from us while the trial was ongoing might risk causing him annoyance or unwanted stress. On the other hand, Brearey's time in the witness box was over and we had to try to get the story – whatever it was. So we took a chance and wrote to Brearey one more time to see if he would speak with us.

It was a Thursday afternoon in late April 2023. Jonathan was driving to film an interview when the phone rang. 'Hi, Jonathan,' said the caller from the unknown number. 'It's Steve Brearey.' Jona- than pulled off the road and skidded to a stop. The lead consultant from the unit was ready to talk.

Over the coming months, we sat for hours with Brearey and other medics from his unit, piecing together their story of how doctors, nursing staff and managers had reacted to the deaths. Some of the medics we met were passionate and angry. Some were reserved. Some were terrified.

Ravi Jayaram was another of the seven consultants working on the unit. Ravi and Steve were a kind of double act. In time, Lucy Letby would complain that she was a victim of a conspiracy within the hospital, orchestrated by a 'gang' of consultants. Steve and Ravi were the alleged ringleaders.

Ravi was an unusual case. By his own admission, he was something of a Z-list celebrity. He'd appeared as a TV doctor on *The One Show* and *This Morning*, and he clearly enjoyed the limelight. His response when we asked him if he'd do an interview was memorable. 'I don't want to sound wanky,' he said. 'But can you talk to my agent?'

Steve was different. The man seemed to be without ego. He was thoughtful and quietly spoken. He didn't crave the limelight. In fact, he probably hated it. Occasionally, when we spoke to him on the phone, he'd be in a remote part of Scotland or Ireland, cycling with his wife, away from the madding crowd.

We first met Steve Brearey and Ravi Jayaram in a hotel on the outskirts of Chester. Ravi seemed confident and telegenic. Steve arrived in a sweat-marked grey T-shirt, cycle helmet in hand. He'd biked it straight over from the hospital. There were no airs or graces. There was something rather spartan about him.

Brearey had originally been in the RAF before retraining as a paediatrician. He'd been around and seen plenty. He also felt the tragedy of the unexplained baby deaths. All of the medics did. But you could see it on Brearey's face and hear it in his voice. These deaths haunted him. It was impossible to meet Steve Brearey and not feel convinced that this was a man of integrity, driven by conscience and the truth.

In the end, this search for truth would divide the neonatal staff at the Countess of Chester Hospital into factions – each with its own view of the bland, well-spoken nurse from Hereford. Good people and good medics would find themselves on opposing sides of the argument. Many of the nurses who worked with Letby every day believed there was no way she could harm babies. A minority of others – most notably Brearey – dared to think the unthinkable as the months rolled by and babies kept dying or collapsing: that

Letby might be a killer. Even the conclusion of Letby's trial and her conviction hasn't healed the rift within the neonatal unit at the Countess of Chester Hospital.

And then there were the senior bosses running the hospital. It's hard to know exactly what they thought or believed. It's not unreasonable to suppose that they saw the consultants as conspiracy theorists. What would you think if someone told you that one of your colleagues was a serial killer – without hard proof? But these are speculations. What is apparent is that senior managers were unsympathetic to the consultants' concerns. Their priority seemed to be simply to move on. Had that been the end of it, Lucy Letby might still be living in quiet obscurity. No police investigation, no trial, and no answer to the question: was Lucy Letby a killer?

By the end of June 2016, all seven consultants on the neonatal unit had arrived at pretty much the same conclusion. A 'tipping point' had been reached after the death of the second triplet, according to consultant John Gibbs.

Dr Gibbs was the longest-serving consultant on the unit. He'd worked closely with Letby and had been present for no fewer than ten of the incidents for which she would later be charged. Like his colleagues, Dr Gibbs' concerns about Letby had developed gradually. A photograph from 6 August 2015 – two days after the fourth unexpected baby death – shows Letby and Gibbs standing beside each other, smiling as they celebrate reaching the halfway mark in the hospital's campaign to raise £3 million for a new neonatal unit. The idea of Letby as a killer was still unformed.

But by the following year, Dr Gibbs had a very different view of the nurse. On 25 June he was on shift when yet another baby boy collapsed. It was the day immediately after the second triplet had died. Three unexpected medical emergencies in three days – two of them fatal. Something was clearly wrong and Gibbs knew it. He pulled one of the nurses, Mary Griffith, to one side in the neonatal unit storeroom to ask her who'd been in the nursery when the latest crisis happened.

As they were speaking, Lucy Letby came in and heard the conversation. She told Dr Gibbs that she'd been the baby's designated nurse but she'd popped out for a few minutes in the knowledge that Mary Griffith was there, and the shift leader was just outside.

Letby was clearly shaken by the inquisitive consultant's question. It bothered her enough to provoke a late-night message to her close friend, the married registrar. 'Do I need to be worried about what Dr Gibbs was saying?' she ventured.

'No,' her confidant reassured her. 'He was asking to make sure that normal procedures were carried out.'

They discussed what exactly had been said in the equipment storeroom, and the fact that Lucy Letby hadn't been with her patient when the alarms went off because she'd gone to look after another child.

Dr ■■■■: There is nothing to worry about . . . You can't be with two babies in different nurseries at the same time, let alone predict when they're going to crash . . . . . .

Letby: I know, and I didn't leave him on his own . . . Feel better now

Dr ■■■■: Nobody has accused you of neglecting a baby or causing a deterioration.

Letby: I know. Just worry I haven't done enough

Dr ■■■■: How?

Letby: We've lost 2 babies I was caring for and now this happened today, makes you think 'am I missing something/ good enough'

If Letby was hoping for reassurance, she was in the right place. Clearly her friend couldn't imagine she would be guilty of anything of the sort – much less anything more sinister.

Dr ■■■■: Lucy, if anyone knows how hard you've worked over

the last three days it's me . . . If **anybody** says anything to you about not being good enough or performing adequately I want you to promise me that you'll give my details to provide a statement. I don't care who it is, and I don't care if I've left the trust. Promise?

Letby: Well I sincerely hope I won't ever be needing a statement
But thank you, I promise

The registrar gave the situation some more thought. Dr Gibbs had been asking questions, he suggested, because the mortality rate in Chester was higher than the regional average. 'It makes people (consultants) look at trends and patterns. That might have been why Dr G came to ask,' he surmised.

The reassurances kept coming.

Dr ███: You didn't miss anything that I would expect an experienced itu [intensive care] trained nurse to spot . . . you were flawless. It's why I am so happy to work with you. You don't flap, you give perfectly sensible suggestions and things run seamlessly . . . No more doubt – it's not you, it's the babies.

Letby: Thanks, really appreciate you saying that . . . So relieved that it's you who has been there throughout.

Warming to his theme, the registrar went on:

Dr ███: It's true. You are one of a few nurses across the region (I've worked pretty much everywhere) that I would trust with my own children. If you're worried – I'm worried. You should do the APNP [Advanced Paediatric Nurse Practitioner] course. You'd be excellent.

Letby: Don't know what to say Thank you

Dr ██: Self doubt finished?

Letby: I think so, thank you ++

All of the staff on the unit were talking about the events of that week. Three emergencies in three days, including two unexpected deaths, had prompted everyone to question what on earth was going on. It was her day off, but Lucy Letby joined in the discussion in a series of texts, advancing various theories.

Perhaps the unit was admitting too many babies. 'We're way over capacity,' she said in one message.

Another nurse suggested that an infection on the unit could be to blame. 'Yeah I think it needs looking at,' Letby agreed. 'There was shit coming out of the sink in [room] 2 on Sat and the toilet overflowing . . . I think the unit needs properly assessing, I don't think equipment gets cleaned properly . . . and we haven't got the space, facilities etc to maintain hygiene.'

Could it be because there weren't enough nurses? '[I]t's staffing [the ward manager] needs to look at,' she said.

All of Letby's colleagues were racking their brains to try to get to the bottom of what lay behind the crisis, but no one really had a clue. On 27 June 2016, two days after the last unexpected baby collapse, Letby got her uniform ready for that night's shift and prepared to go back into work. But a couple of hours before she was due to clock on, the phone rang. It was the unit manager, Eirian Powell, telling her not to come in that evening after all.

The phone call came like a bolt out of the blue. Letby must have sensed the groundswell of worry on the unit – the chatter among staff, the conjecture, the speculation. But it wasn't aimed at her, she'd told herself. It was no more than an undercurrent of general concern and guesswork. Everyone was in the same boat. Dr Gibbs asking pointed questions was unwelcome, but the married doctor had reassured her it was nothing to worry about.

The unexpected call telling her not to come in had brought her back down to earth, and her mind was racing. Why had her shift been cancelled? Why was she contacted at such short notice? What was being said about her?

She needed reassurance, and turned to the two people she knew would offer it – the married registrar, and her closest nursing pal.

Letby: E [Eirian] just phoned telling me to do days this week and not Go in tonight as trying to protect me 😔 . . . Asked if there was a problem and she said No just trying to protect me as had a difficult run . . . less people on nights etc and we can have a chat etc tomorrow. But Im worried Im in trouble or something

Friend: Don't worry, how can you be in trouble you haven't done anything wrong. Just very unfortunate.

Letby: I know but worrying in case they think i missed something or whatever. Why leave it til now to ring.

Friend: It is very late I agree. Maybe she's getting pressure from elsewhere?

Letby: She said it's busy so more support for me on days . . . She was nice enough I just worry. This job messes with your head

The married doctor told her that as he had been the medical lead on both days when the triplet boys had died, he was also expecting an uncomfortable conversation with his superiors, and that one of the consultants had already met the medical director to discuss things.[1]

'I can't do this job if it's going to be like this,' complained Lucy Letby. 'My head is a mess. Why is she ringing at this time? There must be a problem.'

'Lucy – you did nothing wrong at all,' he soothed. 'It is an odd time to ring, but you've had a rough few days and a good manager would realise that.'

The registrar went on to say that the unit's low staff turnover suggested it was well run, and Lucy Letby's manager was probably just checking how she was, as she hadn't looked well at the weekend. The nurse felt better. 'No, you are right,' she said gratefully. She acknowledged that she may be asked why she'd been given responsibility for the two remaining brothers on the day after the first triplet had died – and why she'd also been in charge of the unrelated baby who collapsed on the day after that. But there were reasons for it all, she said.

Letby's nurse friend texted again. 'Try not to worry too much,' she advised. 'At the end of the day there's been no common factors in any of it and a lot of other people involved.'

Lucy Letby's mood improved. Her close friends, at least, still supported her. What she didn't know was the extent to which the consultants were now conferring about her.

Murthy Saladi was another of the seven neonatal consultants. On 29 June 2016, Saladi emailed his colleagues, along with the hospital's medical director Ian Harvey and head of nursing Alison Kelly. 'Should we refer ourselves to external investigation?' read the subject line. Saladi was clear about what he had in mind.

'I believe we need help from outside agencies,' he wrote. 'At the moment we are all under suspicion and the only agency who can investigate all of us I believe is the police . . . I think we should pro-actively seek their help before we are forced because of further deaths.'

Fellow consultant Ravi Jayaram responded with his take on the situation. Hospital executives, he said, 'do not seem to see the same degree of urgency as we do.'

Medical director Ian Harvey responded defensively. 'Ravi – this is absolutely being treated with the same degree of urgency,' he snapped, before demanding that all email communications on the subject should stop. '[A]ction is being taken. All emails cease forthwith.' It was an early sign of what was to come. It was clear to the consultants that, for Harvey, their worries about Letby and talk about getting the police involved had to be managed and contained.

Two days later, Harvey met with Steve Brearey, Ravi Jayaram and Murthy Saladi. He also brought along the hospital's head of corporate affairs and legal services – an ex-police officer called Stephen Cross. The question of whether to call the police was top of the agenda – and, according to the consultants, Cross left no doubt about where he stood on the matter. Calling the police, he said, would be catastrophic for the trust. The neonatal unit would be closed and turned into a crime scene – an image that would clearly unnerve the consultants.

Ian Harvey and Stephen Cross were of one mind. But what about their boss – the hospital's CEO? Tony Chambers had been CEO of the Countess of Chester Hospital since 2012. Chambers was a classic NHS manager. He'd trained as a nurse before pivoting into management. Some say he wasn't a natural fan of doctors – stemming from his days as a trainee nurse. But compared to the urbane and allegedly haughty Ian Harvey, Tony Chambers seemed genial and down to earth. There was something of the pub manager about him – right down to the five o'clock shadow.

Like all good NHS managers, Tony Chambers always made himself available for a photo op or a puff piece about his hospital. In 2014 he enjoyed showing the Duchess of Cornwall around the place, cameras flashing, as she opened a new building. Two years later, his hospital's neonatal unit was in crisis. Thirteen babies had died in thirteen months – five times the annual average death rate. Many of the deaths were unexpected, one nurse had been there for nearly all of them, and the lead consultant on the unit believed she might be a murderer. You'd think the CEO would be engaged. But somehow, Tony Chambers had managed to avoid the drama – until now.

It was the last week of June 2016. Lucy Letby's managers looked at the rotas. She had three long day shifts left to complete before her annual leave was due to begin. They allowed her to work on all three days, and then she turned on her 'out of office' and set off for Torquay for a long-arranged holiday with her parents. That suited her managers just fine. Difficult conversations could be postponed – at least for now. The hiatus also gave senior staff a bit of space to work out what to do next. Letby wasn't to know that she'd never return to work on the unit, or as a nurse at all, ever again.

On 4 July 2016, as Lucy Letby was just starting her holiday, Tony Chambers met with the consultants from the neonatal unit for the first time since the first suspicious baby deaths more than a year earlier. Ian Harvey and Alison Kelly also attended the meeting. The mood was uneasy. The bosses knew they had to do something, so they promised a thorough 'forensic' review of the baby deaths. The review would look at the circumstances of the deaths, including staffing and the severity of the babies' pre-existing health conditions. It was also agreed that the neonatal unit would be downgraded to a 'special care unit'. Only babies who didn't need intensive care would be kept there from now on.[2]

The consultants agreed. But from where they were sitting, the bosses still weren't listening. The unexpectedness of the baby deaths, along with the fact that the babies hadn't responded to resuscitation as doctors expected, pointed to something truly out of the ordinary. It was only a matter of time before Lucy Letby's name was mentioned.

'I can remember describing the concerns that we had about Lucy Letby and the possibility of harm being done to these babies,' recalled Steve Brearey. Tony Chambers' response was telling. Blaming Letby, he said pointedly, would be 'very convenient', according to Brearey's recollection. The insinuation was clear: the consultants were using Letby as a scapegoat for other failings on the unit – possibly failings of their own.

While we were making our BBC *Panorama* documentary, we wrote to Tony Chambers and put it to him that he had described the consultants' concerns as 'very convenient'. He didn't deny it, but he said this was 'a one-sided account of the meeting where what I said has been taken out of context'. He added: 'I also said that there were a significant number of factors to consider, including demand, acuity, clinical care, staffing and environment.'

Chambers also echoed what his former colleague Ian Harvey told us. The laboratory evidence that a baby had been poisoned with insulin had been overlooked by a consultant. According to

Chambers, these blood test results were 'the only strong evidence of potential harm and would have materially altered the focus of subsequent enquiries and actions if they had been raised with me or any other senior manager in August 2015'.[3]

Chambers says that the consultants' 'serious concerns' were escalated to him for the first time in June 2016, at which point the board of directors was informed and 'prompt action was taken to maintain Neonatal Unit safety'.[4]

But the consultants left the meeting with Tony Chambers unsatisfied. Dr Brearey and Dr Jayaram had a further meeting with Ian Harvey and corporate affairs chief Stephen Cross in which they repeated their opposition to Letby's return to work. Judging from the accounts of the consultants, Harvey seemed almost nonchalant. 'She won't stay very long,' he said. The suggestion that Letby might be a serial killer didn't appear to be a serious consideration.

The Letby family's holiday hotel in Torquay felt a world away from Chester and all its conjecture. Lucy Letby tried to relax. But it must have been difficult to put thoughts of work out of her head entirely. She knew that, in her absence, doctors' meetings were being held and debrief conversations conducted. How could she not wonder what was being said? She didn't have to wait long. At 00.54 am on 6 July 2016, her phone pinged: a text from her friend, the married registrar. He'd been at a debrief:

> Dr ▆▆▆: You need to keep this to yourself.
> The meeting this afternoon looked at everything with [the triplets] from birth onwards.
> We reviewed everything. Room / meds / medical reviews and actions. We looked at all documentation med & nur [medical and nursing] . . .
> There is absolutely nothing for you to worry about. Please don't.
> There are going to be some recommendations based on staffing / kit but there was no criticism of either resus.

This is staying quiet until has been to exec's.

E [Eirian] had nothing but good things to say about you.

Letby: Ok . . . . . .

I Really appreciate you telling me – it won't go any further. I was one member of a huge team effort, but you know I've been carrying the worry of the 'what if I wasn't enough' – it's reassuring to hear that it doesn't appear that anything could have been done differently, or that I didn't act on or do something I should have.

Thank you.

The registrar was glowing. He told Lucy Letby that he'd been invited to the meeting as it was thought to be a good chance to help him prepare for becoming a consultant.

Dr ███ : There were a few questions which were easy to answer, but the constant theme was how well you and I dealt with [the first triplet's] deterioration and with [the second triplet's] resus. I felt proud for both of us.

Letby: That's good to hear. I'm glad you've had positive feed-back too – You were fantastic, it was an awful situation but I wouldn't have wanted anyone else to be there.

Dr ███ : Thank you – I wouldn't have wanted anyone else but you to be looking after [the triplets]. We do work well together!

The registrar mentioned the first triplet's liver injury as something believed to be related to the resuscitation or a disease process, rather than the cause of his deterioration. 'It's not thought to be significant,' he revealed. But there was a kicker. 'There will be an inquest,' he warned. 'We may have to attend.'

It was after 1.30 in the morning, and the registrar confided some more.

Dr ▮▮: They're looking at me because I was involved in all.

Letby: Have they said that?

Dr ▮▮: Not in so many words. I document clearly and contemporaneously. It's difficult to pull my work apart but there were a couple of comments – which is fine as long as I get the chance to talk through the process.

Lucy Letby agreed that they were in the same boat:

Letby: I imagine they will look at us both (as E [Eirian] has done with me for previous babies).

At the very least, Letby knew she had the solidarity of the married registrar. She even felt secure enough to offer him some comfort:

Letby: Try not to worry about it unless anything is said – they will be covering all areas.

Dr ▮▮: I know. I'm not worried.

The next night, the registrar opened up his messaging app again to forward an email to the nurse which he thought she might want to see. It was from the lead neonatologist Dr Steve Brearey, suggesting that he should prepare a written statement for the inquests, 'now, while everything is fresh in your mind'. The registrar confessed that he felt a bit upset at the prospect:

Dr ▮▮: The meeting yesterday found no issue with management or drugs etc – but doing this in a court is going to be uncomfortable.

Letby: It's a bit of a worry if it's going that far. Do you think I'll be involved?

Unlikely, answered the married registrar. His guess was that the inquest would probe management procedures, and rely on documents rather than a statement from her.

Letby: I don't know what to say. Feels like a bit of a blow considering everyones hard work etc

Dr ███: I feel the same . . . I know you won't say anything – this email has to stay between us, is that OK?

Letby: Of course, 100%

Lucy Letby's holiday was coming to an end, and she was due back at work on the neonatal unit the following week.

It was mid-July, and the initial findings of the promised 'forensic' review into the baby deaths were ready. Ian Harvey had done the review himself. For the consultants, his conclusions were unsurprising and disappointing. The baby deaths were 'multifactorial' he said – medical speak for 'caused by different things'. Staff numbers and the severity of pre-existing medical conditions in the babies were among this multiplicity of factors. As for Lucy Letby, she would return to work under one-to-one supervision. That was the decision of Harvey and his fellow managers. And so a possible baby killer would be back on the unit.

For a nurse of Letby's experience, one-to-one supervision was highly unusual, but unit manager Eirian Powell did her best to make it look routine and unremarkable. In an email to nursing staff, she said all staff would need to undertake a period of clinical supervision. According to the email, it had been 'decided that it would be useful to commence with staff who have been involved in many of the acute events facilitating a supportive role to each individual'. Powell's email continued:

Therefore Lucy has agreed to undergo this supervision first commencing on Monday 18th July. I appreciate that this process may be an added stress factor in an already emotive environment but we need to ensure that we can assure a safe environment in addition to safeguarding not only our babies but our staff. This is not meant to be a blame or competency issue but a way forward to ensure that our practice is safe.

Nothing to worry about. Nothing to see here. This isn't a reflection on Lucy. That was the message. But Letby herself could see through the window-dressing. She knew she was under suspicion and she'd already begun her fightback. On the same day as Eirian Powell's email, Letby messaged a nursing friend from the unit. 'I've done a timeline of this year,' she wrote.

'Fab,' replied the friend, adding: 'quite a few babies weren't compatible with life anyway. I wonder if midwives get this with amount of stillbirths . . .'

Letby appreciated the support: 'Yeah and some went off within hours/on handover. Or were already acutely unwell when I took over . . . Hoping to get as much info together as possible – if they have nothing or minimal on me they'll look silly, not me.'

Holiday over, Lucy Letby was back in Chester, and ready to go back to work. But before she could lay out her uniform and pack her work bag, she was told there had been a change of plan. Her managers had had a rethink. On reflection, they'd decided it would be best to move Letby off the unit and into an office job within the hospital until arguments about the baby deaths calmed down.

Once again, the decision was given full window dressing. On 9 August 2016, Eirian Powell emailed staff: 'Lucy is currently seconded to the Risk and Patient Safety Office for a period of three months.' By any measure, it was a bizarre move. Lucy Letby had been identified by consultants as a potentially serious risk to the neonatal unit. The Risk and Patient Safety Office seemed like the last place she should be. It was, perhaps, an indication of wider dysfunction within the hospital. 'The Risk Department was a disaster,' one hospital insider told us. 'This department is where they moved awkward nurses to.' It also appears to have been clueless when it came to assessing risk. The same insider told us: 'There was a point where they wanted to make [Lucy Letby] risk lead for neonates.'

It was a reflection of just how differently senior managers and consultants saw Letby. For Eirian Powell and the hospital's executives, Letby was the unfortunate target of a misconceived theory of foul play. By contrast, as far as the consultants were concerned, a suspected baby killer was now going on 'secondment' to the hospital's Risk and Patient Safety Office. Here, Letby would have privileged access to documents and files potentially relating to the neonatal unit and her case. She would also enjoy greater access to senior hospital managers, including some of those involved in investigating her.

But Letby was under no illusions about what the move meant. She was being suspended from duty – and she was furious. Shortly after Eirian Powell's email landed, Letby texted one of her nursing pals on the neonatal unit. 'Omg She's sent email about secondments!'

Letby wasn't the only one talking about it. 'Email is on fire!' replied her friend.

'Bloody hell fuming,' Letby texted back. 'I'm in email and makes it sound like my choice.'

'Feel a bit like I'm being shoved in a corner and forgotten about by the trust. It's my life and career,' she seethed in another message.

These texts were a foretaste of what was to come. Much later, in police interviews and in court, Letby would seem dispassionate, aloof – even cold. But in the fog of suspicion, uncertainty and division that had descended over the neonatal unit in the summer of 2016, Letby's was a clear and passionate voice to anyone who would listen. She was a good nurse. She'd done nothing wrong. Even a temporary 'secondment' to a hospital office job was an egregious injustice – a smear on her integrity and the career she'd worked so hard to build.

For Letby's fellow nurses, it was the first indication that Letby's practice was being questioned. 'When Lucy moved to the Risk and Patient Safety Office, there were a lot of questions and a few whispers – you know, suspicions,' recalled one nurse who worked on

Letby's unit. But even now, none of Letby's rank-and-file nursing colleagues had any real idea of the seriousness of the suspicions against her. The desperate conversations about Letby between the consultants and senior managers were kept under wraps. Even the junior doctors were in the dark. Many would have to wait until Letby's trial was well under way before learning what the consultants were thinking and saying about her. 'It's striking, knowing now that there were conversations going on,' one medic from the unit told us. 'I'd feel more comfortable sitting here today if we'd been made more aware – had been more involved.'

Behind the scenes though, the consultants and the hospital bosses were readying themselves for the next round in their contest over the truth. Earlier in the summer, medical director Ian Harvey had reached out to the Royal College of Paediatrics and Child Health. The College was independent of the hospital and generally had the confidence of consultants and hospital bosses alike. We don't know exactly what Harvey told the College. He certainly didn't mention Lucy Letby. But they were informed about the increased deaths and it was agreed that the College would visit the hospital and conduct 'an invited review of the [hospital's] neonatal service' and 'provide a view on whether there were any contributory factors in the deaths or missed opportunities'.[5]

On 1 September 2016, the team from the College made their way to Chester. They spent two days on the neonatal unit, gathering information and talking to staff. Steve Brearey recalls the visit clearly.

'They asked to speak to myself and Dr Jayaram for a couple of hours,' he told us. 'We explained to them at length the deaths and our worries about the deaths. They spoke to the other five consultants who, as well as telling them about the general care of the neonatal unit, also expressed their concerns about the deaths and the association with Lucy Letby. The reviewers were in no doubt about the clinicians' concerns about the association between Lucy Letby and the deaths.'

But the team from the College had more routine priorities. Their job was to examine everyday issues – like staffing levels, competency, protocols and the quality of service on the unit as a whole. And that was the flavour of its report following its review of the neonatal unit. No explanation for the increase in baby deaths was offered, but the report did highlight systemic shortcomings like staffing levels, intra-departmental communication, and reporting procedures following deaths or serious incidents. Whether a member of staff was harming babies was not a question that the College was geared up to answer – and its report made no attempt to do so.

Even so, the College's report was strikingly anodyne. The consultants had told the team from the College that they were worried there was a link between the baby deaths and a particular member of staff, and yet there was no mention of this anywhere in the College's report. There was no reference to Lucy Letby, even anonymously, or the fact that senior medics were worried about the possibility of foul play. Here was another review – to add to the others from February, May and July of the same year – in which consultants' worries about Lucy Letby were quietly set to one side. The closest the report came to acknowledging these worries was to recommend 'a thorough external, independent review of each unexpected neonatal death between January 2015 and July 2016 to determine any factors which could have changed the outcomes'. The review should include 'obstetric and pathology / post-mortem indicators, nursing care and pharmacy input'. So – a review calling for another review.

At one level, the narrowness of the Royal College report was unsurprising. But such was the distrust now between the consultants and senior managers that Steve Brearey and his colleagues began to suspect that the College's findings had been deliberately sanitised to suit hospital bosses. We understand that in the two months between the College's visit to the Countess of Chester Hospital and the publication of their report, the hospital's medical director Ian Harvey held numerous communications with the College team about what would be included in the final report.

In the end, and unbeknown to the consultants, two versions of the report were prepared. One was for public consumption. The other was kept secret. In ordinary circumstances, this would be unremarkable. Official reports often contain information that is not suitable for widespread dissemination, such as private HR-related information. In such circumstances, more than one version of a report may be produced with private information restricted for a narrower readership. But it's the nature of the information that was omitted from the public version of the RCPCH report that is notable. Unlike the public version, the secret version of the report did make reference to the consultants' concerns about Lucy Letby. They're set out in several paragraphs excluded from the public report. We managed to get a copy. Here's some of it:

> The neonatal lead, in an effort to be thorough and explore all possibilities, had identified that one nurse had been rostered on shift for all the deaths although the nurse had not always been assigned to care for that specific infant. Subsequently the paediatric lead and all the consultant paediatricians had become convinced by the link. Although this was a subjective view with no other evidence or reports of clinical concerns about the nurse beyond this simple correlation an allegation was made to the Medical Director and Director of Nursing . . . The consultants explained that their allegation was based on the nurse being on shift on each occasion an infant died (although not necessarily caring for the infant) combined with 'gut feeling'. There was no other evidence or history to link Nurse L to the deaths, and her colleagues had expressed no concerns about her practice.

It's hard to be sure about the real author of this unpublished extract. On the face of it, it was written by the College, but it's hard not to wonder how much of it had come from Harvey himself. It oozes with scepticism for the consultants' point of view. Their suspicions about Letby were 'a subjective view' based on 'gut feeling', with no supporting evidence apart from the fact that Letby had been on duty when the deaths had occurred. The fact that the consultants regarded the deaths as unexpected and that babies had not responded properly to resuscitation were factors that, in the consultants' minds at least, were further evidence underlying their suspicions. But these factors appeared to be disregarded.

But there's more to the unpublished section of the report by the Royal College. As well as claiming that the consultants' suspicions about Letby were unfounded, the extract included a glowing assessment of Letby as a nurse. She was, according to what the College had been told,

> [a]n enthusiastic, capable and committed nurse who had worked on the unit for four years . . . The [hospital's] Directors understood there was nothing about her background that was suspicious; her nursing colleagues on the unit were reported to think highly of her and how she responded to emergencies and other difficult situations, especially when the transport team were involved. There were apparently no issues of competency or training, she was very professional and asked relevant questions, demonstrating an enthusiasm to learn along with a high degree of professionalism.

To add insult to the perceived injury against Letby, she had – according to the unpublished section of the report – been denied due process. The implication was that the consultants' determination to get Letby off the unit was a breach of the nurse's rights, as well as being traumatic for her nursing colleagues on the unit. Letby had, it was claimed, been moved off the neonatal unit 'without explanation nor any formal investigative process having been established'.

> [T]he Director of Nursing considered supervised practice for the nurse but the consultants would not accept this and required the nurse be removed from the unit. Senior operational staff on the unit reported being very upset at the situation and the neonatal nurse manager in particular explained the difficulty of wanting to support the nurse and managing morale and anxiety among the other nursing staff who were not aware of the allegation . . . On her return [from holiday] she was told that she would be supervised for a period and that others were also being supervised. She was not told of the specific

allegation but she was made aware that there were concerns that she was on duty for each of the deaths. At a subsequent meeting, accompanied by her Union representative she was advised that supervision was not possible (due apparently to 'staffing levels') and she would be temporarily redeployed. She was apparently advised again that this would also happen to other members of staff. She was told not to make contact with staff on the unit . . . No formal HR process had been put in place for the ten weeks between the redeployment and the RCPCH visit. The RCN support to the nurse had, up to the RCPCH visit, not been very active but it was expected that the nurse would raise a grievance.

Perhaps most interesting of all is what the unpublished report extract reveals about what Letby was saying herself. Like Brearey and the other consultants, she too had met with the review team from the Royal College – and she had used the opportunity well. According to the text: 'She herself explained to the review team that she was passionate about her career and keen to progress. She regularly volunteered to work extra shifts when available or change her shifts when asked to do so and was happy to work with her friends on the unit.'

Several months would pass before the consultants were allowed to read the unpublished section of the Royal College report. The hospital's CEO Tony Chambers would later tell the consultants that all of the 'redactions' from the public version of the report were made at the request of the RCPCH and 'purely because they related to HR concerns'.[6] But the battle lines had been drawn and they already knew where they stood in relation to Ian Harvey and the other hospital bosses. They were the bad guys – accusing a young nurse on the basis of gut feeling and coincidence. Letby was a victim – and the bosses were backing her.

On 7 September – less than a week after her meeting with the team from the Royal College – Letby initiated a grievance procedure against the consultants. That same month, the Royal College of Nursing wrote to her to let her know about the concerns that had been raised about her. But she wasn't alone. She had powerful friends within the hospital. None more so than Karen Rees – the hospital's lead nurse for urgent care.

Even after the death of the triplets in June 2016, Rees had resisted demands from Steve Brearey to remove Letby from the neonatal unit. When she was finally moved to the hospital's Risk and Patient Safety Office, Rees became a lifeline for Letby. Over the next two years, Letby and Rees grew close. It was rumoured that Letby even attended barbecues at Karen Rees's home.

According to Rees, Letby was emotional and utterly believable. 'I witnessed her in complete distress, crying and swearing her innocence. She was very convincing,' Rees later recalled.[7]

> If I think back to all the times when I have seen her really, really upset – I wouldn't say hysterical, but really upset – and I would think: how can somebody continually present themselves in that way on a near weekly basis for two years? I find that really difficult and I think, 'Oh my gosh! Would she have been that good at acting?' . . . She was just looking at me as if to say: 'Why?' Her mantra was: 'I'm not going to be forced out of the job I love. I've done nothing wrong.' And she kept saying this. She never changed that mantra.[8]

Rees would believe in Letby's innocence even after her arrest in 2018 – right up until her trial in 2022.[9] Rees now says she was duped by Letby,[10] but it's hard to resist the impression that, privately, Rees still isn't completely sure that Letby is guilty.

Rees wasn't the only senior hospital manager to be persuaded by Letby's protestations of innocence. As Letby's grievance procedure got going, Letby's father John came to Chester to support his daughter in her hour of need. And he didn't stay on the sidelines. He went straight to the boss of the hospital. Tony Chambers later acknowledged that he spent hours with Letby and her father. Letby's father was as adamant as his daughter: Lucy had done nothing wrong.

As the bosses lined up in support of Letby, life for the seven consultants on the neonatal unit was becoming increasingly uncomfortable. Most of the nurses – unaware of exactly what Letby was suspected of – felt that she was being victimised. And they weren't alone. In November 2016, the neonatal unit's lead consultant Steve Brearey was summoned to an interview by HR. It was chiefly because of Brearey that Lucy Letby had been removed from the neonatal unit. Letby was fuming, and now Brearey himself was under investigation.

It was clear where Ian Harvey's sympathies lay. As far as he was concerned, the case against Letby was flimsy. But the consultants weren't about to back down, and Harvey knew that he and the other hospital managers had a fight on their hands. Harvey also knew that further investigation into the baby deaths was needed. The Royal College report, for all its inoffensiveness, had called for 'a thorough external, independent review of each unexpected neonatal death between January 2015 and July 2016'. A demand like this couldn't be ignored.

In the autumn of 2016, Ian Harvey asked a London-based neonatologist called Jane Hawdon to review the cases of the babies who had died – thirteen in total. Dr Hawdon agreed to look at the babies' case notes and prepared a professional but sparse twenty-page report setting out her findings.

Whatever its merits, Dr Hawdon's report wasn't the thorough review into the baby deaths that the Royal College had called for. She didn't visit the neonatal unit or talk to any of the consultants. Her report was based exclusively on medical notes, and insiders say it was prepared over a single weekend. Dr Hawdon didn't promise more than she delivered. Indeed, she was perfectly candid about the limits of her review. She made clear that she didn't have the time to carry out an in-depth examination of the cases. Her conclusions, she said, were, 'her opinion', presented 'to inform discussion and learning'. Moreover, the report 'would not necessarily be upheld in a coroner's court or court of law'. Crucially though, Dr Hawdon said more investigations into some of the deaths were needed. In her conclusions, she singled out four baby deaths that she said were 'unexplained' and should, as long as the coroner's reports didn't say otherwise, be subjected to 'broader forensic review'.

If Ian Harvey had been hoping Dr Hawdon's report would bring closure to the debate about what had caused babies to die on the neonatal unit, then he may have been disappointed. But judging from what happened next, it appears that Ian Harvey felt the time had come for everyone, including the consultants, to move on.

In early January 2017, Ian Harvey met with the board of the Countess of Chester Hospital. The meeting was for senior bosses and non-executive directors only. The consultants weren't invited. The main item on the agenda was the increase in deaths on the neonatal unit. Harvey did most of the talking, and his focus was the two reports that had been prepared by the Royal College and Dr Jane Hawdon.

Both reports, he noted, had highlighted issues of 'leadership, escalation and timely intervention' – in other words, systemic failings on the neonatal unit. He also pointed out that neither report had highlighted any single individual. All true, but neither report amounted to a forensic review of the baby deaths. Indeed, both the Royal College and Dr Hawdon had also called for further and more thorough investigation of the deaths. Dr Hawdon in particular had singled out four that she said were 'unexpected and unexplained' and required 'broader forensic review'. And yet it seems that this was not the message that the board heard. We understand that Ian Harvey's presentation to the board suggested that the reviews by the Royal College and Dr Hawdon were comprehensive and that the outcome of these reviews was that no one person was to blame.

Years later, the board's Chairman Sir Duncan Nichol had scathing words about the information that he and his fellow board members had been given: 'I believe that the board was misled,' he told the BBC.

Harvey disagrees. 'The statements I gave to the board were true to the best of my knowledge,' he said. In an email to us, he also said: 'In January 2017 we could not link any one member of staff to all of the cases that we had reviewed, so I believe that this was correct at that time.' Tony Chambers feels the same. He told one of our colleagues that 'what was shared with the board was honest and open and represented our best understanding of the outcome of the reviews at the time'.

The two reports by the Royal College and Dr Hawdon weren't the only thing discussed at that closed-door meeting with the hospital board in January 2017. Lucy Letby was discussed too – not as a plausible murder suspect but as a victim. An impact statement from Letby herself was read aloud. In it, she described how being under suspicion had affected her life. She also declared her wish to return to the unit. And Harvey was backing her all the way. The consultants, he said, should apologise to Letby. Enough was enough.

With the board now onside, it was time to deal with the consultants once and for all. On 27 January 2017, all seven of the consultants on the neonatal unit were summoned to a meeting with senior managers. All of the top brass were there – Tony Chambers, Ian Harvey, Stephen Cross, Alison Kelly and Karen Rees. As with everything else in this story, there are competing versions of events, but all seven consultants say they are sure about what they heard.

Ian Harvey repeated what he had told the hospital board a few weeks earlier: the reports by Dr Hawdon and the Royal College had highlighted poor leadership and issues with medical care on the neonatal unit. Once again, according to several of those present, there was no mention of Dr Hawdon's call for four of the deaths to be investigated further.[11]

Lucy Letby's impact statement was also given another reading. This time, Karen Rees was the one to read Letby's words aloud to everyone in the room. She'd been found innocent of all allegations, Letby claimed. She'd also been the target of verbal slurs by some of the doctors. Some of the paediatric trainees had reportedly referred to Letby as the 'angel of death'. There was even a reference to Letby and suicide, although the context and precise content of what was said is unclear. For those at the meeting who believed Letby was innocent, her words were an indictment against the consultants who, she said, had made her life a misery.

But for the consultants, Tony Chambers was the one who delivered the most memorable lines. He talked about the hours he had spent with Letby and her father. She was adamant that she had done nothing wrong. The board had upheld Letby's grievance procedure and she would therefore be returning to work on the neonatal unit. And there was more. The consultants were to accept the findings of the board. They would also have to apologise to Letby for their actions. 'You will draw a line under this,' Chambers declared. 'And if you cross that line there will be consequences.' The hospital's most senior figure had spoken. Lucy Letby had been declared the victor in the battle for the truth. The consultants had been wrong to suspect her and her slate had been wiped clean.

Tony Chambers disputes the consultants' account of the meeting. He later told the consultants that his reference to 'drawing a line' was 'never meant to imply that we had "drawn a line" under requirements for further investigations'. He also said that he hadn't meant to be aggressive or threatening.[12] In correspondence with us, Chambers said that he had explained to Letby and her father that the fact that her grievance procedure had been upheld wasn't the same as exoneration. 'I made no comment,' he said. He also disputed the consultants' account of the tone of the meeting. He told us the meeting had ended on a conciliatory note. According to Chambers' recollection, Ravi Jayaram had 'thanked the Board' and said that the consultants looked forward to working together with senior management before adding: 'We [the consultants] have not been as good at that as we could have been.'[13]

But despite Ravi Jayaram's diplomatic pleasantries, the consultants were now more isolated and vulnerable than ever. They took Chambers' insistence that there would be consequences if they didn't draw a line under things as nothing short of a threat: keep asking questions about Lucy Letby and you will be in trouble.

That evening, after the meeting, one of the consultants was so concerned about the implications of what Chambers had said that she sat down with her husband 'and worked out how long we could pay the mortgage after I lost my job'.

And yet the consultants' suspicions about Letby hadn't gone away. They couldn't simply wish them away. If anything, their suspicions had hardened. Since Letby's removal from the neonatal unit in July 2016, not a single baby had died. Of course, the unit had also been downgraded at the very same time, which meant it no longer cared for very sick babies. In other words, the death rate was bound to come down. But zero deaths in eight months? Was that really nothing to do with Letby's absence? The consultants still believed Letby was the problem. But they hadn't a shred of proof. Their case against Letby, if you can call it that, had fallen short. They were running out of options.

On 28 February 2017, the consultants did as they had been asked and wrote a letter of apology to Letby. 'Dear Lucy,' it read:

> The increased mortality on the neonatal unit and subsequent reviews and re-designation of the neonatal unit has been a very stressful time for all staff and parents. We understand that it has been an exceptionally stressful time for you. We would like to apologise for any inappropriate comments that may have been made during this difficult period. As you will be aware, emotions have run high. We are very sorry for the stress and upset that you have experienced in the last year. Please be reassured that patient safety has been our absolute priority during this difficult time.

All seven consultants signed the letter – even Steve Brearey. Brearey later described it as 'a way of appeasing [the bosses'] request but not actually giving a genuine apology.' But for the hospital's HR officials, this was only the first step on the path to reconciliation between Lucy Letby and the consultants. In March 2017, Steve Brearey and Ravi Jayaram were invited to participate in mediation with Letby. It wasn't an ordinary invitation though. According to Brearey, Ian Harvey had indicated that failure to take part in the mediation could result in referral to the General Medical Council for professional misconduct. Brearey noted as much at the time, citing '[an] email from the medical director suggesting GMC referral might follow from someone if I don't engage'. Brearey's back was against the wall, and the HR department knew it. On 1 March 2017, Brearey emailed HR with the following: 'I would like to re-iterate Dr Jayaram's comments that I feel it is inappropriate to hold this mediation at this time when the board are aware of all the consultant paediatricians' concerns.'

Brearey went through the motions, but he stopped short of meeting Letby face to face. There were just too many unanswered questions. Ravi Jayaram was more willing. He sat down with Letby to discuss her return to work. After her trial, Jayaram offered this account of the meeting:

It was bizarre. And of course, to listen to her saying, 'I'm coming back next week. Will you work with me?' And of course, I was having to say, 'Well, if the trust have deemed that you're coming back to work, I will work with you, yes.' 'But will you be happy to work with me?' [she asked]. 'I will work with you if you're on shift,' [I said]. Because no, I wasn't happy.[14]

For Brearey though, sitting down with Letby was too much. Deep down, he believed, or at least feared, that Letby was a killer. Whether or not he was right, making nice with her simply wasn't something he could bring himself to do.

But Brearey had other reasons too. Despite the warnings and threats from senior managers, Brearey and his fellow consultants hadn't stopped asking awkward questions – starting with some of the pronouncements from Ian Harvey that had clearly shaped the thinking of Tony Chambers and the hospital board. In his meetings with the board and later with the consultants, Harvey had highlighted poor leadership and issues with medical care on the neonatal unit. He'd also suggested that adequate enquiries into the baby deaths had been made. He cited not one but two reviews that he had personally commissioned – one from the Royal College of Paediatrics and Child Health and the other from respected neonatologist Dr Jane Hawdon.

But the consultants weren't convinced. None of them had seen the uncensored version of the Royal College report. And none of them had seen Dr Hawdon's report either. In the weeks following the January showdown with Tony Chambers and the bosses, the consultants wrote to Chambers demanding to see both reports. In early February, they got their wish. The report by the Royal College was largely unsurprising. It was never going to get to the bottom of the baby deaths – and so it wasn't a surprise that it didn't. The Hawdon report was also inconclusive, but one aspect of it leapt out. Four of the baby deaths, according to Dr Hawdon, were unexplained and should be investigated further. Despite what the consultants saw as the efforts of Tony Chambers, Ian Harvey and the other bosses to shut down further questions, here was a clear, independent recommendation to keep digging.

On 9 February 2017, Steve Brearey and Ravi Jayaram met with Ian Harvey. Harvey offered reassurance: the recommendation in Dr Hawdon's report was in hand. But the consultants weren't taking any chances. They'd stopped trusting their bosses months ago. It was now time to look for outside help.

There aren't many neonatal consultants in the North West of England. It's a small world in which most people tend to know each other. Everyone knew Dr Nim Subhedar. Nim was the 'lead neonatologist' for the Cheshire and Merseyside Neonatal Network – an umbrella organisation for neonatal units across the North West. Nim was respected by pretty much everyone. He was also familiar with what had been going on at the Countess of Chester Hospital.

Almost exactly a year before, Steve Brearey and his colleagues had made their first concerted attempt to explain the deaths by looking for common themes. They'd found nothing to go on, apart from the fact that most of the babies had died unexpectedly during the night. It was a frustrating exercise, conducted without any input from senior management. But Nim Subhedar had stepped up to help. He joined in with Brearey and his colleagues – discussing and analysing the deaths and lending whatever insights he could.

Twelve months later, those same questions were still un-answered. Each successive review had called for further investiga-tion. Dr Hawdon's report was the latest in the grim series, but Brearey and his colleagues wanted another opinion. Nim was the obvious choice.

Subhedar wasted no time. On 10 February, Subhedar emailed Ian Harvey with his take on Dr Hawdon's report. 'My own interpretation of the 13 deaths included in her review suggests there were 4 cases in whom there is no clearly identified cause of collapse/death, and a further three cases where the cause of the initial collapse leading ultimately to the baby's death remain unexplained,' he wrote. 'The single most important and relevant recommendation . . . advises "broader forensic review" of the cases in whom the death/collapse remains unexplained. I would recommend extending this to . . . 7 cases . . .' Subhedar subsequently added another death to this list. In his view, no fewer than eight of the baby deaths on the neonatal unit should be investigated further.

By the end of March 2017, a crisis point in the dispute between the consultants and hospital managers had been reached. Despite multiple reviews, there were as yet no satisfactory answers about why so many babies on the neonatal unit had died. The latest external advice was that eight of the deaths should be investigated. But still, no one was investigating properly. Ian Harvey had left the hospital board in the dark. Meanwhile, Lucy Letby was getting ready to return to work. She'd already visited the neonatal unit and clearly enjoyed the support of many of her old nursing colleagues. The stage was set for her comeback.

On 27 March, Steve Brearey and Ravi Jayaram met again with Ian Harvey and Tony Chambers. This time, Brearey was the one making demands. Previous reviews had failed to explain the deaths. In-house options had been exhausted. It was, Brearey said, time to call in the police. Nine months had passed since the suggestion of getting the police involved had first been mentioned to senior management, and by now even Tony Chambers could see the argument. He agreed to Brearey's request, promising to clear his diary and make it a priority.

But Ian Harvey – the hospital's most powerful doubter of the consultants and their suspicions of Letby – wasn't quite ready to concede, or so it appeared. In early April 2017, Harvey approached Steve Brearey and Ravi Jayaram and invited them to meet with a criminal barrister. Harvey chose the barrister and co-ordinated the meeting.

Harvey assured Brearey that nothing had changed. The plan was still for the hospital to call in the police. The barrister's job was just to work out how. But the barrister had a different impression.

On 12 April, the barrister and all seven consultants got together. The barrister opened proceedings. He'd been instructed by the hospital, he explained, to advise on *whether* the hospital should call in the police. Despite the assurances from Ian Harvey and Tony Chambers, the decision to involve the police had apparently not been finalised.[15]

To the consultants, the meeting with the barrister looked like another attempt by senior managers to find a way to keep the police from getting involved. But by the end of the meeting, the barrister himself had read the situation. The police had to be involved – and the barrister had a plan for making it happen. It was called CDOP.

'CDOP' stands for Child Death Overview Panel. It's an official forum for looking at child deaths and the reasons for them.[16] On the face of it, it looked like just another talking shop. The difference with this one, though, was that the hospital managers wouldn't be in charge. The meeting would be chaired by a senior officer from Cheshire Police called Nigel Wenham.

It was a big moment. In just a few days' time, Letby was due to return to work. The CDOP meeting was the consultants' last chance to stop her. But for Steve Brearey, the timing was unfortunate. He was heading to Uganda for a medical trip. For two years, he'd been carrying the burden of the unexplained baby deaths. Now, here was his first opportunity to kick-start a real investigation – and he wouldn't be there to take it.

On the day of the CDOP meeting, Brearey was sitting on the banks of Lake Bunyonyi when his phone pinged. A text from Ravi. The meeting had gone well:

I won't bore you with the details but in terms of outcomes both the policeman and the lay chair immediately understood our concern that we did not feel that the right questions had been asked yet. Superintendent Wenham is going to discuss with his superiors but his feeling is that at the very least there should be some official 'scoping' of whether an investigation is justified and if so how it should be done . . . For the first time I feel that there is a chance that the concerns we have might be investigated appropriately . . .

Four thousand miles away, it was the news Steve Brearey wanted to hear. For Lucy Letby though, it was a devastating development. With the police now involved, her return to work on the neonatal unit was out of the question. That was CDOP's advice to the hospital, and this time, the bosses had to accept it.[17] For them, the time for delay and prevarication had finally run out. On 2 May 2017, the CEO of the Countess of Chester Hospital, Tony Chambers, wrote to Cheshire Constabulary to ask formally for an investigation into the baby deaths. Within days, a police investigation was launched. It would be called 'Operation Hummingbird'.

Chapter 5

Operation Hummingbird

Judging from the size and location of its HQ, you'd think Cheshire Police was MI5. It's basically a huge fortress in the middle of nowhere, half an hour's drive from Chester. But relatively speaking, Cheshire Constabulary isn't one of the bigger forces in the North West of England. High-profile serial murder cases weren't exactly familiar territory and this one – if it even was a murder case – was far from straightforward. It would take five years and dozens of officers to get enough evidence to bring Lucy Letby to trial. Even then, there were no certainties about what the jury would make of it all.

Nigel Wenham – the police officer who'd chaired the CDOP meeting in Chester – had promised the consultants a 'scoping' exercise to see if a police investigation was needed – nothing more. And although Tony Chambers had formally asked Cheshire Police to investigate, his letter to Chief Constable Simon Byrne suggested he wasn't expecting the police to find anything. The investigation, as far as Chambers was concerned, was to 'put . . . minds at rest'.[1] Ian Harvey had a similar view. He told us:

> When we met with the police, we did not have anything but limited circumstantial evidence to report. We did say that we had explored every other avenue and that a formal police investigation was the only way to confirm whether or not the deaths were due to natural causes.[2]

Harvey would continue to believe for many months that the police investigation was a formality that would find nothing of concern.

Detective Inspector Paul Hughes was the man inside Cheshire Police given the job of 'scoping' things out.[3] Hughes was head of the force's major investigation team. It was now up to him to figure out whether a police investigation was needed at the Countess of Chester Hospital.

It didn't take him long. Steve Brearey had returned from his trip to Uganda, so on 15 May, Hughes and his colleague Nigel Wenham met with Brearey, Ravi Jayaram, John Gibbs, and one of the other consultants. The venue was familiar territory for the consultants – a drab conference room next to the Women and Children's building at the Countess of Chester Hospital.

Steve and Ravi did most of the talking. 'We sat down with two senior police officers and told them of our concerns,' Brearey recalls. 'And they were astonished. Their keyboards were going rapidly, trying to minute everything that we were saying.'

Naturally, the two police officers in the room had no idea about what goes on in a neonatal unit – or what to expect, so the consultants made it as simple as they could. Babies generally don't collapse unexpectedly, and when they do, doctors are usually able to explain why. For the consultants, that's what made these baby deaths and collapses different. They were unexpected and unexplained.

They also explained the connection between the incidents and 'a nurse' on the unit – and how the deaths had stopped ever since her removal. That alone looked suspicious, but Detective Inspector Hughes was wary of jumping to conclusions. Reflecting on the case later, Hughes said:

'My first thoughts were, as [Senior Investigating Officer], that if I had been doing something and somebody else had been moved, then I would stop as well. So I didn't [get] drawn into much about what that meant.'

Even so, what the consultants were saying was alarming. 'It was very clear from the end of that meeting that there was plenty of substance for them to justify a police investigation,' Brearey recalled.

But no one had seen or found hard evidence of foul play, so it was far too early to talk about suspects. For Detective Inspector

Hughes, establishing whether a crime had even been committed was the first step – and that was no easy task.

There's a reason why medics spend so many years in training. Medicine is a complex business – full of jargon and complicated science – so this was always going to be a difficult case, in need of expert guidance and opinion. Of course, Steve Brearey and the other consultants knew their stuff. But they were witnesses, and so they weren't independent. What Cheshire Police needed was an independent expert to take a look at the cases, guide them through what was going on medically, and ultimately form a view on whether babies had been harmed.

Cheshire Police had never had a case like this one before so they reached out to their friends in the National Crime Agency in London. The NCA was used to complex cases and had a database of experts to draw on.[4] One of those was Dewi Evans. Evans was a retired paediatrician[5] based on the other side of the English border in the southern Welsh town of Carmarthen.

Evans knew his way around the criminal justice system. He'd been an expert witness in medical negligence and child abuse cases for twenty years. Indeed, it had been his main line of work since his retirement from clinical practice in 2009. He also had a bullish attitude towards barristers. 'Bombast, bluster and belligerence forms part of their armoury,' he once said. 'They are who they are. The degree of aggression one experiences is usually inversely proportional to their understanding of the particular case.'

In May 2017, the same month that Cheshire Police launched their investigation, Dr Evans emailed one of his contacts at the NCA. He'd heard rumblings of what had been going on at the Countess of Chester Hospital – and he sensed an opportunity. 'I've read about the high death rate for babies in Chester and that the police are investigating,' he wrote. 'Do they have a paediatric/ neonatal contact? . . . If the Chester police had no one in mind I'd be interested to help. Sounds like my kind of case.'

Evans had been a consultant paediatrician with decades of experience in looking after babies and children. He'd pioneered a neonatal intensive care service in Swansea and had held the position of clinical director there before he retired. His experience was unquestionable, but he wasn't technically what medics call a neonatologist – an officially recognised specialist in the care of newborn babies. For Evans, this was just a label. Neonatology wasn't a distinct field in Swansea when he began his practice, but he maintains that his expertise and experience matched that of a consultant neonatologist. Later on, during the trial, Letby's defence team would launch various attacks on Evans' expertise and credibility, as well as his motives. Right now though, he looked like just the man Cheshire Police needed. The National Crime Agency made the introductions and one sunny day in early July 2017, Dewi Evans drove up to Chester to meet with officers from Cheshire Police.

Blacon police station was unprepossessing. It looks a bit like a secondary school – a far cry from the force's imposing HQ in Winsford. But it was right next to the Countess of Chester Hospital and it had already become the nerve centre of Operation Hummingbird. Inside, Evans sat down with Paul Hughes, the man leading the investigation, and a handful of Hughes' senior colleagues. It was too early to jump into the weeds on such a vast and complex investigation. Instead, Evans asked to see the medical notes of one of the babies that Cheshire Police was interested in.

They picked one of the last baby deaths in their timeline – one of the two triplets who had died in June 2016. Consultants had cited the triplet deaths as a tipping point in their concerns about Letby. Steve Brearey himself had been personally involved in this one. But Evans was told none of this, and he would always maintain that he knew nothing about Brearey or the battle between the consultants and senior managers at the hospital. All he had to go on were the clinical notes – and a cursory examination at that. And this alone was enough to make him alarmed. 'The medical records noted that the baby had died with bleeding into the liver and the abdominal cavity,' he recalled. 'And there was a mark on the skin just over where the liver was. It was pretty apparent to me that this baby had suffered trauma – deliberately inflicted trauma.'

The police wanted to know more – and Evans was happy to assist. But he'd spent enough time with criminal defence barristers to know that if this case and his opinion ever got near a court, his impartiality would also be on trial. If he knew before reading the medical notes that allegations or suspicions had been levelled against a particular nurse, he might leave himself open to the accusation that he wasn't approaching the evidence objectively with an open mind. So before going any further, he made his position clear to the cops. 'If you have a suspect, I don't want to know,' he told them – and they were more than happy to agree.

Evans knew the time period that the police were investigating – January 2015 to July 2016. But he didn't know how many cases they were focusing on – and he didn't want to know that either. Rather than limiting himself to particular cases, Dewi Evans asked the police to send him everything – medical records for 'all the babies who died and all the babies who suffered a life-threatening problem' between January 2015 and July 2016. The police agreed, and in September 2017, Evans received a memory stick containing the documents he'd asked for. He was now part of the team – Operation Hummingbird's go-to expert.

Evans had his work cut out for him. The medical notes from the hospital had been dumped on the police with no ordering or organisation. 'They were a mess really,' Evans reflected. 'Getting them into order was a job in itself.'

Over the next two months, Evans reviewed around thirty individual cases. He says he approached the case with an open mind. He wasn't setting out to uncover a crime. 'I was a blank sheet of paper,' he said later. 'My state of mind was very clear. Let's find a diagnosis. Nothing to do with crime. Let's identify any specific collapse and see if I can explain it.'

He started with the babies who'd been born first, and the first three he looked at were all deeply troubling. The first baby had projectile-vomited before she collapsed and stopped breathing. The fact that there were no prior warning signs wasn't the only indication that something wasn't right. The baby had vomited milk so forcefully that it had left her cot and landed on the floor. It didn't make sense. The baby had been receiving milk feeds through a plastic tube running through her nose and down into her stomach, but the amounts were very small and the timing of them very specific: 45 millilitres – roughly a double whisky – every three hours. The feeds were gentle, without any force. The milk travelled down the tube under gravity and took about an hour to complete. However, even after the baby had vomited, 45 millilitres of milk was found remaining in her stomach. The conclusion seemed inevitable: the baby had been force-fed much more milk in a way that was so harmful to her that it caused her to vomit with staggering force before collapsing. The baby did survive, although she later suffered irreversible brain damage. For Evans, it was clear that the baby had been deliberately harmed.

The next case was more shocking still – the first of a set of twins born in June 2015. According to Evans' reading of the notes, the baby had been well before collapsing suddenly and without warning. As a paediatrician with nearly thirty years of practice behind him, Evans had seen his fair share of baby deteriorations. 'They don't come out of nowhere,' he said. 'And they aren't sudden either. Babies generally decline gradually rather than suddenly.' Steve Brearey had said exactly the same thing. But it was what happened after the collapse that seemed to confirm to Evans that the baby had been harmed. 'Babies do stop breathing,' Evans told us. 'But you can generally reverse this with resuscitation.' In the case in front of him though, the baby hadn't responded to resuscitation and died – to the surprise and dismay of everyone on the unit. Evans' conclusion about what had caused the baby to die would ultimately come to define much of the case against Lucy Letby and the science used to convict her. Evans concluded that the baby's collapse was 'consistent with his having received a bolus of air intravenously' – in other words the injection of air into his circulation. The baby's twin sister also collapsed the following evening, and although she survived, Evans' preliminary analysis of what had caused her collapse was the same.

In medical speak, it was known as air embolism – a blockage caused by an air bubble in the blood circulation. Even the most junior medic knows that an air bubble in a blood vessel can be fatal. It can cause the heart and the respiratory system to stop working. From the medical notes he was reading, Evans believed someone had been harming babies by deliberately injecting them with air.

It's easy to understand in the abstract: air injected into a blood vessel can kill. But how might it happen on a neonatal unit? What was the set-up and what equipment would be needed? Would it be easy to inject a baby with a fatal dose of air and how difficult would it be to avoid getting caught?

We had to know, so we persuaded a respected neonatal nurse and university lecturer, Allison Mitchell, to demonstrate for us on camera. The model baby was a tiny doll used for teaching nursing students. The incubator looked high-tech, but it was essentially a heated box. There were various tubes attached to the baby as well, including several intravenous lines.

'Can you show me how you could inject air into the baby?' Judith asked tentatively. Allison took a deep breath and reached over to a shelf beside the incubator where she had placed several unopened syringes in paper packets. She picked one up, ripped it open and withdrew the plunger. 'So this syringe is actually full of air now,' she said before opening the two circular Perspex doors at the side of the incubator.

Our cameraman followed her hands as they entered the incubator. She removed the needle and attached the plastic syringe containing the air to a nozzle on one of the lines running into the model baby's bloodstream. Allison pressed the plunger and the air left the syringe.

'Simple and quick,' Judith remarked.

'Very quick,' said Allison.

It was chillingly simple. Syringes like the one Allison used are everywhere on neonatal units. No one keeps tabs on them and, once they're used, they're disposed of immediately. It seemed to be the perfect method of murder for a nurse who wanted to kill.

We could tell that Allison was uncomfortable. She'd never been asked to do anything like this before.

'It isn't on any nurse's radar to do this,' she said, shaking her head. 'It's difficult. To actually consider injecting air is totally alien. It's not something you would do.'

But looking at the medical notes in his study in Carmarthen, that is what Dewi Evans believed had been going on at the Countess of Chester Hospital. As Evans went through the notes, he identified other babies that in his opinion had also been injected with air. He also identified possible evidence of deliberately inflicted trauma and the injection of air into babies' stomachs. 'A pattern became apparent in the cases,' he later explained during questioning in court. The pattern, he said, was 'quite disturbing and quite unusual . . . There were occasions where I couldn't explain it, and occasions where I found something deeply suspicious . . . There were incidents I found disturbing.'[6]

In November 2017, Evans presented his findings to Cheshire Police in a series of preliminary reports. No two examples were exactly the same, but Evans identified fourteen cases where he believed babies had been 'placed in harm's way'. Seven of these had died. It was a pivotal moment. The expert on the case believed there was evidence that crimes had been committed. Operation Hummingbird was no longer a scoping exercise.

But Evans was just one man and one opinion. What if he was wrong? After all, experts get things wrong all the time and Cheshire Police had no prior experience of Dr Evans. Evans himself knew the system well enough to know that his reports on their own weren't enough, so he advised the police to find a second expert to review his work – someone he didn't know. In early 2018, Cheshire Police approached a Newcastle-based consultant called Martin Ward Platt. Ward Platt was a respected neonatal paediatrician with an impressive academic background. He'd been an editor at the respected journal *Archives of Disease in Childhood.*[7] He was also an expert in hypoglycaemia in babies.[8]

Ward Platt looked at Evans' preliminary reports and the medical records on which they were based. In his review, Evans' conclusions were sound. If anything, they were a little on the cautious side. We've seen Martin Ward Platt's review of Dr Evans' reports. It's short – just seven pages – but for Cheshire Police, it was a game-changer. They now had two independent experts telling them that they believed that babies on the neonatal unit at the Countess of Chester Hospital had been harmed – some fatally. 'The police now had a case,' Evans reflected.

We asked Evans when he first heard the name Lucy Letby. He'd seen her name on the medical records he'd been analysing. But he had no idea she was a suspect. 'There were forty nurses on that unit,' he said. 'I saw her name along with all the others.' Didn't he spot Letby's name cropping up again and again in the cases that alarmed him? 'No,' he told us. 'I was focusing on the medical records, not the staff.' According to Evans, the first time he heard that Lucy Letby was a suspect was when she was arrested in July 2018 – eight months after preparing his initial reports for the police.

But Cheshire Police had more pieces of the jigsaw than Evans. On Evans' suggestion, they prepared a grid showing which staff had been on duty at the time of the incidents identified in his reports. The data pointed squarely to one person: Lucy Letby. She always seemed to be there – at the scene of the crime.

Was there definitely a crime, though? Both Evans and Ward Platt had highlighted the evidence. But this wasn't like DNA evidence. If your DNA is found on the gun, then it's hard to argue that you never touched the gun. Evans' air embolism explanation was different. It was an opinion – a *theory*, albeit an expert one, and the fact that Martin Ward Platt agreed with him didn't mean that the police were home and dry. The research on air embolism in premature babies was virtually non-existent, and even though the police had two experts who broadly agreed with each other, there was no guarantee that this would meet the demanding standard of criminal proof: beyond reasonable doubt. Then tragedy struck. Martin Ward Platt fell ill and was forced to bow out of the case. He died just months later.

Without a second expert, there was too much resting on Dewi Evans – even with Martin Ward Platt's own supporting review. And if Evans was wrong, the entire investigation would be based on a false premise – that babies had been killed and a murderer was at large. There was no smoking gun. Indeed, it wasn't certain that there was even a smoking gun to be found.

But in February 2018, that changed. Nine months had passed since Steve Brearey and Ravi Jayaram had first sat down with Cheshire Police. Since then, news had spread that the police were investigating, and parents were worried. Some had babies who'd spent time on the neonatal unit and they wanted to know if their babies may have been mistreated. Brearey and Jayaram took many of the calls – offering reassurance where they could and passing any worrying cases on to the police.

The police were glad of the help, but they needed more. Several of the babies who Dewi Evans believed had been murdered were twins and had twin siblings who'd also spent time in the Countess of Chester Hospital. The police wanted to know if anything suspicious had happened to these siblings as well, so they asked Brearey and Jayaram to take a look. It was a big job with long hours and late evenings spent poring through old medical records.

One evening in February 2018, Dr Brearey was going through the file of one of the twins. The baby's twin brother had died – suspiciously and without obvious explanation, according to Dewi Evans' analysis. The surviving twin had suffered life-threatening episodes of low blood sugar – hypoglycaemia – but he had recovered and was discharged. We touched on his case towards the end of Chapter 2. He was one of the two babies whose lab test results indicated that he had been poisoned with insulin. The results had been seen by a consultant but they weren't followed up – until now.

As Brearey reviewed the baby's notes, he couldn't believe what he was reading. At 17.56 on 5 August 2015, following sustained hypoglycaemic episodes, a blood sample had been taken from the baby and sent off to the Royal Liverpool Hospital for analysis. The analysis showed high levels of insulin in the baby's blood. Insulin lowers blood sugar, so that explained the baby's dramatic drops in blood sugar. But the blood analysis revealed something else as well. It showed an abnormally low reading for something called C-peptide. C-peptide is a substance that the body produces when it produces insulin. Where you get naturally produced insulin, you get C-peptide. You don't get C-peptide, however, when synthetic or laboratory-produced insulin has been administered. C-peptide is therefore a marker of naturally produced insulin. Where there is insulin without corresponding C-peptide, the obvious conclusion is that the insulin isn't natural and has been administered externally – what medics call 'exogenous insulin'. The high insulin and low C-peptide reading in the baby's blood test pointed to one conclusion: the insulin in his blood wasn't natural. It was exogenous. It had been given to him.

There was no way that an insulin overdose could have been an accident. The quantity of insulin was far too high and no insulin had been prescribed.[9] In fact, none of the babies on the unit at the time had been prescribed insulin.[10] Even if they had been, the procedure for administering it is strictly controlled. There appeared to be only one explanation for the results of the blood test: the baby had been poisoned.

It was the closest thing to a smoking gun. 'It made me feel sick actually thinking about it,' Brearey told us. 'The realisation that after a year of worrying about what sort of mechanism might have caused these deaths, there was a baby case in front of me in which it was quite clear that this baby had been poisoned by insulin. And the nursing record supported the fact that Lucy Letby was present on shift at the time.'

For Brearey, it was confirmation of what he'd suspected all along. Lucy Letby had been harming babies. 'That was my movement from being fairly convinced that harm had been done to losing any iota of doubt about her guilt really. I couldn't see a scenario where these babies couldn't have been poisoned.'

Unbeknown to Steve Brearey, Dewi Evans had also been reviewing the same medical notes – and he too had reached the same conclusion – that babies had been poisoned with insulin. In all, Evans and Brearey identified three babies who they believed had been harmed using insulin, although only two would be included in the court case against Letby.

Back at the Countess of Chester Hospital, the wider staff and even the bosses were unaware of what the police were unearthing. Meanwhile, Letby continued to work there and would go on doing so for another five months. Sure, she was off the neonatal unit. But she carried on going about her duties every day like any other hospital employee, passing her time in the hospital's Risk and Patient Safety Office. It was a surreal situation. It was as if the hospital and the police were operating in parallel universes.

Letby's supporters in management remained onside – none more so than lead nurse for urgent care Karen Rees. Rees still believed in Letby. She would later admit that '[p]rior to [Letby's] trial, I had thought that she was innocent.'[11] The hospital's occupational health manager Kathryn de Beger also appeared to be an ally – at least in Letby's mind.[12]

The hospital CEO seemed relaxed about Letby too. In the spring of 2018, Tony Chambers told a local newspaper: '. . . there were just a few niggles that our clinicians said, look, we think we have got 90 per cent of the answers but there are still bits that we need to in a sense be clear that we have not missed anything.'[13]

Even the hospital's medical director Ian Harvey appeared to be unaware of the alarming evidential picture that Cheshire Police was assembling. In April 2018 – five months after Dewi Evans had officially given Cheshire Police his bombshell analysis of the baby deaths – Harvey met with Steve Brearey and Ravi Jayaram. The two consultants asked him why he thought the police investigation was taking so long. 'It takes a long time to prove a negative,' he answered, according to the two consultants. It appeared that Harvey still believed the police investigation would give the hospital and Lucy Letby the all-clear.

By June 2018, Cheshire Police had a weighty dossier of circumstantial evidence pointing to Lucy Letby: the insulin cases looked like proof that there was someone in the hospital harming babies on the neonatal unit. Letby had been on duty at key points in each case. Then there were the seven deaths and seven further baby collapses – all suggestive of foul play, according to Dewi Evans and Martin Ward Platt, with Letby on duty for every one of them. An eighth death was later added to the list.

But there was still no direct evidence against Lucy Letby. Not one of her colleagues could say they had seen her harming a baby and there was no CCTV on the neonatal unit. There was no incriminating DNA evidence either. The police needed another piece of the puzzle: evidence from Letby herself. What did she have to say about the deaths and collapses? Would she admit to anything or accidentally reveal something that proved the case? What about her phone or personal laptop? Look inside anyone's phone or computer and you'll find their secrets and maybe even their confessions. What did Lucy Letby's contain?

Arresting her would provide answers, but it wasn't risk-free. Once she was arrested, all hell would break loose. Her name would appear in every newspaper and on every TV channel. Parents of other babies who'd spent time in the Countess of Chester neonatal unit would worry. Talk of a serial killer would stir up panic, horror and grim fascination among the public. The police themselves would no longer have the luxury of working quietly at their own pace. The world's eyes would be on them. Letby was innocent until proven guilty, yes. But once the police announced they had reason to believe she was a serial killer, the pressure to prove their case and bring home a conviction would be immense.

It was a big decision, but the momentum of the investigation was pointing in only one direction. On 3 July 2018, detectives from Cheshire Police knocked on Lucy Letby's door on Westbourne Road in Chester as the sun was rising. It was just after 6 a.m. and most of the street was still asleep, so the nurse's neighbours missed the sight of her being led out of the house in a blue tracksuit and handcuffs, and being put into an unmarked police car. Letby's dad John was staying with her at the time, and he managed to avoid being spotted too.

It wasn't long before the world found out though. The babies' families had been told first and were trying to absorb the seismic news. Until that point, they had no idea that anyone was under suspicion at all – much less that a nurse was wanted for potential murder. They didn't know about the internal hospital battles between the consultants and senior managers, or the suspicions that had led detectives to the nurse's door. When the name Lucy Letby was mentioned to them, many struggled to put a face to it.

The mother of twins E and F told us how her family felt when they were told that a nurse called Lucy Letby had been arrested on suspicion of murder:

I thought, the hospital's old, it's not very nice. It was dirty, and I thought it was along the lines of medical negligence. It never entered my mind that there was somebody intentionally harming babies. I never thought that. So getting that phone call, it was a shock. I was totally taken aback, but then afterwards, when I did reflect on it, it actually all fitted together. It was almost like the penny dropped, [about] the way [Letby] had behaved with me.[14]

Meanwhile, the news was also sinking in on the neonatal unit. While the arrest was no surprise to the consultants, the nursing body had largely been in the dark. How did her fellow colleagues react? 'Shocked!' one nurse told us. 'Horrified. I don't think anybody saw it coming. Maybe some did. I didn't. It was shock and horror that she was arrested and that these were the suspicions that people had about her. I don't think anybody could believe that somebody could do that.'

The story was everywhere within no time: Lucy Letby, a nurse at the Countess of Chester Hospital, had been arrested on suspicion of murdering eight babies and attempting to murder six others. News cameras turned up outside her house and the street swarmed with reporters. The neighbours were bemused – they hardly knew the nurse, they said. She hadn't lived there long. She was often at work. She kept herself to herself. They couldn't imagine anything more horrific – and to think it might involve someone from their road! Awful. Thanks for knocking, but we really can't help you. Kindly leave us alone.

From the street outside, journalists could only guess what was going on in the house as officers in overalls and plastic gloves worked their way through it. Publicly, the police had only announced that a 'healthcare professional' had been arrested. But it hadn't been hard to work out who she was and where she lived. Hers was the house with the crime-scene tape all around it and a blue police tent in the driveway.

What does the house of a suspected baby killer look like on the inside? Until now, the police had wondered the same thing. Would

Letby's dark side – so far unseen by anyone, including her closest friends – finally be revealed? In 2022, another young woman in her twenties called Shaye Groves stabbed her boyfriend to death. When police visited her home, they found framed pictures of serial killers on her walls, as well as knives, axes and a bookcase shaped like a coffin. Joanna Dennehy was another vicious killer who posed for selfies while brandishing a knife. Would Lucy Letby's private world reveal similar signs of a depraved mind?

Inside, the house was plain and a little unloved, but judging from appearances, this was no serial killer's lair. Having packed Letby off in a police car, the detectives went through her home room by room.

Her bedroom looked like that of an average girly girl – a bit messy, lots of pink stuff, and slightly childish creature comforts. Fluffy dressing gowns, with sparkly spots. Cuddly toys. Butterfly-prints on the bedclothes, and 'sweet dreams' on the pillowcase. The bed was still messed up – a freeze-frame of the moment the police had knocked at the door.

The bedside tables were covered with standard clutter – hairspray, tissues and lip balm. Medication, possibly for her thyroid issues. A water glass and a remote control. It couldn't have been more normal. Her reading matter made an interesting find. Two books sat by the bedside. *In Shock*, a doctor's memoir about being dangerously ill after a miscarriage, and *Never Greener*, a novel about a young woman who had an affair with a married man.

The furniture was cheap. A functional chest of drawers. A mirror leaning against the wall. A single red plastic flower poking out of a nondescript glass vase. Mass-market art – framed prints of trite sayings – 'Shine Bright Like a Diamond' and 'Leave Sparkles Wherever You Go'.[15] A string of twinkly lights entwined around the bed frame, and a pink hoodie hung at one end. Handbags dotted around – faux leather, like something a teenage girl might pick up at a market stall. One looked like an 'everyday bag', another for nights out. There were pink suitcases too – Letby had just got back from her holiday and would barely have had time to unpack before the cops came knocking.

Letby's two cats – Smudge and Tigger – were in the house when the police came. They were rescue cats, according to Dawn, Letby's steadfast old friend from Hereford. 'They were her whole world,' she told us.

You could hardly imagine a more ordinary-looking home for a single young woman. The cuddly toys and all that pink suggested a childish, saccharine temperament – as if Letby hadn't quite grown up. On one wall there was a little scene of a yellow bird sitting on an ornate branch with bright green leaves and pink flowers. It was almost as if Letby's home was a continuation of the neonatal unit where she worked – sweet and babyish but also rather bland and nondescript.

One of the odder items, though, was a black paper shredder tucked away in the corner of one of Letby's rooms. The question was obvious: had she been shredding evidence?

If she had, there was still plenty left to be found. Underneath the bed was a large carrier bag with 'IBIZA' written on it, and the police were very interested in what was inside – four 'handover sheets' from the Countess of Chester Hospital. The dates were of particular interest: 23 and 24 June 2016 – that's when the two triplets had died. 24 June – that was when Steve Brearey had tried – unsuccessfully – to get Letby kicked off the unit. And 25 June was the last of the baby collapses before Letby's exclusion from the unit in July 2016. A further thirty-one handover sheets were found in a Morrisons bag, along with a blood-gas reading for one of the babies Letby was suspected of attacking. There was also a paper towel with handwritten resuscitation notes scrawled on it.[16]

But there was more. Inside Letby's chest of drawers was a diary. From the outside, it looked as sweet and innocuous as everything else in her house. There was a cartoon of a teddy bear on the front cover and a smattering of childish motifs with the imploring slogan, 'Have a lovely year!'

Inside there were references to Letby's social life in pink writing. 'Wednesday 6 April: Salsa', recorded one activity. But there were also references to babies from the neonatal unit. 'LD (extra) twins resus,' she'd written.[17] Letby later told police 'LD' stood for 'long day'.

Then, as a latex-gloved forensics officer leafed through the diary, something much more disturbing was revealed. Tucked inside the journal was a green Post-it note covered from top to bottom in handwritten scrawl. At the top was written NOT GOOD ENOUGH in capital letters – all underlined. For many people who followed Letby's trial, this note would become one of the most memorable pieces of evidence in the case. It would also be a focal point of debate and conjecture about Letby's personality and state of mind.

'There are no words,' it read.

I can't breathe . . . I can't focus . . . Kill myself right now . . . overwhelming fear / panic

Police investigation . . . All getting too much . . . I feel very alone + scared . . . what does the future hold . . . how can I get through it

NO HOPE . . . DESPAIR . . . PANIC . . . FEAR . . . LOST

Letby's defence team would argue in court that this note was an outpouring of anguish – and it was certainly that. But the note also included statements that appeared to be direct responses to the accusations. 'I haven't done anything wrong,' it reads. 'Slander . . . Discrimination . . . victimisation.'

In the bottom half of the green Post-it note, the word 'HATE' is written and circled, almost maniacally, in thick black ink. Then, at the bottom, this:

I killed them on purpose because I'm not good enough to care for them + I am a horrible evil person . . . I AM EVIL I DID THIS.

I killed them – on purpose. It was an extraordinary find. For the police, the suspect they'd spent more than a year investigating had written what appeared to be a confession note.

There were other notes too. Some suggest a tortured and

confused mind: 'I killed them. I don't know if I killed them. Maybe I did. Maybe this is down to me.'

Letby's desperation is clear. In some notes, she writes the names of her closest allies at the hospital. Karen Rees's name is scrawled over and over again. So too is Kathryn de Beger, the occupational health manager that Letby was seeing. There are even messages for Letby's cats – Tigger and Smudge – and her childhood dog Whiskey. But the notes also contain references to Letby's accusers. 'BASTARDS', screeches one in capital letters. Another refers directly to the consultants, the mediation process and the police.

The scenes of crime officers seized this trove and sealed the notes inside see-through exhibit bags. The detectives working on the case were staggered at some of what had been found. Paul Hughes later told us:

> She obviously collected a lot of stuff. Lucy Letby is clearly someone who keeps things – medical records, handover sheets, diaries and notes. And it surprised me because she would have been aware that we were going to come and speak to her at some point. So it was surprising that when we did go and knock on her door and arrest her . . . that there was so much material, graphic in its nature, that was almost presented to us when we arrived.[18]

The police also searched Letby's parents' home in Hereford where they found more handover sheets. They raided her desk inside the hospital 'Risk Office', and there were more notes there too. 'I really can't do this anymore,' laments one.

> I just want life to be as it was . . . I want to be happy in the job that I loved and a team I felt a part of. Really I don't belong anywhere – I am a problem to those who do know me + it would be much easier for everyone if I just went away.

There's a reference to a male doctor on Letby's unit. Beside his name, Letby writes: 'Please help me . . . You were my best friend . . .

LOVE.' Who was this man? And what was Letby's relationship with him?

While the world's media traded titbits and speculated about the nurse who'd just been arrested, Letby was in an interview room in Blacon police station in Chester. She already looked like a convict. The blue hoodie she'd been wearing during her arrest, with the girly pink writing on the front, had been replaced by a standard-issue dull grey sweatshirt.

Just one case of murder or attempted murder is an investigation in its own right. Here, there were fourteen – all of them several years old and all dense with medical and scientific detail and complexity. There was no quick way to do this. Every event – each blood transfusion, each time a baby was fed, each time a nurse or a doctor made a note – had to be gone through.

'Did you have any concerns that there was a rise in [the] mortality rate?' the female detective on the other side of the table asked.

'Yes,' Letby replied.

'OK, so tell me about that – what concerns did you have?'

Letby kept her eyes lowered as she began to answer. 'I think we'd all just noticed as a team in general, the nursing staff, that this was a rise compared to previous years.' She spoke softly – as if in a state of shock. Her shoulders were hunched – crumpled almost. But you could tell that the cogs in her brain were turning. Every word was carefully chosen – clear and unhurried.

'Are you responsible for the attempted murder of ████?' came the question. 'No,' Letby replied. 'Did you inject insulin into ████?' 'No.' Then it was Letby's turn to interrogate the police. 'Can I ask a question?' she asked meekly. 'The bag – was it kept or checked post-event?' It was an astute question. The insulin evidence appeared to establish that someone on the unit had been harming babies. The police believed that intravenous nutrition bags had been deliberately contaminated – by Letby. But did they have the bags to prove it? As it happened, they had long been disposed of.

There's something in this tense exchange that captured the dynamic of the entire case, and the bitter wranglings over the truth that would follow – right up to the present day: a police force swimming in an ocean of scientific questions and complexity; and an inscrutable murder suspect. This wasn't the Lucy reflected in girly text messages, cuddly toys and pink bedroom ornaments. This Lucy was rational, composed, and – however fearful she felt – quietly steely.

To her police interrogators, it was clear that Letby wasn't your regular criminal suspect. If she was guilty, she was going to be a formidable adversary. She admitted nothing. She knew her job backwards. She knew the rules inside out and she had an answer for everything. She didn't attempt to hide behind guilty 'no comments'. There were no meltdowns or panic attacks. And there were no obvious lies. Letby seemed to be a model of compliance. 'She was comfortable,' recalls Paul Hughes, one of the detectives who interviewed her. 'She'd go through medical notes, she would talk to us, she was co-operative, she engaged.' But she didn't over-elaborate either. Letby had looked after hundreds of babies, and many of the events she was being asked about were years old. Anyone would forget small details – and Letby forgot plenty. The police showed her medical notes in an effort to jog her memory, but some details were simply too difficult to recall. If it was a deliberate strategy on Letby's part, it was a shrewd one. Better to say you can't remember than be caught in a lie.

She claimed ignorance too on one of the biggest allegations in the case. The police's experts had told them they believed babies had been injected with air, but Letby said she hardly knew anything about air embolism. Whether that was true is a subject we'll look at in Chapter 8.

As careful as she was though, Letby's story still had wrinkles in it. Initial examinations of her phone and tablet revealed that she'd done social media searches on the parents of some of the babies she was suspected of murdering. It's the kind of thing you'd think you'd remember doing – but when her police interrogators confronted her about it, she said she couldn't remember. She also told them that she had no memory of one of the baby girls who died, though her phone revealed that she'd texted a colleague about her, and searched for the baby's parents online.

By and large, Lucy Letby's answers were consistent with each other, but at times she contradicted her colleagues' recollections of key events. The first baby to die, for instance, had collapsed shortly after an intravenous line had been attached. She claimed her colleague was the one who fitted the line, but according to her colleague's recollection, it had been Letby.

Letby was careful not to talk about things she didn't know about, but occasionally she offered dubious explanations for some of the events she was being asked about. One of the babies had been found with excess air and milk in her stomach. According to Letby, the air might have got in there because of vomiting or infection – an unconvincing explanation, according to one of the prosecution experts whose evidence would later help convict Letby. 'Babies do not take in air when vomiting,' the expert later remarked. 'If you are vomiting, things are coming out, not coming in.'

She was asked whether bad luck was to blame for the fact that so many babies had died on her watch. 'Yes,' was her answer. She highlighted poor staffing levels and the fact that the unit was stretched – both powerful points – but they didn't amount to a clinical explanation for the deaths. Of course, if Letby was innocent, why should she have answers that even the hospital's senior doctors had struggled to find? And yet, according to the detectives who interviewed her, her denials seemed devoid of passion or emotion.

Time and again, Letby had been the only one in the room when babies had collapsed. On its own, this proved nothing, but it looked bad. Did Letby get this? It was hard to tell. She was almost impossible to read.

What about the 'confession' note? What did Letby have to say about that? Yes, the notes recovered from her house and office contained mixed messages, but what innocent person writes 'I killed them on purpose because I'm not good enough to care for them + I am a horrible evil person . . . I AM EVIL I DID THIS'?

Letby explained she had written the note shortly after being removed from the neonatal unit in July 2016. The timing is interesting. No one had formally accused Letby of a crime, let alone murder at that point. The police hadn't been called, and the hospital bosses were still largely on her side. Why write a note like this?

'I just wrote it cos everything had got on top of me,' Letby said.

> They were telling me my practice might be wrong, that . . . my practice might not have been good enough. So I felt like people were blaming my practice, that I might have hurt them without knowing through my practice and that made me feel guilty and I just felt really isolated. I was blaming myself but not because I'd done something [but] because of the way people were making me feel.

So had she made any mistakes?

'No,' replied Letby.

But the note says 'police investigation'. Why would doubts about Letby's competence lead to a police investigation?

'I'm not sure,' Letby answered. 'I thought they might refer me to the NMC [Nursing and Midwifery Council] and I didn't know if that went to the police.'

'What's the difference between being incompetent or criminal in your world?' asked the detective.

'Criminal is something that's done deliberately,' Letby answered. 'Whereas you not being competent would be that you're not competent in something that could give you a result that wasn't intentional.' It was a flawless answer straight out of a textbook on criminal law. The cogs were still whirring. Letby was no idiot.

'How would you describe [the note] as a whole?' she was asked.

'It was just a way of me getting my feelings out on to paper, it just helps me process it a bit more,' she told the detective.

'Lucy, you then go on to say, "I don't deserve to live. I killed them on purpose because I'm not good enough to care for them. I am a horrible evil person."'

'I didn't kill them on purpose,' Letby replied. 'I felt if my practice hadn't been right then I had killed them and that was why I wasn't good enough.'

'Do you believe that there's a potential that you caused their deaths?' asked the detective.

'Not intentionally.'

For three days it went on like this – question and answer in a cramped windowless police interview room.

At times, Letby was asked point-blank: did you harm this baby? Her answer was always the same: no. If the police had been hoping Letby would crack, they'd have been disappointed. Even the 'confession' note – as compelling as it was – wasn't proof. Letby had given her explanation and defence lawyers would no doubt be able to marshal arguments about it too. The case against her was far from complete.

On 6 July 2018, Letby was released on bail. In many ways, the world that was waiting for her outside was far worse than what she'd just been through in police custody. Her name was everywhere. Her Facebook account had been plundered with pictures going back to her childhood splashed in every tabloid newspaper.

Now that she was a murder suspect, even her most supportive backers among the management at the Countess of Chester Hospital cut her off. Letby was officially suspended from all duties while the police inquiry was under way. She couldn't go back to her house in Chester either. It was part of the police investigation and therefore out of bounds. In any case, the world now knew where Letby lived. Her home address was public knowledge. Her parents' address in Hereford was out there too. But right now, it was the only safe place she knew. And so after her release, Letby returned to Hereford to the home and the childhood bedroom where she'd grown up.

Only Lucy Letby and her long-suffering parents John and Sue will know what was said within those four walls, but there were surely many agonised conversations and bitter tears as their world imploded. Did John and Sue ever doubt their daughter? No – at least not now. Nor did Letby's old friends in Hereford. Her old friend Dawn claimed to speak for all of them when she told us:

We know she couldn't have done anything that she's accused of, so without a doubt we stand by her. I've grown up with Lucy, and not a single thing that I've ever seen or witnessed of Lucy would let me for a moment believe that she was capable of the things she was being accused of. Unless Lucy turned around and said, 'I'm guilty,' I will never believe that she's guilty.

Unsurprisingly, Letby went to ground. She even steered clear of her old friends in the aftermath of her release. Meanwhile in Chester, the police were regrouping and working their way through a ton of new material. The searches of Letby's addresses, on their own, yielded half a million pages of evidence. In addition to the hand-written notes and diaries, there were no fewer than 257 handover sheets that Letby had taken home with her from the neonatal unit. Then there were Letby's phone and Facebook messages – enough to fill a book. Every one had to be catalogued, analysed and cross-referenced with the timing of the baby deaths and collapses. Perhaps, in these messages, she'd let something slip. Many of us share our deepest secrets over WhatsApp, and who expects their private messages to be read by the police? Would Letby's messages reveal that she had a hitherto hidden dark side?

In early 2024, Judith reported on the trial and conviction of two teenage killers who murdered sixteen-year-old Brianna Ghey. Out-wardly the killers seemed harmless enough, but their text messages and online search habits revealed a horrifying fascination with tor-ture and murder. Would Letby's phone reveal a dark truth behind the mask? Maybe she too was secretly fascinated with murder. Or perhaps she confessed to a friend or let something slip that proved that she was a baby killer.

For months, the police scoured Letby's digital footprint. They now could see what she was texting before and after the baby deaths and collapses. Some of the messages look sinister in the light of her convictions, like the one about fate, sent shortly after one of the deaths in June 2015: 'I think there is an element of fate involved. There is a reason for everything.'[19] Others could be read as Letby covering her tracks with innocent explanations for the deaths – 'gaslighting' her colleagues, as the prosecution would later put it in court. 'He was IUGR [intrauterine growth restriction] & REDF [reverse end diastolic flow], plus prem & ?downs so guess he was very high risk,'[20] she wrote to one nurse.

In other texts, she expresses bewilderment – just like everyone else on the unit, like one written in June 2015 – after the death of a baby who Letby later told police she didn't remember:

[O]n a day-to-day basis it's an incredible job with so many positives. But then sometimes I think, how do such sick babies get through & others just die so suddenly & unexpectedly? Guess it's how it's meant to be[21]

Seeing these texts, through the prism of Letby's conviction, it's hard to read them as anything other than a deliberate attempt to confound and divert attention away from herself. But on their own, the texts proved nothing. A perfectly innocent nurse could have written them. Indeed, for the most part, Letby's messages were what you might expect from a nurse experiencing a run of bad luck and death.

The police knew that to present them in court, they'd need to make sense of them. They began work to create a timeline of the texts which could be woven into the chronology that they were building up of the baby collapses on the unit.

Letby's non-work messages seemed benign. She chatted to her pals about innocent activities like dancing lessons and hula-hoop practice.[22] She watched run-of-the-mill mainstream TV shows, like *Strictly Come Dancing*[23] and *Love Island*.[24] After the death of the first baby, she texted: 'Watching an hour to save a life about neonatal unit x'. Thinking of Letby as a child killer, it's unnerving to imagine her watching a fly-on-the-wall documentary series about saving babies' lives. But no one thought to read anything into it at the time, and that fact is relevant too. Nothing in Letby's personality aroused suspicion. She didn't have a visible dark streak.

Letby's search history was mostly unremarkable too. She wasn't part of any dubious online networks or communities of disturbed individuals. There were no searches for 'how to kill a baby' or 'how to get away with murder'. She didn't visit macabre websites or watch disturbing content.

There was, however, one unsettling aspect of Letby's otherwise vanilla online life. Time and again during that harrowing year, June 2015–June 2016, Letby had done social media searches for the parents of babies that had died or collapsed while she had been on duty. She searched for the parents of all three babies who died in June 2015.[25] She searched for the parents of the twins she had cared for in August 2015, one of whom had died and the other of whom she would later be convicted of poisoning with insulin. In September 2015, a baby collapsed and was left brain-damaged as a result. Letby searched for her parents too. A month later, she searched for another baby who died and whom the police believed she had murdered. The pattern continued. In some cases, it was obsessive. There were multiple searches for the parents of the August 2015 twins. Letby even looked them up on Christmas Day.[26] She remembered the anniversaries of the babies who had died and in one case, she marked the occasion by searching online for the baby's surname.[27] These searches might look morbid and weird. But what did they prove? Letby would probably argue she'd conducted them out of concern for the parents or babies who had survived. She'd also done repeated searches for the families of babies whom she wasn't accused of harming – lots of them.[28]

The truth was that Letby's text messages and search history, as interesting as they were, didn't reveal an obvious dark side. Odd, maybe. Obsessive, perhaps. But on their own, they didn't establish that she was a murderer.

The police knew, as they had done right at the beginning of their investigation, that science would be key to explaining why so many babies had died and whether Lucy Letby was responsible. They already had one set of expert opinions in the bag. Dewi Evans had given the police his view in a series of preliminary reports. He believed babies had been deliberately harmed, and he had given his assessment of the methods of harm involved. Including the two insulin cases, Evans' analysis now pointed to seven murders and ten instances of attempted murder. Their second expert, Martin Ward

Platt, had agreed with Dr Evans' initial reports, but after he died, the police had to think again. They knew that, without another expert backing Evans up, their scientific case would be weak. It was a delicate situation. Experts can be unpredictable. They disagree, and while most strive honestly for objectivity and impartiality, they are, after all, human. Some are intellectually cautious. Others are bullish and sometimes shoot from the hip. Some are naturally collegiate and consensual, respecting the opinions of their colleagues. Others are contrary, with a natural appetite for spotting mistakes and sloppy reasoning among their peers. The case now hung on finding another expert who would agree with Dr Evans. Having only one expert was far from ideal, but what if the police's second expert disagreed with him? The scientific argument against Letby would be inconclusive, and the entire case would be in trouble.

As an expert in neonatology, Sandie Bohin was good news. She'd been head of Neonatology at University Hospitals Leicester before moving to Guernsey to continue her practice in paediatrics there. Her professional accreditations were impressive too: Fellow of the Royal College of Paediatrics and Child Health and a member of the British Association of Perinatal Medicine. Like Dewi Evans, Bohin had plenty of experience of the courts and working with law enforcement. She'd provided expert opinions for the National Crime Agency and HM Coroner. She was also fresh to the case. She didn't know Dewi Evans and he didn't know her, and the fact that she was based in Guernsey meant she was well removed from the small world of neonatal practice in Chester and the North West.

In early 2019, Cheshire Police contacted Dr Bohin and asked if she'd take an independent look at the cases. She agreed. Cheshire Police followed up by sending Bohin the medical notes for the cases that Dewi Evans had examined. But the job they gave her wasn't exactly the same as the assignment they'd given Dewi Evans in 2017. Rather than simply asking her to come up with her own theories, Cheshire Police asked Dr Bohin to review Dr Evans' reports and determine whether she agreed with them or not.

Some of Letby's defenders would later question this approach. Dr Bohin, they would argue, should not have been allowed to see Dr Evans' theories before developing her own first. Knowing what her colleague Dewi Evans had said might influence her own thinking on the issues. But that's the way the police wanted things and Bohin herself had no doubt about her own independence of mind. Later, in court, she gave this account of her assignment: 'I was asked to peer review statements made by Dr Dewi Evans, and give a view on whether I agreed, disagreed or had an alternative view.'[29] She brought her own professional view, she said. 'It was as though I was doing it from scratch.'[30]

In March 2019, Dr Bohin delivered her first set of reports.[31] For the police, it was a make-or-break moment. When Bohin's reports landed, there were sighs of relief at Cheshire Police HQ. For the most part, she agreed with Dr Evans. Naturally, there were small points of difference between the two, but by and large, her conclusions were similar to Dr Evans': she concluded that several babies had had air deliberately injected into their bloodstreams while others had had air or milk – sometimes both – injected into their stomachs; a further two babies who had suffered non-fatal collapses had been poisoned with insulin; the others had been deliberately harmed by a variety of other means (although the precise means wasn't specified in every case). For the police, it was a game-changer: the experts agreed! Eighteen months of painstaking police work hadn't been wasted. The case against Letby had now entered a new phase of intensity.

Former colleagues of Lucy Letby's also gave accounts to the police that raised further concerns, like that of Ashleigh Hudson – the nurse who found Letby standing by a dark doorway remarking that a baby looked pale. How could she tell when the lights were off? When Nurse Hudson turned them on, she found that the baby had stopped breathing.

But it was evidence from one of the bereaved parents that raised the most serious challenge to Letby's version of events. It came from the mother of twins who we later interviewed for *Panorama*. She spoke to the police and took them through the events of the evening when her first child died. She remembered hearing her baby screaming from the corridor of the neonatal unit and seeing blood around his mouth. She remembered seeing Lucy Letby in the nursery, trying to look busy but doing nothing to help her baby. She remembered Letby suggesting that the baby boy's feeding tube had been the cause of the bleeding and urging her to go back to the ward where she had been convalescing. And she remembered all of it with minute-perfect accuracy – so much so that Letby's own medical notes of that evening appeared to be inaccurate. The mother had turned sleuth herself, sourcing her mobile phone records to verify the timings that she remembered. It was dynamite.

By June 2019, the police were drowning in evidence. They'd found more cases of attempted murder, which meant more bundles of dense, jargony medical notes. They'd also continued interviewing people connected to Letby – which translated into piles of transcripts and witness statements. And then there were the thousands of pages of evidence from Letby's phone and tablet. Almost a year had passed since Letby's first arrest. If the initial searches of her home were anything to go by, there may be more notes and diaries still to find.[32] Maybe she'd kept writing – kept pouring out her thoughts and feelings. If she had, what would she reveal this time? The time had come to bring her back in for questioning and do another search of her home in Hereford.

On 10 June 2019, Letby was rearrested at her parents' home in Hereford and driven to Chester. In the interview room, she was asked again about air embolism – the main cause of death in the cases identified by Dr Evans and Dr Bohin. As she had done a year beforehand, Letby claimed not to know much about the visible effects of injecting a baby with air, but she ventured that it would be very difficult to push air into a baby through an intravenous line. For every case, Letby was asked if she murdered or attempted to murder the baby concerned. As before – and as she would continue to do right up to the present day – she denied everything.

Letby engaged with her interrogators, but 'I don't know' or 'I can't remember' featured frequently in her answers. Was that unusual? Perhaps not. She was being asked about individual times and events going back four years. How well do any of us remember what we were doing at a particular moment four years ago? She was also unable to offer explanations for some of the unexpected collapses that happened on her watch. Then again, no one else could either, including the consultants. But she did make some important concessions. A combination of Letby's phone records and testimony from one of her colleagues had placed her in the room immediately before the second baby died in June 2015. Letby agreed: she had been the only person in the room when the baby collapsed. In fact, she was beside his cot. When asked why she had been in the room, she couldn't remember. She also agreed that the baby had been stable before his collapse. He later died.

Letby also agreed with the police's assessment of the insulin evidence. The blood tests from the two babies concerned appeared to show that the babies had been given high levels of insulin. And Letby agreed that the insulin could not have been administered by accident. In other words, whoever was responsible had done it deliberately.

The case of the baby who had projectile-vomited milk was also discussed. The police believed she'd been force-fed excess milk and air through a tube running through her nose into her stomach. Letby agreed that this baby too had been stable. She also agreed that air had entered the baby's stomach through a feeding syringe, but she denied being responsible.

But it was the vivid and precise testimony of the young mother of twins who'd seen blood around the mouth of her baby boy in August 2015 that continued to present the biggest challenge to Letby.

'Do you agree that it [the mother's account] paints a different picture to what it says in the notes?' the detective asked Lucy Letby.

'Yes,' she answered.

By now, Cheshire Police felt they had built a strong case against Letby. But the decision on whether or when to charge her wasn't their call. It was up to the Crown Prosecution Service. Pascale Jones was the CPS lawyer in charge of the case. Pascale was a somewhat brusque Frenchwoman who seemed to have little interest in ingratiating herself with the media. But she had lived and breathed the case since it had first landed on her desk. She knew it would probably be the biggest job of her career, and she was determined to bring it to trial with the strongest possible case for a conviction. But that required patience. The police had gathered a mountain of evidence, but for Pascale and the CPS, it still wasn't quite enough to press charges.

On 13 June 2019, Letby was released on bail – again. For the parents of the babies in the case, it felt like torture. For over a year, they'd known that Lucy Letby was suspected of killing their babies. The story was all over the news, and yet Letby was still free. Would she at least face trial? They didn't know. She hadn't even been charged with a crime. Another seventeen months would go by with no news and no charges.

The twins' mother told us that the prolonged nature of the police investigation was hard to live with. She explained, 'Until Lucy was charged, we lived our lives in three-month cycles, anxiously waiting to see if her bail would be renewed and what would happen next. Life moved forward, but a dark cloud loomed over us.'

By now, the police had obtained further expert opinion from a pathologist that fitted with the analyses of Dr Evans and Dr Bohin. An expert radiologist was also consulted and he too reinforced the prosecution case. Virtually all lines of enquiry had now been exhausted and, from the point of view of both the police and the CPS, there was probably enough for Letby to be charged without further delay. But there was a cost to doing so. Once a suspect is charged, investigative questioning of the suspect has to stop. Charging her now would mean no more interrogation time – and that was far from ideal as both the police and the CPS had more questions for Lucy Letby. Despite the mountains of evidence, the case against Letby was entirely circumstantial. Beyond reasonable doubt – that was the standard of proof that a jury would apply if the case was brought to trial. There were still too many unanswered questions. Maybe another round of interviews would give the police the slam-dunk evidence that they so badly wanted. Maybe Letby would finally crack – confess to everything and validate years of painstaking police work. How could they know unless they questioned her further? So they decided to re-arrest her and question her a third time before making any decisions about charging.[33]

Early on the morning of 10 November 2020, a team from Cheshire Police drove down to Hereford and pulled into the tranquil cul-de-sac where Lucy Letby was staying with her parents.

One of the arresting officers later gave this account in a carefully curated PR film produced by the Cheshire Police press office:

> When we knocked on the door, Mr Letby opened the door. It was all very low key . . . We went in, we explained why we were there. They knew because they'd been through it twice before. Miss Letby's mum was very distressed but Miss Letby herself complied and was very subdued . . .
>
> I do remember the door closing on the BMW that she was going to be driven back up to Chester in, and her pulling away and me phoning Detective Inspector Hughes, as he was at the time, and saying: 'Yep, job done. She's in the car. She's on the way.'[34]

Back in Chester, in the police interview room, Letby's position remained unchanged: she said she hadn't harmed any babies and for those who had been harmed, she had no knowledge or explanation to offer. But some of her answers appeared to add to the general impression that she wasn't being truthful. She was asked again about her repeated social media searches for parents of babies who had died. It seemed like something anyone would remember doing. But Letby told police she had no recollection of doing the searches – or why she had done them. It was hard to avoid the conclusion that Letby was lying.

The interview process had now been exhausted. It was crunch time. Operation Hummingbird had been running for three and a half years. Once again, it was over to the CPS to decide whether to charge Letby or release her once again.

It's hard to believe that the police didn't have an idea of what Pascale Jones and the CPS were going to do next, but the tension among the investigative team was palpable nonetheless. One of the detectives on the case was sitting at his desk when his senior colleague Nicola Evans got the call. 'I remember the phone ringing,' he recalled. 'Nicola Evans sat opposite me. She picked up the phone and you could tell from the conversation she was having that the CPS were telling her that the email was on its way to her with the charging advice . . . There was then maybe a minute . . . of silence while she read it, and I remember her just looking at [Detective Inspector] Paul [Hughes] and saying: "All of them. She's charging all of them."'

Eight counts of murder and now ten of attempted murder. Detective Constable Danielle Stonier was in the custody area where Letby's cell was located when the news came through.

'Lucy Letby was brought out of her cell,' she recalled. 'Another colleague . . . read out those charges to her . . . It took a while . . . Hearing those names and hearing each individual charge was – it was a bizarre feeling.'

This time, there would be no going home for Lucy Letby. On 12 November 2020, two days after officers had appeared at her parents' home in Hereford, Letby was taken to a room in Blacon police station for a short court appearance via video link. Just three evenings earlier, she'd been at home having dinner with her parents in Hereford. It was Lucy Letby's last night of freedom. From now on, her world would be a prison cell.

Chapter 6

The Trial

The first time we saw her, it was underwhelming. We'd had two years to conjure up our own imagined spectre and now, as the courtroom TV spluttered into life, the woman who appeared with lank hair and grey custody-issue sweater didn't match whatever it was that we'd been expecting. She seemed meek, not murderous. Wholly out of place at the 'accused' end of the video link, and doubtless unaware of the serried ranks of reporters at the other end – sitting on the press benches of the court, craning to get a view. We'd heard and read her name countless times by now, but this was the first opportunity to size up Lucy Letby for ourselves.

Warrington Magistrates Court was a nondescript venue. The building, sandwiched between a Travelodge and a shopping mall, could just as easily have been a call centre. A regular clientele of petty criminals spun through the revolving doors, accused of shoplifting, driving offences and other low-level misdemeanours. The press benches were usually empty, save for the occasional local newspaper reporter sent to fill column inches by scraping colourful detail from the daily despair.

12 November 2020 was different. Satellite trucks and camera crews formed a guard of honour outside. A huddle of reporters from national titles joined TV and radio correspondents in the queue for the bag check. The hearing wasn't expected to last long – a few minutes at most – just long enough for the accused to be produced for public appraisal, and for the basic details of the allegations to be read out. This was far too serious a case to be dealt with by magistrates, and as expected Lucy Letby was told she'd have to appear at the Crown Court on the following day. The whole thing only took twelve minutes before the nurse was taken

back to her cell and the video feed was cut, but that was more than enough time for the press to peer at her and listen to her quietly confirming her name and address, and for the court artists to get the measure of the woman and go off to draw her.

The next day, the transit van carrying Lucy Letby drove through the stone arches underneath Chester Crown Court and into the secure loading area of the nineteenth-century building. This setting generated a greater sense of occasion – it was where the Moors Murderers Ian Brady and Myra Hindley had been put on trial – a court well used to hosting large-scale cases attracting sizeable public interest. Again, the reporters queued up for a seat, and this time Lucy Letby's parents were there too, up from Hereford, to see their daughter led into the dock of a court for the very first time. They sat uncomfortably in the jury box, given a ringside seat for this hearing before the red-sashed Recorder of Chester, Judge Steven Everett, who peered down from the judicial bench of courtroom two. Although he wasn't to preside over the trial itself – which was still two years away – other main roles were already being cast, and the reporters looked across at the wigs and gowns on the legal benches with interest.

Lucy Letby's defence barrister, Ben Myers QC,[1] was instantly recognisable. He'd represented David Duckenfield, the police officer who was in charge at the Hillsborough football disaster – successfully defending him against charges of gross negligence manslaughter. Myers was known as a charismatic performer – a box-office hire for a case of high profile, and he came with a colourful CV which included active service as a troop commander in the First Gulf War, and some success as the author of a series of children's books.

His opposite number on the prosecution benches was a far less spirited proposition. Some of the reporters remembered Nicholas Johnson QC as the barrister who'd prosecuted the paedophile football coach Barry Bennell, but he wasn't the kind of man who courted publicity. Indeed, he was so averse to it that his photograph didn't appear on his own chambers' website, and he had a habit of arriving early at court to avoid TV cameras. His reputation was for meticulous preparation and an unflappable manner. A safe pair of hands for a prosecution which promised to involve months of evidence of the highest complexity.

The wheels of justice grind slowly, and right now it was far too early in the process for Lucy Letby to be asked to enter a plea. We'd have to wait to hear her declare her position, guilty or not guilty. Other than confirming her name, she sat mute at the epicentre of the spectacle, incongruously informal in pink T-shirt and grey tracksuit.

It was all standard procedure for the lawyers and reporters, but Letby's parents looked well out of their comfort zone. They sat silently and awkwardly as the lawyers discussed dates, and the next years of their lives were mapped out for them by people they didn't know. It was no place for emotion, yet this was the first time that Sue and John Letby had been in the same room as their daughter since she was charged, and they engaged in an excruciating game of mimed charades. Mrs Letby made a heart sign with her fingers, gesturing twice for emphasis. Mr Letby mouthed 'I love you' and locked eyes with the nurse, who shook her head at her parents and nodded as she was taken back down to the cells.

Months went by. The courts were still fighting through the backlog of cases created by the Coronavirus pandemic, and at the best of times, trials of the scale of Lucy Letby's involve a lot of housekeeping before they get going. Even by that measure, progress felt glacial. There were another eleven preparatory hearings over the following two years, dealing with everything from the location for the trial, to the experts being instructed and the mental health of the defendant. At one stage, we learned that Nurse Letby was in a bad way, having been moved from one prison in Surrey to another in Yorkshire without her medication and belongings. She was apparently so disorientated by the move it had rendered her incoherent, and she was being assessed by forensic psychologists and a psychiatrist from the high-security Ashworth Hospital. There was no suggestion though that the case wouldn't go ahead; her QC told the court, 'She wants to have her trial. We want her to have her trial – this isn't a preamble to her defence. Our concern is that she's able to participate properly.'[2]

The prosecution had a team of three barristers working flat out on the case, but Team Letby only consisted of Ben Myers and his junior, Michael Maher. That was all the legal aid funding had allowed for, and the defence clearly felt outgunned. They successfully applied for more money to pay for a third advocate – the costs would eventually exceed £1.5 million[3] – and very late in the day they were joined by Fiona Clancy, the only woman on the barristers' benches, who suddenly found herself with a massive pile of reading to get through at very short notice. The team was complete, and the stage was set. Finally, more than five years since police first started investigating the unusual number of baby deaths in Chester, the nurse charged with their murders was about to stand trial.

Monday, 10 October 2022 was an average kind of news day. Internationally, Vladimir Putin was accusing Ukraine of terrorism for attacking the Crimea bridge. In the UK, it was the month after the death of the Queen, and the Conservative Party was embroiled in in-fighting during Liz Truss's short tenure as prime minister. There was space on the front pages and on the airwaves for other domestic stories.

The first satellite trucks pulled up outside Manchester Crown Court just as it was getting light. The 1960s court complex wasn't designed with live broadcasting in mind, and the vans and dishes had to jostle for space along the thin strip of road next to the building. A curry house on one side and a noisy bar at the end meant that there were few prime spots available, and the more experienced camera crews knew that they had to arrive early to claim their position. A forest of tripods sprang up at the base of the courthouse steps alongside a phalanx of reporters cradling takeout coffee, bantering about recent stories and sharing predictions for the day ahead.

The crews swung their lenses around. They'd spotted some of the protagonists arriving. Lucy Letby's barrister Ben Myers KC[4] strode in – business-like, briefcase in hand and ready to do battle. There was no sign of his opposite number, Nicholas Johnson KC – the man whose job it was to send Letby to prison. He was already inside the building, having slipped in without being filmed.

The crews stayed poised – they were waiting for Letby's parents to arrive, and it wasn't long before they got their quarry as the couple rounded the corner and moved into view, walking under the colonnade holding hands. Their dour expressions matched their dark suits – grey for him, black for her – suitably sombre for a day which doubtless they'd been dreading. Their daughter was already inside, having left prison near Wakefield before dawn to be driven for an hour or more over the Pennines to Manchester. As the van approached court, press photographers held their cameras up to the windows, flashing away in the hope of picturing the nurse-prisoner inside. But they weren't quick enough – the court authorities were wise to this well-worn dance, and the shutter entrance was already cranked up so that the transit van could sweep inside and drive out of sight under the building.

Inside the courtroom, the seating plan had been carefully worked out. First and foremost, there had to be enough space for the babies' families and the police officers who accompanied them. Then there was the question of where to put Mr and Mrs Letby. They were entitled to their own space too, but it wasn't a big room and they were given seats on the opposite side of the public gallery to the babies' families – the central aisle between them acting as a physical and metaphorical divider.

The Letbys wanted to be able to see the dock clearly. They asked for a screen to be moved out of the way so they could keep eyes on their daughter and it wasn't long before they were rewarded with the sight of her being brought in by the dock officers, who led her to her seat in the centre of the secure area.

The room started to fill up. The legal benches were fully popu-lated – two monochromatic rows of black gowns, and behind them another row of solicitors and support staff. At exactly half past ten, the judge's clerk rapped on the door and the room rose as one, hinged seats flip-flapping upwards as Mr Justice Goss entered, red-robed and eminent, to preside from his elevated perch above the barristers' benches. He was there, as the royal coat of arms behind him illustrated, to dispense justice on behalf of the monarch. It was, after all, the King v Lucy Letby, but it was the courtroom of

Judge James Goss, and once reseated, the room fell respectfully silent.

The judge looked across at the defendant, who was behind the glass window of the dock directly opposite him. Lucy Letby had smartened up since her first court appearances in a prison tracksuit and was deferential in a sober navy blue suit and black shirt. She was asked to stand.

The clerk adjusted his wig and began to work his way through the litany of charges. Twenty-two times he asked the nurse, 'Do you plead guilty or not guilty?' It was a required formality – we knew what her answers would be because if she'd previously indicated her intention to plead guilty, there would have been no need for a trial. Yet despite the predictability, there was a barely perceptible intake of breath each time a charge was put to her. The parents of the babies listened out for their child's name, and the corresponding crime. Seven counts of murder, fifteen counts of attempted murder. 'Do you plead guilty, or not guilty?' she was asked, again and again. 'Guilty!' thought the parents, silently. 'Not guilty,' answered Lucy Letby each time.

The battle lines drawn, there was an air of expectation in the room as Nick Johnson KC got to his feet to open the case for the prosecution. He cleared his throat. He'd worked meticulously through thousands of documents to prepare for this trial. The devil was in the detail and there would be many details to recount and dissect over the coming months. All in good time – this wasn't the moment to frighten the jurors with granular information. Johnson knew that to draw them in, he needed to tell the story of the case, and he began by setting the scene.

'The Countess of Chester Hospital sits on the edge of the city of Chester. It is a hospital like many others in the UK,' he told them. Then he paused and glanced at the dock. 'Unlike many others, within the neonatal unit at Chester, there was a poisoner at work.'

Like a good crime writer, Nick Johnson knew that he had to whet the jury's appetite for more information. He wouldn't disappoint on that front – his opening speech stretched across ninety-four pages, taking three days to deliver, carefully previewing the prosecution case, baby by baby. Over on the press benches, the reporters were trying hard to keep up with his brisk oratory. Although the babies couldn't be identified publicly, they were spoken about freely in the courtroom, and the speech was peppered with the names of the children and their parents. To the public, they would be known only as babies A to Q. To this day, their identities are protected. Judith was one of the only reporters live-blogging from inside the courtroom. She kept the list of names and their corresponding letters close to hand. One slip-up would be a disaster.

Johnson's speech was heavy-going, but it made headlines. After the first day, the next morning's front pages had splashed with 'Poisoner on the Baby Ward', and 'Malevolent Nurse' – the barrister wasn't averse to dropping in the odd sound bite, though he was no showboater. He wasn't playing to the media gallery – the only audience members he cared about were the eight women and four men in the jury seats, and after speaking for more than ten hours, he knew that he had to leave them with a flourish. He explained that after the nurse's arrest in 2018, the police had searched her house and they'd found some interesting things.

'Mr Murphy . . .' he said, turning to the technical operator whose job it was to present the evidence, 'would you please show exhibit number J312?'

A striking image flashed up on the display screens which were positioned all over the court. Each juror had their own monitor, and there were more in front of the dock, the legal benches and the public galleries. It was faintly reminiscent of a TV showroom with all televisions tuned to the same channel, only this time rather than the racing or a soap opera, the display was of an enlarged photograph of a scribbled note. It had been blown up to fill the screens – a sea of black ink on green Post-it note paper. We craned to make out the phrases. Nick Johnson was ahead of us and had picked out the ones he wanted to emphasise. 'I don't deserve to live . . . I killed them on purpose because I'm not good enough . . . I am a horrible evil person . . .' he read out, and then pointing to a phrase in capitals, 'I AM EVIL I DID THIS.'

The barrister had his flourish, playing the note like it was the ace up his sleeve. 'That, in a nutshell,' he told the jury, 'is your case.' It was an unexpected finale, and he waited a moment for them to take it in. Then, leaving them in no doubt about their weighty responsibility, he said softly, 'Whether or not she did these dreadful things is the decision you will have to make when you have heard all the evidence.'

Johnson sat down and took a sip of water. He had laid out all his wares and he would spend the next six months presenting his evidence, but before he could begin, it was the turn of Letby's barrister Ben Myers to have his say. The prosecution had spent most of the week painting the defendant as pure evil, and now the defence began a rebranding exercise. 'Lucy Letby was a dedicated nurse,' Myers told the court. 'She loved her job. She cared deeply about the babies and also cared for their families . . . The defence say she is not guilty of causing intentional harm to any baby or of killing any baby.'

Conscious that the jury had just been shown what looked very much like a confession note, Ben Myers asked for the document to be displayed again. Was he about to suggest that the words hadn't come from the pen of Lucy Letby? Was he going to tell us that there'd been some mix-up, and the writing was someone else's? No. The note was hers all right, but he said it was important to look even more closely at it. He pointed out some of the other phrases – 'Not good enough'; 'I will never have children or marry'; 'Despair'; 'I haven't done anything wrong.'

Myers might have been expected to skip quickly over the text, so troubling did it seem. But he allowed the court time to absorb it, and let the jurors run their eyes up and down the scrawl. 'We suggest that anyone who reads this fully with an ounce of under-standing will see that it's the anguished outpouring of a young woman in fear and despair, when she realises the enormity of what's being said about her, in the moment to herself,' he said.

Baby by baby, Mr Myers offered alternative possible explanations for what had happened, from understaffing and sub-optimal care by the hospital, to underlying health problems that the babies had been dealing with before they came anywhere near Lucy Letby. He summarised, 'There is no evidence of her actually doing harm to any child,' and provided his own verbal flourish. 'Using syringes to inject air? No, we say! Tampering with bags of fluid? Again, no! Or in some way poisoning them? Physically assaulting children? Smothering them? No!'

The KC finished by leaving the jurors in no doubt that, whatever the merits of either side, this wasn't going to be an easy process. 'This is a complex case,' he told them. 'It's not straightforward. And in that dock is a young woman who says this is not her fault.'

Myers had acted as Lucy Letby's mouthpiece, advocate and champion. It was a spirited performance, but his energy wasn't matched by the nurse's expression. Hard to know what she was thinking during that passionate oration on her behalf – she looked as unmoved now as she had earlier, when she was being portrayed by the prosecution as evil incarnate. It was as if the words being spoken were washing over her, and they were all about somebody else.

Both Nick Johnson and Ben Myers had done their persuasive best. But their speeches were no more than an overture. This was a trial which would rest on the detail. Mr Myers had said as much when he dismissed the prosecution's presentation of the scribbled notes, Facebook searches and text messages as 'amateur psychology'. He had urged the jury, 'what the case will come down to is the medical evidence and what it can safely prove and what it can't, and what we can safely conclude.'[5]

The prosecution team had the medical evidence firmly in mind too. Mindful of the amount of dense information and complex jargon coming the jury's way, they'd put together a glossary of terms, running alphabetically across twenty-five pages, from A (Abdominal distension, Acidosis, Actrapid, Adenosine, Air embolism) to V (Vagus nerve, Vena Cava, Ventilatory support, Volvulus). They had also appointed a range of expert witnesses in fields including paediatric radiology, endocrinology and haematology.

The expert evidence would be vital. Would this panel of medics offer hypotheses which would convince the jury that the babies had been attacked, or would the defence be able to pick holes in their arguments and present alternative expertise to show that there had been other causes? What about those who'd worked alongside Lucy Letby? A procession of doctors and nurses would filter in and out of the witness box, but would any of them be able to shed empirical light on what was alleged to have been going on under their noses at the Countess of Chester Hospital?

Then there were the families of the babies, who were by no means an afterthought and whose testimony could prove crucial. They had all provided powerful statements to the police. Some of them were being lined up to come and give first-person evidence in court too. Doubtless it would be emotional, but would it prove anything? How many parents would come and testify, and what bearing would their accounts have on the case?

And what about motive? Before the trial began, Cheshire Police and the Crown Prosecution Service held a briefing for journalists. They were asked whether Lucy Letby's psychology and motivation would form part of the case and they replied that it wouldn't – it wasn't considered to be a necessary strategy. But would that satisfy the jury? Could they convict the nurse without any clue as to her state of mind? Would they struggle to link her to every one of the individual allegations, without an overarching motive to suggest some continuity of behaviour?

The case got going and the court settled into a rhythm. Regular witnesses, like the paediatric experts Dewi Evans and Sandie Bohin, became familiar faces. Terminology that felt foreign to begin with soon tripped off the tongue, rendering the reference glossary redundant. Documents that originally appeared unfathomable to the non-medics present became easier to decode.

Letby too had her own routine. There was a 'Groundhog Day' aspect to her arrival each morning, accompanied by a small cast of dock officers who were becoming familiar faces in their own right. She always sat in the same seat in the centre of the enclosure, often nodding at her parents as she entered, but otherwise avoiding eye contact with anyone. She rotated a small wardrobe of sober clothes – bank-teller polyester suits, dark shirts – and her previously dyed blonde hair had returned to its natural brown.

By the time we filed into court at half past ten each morning, she'd already been up for the best part of five hours, having been woken before dawn to be transported the forty miles from prison to court. She didn't look tired, exactly. But there was a weariness to her, as though she was slightly detached from her surroundings. On one hand, she was assiduous about following the evidence, listening via the speaker in the dock, and looking at the same documents on her iPad that the jury was being shown. She would regularly spend time with her legal team during breaks, and at the start or end of the day. She'd pass notes to them, through the slits in the dock window. She was clearly engaged in the process. Yet, at the same time, she seemed remote – detached from the charged emotion of some of the evidence.

The majority of the babies' parents were not required to come to give evidence in person. Their statements were read out by prosecution barristers on their behalf, and because the defence didn't want to query their accounts, there wasn't a need for them to be physically called as witnesses.

Four weeks into the trial, that changed.[6] Baby D was one of the first babies that Lucy Letby was accused of murdering – one of a spate of incidents in June 2015. The little girl died after collapsing three times in one night, and the Crown alleged that the nurse had injected air into her bloodstream. Letby denied it and her defence said the baby could have died from an infection after the hospital had failed to give her mother antibiotics when her waters broke early. Ben Myers KC wanted to cross-examine the woman about her experience, and so she was asked to come to court.

Had the baby lived, she'd now have been in her first year of junior school. Her parents would have had seven years of her childhood to enjoy. Instead, those seven years had been filled with heartache and pain, and now the little girl's mother carried that grief into the witness box of courtroom seven. The technical jargon of the preceding medical evidence felt impersonal by comparison. Who could fail to look at the woman now taking her oath and feel anything other than intense sympathy for her situation?

The mother had done battle with her memories over these last years. Fighting to suppress them when they became too painful, yet simultaneously striving to hold them close as precious validation of her relationship with her daughter. Closure is a concept which the traumatically bereaved reject. Why should they accept any finality? Grief has no end. Yet somehow this woman had learned to live with it, and now she steeled herself. Giving evidence would involve opening up all the wounds she'd tried to heal. She wouldn't have put herself through it were it not for the need to see this horrific legal process through. Justice wouldn't bring her baby back, but perhaps it would help to make some sense of the senseless and give her the catharsis she craved.

The trial was into its second month, but this was the first time that this mother had been inside the court. She'd been required to stay away to ensure that her memory and her evidence didn't become skewed or contaminated by the testimony of others. This, then, was her first opportunity to take in the scene, to acknowledge the jury – sitting directly opposite her, the judge to her right, and the barristers to her left. She was also, of course, aware of Lucy Letby, sitting behind glass at the back. Letby was at the furthest remove from the mother's seat in the witness box, but it must have been unsettling knowing that she was there. The last time the two women had been in the same room together was the night the baby girl had died. Letby's photograph had been plastered, painfully, all over the media since her arrest, but that was a wholly different prospect to seeing her now in the flesh.

If Lucy Letby recognised the baby's mother, her expression didn't show it. She made no move to acknowledge her, looking down at her notes rather than towards the witness box. For her part, the mother tried to fight the urge to glance at the dock, and looked instead at Nick Johnson KC who would be questioning her first, on behalf of the prosecution.

Mr Johnson smiled at her gently. He understood that while the courtroom was his natural habitat, it was likely to be a highly un-comfortable place for the witness and he took a deliberately tender approach, asking her to start by describing her pregnancy.

She allowed her mind to travel back to 2015 – the joy of expecting her first baby, and the nerves that went along with it. She told the story of how her waters had broken early, and how she'd been left without antibiotics for more than fifty hours with the chances of infection increasing all the time. Eventually she was taken for a Caesarean section and her baby was lifted over the screen for her to see after giving birth. It wasn't the precious moment that she'd expected – instead of hearing the baby cry out, there was silence. 'She seemed lifeless. She didn't scream, there was no sound,' she told the court. 'Everything was quiet in the room.'[7]

Her fearfulness was compounded when the baby girl was brought to her chest. 'I had her skin-to-skin,' she recounted, 'but she didn't really have any movement. She looked limp and pale, she struggled to breathe, and she was making a groaning noise. She wasn't really responsive. There was a split second where she opened her eyes and looked at me, and then there was no response. I tried to breastfeed her, but she was completely limp, so I was quite worried.

'I was told by a doctor that I didn't need to worry – she was OK, and her condition was due to her being delivered by C-section. But I didn't believe what he said. I wasn't happy – it was careless and blasé.' It was a poor reflection on the hospital. Could Lucy Letby's barrister be right to blame the baby deaths on poor care?

The baby had been taken to neonatal intensive care, and it became clear that she had picked up an infection – as her mother had feared. Though it was seven years earlier, the woman could still close her eyes and picture the scene. She could still remember exactly how she'd felt physically too. The post-surgery agony – 'ten out of ten pain on morphine in a wheelchair,' she told Nick Johnson. But there was optimism too as the infant had started to improve over the next day and she'd been promised that it wouldn't be long before she'd be able to cuddle her daughter.

Listening to the woman tell her story, it was hard not to will her to give it an alternative ending. How comforting it would have been to hear about the baby's continued recovery, and the proud moment of her parents taking her home. But this was a tale with an ending that everyone in court already knew, and hard though it was to tell, she had to continue along that narrative instead.

Baby D's mother had been asleep on the postnatal ward when she and her husband were woken up in the middle of the night. 'It was about four a.m.,' she told the jury. 'A nurse told us to come quickly as [the baby] was poorly. She was in a panic, and we rushed downstairs and a doctor was holding her and trying really hard to resuscitate her. We were just standing there looking as our daughter was dying.'

It felt like she was reliving that experience. The mother recounted what it had been like to watch the doctor, who seemed agitated, trying to save her daughter as a phone was held to his ear. It was so horrific, she said, that she couldn't bring herself to stay any longer, and she asked to be taken away. It was Lucy Letby who was holding the phone, she said. How did she know? She remembered seeing her on the unit at seven o'clock that evening when she was wheeled in to see her daughter. 'I was pushed in,' she recalled, 'and she was sort of hovering around but not doing much. She had a clipboard to take notes and she was sort of looking at a machine, but I didn't understand what she was doing. I asked if everything was OK, and she said, "Yes, she's fine." I would have expected her to leave us, but she just stuck around and was sort of just watching and looking over us. I wanted to tell her to go away and give us some privacy.'

Then, the most painful memory of all: the moment when doctors stopped trying to resuscitate the baby girl and she died.

'Was Lucy Letby in the room then?' asked Nick Johnson.

'Yes,' answered the mother. Letby was there. Other staff had been there too.

For every witness who appeared in court, Lucy Letby's barrister also had an opportunity to ask questions. And now it was his turn. His client was accused of murdering the woman's child, so the encounter was bound to be uncomfortable. Ben Myers started with an icebreaker clearly calibrated to show compassion. 'What you went through was an awful experience,' he brokered softly. 'I only have one or two questions to ask.'

How did she know that it was seven o'clock when she'd first seen Miss Letby that evening?

'I must have looked at the clock,' came the answer.

'Could it have been another nurse?'

'I don't think so,' responded the witness.

The judge peered down from his bench, up above the witness box. Could she be a little clearer, he asked politely? The baby's mother explained that she wouldn't have known Lucy Letby's name at the time but would have seen her picture after she'd been arrested and made the connection then.

That was all Ben Myers had to ask, and Baby D's mum was released from her duty as a witness and told that she could leave.

Giving evidence hadn't been pleasant exactly, but it was over in less than an hour, and the cross-examination by Lucy Letby's defence barrister was less bruising than it could have been. The next mother to give evidence, however, would have a much different experience – one that still troubles her today.

Her sons, Baby E and Baby F, were the twins whom Lucy Letby was alleged to have attacked in August 2015. Letby was accused of injecting air into Baby E's bloodstream, and somehow hurting his upper gastrointestinal tract to cause bleeding. Then she was said to have poisoned his brother Baby F with insulin on the following day.

Now the jury was going to hear a first-hand account directly from the twins' mother, who was said to have walked in as Lucy Letby was in the process of murdering her first-born son. She was the only one out of all twenty-six parents[8] in the case who had been in that situation, and her testimony stood to be hugely important.

To the public, she was faceless – the anonymous mother of Baby E and Baby F. But those of us in the courtroom saw a person, not a letter – a petite, smartly dressed, composed woman. We heard her name and her voice. We had a glimpse into her world. She took a breath as the prosecutor got to his feet to begin his questions.[9]

The boys were born eleven weeks early, but – she told the court – she thought they were in good condition for their gestation. After they were born, she stayed on the postnatal ward, making regular visits to the neonatal unit.

Seven years on, she remembered those blissful first days of motherhood. She spoke warmly about the twins' health, and how they'd been doing so well that they were about to be transferred to a hospital nearer to home. 'I wanted them to have my breast milk,' she said. 'I was expressing it myself – it was very important to me to provide the milk. It was the only thing I could do for them at that point – I had to do it. It was non-negotiable for me . . . I was still sensitive and sore and fragile, but I was just absolutely over the moon. My two boys were perfect, and I was providing milk for them.'

Nick Johnson looked kindly at her – his opening speech had given the jury a preview of what was coming next, and now he had to guide her through the painful part of her story and take her back to the night the eldest twin had died.

'You went down to the ward with the purpose of delivering the milk for the boys and went into room one. Other than your children was there anyone else in there?'

'Yes.'

'Who?'

'Lucy Letby,' she said. Even uttering the nurse's name sounded distateful to her.

'What could you see or hear as you walked into the room?'

'I could hear my son crying, and it was like nothing I'd heard before, and I walked over to the incubator to see that he had blood coming out of his mouth and I panicked. I was panicking because I felt that there was something wrong.'

'Was Lucy Letby near your son when you walked in?'

'No, she was at the work station.'

Nick Johnson paused. He needed the jury to understand exactly who had been where during this critical time. He asked the technician to play a walk-through video of the neonatal unit. The court had seen it before when being guided through earlier parts of the evidence. But the twins' mother didn't know that it was going to be played, and it threw her. Later, when we interviewed her for

BBC *Panorama*, she told us that being shown the footage took her breath away. It was the first time she'd seen the room since 2015.[10]

As the video was played, she fought back tears. Nick Johnson gently asked her to point out where Lucy Letby had been at the time she'd arrived.

'On the right-hand side of the screen,' she answered.

The camera lens wobbled around the room, showing the two incubators where the twins had been lying.

'Just describe what you could hear.'

'Crying.'

'What sort of crying?'

Finding the right words to capture and communicate that terrible sound wasn't easy. She said the noise was so loud, she'd been able to hear it out on the corridor.

'It was a sound that shouldn't have come from a tiny baby. I can't explain what it was. It was horrendous. It was more of a scream than a cry,' she explained.

The woman said that she'd gone straight to the distressed infant, thinking that she might be able to settle him by laying her hands on him as she'd previously been shown, but she was taken aback by the sight of blood all around his mouth. The police had asked her to show them what she meant by annotating a diagram of a baby's face, and the image that she'd drawn was now displayed on all the screens in court.

Lucy Letby looked at the screen which was provided for her in the dock, angled so that she could see the same images as the jury. She noted the mother's drawing of the baby's bloody face, and looked away again, expressionless.

'Did you ask Lucy Letby about what you could see?' enquired Nick Johnson.

'Yes – and I asked what had gone wrong. She said, "The feed tube from the back of his throat will have been rubbing and that will have caused the blood."'

'Did you accept that explanation?' asked Mr Johnson.

'Yes,' replied the mother.

'Were you concerned about the explanation?'

'Yes.'

'Did Lucy Letby say anything else to you?'

'She told me to go back to the ward.'

'Did you do what you were told by her?'

'Yes.'

'Why did you do what you were told by her?'

'Because she was an authority, and she knew better than me, and I trusted her completely.'

'Did she say what she'd do about the problem?'

'She said the registrar was on his way, and if there was a problem someone would ring the postnatal ward.'

'Did you accept that explanation?'

'Yes.'

Listening to the way this had all played out, it was impossible not to feel for that bewildered new mother seven years earlier, who'd been torn between following her maternal instinct and trusting what Lucy Letby had told her. As it turned out, she'd ended up bowing to both impulses. The woman explained that she'd gone back up to the postnatal ward, as Nurse Letby had instructed, but had run there to call her husband. She said, 'I knew there was something very wrong. I was frightened. I didn't take my phone downstairs and I needed to speak to him. I needed to tell him.'

Nick Johnson KC stopped the witness there. He asked the technician to display exhibit number J2431 on the screens. The monitors soon filled with an image of the woman's mobile phone records, which showed the precise time – 9.11 p.m. – that she'd made that call.

The barrister didn't ask Baby E's mother to go into detail about her son's decline and the fight to resuscitate him. He said simply, 'The medical team were working on him . . . and their best efforts were unsuccessful . . .'

'Yes,' she agreed.

'Once he'd passed away, did you have any contact with Lucy Letby?' he asked.

'Yes, oh yes,' she replied emphatically. 'I was asked if I would like to bathe [my son] and at that moment I didn't feel that I was able to. I was just broken, and I couldn't, so Lucy Letby bathed him in front of me in the neonatal unit, and after he was bathed he was placed in a white gown and I was thankful because we had no clothes for him, because he was so little, and he was given back to us and then went in his incubator and that's where he stayed.'

She added that Lucy Letby had also given them a memory box containing footprints, a lock of hair, a candle and a teddy bear, and the nurse had later sent them a picture of the surviving twin cuddling that bear.

The mother told the court that no post-mortem had been conducted on Baby E, following advice from one of the consultants, but the couple had been so grateful for the care they'd received at the hospital, they later sent a thank you card to the staff. It was displayed on the screens for everyone to see. Nick Johnson had no more questions for the bereaved mother, and he sat down. It was now the turn of Ben Myers, who got on his feet to ask questions in Lucy Letby's defence.

He began as he had done with the mother of Baby D – by offering his sympathies. 'You did all that you could do,' he said solemnly, 'and nothing that is said is meant to suggest anything other than that.'

She nodded. Myers knew that the mother's testimony was powerful for the prosecution, and so he did what lawyers do when faced with a witness who undermines their case: he began to question her reliability. Maybe her account wasn't quite what it seemed. Maybe her memory had become confused.

'Had you spent much time in hospital before this, in capacity with babies?' he asked.

'No,' she responded.

'Do you think that the timings you've given us were correct?'

'Yes.'

'It must have been very intense. Very upsetting,' remarked Ben Myers. He put it to her that she'd got her timings wrong – that she hadn't come down to the neonatal unit and seen Lucy Letby when she said she had.

'I disagree totally,' the mother answered.

'Surely there were other staff around at the time,' said Myers.

'I didn't come into contact with any other staff.'

'No other nurse came in?'

'Not that I'm aware of.'

The mother was unwavering, so Myers changed tack.

'Let me ask you about the crying,' he said. 'He wasn't as upset as to the degree you describe it.'

'It was horrendous.'

Myers persisted. 'I suggest it wasn't as horrendous as you were saying.'

The atmosphere in the courtroom tensed up. The barrister hadn't been anywhere near the hospital that night. Was he really suggesting that he had a better idea of what the baby sounded like than the child's own mother did?

Weeks later, when we interviewed the baby's mother for BBC *Panorama*, she told us how she'd felt when the lawyer made that particular remark to her. She said, 'I know it's the job, but saying that maybe his cry wasn't as bad as you're making it out to be? What a thing to say. I mean, there are so many other ways that that could have been said to get a point across, but that? That will stick with me for life.'[11]

But Ben Myers wasn't finished. What about the blood which the mother had described seeing on her son's face?

'Is it possible that what you saw was a dark liquid with flecks of blood in it?' he queried.

'It was blood,' she asserted.

The mother said that she'd told one of the midwives about it, when she went back upstairs to phone her husband.

'I was distraught,' she said.

'I'm going to suggest that at this time you were worried, and not distraught,' said Myers.

Baby E's mother looked directly at him. 'No, I was distraught,' she said firmly.

The KC put it to her that her recollection of her conversation with Lucy Letby was incorrect – that Letby hadn't told her the bleeding around her son's mouth had been caused by his feeding tube rubbing his throat. And on it went. Piece by piece, fact by fact, he set about challenging the account of the baby's mother.[12]

The woman had been an impressive witness. She stuck to her guns during cross-examination and wasn't cowed by the barrister's efforts to suggest that she'd misremembered details about her own baby – details she'd gone over time and time again.

For a case based on so much circumstantial evidence this would turn out to be crucial. Establishing Lucy Letby as a liar was one of the prosecution team's key strategies. They accused her of falsifying medical records to cover her tracks.[13] They alleged that she lied about remembering some of the babies and parents. They aimed to demonstrate that she wasn't telling the truth about her Facebook searches or the hospital paperwork which was found in her house. Often it was her word against that of someone else, which is why the certainty of parents like the twins' mother was so important.

But as compelling and heart-wrenching as the parents' testimony was, both the prosecution and the defence knew that experts would play a key role in deciding the outcome of the trial. Only they could say what an air embolism was or why a baby's stomach had mysteriously filled with air, or why a baby had suddenly stopped breathing.

Dr Dewi Evans had been involved in the case from the beginning. He was the man that Cheshire Police had turned to, to tell them if babies had been killed. He was the first expert to say that babies had been injected with air. And from the earliest days of the trial, Letby's barrister Ben Myers made it his mission to argue that Dewi Evans was an unreliable witness.

He began by attacking Evans' integrity. Evans, he argued, was compromised from the outset. He'd read about the investigation at the Countess of Chester Hospital in the papers and contacted his mates in the National Crime Agency to see if he could become involved. According to Myers, Evans had 'touted for work'.

Once on the case, his input was biased and unbalanced. He was, Myers argued, a gun for hire – part of the prosecution team rather than a servant of the court.

'You're not independent as a witness, are you?' Myers said.

'That's just insulting,' Evans shot back. 'I'm completely independent. I've been giving evidence in court for a long time. I know about impartiality. I know about the rules. I'm not here for the prosecution, I'm not here for the defence. I'm here for the court.'[14]

Lucy Letby's barrister also challenged the expertise of Dr Evans, who was retired. For Myers, it was an opportunity to accuse Evans of being out of touch with current clinical practices. But Evans gave as good as he got. 'My experience was huge,' he asserted. 'I reckon I could intubate a baby today. It's like riding a bicycle.' No one asked Dr Evans to prove his point by demonstrating the procedure, but it wasn't hard to imagine that he'd be game for trying. He was to become one of the characters of the trial. Some of the reporters nicknamed him the 'Welsh Wizard', and particularly looked forward to when he was being cross-examined by Ben Myers.

But it was Evans' pronouncements on the air embolism theory – the assessment that babies had had air injected into their bloodstreams – that provoked the most aggressive attacks from Letby's defence team.

In January 2023, Ben Myers KC made a formal application to have Dr Evans' evidence excluded from the case. Much of it was directed at Dewi Evans' suitability as an expert witness – whether he had the expertise to back up his all-important assessments of what had caused babies to collapse and die. But Myers also attacked Dewi Evans' integrity and even his temperament. He was accused of being emotive, evasive and obstructive.[15] Evans was a controversial witness. Even the judge agreed that he could be verbose and argumentative. But there was no question of excluding him or his evidence. As far as the judge was concerned, it was up to the jury to decide whether Evans' evidence was credible.

But expert witnesses and parents weren't the only ones who would help determine Letby's fate. Her former colleagues would too. They had worked alongside Lucy Letby, spending hours at a time on shift with her. They'd administered drugs with her, performed resuscitations alongside her, and been involved in myriad conversations and text exchanges. One by one, they came to court to give evidence. Some had very little to say. Others found themselves being interrogated for days on end. Sometimes it became a head-on credibility contest between the medics and the nurse – a he-said-she-said joust.

The cast of medical staff clearly had mixed feelings about being there. Some gave evidence from behind screens, so they couldn't see Letby, nor she they. Others had no problem with being in the defendant's line of sight and sat in her full view, though she never acknowledged them. They might once have worked closely together, but now their lives were worlds apart. None of them came back into court after giving evidence to carry on watching from the public gallery.

Even Letby's friends from Hereford were absent from the courtroom. Not one of them came to watch during those ten months of accusation and incrimination. Later we learned that Letby had told them not to come. Why? Wouldn't she have benefited from their support? Maybe she didn't want them to see and hear about a version of her that she had managed to keep hidden. Or, as one friend told us, perhaps she was just looking out for her friends. Maybe she wanted to protect them from the public glare and the reputational hazard of being associated with her.

There was one exception. Janet Cox, a former nursery nurse who we'd seen pictured with Letby in several Facebook photos. Janet was much older than Letby, but the two were clearly friends. She wasn't called as a witness, although she had been on shift when some of the babies collapsed. But she spent nearly every day in the courtroom, pinning her colours firmly to the Letby mast by sitting next to the nurse's parents, and loyally supporting their daughter. She was the only spectator to do so.

We knew from the outset that Dr Ravi Jayaram would be an important witness. He was one of the consultants who'd fought to get Letby removed from the unit, and the fact that she was now on trial was partly down to him. He'd also seen Letby in circumstances that, according to the prosecution, amounted to an act of attempted murder.

If Dr Jayaram's face seemed familiar to the public gallery, it might have had more to do with his side hustle than his work at the Countess of Chester Hospital. Dr Jayaram dabbled with a bit of TV doctoring and had appeared on *BBC Breakfast*, *The One Show* and *This Morning*, among other programmes. A 'Z-list media medic'[16] was how he styled himself. He certainly had no problem performing for an audience, and he took his place in the witness box with more than a smidgen of self-confidence.

Dr Jayaram had given evidence earlier in the trial, about the first child on the indictment, Baby A, and the aftermath of his death. He spoke then about there being 'talk on the unit' in the summer of 2015, as subsequent babies showed similar symptoms, and how he'd looked up a research paper which described air embolism in newborns.[17] Today he was back under oath again to explain his role in the care of Baby K – a girl whom Lucy Letby was charged with attempting to murder in February 2016.

The consultant told the jury that he'd felt uneasy when he realised the nurse had been left alone with the infant, explaining, 'At this time we were aware of a number of unusual events and of Lucy Letby's presence . . . You can call me hysterical, or irrational. The rational side of me told myself not to be ridiculous. But it kept coming back, so I went to check – to reassure myself.'[18]

Dr Jayaram said he had found Letby standing by the incubator, and although the baby's breathing tube had become dislodged, she wasn't doing anything to help her. He said he had to give the baby rescue breaths and breathing support to revive her.

Only Ravi Jayaram and Lucy Letby had been in the room at the time in question. There was no CCTV. No other eyewitness. It was his word against hers. Months later, when the jury had to work out who was telling the truth, they couldn't decide, and a retrial was ordered on that count.

Jayaram was a commanding witness – often driving the discourse and volunteering information before being asked for it.[19] He was assured enough to allow himself moments of self-deprecation ('call me hysterical, call me irrational . . .') in the knowledge that he had the upper hand. After all, he wasn't the one on trial, and if

Letby was convicted, it would be the ultimate validation of his early suspicions.

But Lucy Letby had not been proven guilty yet, and her barrister Ben Myers KC appeared to bristle at Dr Jayaram's self-confidence. The hostility was mutual.

'In my professional practice we have two-way conversations,' Dr Jayaram snapped at one point. 'It would help me to answer your questions to understand what you're driving at.'

But Myers' point couldn't have been clearer: Jayaram says he suspected that Letby was up to no good – and yet he did nothing.

'You wondered if the tube had been dislodged on purpose?' Myers asked.

'I did wonder that.'

'Did you confront her?'

'Absolutely not – it was my job to deal with the baby.'

'If someone you say is standing there, with all your suspicions, and could have done it on purpose. You'd have asked her.'

'No, I wouldn't,' the doctor pushed back and parried. 'I'm interested in why you say that. Because what I've told you and what I've said is exactly my recollection of things.'

'Did you write it in the notes?'

'Mr Myers, that is not the type of thing that one writes in clinical notes. It's something we [consultants] discussed together and escalated to senior management in the hospital.'

This was new. It was the first time the court had heard anything about the consultants' joint efforts to flag their concerns to management.

'Had you thought someone was harming children on your unit, would you not have informed the police?' Myers asked.

For Jayaram, the question was an affront. Here was Lucy Letby's barrister suggesting that he and his colleagues had sat on their hands. The doctor wasn't going to leave anyone in court with the impression that the consultants had done nothing about their suspicions. It was his moment to set the record straight. The consultants, he said, had flagged their concerns to senior management – but to no avail. They'd escalated things to the director of nursing in October 2015. They'd tried again in February 2016 and alerted the medical director. Dr Brearey had asked for a meeting and – he told the court – they'd waited three months.[20]

Dr Jayaram spoke forcefully. 'We wish we'd bypassed them and asked the police. All we wanted was to be advised on the correct way forward. No way have we played judge and jury. This is an unprecedented situation – we're not trained for this. We work with a certain rule book and playing field – thoughts come into your head and you put them away and then more and more happens. Eventually it reached a point, in June 2016, when we thought things had to change.'

But Mr Myers held firm. 'You made no formal record at the time. You and the other consultants are grown adults who don't have to be trained to ring the police, do you?'

Jayaram shot back. 'We were getting a reasonable amount of pressure from the senior management at the hospital not to make a fuss,' he said. 'We are grown-ups and we should have stood up and not listened . . . In retrospect, if I'm ever in this situation again – and I sincerely hope I never am – I'd have no hesitation about bypassing management.'[21]

It was a tense exchange – a clash of egos as well as competing truths. Lucy Letby was the only defendant in the dock, but this was the first time that there was a sense of the bigger picture. The first suggestion of wider failings. It sounded damning, but would the trial unearth all of the answers to the questions that now reared their heads?

Two weeks later, it was time for the unit's lead neonatal paediatrician Dr Steve Brearey to take his seat in the witness box. In many ways, despite his mild manner, Brearey was Lucy Letby's arch nemesis. On one of her scrawled Post-it notes, Letby had written 'BASTARDS!' in capital letters. Whoever else she had in mind, Brearey was definitely foremost among the 'bastards'. One of Brearey's colleagues told us this whole story was 'Steve's fight' – a seven-year battle to get justice.

Brearey had been on duty for the death of one of the triplets in June 2016. He'd also been there the next day after the second triplet had died. He said that after the second boy died, he spoke to Lucy Letby at the staff debrief.

He told the court:

I asked her how she was feeling, and I can remember suggesting to her that she'd need the weekend off to recover from these traumatic events. She didn't seem overly upset to me, or upset at all, and she told me she was on shift the following day, which was a Saturday. I was concerned about this because we'd already expressed our concerns to senior management about the association between Nurse Letby and the deaths on the unit, so following the debrief I phoned Karen Rees, the senior nurse in the urgent care division who was on call – the duty executive. She was familiar with the concerns. I said I didn't want Lucy Letby to come to work the next day or until this was all investigated. Karen Rees said no to that and that there was no evidence.[22]

Dr Brearey didn't have the same stage presence as Ravi Jayaram and spoke with less panache. But there was a different power in the softness of his tone, and it was interesting to imagine the dynamic that must have existed on that phone call between the quietly determined consultant and the executive at the other end of the line.

You could hear a pin drop in the courtroom as Brearey continued; 'I said, "Would you be happy to take responsibility if anything happened to any of the babies tomorrow?" and she said "Yes," and that's where the conversation finished.'

Between them, consultants Ravi Jayaram and Stephen Brearey had given their answers to some fundamental questions. Had any of Lucy Letby's colleagues become suspicious of her? And what, if anything, had they done about it? But their testimony had also thrown open an entirely new area of speculation – and questions which were likely to fall outside of the trial's remit. The hospital managers were not on trial, but this was the first hint that there would be some big issues for the trust to resolve, regardless of the verdicts. Either a nurse had been attacking babies or there had been a mysterious surge in fatalities. Whichever it was, management did nothing to help, and resisted concerns – according to the consultants. It was hard to see how the Countess of Chester Hospital Trust was going to emerge without reputational damage either way.

The individual details of each baby's decline were harrowing enough for their families to listen to. But along with the media and the public, this was also the first time that they were learning the wider detail, and it was clearly very difficult to cope with. When Ravi Jayaram told the court that the consultants had been under pressure not to make a fuss, one of the parents got up and stormed out of the courtroom. It was simply too much to bear.[23]

Another parent – the mother of twins E and F – later told us, 'Hearing blow by blow for the first time about what happened with [Baby E] was traumatic. It was like it was happening all over again, but I had the knowledge this time. All the things that happened to me were slotting into place, but it was done in open court. You're finding out about what happened to your children at the same time as the rest of the world.'

The mother added that her upset had been exacerbated by seeing online commentary about the case. She revealed, 'There's these people that are sat behind their screens or phones and it's almost like my children aren't human. It's a story to them and they can detach from it but I can't. So all those hurtful things that they're saying, it's real for me because they were small, tiny human beings. My tiny human beings.'[24]

Day after day, week after week, the court heard harrowing evidence about babies dying and parents grieving. And yet, to look at her in court, none of it seemed to be hitting Lucy Letby's sides. She remained inscrutable. Her expression and demeanour remained stubbornly blank. Whatever was going on inside, she appeared unfeeling.

Was it because she'd blocked things out? Was the magnitude of what she was being wrongly accused of too painful to process? Or was she guilty as charged and immune from feeling? We searched her face for expression and usually came away with nothing. Ben Myers' words at the start of the trial – 'You won't get the answers to this case looking at the woman in the dock' – seemed to have been prophetic.

For months, Letby watched as her former friends and colleagues were questioned about her activities. Some cried. Many clearly felt betrayed and traumatised by what had happened. But still, Letby remained impassive. Until one cold morning in February 2023, when a doctor from Letby's unit entered the witness box. He'd asked for reporting restrictions to prevent the media from identifying him and the judge had agreed. He'd also asked if he could give evidence from behind a screen. No one in the court could see him. But when he announced his name, Letby abruptly left her seat, crying as she lurched towards the door. One of the female dock officers intercepted her, and they spoke *sotto voce* for a moment or two before the nurse approached a gap in the window to talk to her legal team. Letby spoke briefly to her solicitor and then Ben Myers KC indicated that she was OK, and the hearing could continue. The defendant resumed her seat and dabbed at her eyes, wiping away tears with a tissue and sipping water as the doctor's evidence got under way.

No one knows for sure what kind of relationship Letby had with the medic behind the screen – the same doctor who she used to text incessantly late into the night. We know the two were in close touch, and friends of Letby suggested she fancied him. She denied it, but they went for walks and had meals together. The anonymous doctor was married with kids, but he spent time at Letby's home. The pair even went to London together for the day in June 2017 – a whole year after Letby stopped working as a nurse. She said they didn't stay overnight.[25]

That was then. Once the legal process got under way things looked very different. Before the trial we learned that the doctor had been the object of unrequited affection from Lucy Letby, who had searched intensely for his wife on social media. It was said that he'd suffered from severe anxiety since the start of the police investigation, with continued underlying stress. Whatever the truth of Letby's relationship with the married doctor, on that February day, the mere sound of his voice affected her in a way that four months of evidence about suffering babies and grieving parents had failed to.

In the scheme of things, it was a modest display of emotion, over almost as soon as it had begun. It didn't disrupt the proceedings for long and the court carried on without taking a break. But given her self-control throughout the preceding weeks, it felt significant – as though the needle had moved for those of us trying to gauge her likely mindset during the case.

If the doctor was similarly moved by encountering Letby, even from behind a screen, it was not apparent. He was there to give factual evidence about his care of Baby L, and he stuck to clinical detail only – disappointing for anyone hoping for something more salacious.

By Easter 2023, it seemed that we'd heard from everyone but the defendant herself. But even at this late stage in her trial, no one knew if Lucy Letby would testify. They say it's the decisive factor in most murder trials. A good performance in the witness box can be enough to get a cold-blooded killer off the hook. But silence is better than self-incrimination. As in every criminal trial, the burden of proof was on the prosecution, not the defence. If she'd felt that the case against her was weak, she might decide there was nothing to be gained by putting herself through the process. On the other hand, she'd sat through twenty-five weeks of prosecution evidence, and this was her chance to meet the allegations head on.

Finally, at the start of May 2023 we had our answer. Ben Myers got to his feet and called the first defence witness. It was Lucy Letby.

Chapter 7

Letby Speaks

If Lucy Letby was feeling trepidatious about making her debut in the witness box, she now had a few days to work on her nerves. As she was driven back to Yorkshire to spend the early May Day weekend in her cell, the rest of the country was in a celebratory mood. The bunting was out for the King's forthcoming Coronation and Liverpool was gearing up to host the Eurovision Song Contest. At New Hall Prison near Wakefield the prisoners were able to watch some of the festivities on TV,[1] and should they have continued channel-hopping, they may also have spotted one of their fellow inmates making the news bulletins again when the trial resumed just after the bank holiday.

On the morning of 2 May there was also a feeling of occasion at the law courts. The media interest in the case had varied over the course of the preceding six months, waxing and waning depending on what was happening on any given day. Some organisations had committed to covering the case every day. But others had dipped in and out, cherry-picking the parts that seemed most interesting, and only sending their reporters to court occasionally. With so much technical detail being repeated from baby to baby, it was sometimes hard to get editors to keep coming back to the story. The scrum of camera crews outside the building at the beginning had mostly dwindled to one or two, and only a handful of journalists were hardcore regulars.

By anyone's standards, however, today promised to be a box-office moment. With the pendulum ready to swing from prosecution to defence, the spotlight was about to swivel too as Lucy Letby came out from behind the glass and moved centre stage.

The manoeuvre itself happened behind closed doors. The nurse's security classification meant that she had to be brought up from the cells and taken through the secure areas at the back of the courtroom while handcuffed to a dock officer. The room was kept empty until she was ensconced behind the desk of the witness box, with an officer on either side. Only then could her shackles be removed and the doors of the court opened for the loitering queue of families, lawyers and journalists. This strict choreography meant that Lucy Letby was never seen publicly in handcuffs. Her team will have been keen to avoid the optics of it in front of the jury, and in any case, she wasn't considered a major 'flight risk'.

Just down the hallway there was another trial running at Manchester Crown Court that spring, with conspicuously higher security. The defendant was a drug dealer accused of shooting a child in Liverpool. There were armed officers on patrol, extra bag searches, a knife arch at the courtroom door, and uniformed police on the exits. None of that was required for the Letby trial. The nurse might have been charged with many more child murders than the gunman down the corridor, but she wasn't assessed as posing a danger to anyone right there and then, in the confines of the court.

No threat perhaps, but once she was in the centre of the room her presence was keenly felt. Until now, there had always been a relaxed atmosphere at the start of each day. The clerk would open the doors and the staff would take their seats while ribbing each other about the previous night's football scores. The barristers would start their banter in the robing room and continue as they carried their files into the courtroom. The reporters would chat while logging on to their laptops, and there'd usually be a low hum of conversation until the loud rap on the judge's door which heralded his arrival.

That morning, everything felt different. The usual customers arrived to find the doors locked, and through the glass slits in the courtroom vestibule we could see there was a swell of movement inside – Lucy Letby was being moved into place. Only when the security staff indicated that they were happy was the green light given for the doors to be opened. We filed in, immediately feeling the change in atmosphere. For one thing, there was an almost reverential quiet – a respect for the gravitas of the moment perhaps, or a spellbound silence. This was our first opportunity to see the defendant outside her usual glass membrane – close up and unfiltered.

And yet, oddly, while it felt momentous, it was also contradictorily underwhelming. Perhaps we'd built this occasion up into more than it deserved, having given it six months' worth of hype. Hard to know what we were expecting, but the sight that confronted us was anti-climactic. Lucy Letby sat waxwork-still in her chair, gazing into the mid-distance, and looking very much as though she'd like the floor to open up. Doubtless she could feel every set of eyes boring into her and, given that her parents were now sitting just behind her, it must have taken a degree of self-control not to look in their direction. It was as though she had an ability to close herself off from her environment and retreat inside her own head.

The customary rat-a-tat-tat on the judge's door broke the spell. Everyone, Letby included, stood for Mr Justice Goss. The hearing was ready to begin. The nurse swore to tell the truth, the whole truth and nothing but the truth, and the barrister tasked with getting her off twenty-two counts of murder and attempted murder went to work.

Ben Myers KC had had two and a half years to prepare for this moment. He'd been leading Team Letby since the first court appearance in 2020, and he was known in legal circles for a strategic ability honed during his time at Sandhurst. He'd long since exchanged his military fatigues for a wig and gown, but he was still fighting battles – albeit on very different terrain. The enemy fire here was verbal, and he knew that it would rain down on Lucy Letby in a few days' time when the prosecution cross-examination got going.

This, then, was his chance to lay early defences, and shore his client up against what was going to come down the track. He made a gentle start – 'Miss Letby, I'm going to ask you about your background,' he began, in an effort to paint a personality that the jury could identify with. He went for the humdrum human details – childhood, schooldays, career ambitions . . . murderous intentions.

It was so casual, the way he slipped it in, that it was easy to miss.

'Did you ever want to hurt any baby?' he asked – a simple question lobbed in among other easy low-balls about her home life and background.

It was an opportunity for Lucy Letby to show some passion and to rail loudly at the very thought of it. Her eyes might have blazed with the indignation of being wrongly accused. She could have vented her fury. Instead, when the words came, they sounded subdued, monotonic and flat. 'No that's completely against what being a nurse is,' she said. 'I only wanted to help and to care for them.' It was a completely reasonable answer of course, and she was stating the obvious – the concept of murdering babies couldn't be more opposed to the vocation of nursing. Lucy Letby knew that what she was saying was correct, and it was what was expected of her too. But it sounded robotic, rehearsed, formulaic.

Ben Myers pushed on. There was a long way to go. In the press seats we listened to each answer as though we were trying to decipher code. We interrogated both what she said and the way she said it. Was she stressed, or was she finding it easy? Was she thinking earnestly about her answers, or just trotting them out? Was she persuasive? Were we warming to her? It was too soon to know yet. She sounded calm and in control. Clear and prepared. Happy to help, within limits. She certainly wasn't evasive, but nor was she loquacious. She was careful, clipped and seemingly devoid of emotion – at least at first.

The tears came after twenty minutes, prompted by questions about how it felt to be taken off duty. Ben Myers had found her Achilles' heel, and he twanged it. 'My job was my life,' she sobbed. 'My whole world was stopped. Everything has changed. Everything about me, my hopes for the future.' She wrung her hands and wiped her eyes. Her earlier composure had deserted her. 'Are you the sort of person who writes things down?' prompted her barrister, segueing smoothly into another area of high emotion.

Letby's notes were no longer the bombshell that they were when first shown to the court, but repeated viewings of them hadn't rendered them any less fascinating. Ben Myers pulled up the green note which had garnered the most attention and picked out the phrases which Letby had scrawled years earlier and which had come back to haunt her ever since her arrest. There was no hiding from them – the barrister and the nurse now had to hit them head on. It was a process she must have practised, playing each one over and over in her mind. Some were particularly thorny: 'I AM EVIL I DID THIS . . . I killed them on purpose . . .' and they were isolated again now for her fresh consideration.

Why on earth had she written those things, if she hadn't killed anyone? Why did she consider herself evil, if she'd never hurt a fly?

There were reasons for it all, she said. Other people had made her feel evil . . . she was worried that she'd somehow hurt the babies through unintentional incompetence. She was in turmoil, and a terrible mental state for two years. 'It was just me processing my thoughts,' she said. 'It wasn't supposed to be read by anyone . . . This is uncomfortable for me. I'm a very private person.'

Very well. Lucy Letby's defence lawyer had no wish to dwell further on the scribblings on the green Post-it either. He'd have to come back to the rest of the notes, but for now he moved back to easier territory – her qualifications to work in intensive care, her willingness to cover extra shifts, her enjoyment of the job. It was an opportunity for the nurse to demonstrate some of her expertise, and she slipped into work mode, explaining processes like blood-gas tests and cardiac observations which were once her everyday reality in a life before cells and handcuffs.

It was as though she was slipping a well-worn sweater back on. This was clearly her comfort zone, and while she wasn't showing off exactly, she did appear keen to impart her knowledge and evidence the years of training she had under her belt. They couldn't talk in general terms forever though, and the barrister tiptoed towards the reason we were all there in the first place.

'The desperately sad nature of this case is that it involves babies who died . . . and I'm going to ask you questions about them,' he ventured with the caveat, 'no insensitivity is intended.' He began by asking what the impact was on staff when a baby died, and whether there was any support. 'It affects everyone on the unit,' replied Lucy Letby. 'There's nothing formal, just the nurses between ourselves supporting each other.'

'Did you send messages to the other staff after the deaths of babies?' he asked.

'Yes, we leaned on each other,' she replied.

'Do you like to message people? Text?'

'Yes.'

Ben Myers was keen to show that his client was one of the team – a woman with functioning relationships and a normal friendship circle.

'What was life like outside work?' he asked her.

'I had quite an active social life,' she answered. 'I regularly used to attend salsa classes, had lunches and holidays with friends, went to the gym . . . My friends were the only support I had.'

In the press seats we all thought the same thing. What about the married doctor? Wasn't he a particular source of support?

Ben Myers got there at the same time and asked Lucy Letby to describe their relationship.

'Was it a friendship?'

'Yes.'

'Was it anything more?' he probed.

'No,' she maintained. 'Sometimes he'd come to my house. We'd go out for coffee or walks. We stayed in touch until it fizzled out.'

That was in 2018 – the year she'd first been arrested, by which point he was working at another hospital. 'Fizzled out' seemed an odd way to describe a purely platonic friendship, but Ben Myers pressed on.

How well did she get to know the parents of babies on the unit? Did she form friendships with them? Did she stop being interested in them once they'd left the unit?

'It was only ever professional when they were on the unit,' she said. 'There have been occasions where I've kept in touch with families once they've left.' She accepted that she used to search for the parents on social media, 'Out of general curiosity . . . and if they'd been on my mind.'

The nurse's Facebook searches had been a running theme of the prosecution case, with the jury regularly being told that she'd looked up one parent or another. 'It was a normal pattern of behaviour for me,' she said. 'It's just what I would do . . . I was always on my phone.' Lucy Letby's voice had thinned out to little more than a whisper and she was asked to speak up. Was she embarrassed by the public exposure of her private social media habits? Searching for the parents of dead babies online appeared voyeuristic, and it must have felt awkward, with some of the families she'd searched for sitting nearby. But her KC didn't shy away from it. Maybe he reasoned it just made her a typical millennial, not a murderer.

He continued with his mission to amplify the nurse's normality. The prosecution had presented the court with photographs of Letby's home, with the master bedroom still dishevelled after her arrest. Like a series of 'before and after' pictures which had had the benefit of airbrushing, Ben Myers now took the chance to look through the keyhole again through a different lens. He displayed a different selection of images, taken on behalf of the defence, after the house had been tidied up and rendered pristine.

Now we in court turned voyeur – feasting on the detail before us. Who would live in a house like this? A neat back garden, with potted shrubs and climbing roses. A tidy sitting room, with corner sofa and trinkets on display. A kitchen noticeboard covered in letters and cards. Up the stairs, past the Disney trinkets on the landing, and into the bedroom. This was the same room we'd seen after the police had come knocking. Afterwards, we were told, Lucy Letby's dad had straightened the place up, and that was the way the defence would prefer that we saw it now, as though the suggestion of a messy bedroom was a criminal allegation too far. The bed had been made, Winnie-the-Pooh and Eeyore sitting atop the ironed bedspread, 'Sweet Dreams' printed on the cover.

'Are you all right looking at these?' asked Ben Myers, who could see that his client was welling up. 'It's just so difficult,' she confessed, starting to cry again. She may have been struggling with being reminded of the contrast between her cosy old room and her current bars-on-the-window billet. Equally, she might have been recoiling at what felt like an invasion of her privacy. If it was the latter, it was about to get worse. The nurse's 2016 diary was displayed on the TV screens in court – the details of her daily life about to tumble out for public dismemberment. It was hardly a remarkable regime, with hair appointments listed alongside reminders to pay car and council tax. Socially, there was 'lunch with Jen at Tatton Park', 'salsa' and a note about a trip to see Ellie Goulding in concert. So far, so mundane, but Ben Myers did another shake of the sieve, and pointed out some finer details that might have otherwise escaped attention. The initials LD and N often appeared – Letby explained that they were there to keep track of her long day and night shifts – and individual names were also recorded. 'Why did you note the names of the babies in your diary?' asked the nurse's barrister. 'For my own reflection,' she replied.

The court was told that when police found the diary, the green Post-it note had been tucked inside, along with a vaccination record for her cats. That little detail prompted more tears from the witness, who confirmed that they were called Tigger and Smudge, and that she'd scribbled their names on one of her notes, together with that of her childhood dog Whiskey. Ben Myers had put his probing about the notes on pause earlier in the hearing, and now came back to them – explaining that others had also been found in Letby's handbags.

One written on yellow paper was enlarged on the screens. We gazed at the looped biro markings, our eyes first drawn to the capitalised HELP in thick ink on the middle of the page, and then moving across the densely packed lines. Letby had written the name of the married doctor next to 'my best friend'. 'Was he your best friend?' asked the barrister. 'Yes, he was a trusted friend,' she answered.

'It says "love is all we needed",' Myers pointed out. 'Where was that expression from?'

'It was the lyrics of a song by Craig David that was in my mind at the time,' she replied.

The KC hadn't finished with the note. He directed his client towards the bottom right-hand corner, where she'd written BASTARDS. Although she was charged with considerably worse, the nurse was at pains to show that she was not someone who made a habit of swearing. 'That's not language I would use,' she said, as if conscious of the need to mollify her parents who were sitting in court and likely to disapprove.

'Why did you use it here then?' asked Ben Myers.

'That's how I felt about people who were accusing me,' she explained, citing two of the consultants, Ravi Jayaram and Steve Brearey.

'Why did you think it about them?'

'Because of the things they'd been saying about me,' she answered.

The barrister asked for a different note to be shown – an A4 screed of tightly rammed markings which appeared almost hieroglyphic at first glance. It was hard not to view it as a textual representation of the inside of Lucy Letby's head – an overspill of chaos, confusion and angst which had been transmitted from brain via biro to paper.

'I don't know if I killed them. Maybe I did. Maybe this is all down to me,' said one line.

'Why did you write something like that?' Myers asked.

'Because that's how I was feeling at the time,' she responded.

'How did it make you feel, wondering if you'd killed them?'

'I hated myself.'

'It says "I want to die". Is that how you felt?'

'Yes.'

'Why?'

'I couldn't see that my life would be the same again.'

It was getting towards the end of Lucy Letby's first day in the witness box, and she had spent all of it dealing with questions about her private life and personal feelings. The nurse may have found it invasive, but Ben Myers hoped that it would help the jury to see her in three dimensions, with hairdresser appointments, meals out, flaws and frailties, just like anyone else. He was conscious, though, that before the court finished for the night, he also needed to leave them in no doubt of her innocence. His questioning had been relatively gentle thus far, but now he switched it up a gear and engaged the nurse in a quick-fire quiz round.

'Let me ask you now,' he began. 'Have you ever tried to kill a baby you've cared for?'

'No.'

'Have you ever tried to harm a baby?'

'No, never.'

'Have you ever tried to force air down a nasogastric tube?'

'No.'

'Have you ever overfed a baby?'

'No, never.'

'Have you ever used insulin with the intention of harming a baby?'

'No.'

'Have you ever physically assaulted a baby?'

'No.'[2]

The barrister reached his finale with a bonus question.

'What have you wanted to do for the babies?'

'Care for them, do my best for them. Help them.'

The nurse met every question with an answer. She got into her stride, and sometimes there was a sense that she was falling back on stock phrases which she trotted out on repeat. It made her sound practised rather than someone who was considering each answer afresh.

'Why did you photograph a card you sent to some of the parents?' she was asked.

'It was just a normal pattern of behaviour for me,' she said.

'Why did you text your friends about the babies?'

'It was just a normal pattern of behaviour for me.'

'Why did you search for the parents on Facebook?'

'It was just a normal pattern of behaviour for me.'

In total, Letby spent five days being questioned by Ben Myers, and by the end she looked well and truly wrung out. She wiped away tears as she whimpered, 'I only ever did my best.' Although she might have felt fed up, she may later reflect that the defence questions had been her time in the sun. Watching from the press gallery, it had been an interesting spectacle, but there was a sense that it hadn't done much to clear the mist. When it boiled down to it, a lot of the nurse's answers were either 'can't recall', or 'that didn't happen'. Much still felt unknown, and the real test would come from seeing how Lucy Letby coped under the pressure of cross-examination by the prosecution.

When Ben Myers finished his questions it was very nearly the end of the court day and, given the fatigue that may well have been setting in after such a marathon, the judge might have been forgiven for sending everyone home for the night. But he was also mindful of the length of time that the trial was taking. When it started the previous October, the jurors were asked to be available for six months until April.[3] That point had been and gone, and we were now in the middle of May with no idea of when the case might finish. Members of the jury had started asking about it,[4] and there was chatter on the legal and press benches about things rumbling on towards the summer, and mutterings about holidays looking in jeopardy.

Mr Justice Goss asked Nick Johnson KC if he wanted to make a start with his cross-examination of Lucy Letby, given that it was nearly home time. Yes – said the prosecutor – he absolutely did. He wasn't necessarily motivated by the need to improve courtroom efficiency. When he got to his feet and bore down on the nurse who was still sitting in the witness box, it was clear that he wanted to mark her card before the court packed up for the day and give her something to sweat about in her cell overnight.

Ben Myers had begun his questions with a long slow run-up and an easy ball, asking the nurse about her childhood. Nick Johnson, on the other hand, went straight for the stumps. He'd been keeping track of the few occasions when Letby had become emotional – when she was asked about being moved from her job; when she saw pictures of her house; and when she heard the voice of her 'trusted friend' – the married doctor.

'Is there any reason that you cry when you talk about yourself, but you don't cry when talking about these dead and seriously injured children?' he asked.

'I have cried when talking about some of those babies,' she retorted.

It was a quick hit – Nick Johnson's first effort to highlight the nurse's lack of emotion. Now he came at her with another fast ball, aimed at showing that she was a liar. He asked for a copy of Lucy Letby's police statement to be put in her hands and asked her if there was anything she'd like to change about what she'd said in the witness box so far. She declined the offer. The pre-trial statement, he suggested, was at odds with what she'd since told the jury. Her story, he claimed, had changed over time. He argued, for example, that she'd said one thing to the police about Dr Ravi Jayaram's allegations and another to the court.[5]

'It's very difficult to recall everything that everyone has said during a seven-month trial,' ventured Lucy Letby.

'I suggest to you that you were lying,' said Nick Johnson.

'No, I'm not lying,' she replied.

The judge called time. It had only been a short skirmish, and Nick Johnson hadn't asked any questions directly relating to the babies, but he sat down again, content to have made a start. Lucy Letby now had a long drive back to Wakefield during which she could mull over their exchange. If she'd taken Johnson's calm and measured tone throughout the trial as a sign that he may take it easy on her, she'd made a major miscalculation. He'd shown himself to be quick, calculated and passive-aggressive. The question was whether she would be able to hold her own at that pace without him getting under her skin.

Having slept on it, the nurse appeared back in the witness box the next morning looking as though she meant business. Wearing a black pinstriped suit,[6] she sat bolt upright and waited for Nick Johnson KC to enter the ring for round two. When he got to his feet, it was clear that the barrister was also feeling energised and ready to spar. He started with a bit of courtroom theatre, returning to the theme of the hospital paperwork found at Lucy Letby's house. He reminded the jury that Letby had previously said that student nurses weren't given handover sheets, and also that she hadn't kept such documents on purpose. He presented the nurse with a piece of paper.

'What's unusual about it?' he asked her.

'I don't know what you mean,' she replied. 'It's a standard handover sheet.'

'It hasn't got any folds on it . . . it's in pristine condition!' he told her.

'Is this the original?' Letby enquired.

'It is the original, yes. Found in a keepsake box in your house.'

Mr Johnson pointed out that police had found 99 handover sheets from Lucy Letby's time as a student nurse, and he accused her of lying. What did this have to do with whether she'd attacked babies? Nothing. But the prosecution barrister had a clear strategy which involved establishing Letby as a habitual liar in the minds of the jury – no matter what the context.

'Are you doing your best to tell the truth, the whole truth and nothing but the truth, Lucy Letby?' he asked.

'Yes,' she answered.

The dynamic between the combatants was establishing itself. Whereas Ben Myers had only ever referred to his client as 'Miss Letby', Nick Johnson styled things differently. There was something of the gowned Victorian schoolmaster about him as he told her off – 'Don't deflect the question!' – and peered at her over his spectacles with his arms folded. 'Is that the truth, Lucy Letby?' he'd ask. 'You're lying, Lucy Letby, aren't you?' There was an edge to the way he said her name in full, as though it carried its own accusatory weight.

The barrister was consistently condescending, almost toying with the nurse on occasion. He sneered about a medical document which she'd kept – 'You fished it out of the confidential waste bin . . . It was for your little collection, wasn't it?'

He pushed her on the inconsistencies between her police statement and court evidence – 'Are you making up bits of evidence as you go along?'

He taunted her about how she'd photographed a sympathy card she'd written to some parents – 'Did it give you a bit of a thrill?'

Letby couldn't do much about Johnson's tone but she wasn't prepared to take his accusations lying down. She often came back at him and tried to match his lawyerly brain with her own wits. Though the push and pull between the interrogator and his subject often made for a gripping listen, it wasn't always clear whether it was helping to illuminate the jury's understanding. Occasionally, however, there were moments that moved the narrative on.

It was Nick Johnson who got Letby to open up fully about the doctors when he asked her if she was alleging that they were in league with each other.

'Are you suggesting that there is some sort of agreement between any of the medical staff who've given evidence in this case to get you?' he asked.

'In the consultant group? Yes, I do believe that,' Letby replied.

'Who is in the conspiracy group?' he probed. 'Which individuals?'

'I believe Ravi Jayaram, Stephen Brearey, John Gibbs and another consultant [whose name is withheld].'

'So, the gang of four?' asked Nick Johnson – coining a phrase which would please headline writers.

'Yes,' agreed Lucy Letby, who went on to suggest that the gang had conspired to blame her as part of a cover-up at the hospital.

It was new information, and the nurse seemed to be on a bit of a roll, which might explain why she felt emboldened enough to meet Nick Johnson head on when he turned to his next subject – the matter of the two babies whom she was accused of poisoning.

'Do you agree that Baby F was poisoned with insulin?' he asked her.

The nurse said yes. This wasn't new – she hadn't disputed the fact that either Baby F or Baby L had received insulin.[7]

'Do you agree that somebody gave it to him unlawfully?' asked Nick Johnson.

This had not been put to Lucy Letby before during the trial.

'Yes,' she said. It felt like a significant concession. It meant that the nurse was confirming that there was a criminally minded poisoner on the unit.[8]

The barrister asked her how she thought insulin had got into the babies' feed. She speculated that it might have happened at 'some point' on the unit, or perhaps when the bag was being prepared beforehand at the pharmacy.

'I don't believe that any staff on the unit would make a mistake in giving insulin,' she said.

'No,' agreed Nick Johnson. 'A mistake isn't an option here. It was deliberate poisoning – but not by you?'

'Insulin has been added by somebody, but I can't say by who – just that it wasn't me.'

One wondered how Letby's colleagues would be feeling on hearing her de facto accusation that one of them had been trying to kill babies. It had the hallmarks of an attempted murder mystery. Given that the three nurses who were on duty with Baby F had all testified to say they had not given him insulin, the pool of possible poisoners appeared to be reducing all the time. Later, it was put to Letby that she was one of only two nurses who'd been on shift when Baby F was poisoned and also when Baby L's feed was contaminated eight months later.

Nick Johnson said to her, 'Isn't the reality that unless there's more than one poisoner, it has to be you or [the other nurse] Belinda Simcock?'

Lucy Letby replied, 'I can only answer for myself and say I've never put insulin into any bags.'

The KC clarified things still further. 'It was never suggested that it was her,' he said.

'I can't answer that,' she responded.

Nick Johnson found another thread to pull – Lucy Letby's memory, or lack of it. 'I can't recall' had become a familiar refrain, but there were inconsistencies between accounts that Letby had given at different times, and the lawyer had a sitting opportunity to make hay from her contradictions.

After her arrest, the nurse had told police that she was in the room when Baby C crashed. Now, in court, she said she no longer accepted that she had been there.

'Do you dispute you were in the room at the time of the collapse?' asked the barrister.

'Yes,' replied the nurse, 'because I have no memory of that.'

'Do you remember being born?' he wanted to know.

'No,' she answered.

'Do you dispute being born?'

'No.'

In interview the nurse had also told police that she had no memory of Baby D. Now, in the witness box, she said that she could remember her.

The KC looked at the witness and said, 'When you said that you didn't really remember Baby D that was a lie, wasn't it?'

'No,' she replied. 'I didn't have any great recollection of the events.'

Johnson pointed out that she had had enough of a memory of the family to search repeatedly for the baby's parents on Facebook.

'Have you got a good memory for names?' he enquired.

'Yes,' she affirmed.

'Would you say you have a good memory?'

'Yeah.'[9]

Lucy Letby seemed to be tying herself in knots. It was one thing for her to feel that she could go up against the barrister on medical topics – that was her profession, not his. But it was another to tangle with his legal intellect, and when she tried it, she invariably came off worse. It was an engrossing spectacle, and sometimes it was as though they'd forgotten that anyone else was watching.

Letby was avoiding looking at her questioner, who was standing to her left, and though her head was angled towards the jury she didn't fix on them either, seeming instead to gaze into the distance. Her eyes often darted about, as though she wasn't focusing, and her expression looked pained, with noticeable frown lines on her forehead. She was clutching her hands under the desk and her voice level had dropped too, and with it, her sense of confidence.

Though she'd always had a staccato delivery, her answers were becoming increasingly monosyllabic. The gulf between the formidable barrister and the struggling witness was widening and she was clearly finding the grilling more and more difficult. Then, for the first time during the trial, she looked up at the judge and asked, 'Please can I have a break?'

There had already been a scheduled morning break, but Mr Justice Goss acquiesced, and the court rose early for lunch. As the legal benches emptied out, some of the prosecution lawyers looked cock-a-hoop, as though they sensed that they had Letby on the rack. Nick Johnson was only four babies in, questions-wise. Was she starting to crack, with another thirteen still to go? The dour Crown Prosecution Service solicitor in charge of their case rarely smiled, but the corners of her mouth turned up slightly, which was sign enough. Her team went out into the late spring sunshine feeling optimistic that they were getting somewhere.

After lunch, we filed back into the courtroom expecting things to pick back up where they'd left off. But Lucy Letby wasn't in the witness box where she should have been and there was a low hum as everyone speculated about what was going on. The defendant was back behind glass in the dock. Our minds raced. What did this signify? Was she throwing in the towel as a witness? No, it transpired, she wasn't. Or at least not for good. She had been assessed by her psychological support worker who'd advised that she shouldn't continue for the rest of the day, but she was expected to return at the next session.

When the court next sat the following week, Lucy Letby was back in the witness box. She got through two more days of punishing cross-examination without major issue, until she was asked about Baby I – who'd been described at the start of the trial as 'an extreme example, even by the standards of this case'. Letby was accused of trying to kill the baby girl three times and succeeding on the fourth.

The court had previously heard evidence focusing on the second alleged murder attempt, from the baby's designated nurse Ashleigh Hudson. Nurse Hudson said that she'd asked Nurse Letby to keep an eye on the infant while she went to help a colleague with a routine procedure elsewhere. When she returned, she said, Letby was standing in the doorway at a distance from the baby's cot. The crib was in the dark and covered by a canopy, but Letby remarked to her colleague that the little girl looked pale. Nurse Hudson said the lights had been switched off in the nursery at the time. Lucy Letby had originally agreed that the lights were off but had since changed her account and was now saying that they had been on a low setting. Nick Johnson pointed out that either way, she'd have just gone into the dim room from the brightly lit hallway outside.

'If you go from the light corridor to the dark nursery, does that make your eyesight really good?' asked Nick Johnson.

'I don't understand,' Lucy Letby said.

'Oh . . . I think you do,' goaded the barrister. 'What effect does coming from a very bright corridor into a dark nursery have on your eyesight?'

'I don't know.'

'You really don't know?'

'No.'

'You're a nurse!' he pointed out. 'Everybody knows, don't they? If you go from bright into dark, what capacity does that have on your ability to see in the dark?'

Letby thought about it. 'It would depend on the brightness of the light, but . . . yes . . . you wouldn't be able to see as well.'

Letby had told the police, 'Maybe I spotted something Ashleigh had not been able to spot.'

'You don't have better eyesight than Ashleigh, do you?' enquired Nick Johnson.

'No,' she replied.

'You were putting all this down to your greater experience, is that right?' he asked.

'No.'

'How would you be able to spot the colouring then if Ashleigh couldn't? If you were in the same place?'

'I'd had more experience, so I knew what I was looking for.'

Nick Johnson leapt in. 'Knew what you were looking *for*? What do you mean by that?' he probed.

There was a pause while the penny dropped and Lucy Letby realised her misstep. 'I don't mean it like that,' she said. 'I'm finding it quite hard to concentrate on all of the dates at the minute . . .'

The judge intervened. 'Having observed the witness, it's been a long day for her. I'll stop the proceedings for this afternoon.' It was the second time that things had become too much for Lucy Letby during cross-examination, and the court finished early for the day, again.[10]

It was another interruption to Letby's evidence, and the stop-start upheaval continued into June. The nurse had started in the witness box a month earlier but had only completed ten days of evidence in four weeks. Juror illness, three bank holidays and her own issues had all been factors, and the strain looked like it was telling on her, especially as legal rules meant she was still unable to discuss her evidence with anyone, so was shouldering the experience alone. She couldn't confide in someone, in the way she used to in the married doctor.

The prosecutor had already mined the topic of the nurse's relationship when he read out text messages that Letby had received from a nurse who was teasing her about having a crush on the doctor. It was pure prosecution point-scoring and it had led to the most comically surreal exchange of the trial.[11]

Lucy Letby had told the other nurse that she'd just received a message from the registrar on Facebook. 'Did u? Saying what?' her friend had replied. 'Go commando? 😂' Letby sent four laughing emojis back and texted denials that she'd been flirting with the medic.[12] It was just banter between two girlfriends, and doubtless Lucy Letby never thought anyone else would read the messages. Now, here she was, having to explain them to a packed courtroom, complete with smirking reporters on the press benches who were lapping up such golden material. Nick Johnson seemed to be enjoying himself too. '"Go commando?" What does that mean?' he asked. 'Is it a reference to the Royal Marines?'

'I don't know,' squeaked Letby, who wasn't enjoying herself at all.

Johnson played to the crowd. 'You don't know? You don't understand what that means? You must have understood it as you found it highly amusing. So, what did you understand the message to mean?'

'I don't know. I can't say right now. I don't know,' she said.

The KC wouldn't let it drop. 'Do justice to yourself. What did you understand "Go commando" to mean?'

'I don't know,' she said again, looking increasingly downcast.

Johnson had done his military barracks research and went for the punchline: 'Do you think it's an army reference? With you being from Hereford?'

'I don't know,' was all Letby could bring herself to say.

Nick Johnson pointed out that the two nurses had continued texting each other about flirting. 'Are you still saying you don't know what "going commando" means?' he asked, giving her one last chance.

Letby wasn't going there. 'Yes,' she said.

The judge signalled that it was time for a break. Lucy Letby had never looked so relieved at the prospect of leaving the witness box.

Other than the entertainment value, there were some who wondered what the point of all the mickey-taking had been. It didn't seem to have anything to do with whether the nurse had attacked babies – at least not at first glance. But Nick Johnson was laying his kindling for a fire he'd ignite later.

The next morning, before the jury filed into their seats, Ben Myers KC told the judge that his client hadn't eaten that morning and wasn't feeling well. She'd said she wanted to continue with her evidence, but her browbeaten expression didn't seem to tell the same story.[13] Perhaps she'd anticipated further questions about her relationship, and it wasn't long before Nick Johnson came back to the subject. He was moving on to cross-examine the nurse about the deaths of the two triplet brothers on consecutive days in June 2016.

Letby had just come back from holiday in Ibiza and was on shift on both days – as was the registrar, although he was on duty away from the neonatal unit.

'Did you want to get his attention?' asked the prosecutor.

'No,' she replied.

'Is that the reason you sabotaged [Baby O]?' he suggested.

'No,' she repeated.

The married doctor had been called to help with the resuscitation efforts. 'Was it you that called him?' Nick Johnson asked Lucy Letby.

'From my memory,' she agreed.

'Were you trying to get his attention?' he enquired again.

'Yes. I wanted him to help [the baby].'

'But his personal attention?'

'No. He was the registrar on the unit that day.'

'Did you enjoy being in these crisis situations with [the doctor]?' asked Nick Johnson.

'No,' Lucy Letby replied.

'Did it give you something to talk and message him about?' he speculated.

'No,' she said again. 'He and I were friends.'

Letby agreed that she had a very active social life, and that she and the registrar had gone to London for a day out together when she was no longer working as a nurse. Nick Johnson pulled up texts with heart emojis, which the pair had exchanged after the trip. He asked again if he was her boyfriend and she replied, 'He's a married man. It was not a relationship at all. It was a friendship.' But a few minutes later, she agreed with the barrister, when he put it to her that she 'had a house, a car and a boyfriend' during the period when she was writing *cri de cœur* notes.

The prosecutor suggested that Letby had 'deliberately misled' the jury on a number of occasions during her trial.[14] He had finished asking her about each of the seventeen babies, and he worked his way towards a finale.

'You're a very calculating woman, aren't you? And you tell lies deliberately,' he said.

'No,' she replied.

'And the reason you tell lies is to get sympathy and attention from people . . . And killing these children, you got quite a lot of attention, didn't you?' It was as close as the prosecution would come to suggesting a motive.

'I didn't kill any children,' said Lucy Letby.

'You're getting quite a lot of attention now, aren't you?' observed Nick Johnson.

The nurse didn't answer, although she could hardly have disagreed. The trial was headline news everywhere.

The KC got ready to sign off. 'You are a murderer,' he said simply, looking down at the woman sitting below him.

But Letby was intent on having the last word. 'I have not murdered or harmed any child,' she said.

Lucy Letby's marathon stint in the witness box was over. Over a period of six weeks, she'd spent a total of fourteen days giving evidence.[15] It had been an enormous gamble for her – she knew that if she agreed to speak as a witness in her own defence, she'd have to be cross-examined on it by the prosecution. Perhaps she reasoned that the two sides were likely to need equivalent time and their questions would present similar challenges. In reality, she spent five days answering the defence points and nearly twice as long under fire from the prosecution. She returned to the dock fervently hoping that the risk had been worth taking.

Now the question was whom the defence team were planning to call next. Given that the prosecution had fielded a panoply of medical experts, there was an expectation that the scales would be balanced with opposing clinical erudition. The court rose for a few days to enable Ben Myers and his juniors to speak to the nurse. It was the first time they'd been able to take instructions from their client since she started her evidence, and Team Letby was now able to regroup.

They decided that there was another witness whom they wanted to call, but when the trial resumed, there was no professor of paediatric pathology or consultant neonatologist to be seen. Instead, the man in the witness box had a very different professional background. Lorenzo Mansutti was the hospital plumber. He was the final witness in the trial and was to give evidence in relation to the sanitation of the building.

Under questioning by the prosecution, Lucy Letby had alleged that raw sewage used to come out of the sinks in the intensive care room, and dirty conditions may have contributed to babies dying. Mr Mansutti confirmed that there had been one occasion when human waste had backed up through a sink in that nursery, but work had been done to relocate sewage pipes so that it couldn't happen again. He described it as a 'one-off', although he said he'd be called out on a weekly basis to fix drainage problems across the estate, which was built in the 1960s.

Plumbing evidence over, the defence case was also complete. There were no plans to call any other witnesses and the jurors would have to make their decisions about the nurse's side of the case based predominantly on her word against the weight of the prosecution evidence. To those of us watching, it was a baffling finale. The prosecution had called dozens of witnesses, including several experts, over a period of seven months. Now it was the turn of Letby's team and the best they could was do was the hospital plumber. Not a single defence expert to argue that the prosecution's science was wrong or fell below that all-important threshold of beyond reasonable doubt. No character witnesses to rebut the prosecution's portrayal of Letby as a deceitful killer. What was going on? Was Letby simply going through the motions? Did she and her legal team think they could win without witnesses of their own? Mr Justice Goss told the jurors that was it and instructed them, 'You decide the case on and only on all the evidence placed before you.'

Although there was no more evidence for them to hear, it would be the best part of another month before the jury started deliberating. Having opened and then presented their cases, both sides were entitled to make closing speeches too, after which Mr Justice Goss would sum up the proceedings from a neutral perspective. The court had grown well used to hearing the voices of both Nick Johnson and Ben Myers – but this was oration of a different flavour – sharply scripted, but with something of the soapbox about both performances.

Nick Johnson KC went first, angling himself away from the witness box, where he'd borne down on the defendant, and pivoting towards the twelve jury seats on the other side of the room. He dismissed Letby's allegation of being scapegoated by a 'gang of four' consultants as 'a conspiracy theory', and he raised the case of Baby E, whose mother testified that she'd walked in on the nurse in the aftermath of an attack. 'Have [the parents] made that up to get at Lucy Letby too?' he asked. 'Are they in on it? Are they a sub-gang of two?' He told the court that it was a 'head-on credibility contest' between the mother's 'powerful evidence' and the nurse's denials.

He told the jurors not to ignore the 'constellation of coincidences', and to 'put all the pieces of the jigsaw together' to see that the 'cumulative picture' only told one story.

'All the clues point in one direction, don't they?' he reasoned. 'She's sitting in the back of the court.'

Then Ben Myers KC showed the court the same events through the other end of the binoculars. He alleged that the 'gang of four' doctors had stitched up the young nurse to cover their own failings.

The nurse started to cry again as her lawyer told the jurors that the case against her was 'driven by a relentless presumption of guilt'. He told them to 'apply a presumption of innocence' to the allegations instead, and with 'no direct evidence' that she'd harmed anyone, implored them to find her not guilty.

There was nothing more that either barrister could say to persuade the jury of their point of view. The judge embarked on his own summary of the evidence, which took another five days, at the end of which it was finally time to send the jurors out. Mr Justice Goss looked across his courtroom at the eight women and four men who held the nurse's future in their hands and told them to respect each other's opinions, and feel under no pressure of time. He knew that the task of wading through nine months of multifaceted material to reach a position of certainty was burdensome enough, without making them race through it.

Legal rules preventing jurors from ever revealing their discussions mean that no one will ever know what process the group followed backstage. Their debates, divisions and disagreements will forever remain known only to them. The only question was whether they would manage to reach the common ground required for them to deliver verdicts on every count – unanimously, as the judge had specified at first.

Front of house, we could only wait and kill time by speculating. The clerk locked the doors of courtroom number seven and the place emptied out – the barristers in their wigs and gowns tipping out into the corridor along with everyone else, before melting away to backroom offices and conference rooms. No one expected anything to happen quickly – the seasoned hacks among the press pack compared war stories about long-running trials they'd covered in the past, involving weeks of jury deliberations. This one, they reckoned, could beat the lot. With twenty-two counts to be considered, anything more than a day per count would result in more than a month's worth of waiting.

For the babies' parents it was a new agony, layered on top of all the others they'd endured. After months of information overload, there was nothing but silence – a vacuum which would naturally be filled with overthinking and worry. In another life you could imagine these couples having met through baby swim classes, or at a crèche group. Instead, they'd got to know each other through the tragic inversion of that parental experience, bound by the baby milestones they hadn't shared. They were only thrust together through circumstance but had forged friendships born from unfortunate common understanding. Now they clung together as the hours ticked by, making small talk in a backroom with their police support officers as they tried not to think about what the jury was doing.

On the other side of the parental divide, Sue and John Letby were going through their own torment while their daughter's future was decided. The long, open concrete and glass corridors of the Crown Court building offered little seclusion, and though there was nowhere for them to take refuge, they had no wish to socialise with the reporters who'd set up camp in the hallway outside courtroom seven. The Letbys took themselves off to the furthest part of the public area – an island of two locked in their own unique misery.

There was one other member of the Letby entourage, and it was hard to know what to make of her. Nursery nurse Janet Cox had been friendly enough with Lucy Letby to be tagged in social photos with her on Facebook – smiling for the camera with colleagues in Christmas jumpers, at a hen party, and as guests at the same wedding. She didn't seem to have been a close confidante of Letby's though – she didn't feature in the text messages which the nurse exchanged with her inner circle. Yet Janet Cox attended court nearly every day, for nearly the entirety of the ten-month trial. It seemed that she had retired from the unit and was dedicating all of her time – and some considerable expense – to the cause of supporting her fellow nurse. The enterprise involved an early start every day, a long commute, and countless hours inside the court building – a commitment to Lucy Letby unmatched by anyone else other than her own parents and her lawyers – who were being paid to be there. Although she made it quite plain that she was not interested in talking about her friend the defendant, Janet Cox didn't share the Letbys' aversion to reporters and often sat next to the journalists who were stationed near to the courtroom door, showing an interest in their work and offering her own line in sunny small talk while filling in puzzle books.

The hours ticked by, punctuated only by the bookending of each day, as the jurors were brought into court every morning and sent out home again each night. We tried to read the runes by searching their expressions as they filed in and out, but it was a fool's game. We wondered how they were approaching the task of working through the charges. Had they started at the beginning with Baby A, working through things chronologically – as the trial had done – until they reached Baby Q? Or had they grouped the infants by their alleged causes of death, starting with the poisoning cases, as Nick Johnson had suggested they should in his closing speech, when he described the insulin as 'the best bit of evidence' in the case?[16]

Outside the courthouse, the forest of tripods had respawned, and a cast of reporters, producers and technical staff kept a loose vigil, knowing that texts from their colleagues inside the building could land at any time, signalling the need to get ready for breaking news.

And what of the protagonist in a holding cell downstairs? Other than occasional welfare visits from her lawyers, conducted in a room with bolted-down furniture, and the oversight of the dock officers whose job it was to escort her, she was left to her own devices. As she sat out the hours in a space expressly not designed for comfort, what was going through her mind? How could she bear to think about the jury's progress during those long days of deliberation? How could she not?

Then, at the start of August, it became clear that one of the women on the jury wasn't able to continue. Accepting that she had good personal reasons for having to leave, and that it wasn't possible for her to carry on, the judge discharged her and thanked her for her months of diligence.[17] By this point the panel had been deliberating for more than sixty hours, and he sent them back out to keep going as a group of eleven.

The jurors were still expected to be working through each count with the aim of returning unanimous verdicts on the whole lot. We reasoned that it was possible they had agreed on some charges but were stuck on others. The question was, where were they stuck – and by what margin? Were they completely gridlocked? Whatever was going on inside the jury room, it looked as though it was going to need some judicial intervention to force the cork out of the bottle.

Mr Justice Goss had read the situation. The jury had been going for seventy-six hours, and it was time to call them in and ask if they'd reached any unanimous verdicts before telling them that they could also now make decisions by a majority of 10-1. He imposed a court order preventing the media from reporting this new development. Any verdicts would have to stay under wraps until the end of the whole trial.

The court reconvened – Lucy Letby was back inside the glass dock, with her parents shaking in their seats on the other side of the room. The babies' parents held hands, praying silently for an outcome that would give them some comfort. The defendant was asked to stand.

'Have you reached any verdict on any count, upon which you are all agreed?' the clerk asked the jury foreman.

'Yes,' came the answer.

A new tension gripped the room.

The foreman gave the details. There were only two unanimous verdicts so far, and they related to the two babies alleged to have been poisoned with insulin.

The clerk cleared his throat. 'On count number six, the attempted murder of Baby F in August 2015. How do you find the defendant? Guilty, or not guilty?'

There was an almost unbearable pause.

'Guilty.'

Gasps from the families. Loud sobs from Lucy Letby. Inconsolable crying from her mother.

'On count number fifteen, the attempted murder of Baby L in April 2016. How do you find the defendant? Guilty, or not guilty?'

'Guilty.'[18]

More emotion. A rush of feelings, and a moment of clarity. Only two of the twenty-two charges had been decided, but it was an answer to the most basic question of all – Lucy Letby had intended to kill babies. In the eyes of the law and the criminal justice system, this was now a fact.

The nurse looked as though she had been hit by a bus. On hearing that verdicts were imminent, she must have known that one of only two potential outcomes would follow – it was a binary choice between guilty and not guilty. Yet, when the word 'guilty' left the foreman's lips, hanging in the courtroom air as it was absorbed by those assembled, it didn't seem to have occurred to her as a possibility. For a fraction of a second, she looked utterly stunned, before the tears came. Any hope the nurse had harboured of one day being able to leave the court by the front door had just disappeared. She was led out of the rear of the dock and taken back down to the cells, a convict now – not just a suspect.

The impact on the rest of the room was also palpable. The babies' families were in quiet turmoil. There had been partial answers for two sets of parents, but they and every other family still had charges that were under consideration. However, the verdicts meant that the jury had cleared the highest hurdle – the fundamental

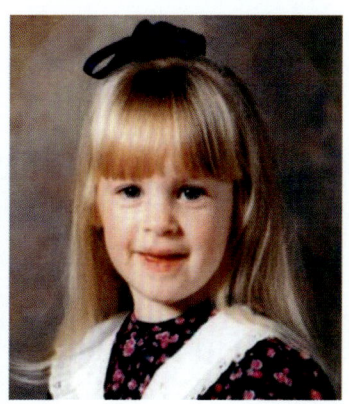

The young Lucy Letby. This photograph also appeared in the *Hereford Times* on 30 December 2010 in advance of her twenty-first birthday on 4 January 2011.

Lucy Letby, age 11, Aylestone School photograph, 2001.

Seventeen-year-old Lucy Letby, still attached to her childhood teddy, and surrounded by her close-knit group of friends.

'Inside the safety of our group, she sort of lets her hair down a bit more and is goofy and makes us all laugh,' according to Letby's childhood friend Dawn.

Carefree days growing up in Hereford.

The Hereford gang having fun with Letby centre stage.

Graduation photo placed in the *Hereford Times* in December 2011 by Lucy's parents, John and Sue. 'We are so proud of you after all your hard work. Love Mum and Dad.'

Lucy Letby's childhood home in the cathedral city of Hereford. Pictures of Letby adorned the walls.

A picture of normality. Letby smiling on a night out.

As a student nurse at the University of Chester. Her chosen course was Child Nursing.

A young Lucy Letby having fun with no hint of a hidden dark side.

With work colleagues on a hen weekend, June 2015. Letby was later convicted of murdering three babies and attempting to murder a fourth in this same month.

Letby on a day out with friends.

At a wedding, with friends including Janet Cox (*far right*), an older friend who later attended court nearly every day in support of her fellow nurse.

the standard

Staff Profile – Lucy Letby

How long have you worked here?
"I qualified as a Children's Nurse from The University of Chester in 2011 and have been working on the unit since graduating. I also worked on the unit as a student nurse during my three years of training."

What would a typical day in the neonatal unit involve?
"My role involves caring for a wide range of babies requiring various levels of support. Some are here for a few days, others for many months and I enjoy seeing them progress and supporting their families. I am currently undergoing extra training in order to develop and enhance my knowledge and skills within the Intensive Care area and have recently completed a placement at Liverpool Women's Hospital."

What will having a bigger neonatal unit mean to you?
"I hope the new unit will provide a greater degree of privacy and space for parents and siblings."

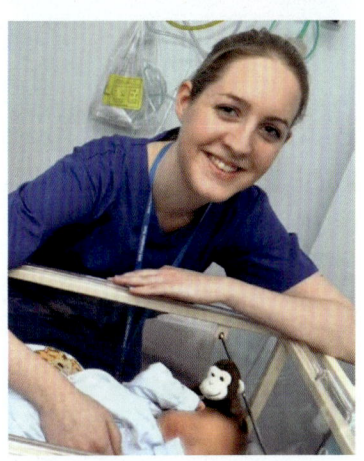

At work (*right*). This photograph appeared in the Countess of Chester Hospital annual report in 2012.

Lucy Letby staff profile in the *Chester Standard*, March 2013.

Publicity photograph for a hospital fundraising campaign, August 2015. This is the month that Lucy Letby was convicted of having attacked Babies E and F. She is pictured standing next to consultant Dr John Gibbs.

Lucy Letby being arrested for the first time at her home in Chester on 3 July 2018.

Police mugshot.

Lucy Letby being interviewed by detectives.

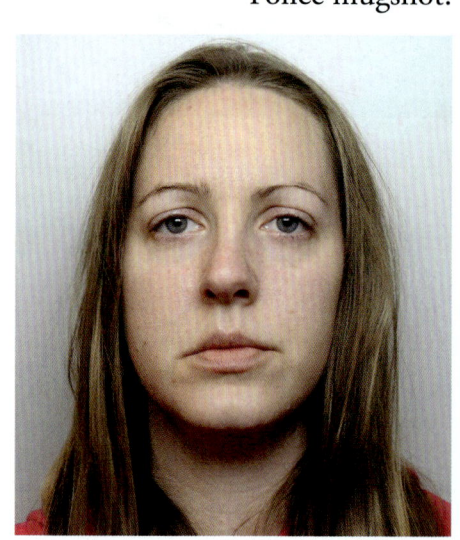

Lucy Letby's house during police search.

Her bedroom, as photographed by police.

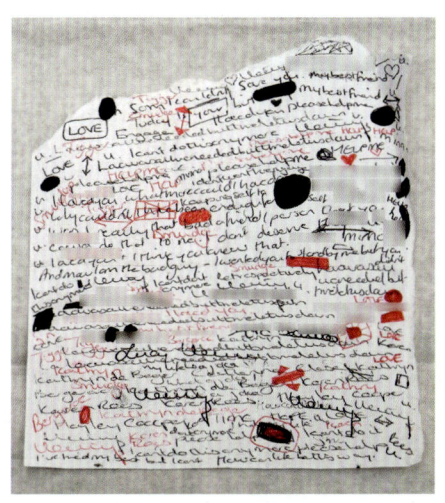

Letby's 2016 diary and her private handwritten notes were found and seized by police after her arrest.

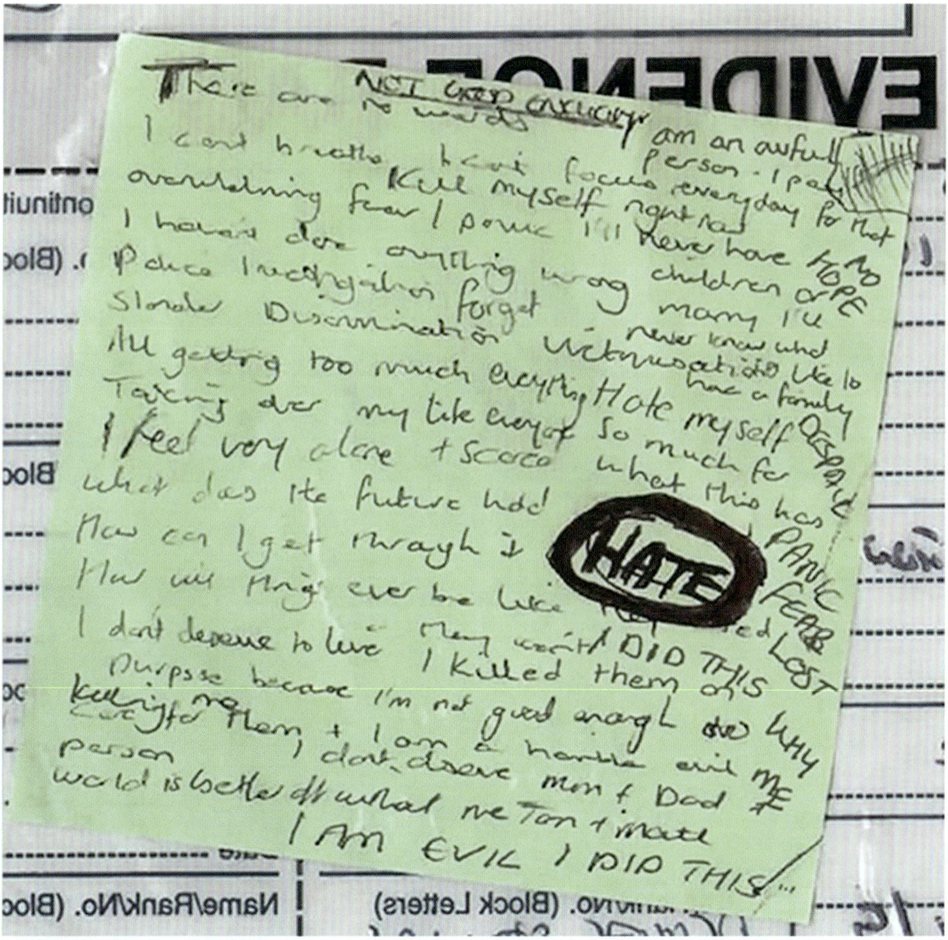

This green Post-it note was found inside Letby's diary.

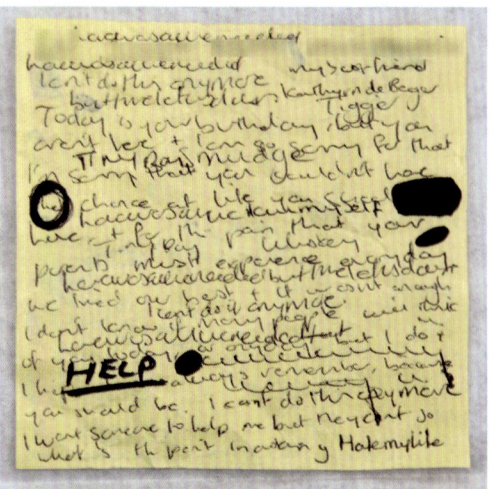
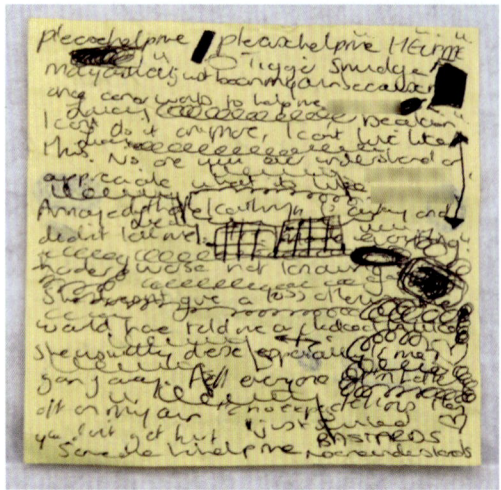

Do Letby's private handwritten notes contain any answers or were they just an outpouring of anguish?

Manchester Crown Court, where the trial of Lucy Letby began on 10 October 2022.

John and Sue Letby arriving at Manchester Crown Court on 21 October 2022.

Dr Stephen Brearey, lead neonatal paediatrician, Countess of Chester Hospital.

Dr Ravi Jayaram, lead paediatrician, Countess of Chester Hospital.

Dr Mike Hall, retired consultant neonatologist and defence expert. He was not called to give evidence in court.

Dr Dewi Evans, prosecution expert paediatrician.

Tony Chambers, former chief executive, Countess of Chester Hospital.

Ian Harvey, former medical director, Countess of Chester Hospital.

Karen Rees, lead nurse for urgent care, Countess of Chester Hospital.

Court artist portrays Lucy Letby crying as she is being questioned by her barrister Ben Myers KC during the first trial, May 2023.

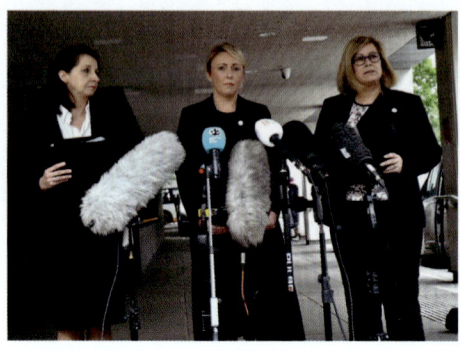

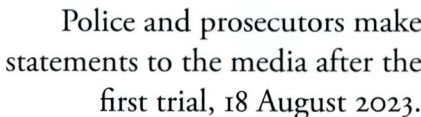

Police and prosecutors make statements to the media after the first trial, 18 August 2023.

Lucy Letby is driven away from court, 21 August 2023. She was found guilty of seven counts of murder and six counts of attempted murder.

'Justice for Lucy Letby' protesters outside the Court of Appeal, London, April 2024.

Camera crews and reporters gather outside Manchester Crown Court on the day of Letby's retrial verdict, 2 July 2024.

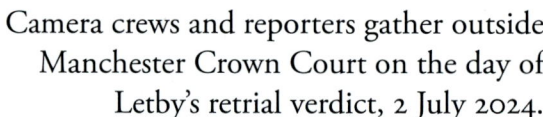

Court artist's sketch of the moment Letby says 'I'm innocent', as she is taken to the cells after being convicted of the attempted murder of Baby K, 5 July 2024.

question of whether Lucy Letby had a murderous mindset at all. Now that they'd decided she did, it didn't feel like as much of a leap to consider whether she'd also harmed the other babies. That said, the families knew that the evidence varied from child to child, and while the jury had made unanimous decisions on the attempted-murder insulin charges, it was possible that they were finding the science around air embolism much harder to deal with.

Court number seven emptied out again and the corridor-dwellers resumed their positions, watching the clock tick towards home time each day, with half an ear permanently on the tannoy system. There were occasional breaks in the tedium when drama overspilled from other courtrooms. An angry defendant loudly berated his barrister after being denied permission to have an ankle tag removed. A woman pushing a buggy with a toddler in tow became upset when told she couldn't take her children into court. A man in need of mental health support paced the hallway demanding to see the King. Court security came down to explain that, although Rex was on all the case listings, he wasn't physically in the building. Janet Cox kept up the small talk, but Mr and Mrs Letby were clearly struggling and occasionally rebuked reporters whom they objected to.

The two guilty verdicts may have felt seismic, but the world at large was none the wiser. The result was known to everyone in court, as well as to all those watching on remote video links at one of three annexes in Manchester and Chester. Yet the reporting restriction meant that it had to stay under wraps – out of the papers, off-air and offline too.

Now that the jurors were allowed to operate on a majority basis, there was a school of thought that the dial might move fairly quickly, but it was another three days before the tannoy sounded – 'Would all parties in the case in courtroom seven please return to courtroom seven!'

Lucy Letby was already in the dock when we started filing into our seats. Her parents had raced in too. Now they watched her, and she returned their gaze, mouthing 'I'm OK' to her mum,[19] who was just about holding it together. The room was crammed again, and the jurors re-entered to be asked whether they had reached verdicts on any more counts.

'Lucy Letby, please stand!' came the instruction. The nurse got to her feet and braced herself. The list of charges was read out once more, and each time the jury foreman had a verdict, it seemed to hit her between the eyes, and she lowered her head as the tears poured forth.

The murder of Baby C? 'Guilty!'
The murder of Baby I? 'Guilty!'
The attempted murder of Baby M? 'Guilty!'
The attempted murder of Baby N? 'Guilty!'
The murder of Baby O? 'Guilty!'
The murder of Baby P? 'Guilty!'[20]

Across the courtroom, it was too much for the nurse's parents. John Letby sat with his head bowed, in that moment unable to look at his daughter. Sue Letby howled uncontrollably, 'You cannot be serious! This cannot be right!' Her only child – her pride and joy – whose graduation photo she'd once sent to be printed in the local paper, was now confirmed as a serial baby murderer.

The sighs and gasps from the babies' families marked their very different emotional state. Those whose cases had been decided were reeling at the impact of hearing it made official, while those who were still waiting for answers had to cope with the open-ended painful limbo of it all. No one was jubilant at hearing the guilty verdicts. Everyone was struggling with the enormity of what it meant.

The jurors were sent back out to continue their deliberations, and Lucy Letby was taken back down to the cells. We weren't to know that it was almost the last sight of her that we'd get.

Standing back from the verdicts for a moment, it was possible to work out something of how the jurors had been handling their task so far. It was clear that they were working through things methodically and that they had made progress on the issue of whether babies had been injected with air. They had now convicted Letby of offences across the whole time period in question – from June 2015 to the same month a year later. They had been persuaded that she'd murdered both of the triplet brothers in June 2016, but hadn't yet decided the case of the twin boy E, whose mother was said to have walked in mid-attack (though they had found the nurse guilty of poisoning his brother Baby F). They had only been unanimous on three out of 22 counts – the two insulin cases and the murder of one of the triplets – and had returned the rest by a majority of 10-1. And they still had a lot of work to do – they were yet to make decisions on fourteen of the twenty-two charges on the indictment.

There was a sense that, having managed to reach some verdicts by majority, the split within the jury room wasn't as chasmic as some had feared. Previously, there had been mutterings between the reporters about what would happen if the case ended with an immovably hung jury. It would be likely to result in a rerun of the whole thing, which wasn't a prospect anybody relished. As it was, a retrial on the remaining fourteen counts wasn't out of the question if the jury made no further progress.

The following week, the court was asked to reassemble once more. The barristers put their wigs back on. The families filed back into their seats. The reporters fired up their laptops. John and Sue Letby sat with Janet Cox in the area that had been reserved for the nurse's supporters. But Lucy Letby was nowhere to be seen. The long glass dock was devoid of its defendant, and a lone dock officer sat there with no one to guard. The prisoner had been brought to court but had refused to budge from her cell downstairs, and the hearing went ahead without her. It meant that she wasn't there to hear that the jury had found her guilty of murdering another three babies and attempting to murder two more. She didn't know that she'd now been found guilty of all the murders on the charge sheet, or that they'd cleared her of one charge of attempted murder. She couldn't see the babies' families weeping, and she didn't observe her own parents in tears either. She wasn't in the room when she officially became Britain's most prolific baby killer of the modern era. She had insisted on staying downstairs in the holding cells of the court building, while above her head the room reeled once more.[21]

When the court reassembled the following day, so that the jury could return another verdict (one charge of attempted murder relating to Baby H – not guilty) the nurse was absent again.[22] It transpired that her previous failure to show up was not going to be a one-off. Ben Myers KC told the judge that his client wasn't planning to attend at all for the rest of the proceedings, which meant she had no intention of being there for the eventual sentencing hearing either.[23]

Up on his judicial bench, cloaked in ermine and red, Mr Justice Goss had run the trial with firm efficiency, but his power had its limits. He couldn't disguise his displeasure, but he pointed out that his remit did not extend to being able to compel the defendant to appear before him. However, when he passed sentence, he said he'd be sure to address his remarks to the nurse as though she was present, and she'd be given his comments to read at her leisure.

John and Sue Letby had taken their cue from their daughter, as had her committed friend Janet Cox, who'd barely missed a day of the action. None of the three was anywhere to be seen. If Lucy wasn't going to come into the room, they reasoned, then neither were they, and they walked away from the courthouse never to return. Mr and Mrs Letby were now facing the rest of their days badged as the parents of Britain's worst baby killer – a different, but parallel, life sentence to the one their child was about to receive. They decided to make a quick break for it before the end of the trial, to avoid the cameras which would inevitably follow them up the road otherwise.

The Lucy Letby trial was now one of the UK's longest murder trials. Friday, 18 August marked the end of its forty-first week. The panel had been debating, discussing and deliberating for 110 hours and twenty-six minutes when they ran out of steam and sent a private note to the judge, who was in his chambers behind the courtroom. Eagle-eyed corridor dwellers might have spotted the first clue when Nick Johnson and Ben Myers suddenly disappeared together – quietly spirited away for a few minutes by the judge's clerk. If news was about to come that the jury couldn't progress any further, both sides would be asked whether they agreed it was time to call it quits. Nothing had been said on the courtroom floor yet, but silently, discreetly, the backstage wheels were turning towards the end of the trial.

The court assembled again. Every seat full, other than the ones reserved for Lucy Letby and her parents. There were two dock officers behind the glass, once more flanking an empty chair.

The seven women and four men of the jury were brought into the room, and with six undecided counts of attempted murder left, they were asked if they'd reached any more verdicts. No, said the foreman, they had not. The judge looked at them kindly, as if to acknowledge the hours of effort they'd already put in. He asked them to leave the room for a few moments and discuss among themselves whether any more time would help. The packed courtroom held its breath collectively, waiting in total silence while the eleven jurors held their private summit in an anteroom. Less than five minutes later, the bailiff brought them back. The answer was no – they'd got as far as they could – more time, it seemed, would only send them round in circles again. Wherever the split was within the jury room over the remaining charges, it would require a bridge too far. It was time to stop.

A door banged at the back of the public gallery. One of the babies' fathers stormed out of the room, on hearing that his child's case had been left undecided. Five sets of parents were in the position of having sat through the ten-month trial, without the finality of receiving all their relevant verdicts.[24] Other parents, who did have their answers, were emotional at the completion of the proceedings. They weren't the only ones. Over on the other side of the courtroom, having listened stoically to harrowing evidence for months on end, some of the jurors were crying too. The judge spoke to them gently. 'This has been a most distressing and upsetting case,' he told them, as he discharged them from duty and granted them lifetime exemption from ever sitting on a jury again. Mr Justice Goss thanked the jurors for their 'obvious care, diligence and sense of responsibility' and told them that support would be made available for them if they wanted it.

It was a Friday, ten days since the first verdicts had been returned, and miraculously, despite the drip-drip of results over five separate hearings, the secret had been kept, and the public at large had no idea. Now the judge removed the order which had prevented the media from revealing the story of what had been going on in courtroom number seven in recent days. Within seconds of the veil being lifted, the internet lit up, TV channels went live, and radio broadcasts started rolling. The cork was well and truly out of the bottle, and Manchester Crown Court became the centre of the news universe for the rest of the day. The concrete steps of the courthouse hosted press conferences and statements, and the coverage continued overnight and throughout the weekend as the extent of the story beyond the trial became clear, and the world learned the scale of the scandal. It was a big moment for those of us who had been so close to the proceedings too. The freneticism of covering the verdicts didn't allow for much reflection at the time, but in the days afterwards it started to sink in. It was the poignancy of the moment which registered much more than the news sensation. We'd both followed the trial from the beginning. Judith had been on the story since the very first rumblings of unease at the Countess of Chester Hospital back in 2017. Now, six years later, a young nurse had been convicted. The sense of catharsis among families and witnesses was palpable, but the awareness of the profound tragedy of this story was what really lingered.

Three days later, on Monday morning, the camera crews were back again at the crack of dawn and the high-security van which had carried Lucy Letby from Wakefield to Manchester every day wended its way over the hills for the last time. She may have told her lawyers that she wasn't going to enter the dock, but the prison service still had to produce her for the hearing, and so the roller shutter cranked up once more, and the snappers' scrum held cameras aloft again, flashes firing at the windows as the van drove in.

Inside the building there was some new activity in courtroom seven. Mr Justice Goss had agreed to allow his sentencing to be filmed, and the technical equipment was brought up so that his comments could be broadcast when the time came. One of Lucy Letby's lawyers asked Judith whether the judge's address would be widely available on all TV channels, and online. One wondered whether the nurse had sent word to ask. She may not have been planning to attend the hearing in person, but she'd always have the option of watching it on catch-up in her prison cell.

She wouldn't, however, be able to view the first part of the hearing, as only the judge's remarks were to be filmed. Before he passed sentence, he would hear first from both legal teams, and crucially, from the families of the babies she'd been convicted of attacking.[25] Every parent had been offered the opportunity to tell the court about the impact that Lucy Letby's crimes had had on them, and it promised to be an emotionally charged, and vital, experience.

There'd been evidence from them during the trial of course, but that was of a different order – mostly pared back, factual and designed to assist the jury. Now the floor was theirs, and they spoke from the heart. Most of the parents had written 'victim impact' statements. Some couldn't face the ordeal of reading them out loud, and they listened while a barrister voiced theirs for them. Others felt compelled to speak for themselves – either physically in court, or on pre-recorded video. Not one of them can have found it easy to summon the words. Each statement was heard in total silence, save for an underscored accompaniment of low sobbing, which came from all around the room.

Lawyers struggled to hang on to their professional composure and dabbed damp eyes. Jurors, who didn't have to be there now their function was over, were tearful as the families' full stories came tumbling out. Eight of the eleven jury members had returned voluntarily to see the sentencing, sharing the need many others also felt that day to see the whole process through. Listening to the parents' statements it was clear that 'closure' was not a concept that could ever possibly apply, but the end of the trial felt like a punctuation point, and maybe there was some catharsis in that.

No relief came from being able to direct anger and contempt at Letby though.

Her chair sat empty – she was not listening. As a new reality – a new truth – took root in the public mind, Lucy Letby remained below deck, out of sight.

That, in itself, had given some of the parents pause for thought. The mother of Baby C revealed that she'd wrestled with whether or not to speak. She said, 'I have thought very hard about whether to tell the court about the impact Lucy Letby has had on our family . . . about whether to let Lucy Letby know the extent of our pain.' It wasn't clear if Letby's no-show made it any easier or not.

The decision to speak may have been hard, but once the parents started, the emotional floodgates opened. They spoke of longed-for babies, rounds of IVF, difficult pregnancies and prematurity. They were families who'd already been through the mill before Letby came on to the scene, and they said she was aware of that, and preyed on it. Baby G was born seventeen weeks early after a miscarriage scare. Her father said, 'I would pray to God to save her, and He did. But then the devil found her.'

These were families whose babies' lives were lost or damaged before they'd barely begun. The parents of twins A and B said, 'We never got to hold our little boy while he was alive as you took him away.'

The triplets' mother revealed that she only has one photograph of her holding all three babies and it was taken after two of them had died. She now panics when people ask how many children she has – unable to bring herself to say she gave birth to three, but two were murdered. As he grows, the surviving triplet is starting to ask about his brothers. How to explain all this to him?

The mental health toll was clear to see. They spoke of breakdowns, anxiety, depression and flashbacks. Baby I's mother wore sunglasses for a year after her daughter died 'to hide the pain and tears from my kids'. Some parents needed medicating or turned to alcohol to cope. Two had considered suicide.

The mother of Baby D, who died in June 2015, clutched her baby girl's toy rabbit as she opened up her heart to a room full of people she barely knew, and said starkly, 'I have lost my confidence as a mother, as a woman, as a friend, as a wife.' She described going home with her husband after their daughter had died:

Just the two of us instead of a family of three . . . Our family cleared all traces of baby stuff around the house, removed the baby seat from the car, and her bedroom door remained closed for many months. The funeral service took place the day before her due date . . .

Since [she] passed away I lived beside my own shadow. I have had multiple therapies, panic attacks and dark thoughts. I had a car accident and crashed into a wall. After a nervous breakdown I took time off work. At times it felt like I was losing my mind, my sanity, my worth, myself. I considered ending it all . . . I was hoping so hard that maybe if I went to the other side, I would see my daughter and be with her. Whether this is true or not, I now find comfort thinking that my prayers brought me the strength and courage to stay.

The benches were full of professionals who'd spent years working in the courts – prosecuting, defending, and reporting on serious crime. It's natural for people working in the courts to become a bit numb to it all – but not in this moment. Listening to the raw honesty of this mother's testimony was a different matter. Reporters forgot their typing, and lawyers looked away from their laptops as they sent silent waves of sympathy towards the woman in the witness box.

The triplets' father said, 'I turned to alcohol . . . I was on the edge. One day I took the car keys and had thoughts of ending my life.' He explained that he'd pulled himself back from the brink and then in 2018 the police called to say Lucy Letby had been arrested.

The arrest forced all the parents to rerun every past interaction with Letby through their minds. The triplets' mother said, 'I hate the fact that Lucy Letby was the last person to hold [Baby P]. She has destroyed our lives.' The mother of twin boys E and F said that when Letby was arrested, 'Our world was shattered once again. We felt cheated and deceived and utterly heartbroken once more. The impact on our family was catastrophic.'

Baby C's mother cried in the witness box, explaining that after her son died,

> his hand and footprints were turned into a pendant which I wore around my neck. It made me feel close to him . . . When Lucy Letby was arrested, those few tangible memories I had of my son felt tainted. She took those hand and footprints. I felt so conflicted as to what that meant, I stopped wearing them. I needed to understand what part Lucy Letby had played in the death of my defenceless baby boy . . .
>
> Now we know as much about [my son's] death as I believe we ever will, I feel able to wear his hand and footprints for the first time in five years. I know now that they represent the love I have for my son, and I will not allow evil to taint that. They represent justice and the truth.

The families found the court process a different kind of struggle. The mother of twins E and F said, 'The trial felt like a platform for Lucy to relive her crimes, and it feels cruel that we had to endure it for ten months when she knew all along that she intentionally killed and harmed my babies.' The last time the parents had seen the nurse in the flesh was on the hospital ward. Coming face to face with her again in court floored many of them – some removed themselves from her line of sight.

The families explained that Letby's crimes aren't a matter of past history. They have left a legacy of lasting damage. Their babies have grown into children who are living with terrible consequences. Many of the parents have become over-protective and unable to trust anyone with their children.

Baby F, who survived the insulin attack but lost his twin brother Baby E, now has profound needs. His mum told the court, 'We attend regular hospital visits for his complex and severe disabilities – I never allow him to be alone with medical professionals. It breaks my heart to know that things could have been so different for him. He is without his best friend – his other half. We have essentially grieved for both of our boys and the future we had planned.'

Baby G now needs substantial care. She is registered blind, is nil by mouth, and has cerebral palsy and progressive spinal curvature. She needs surgery but there's concern that she may not survive it. Her parents said, 'She's getting bigger and it's getting harder to carry her. What if she outlives us? Who will care for her then? We see other families and their children fishing . . . playing football . . . other things we can't do. She'll never have a sleepover, go to high school, have a boyfriend, have her first kiss or get married.'

Baby N was the boy with haemophilia whom Letby was convicted of trying to kill in June 2016. His mother said:

He's just turned seven years old. We still have a camera watching him sleep.

I am the only one trained to provide him with his medication. We believe he's had lasting damage as a result of his injuries. He can be sick when he's eating, coughing or running around which can be caused by trauma to the throat.

We do everything possible to keep him safe now. If that means wrapping him up in cotton wool, then that's what we'll do. We know we smother him with love and affection. We don't give him boundaries because we don't want him to be sad and upset. We wanted him to be home-schooled as we don't want anybody else looking after him.

The mother of Baby D told the court that she'd gone on to have another child – a little boy – after her daughter had been murdered. She said, 'One day he asked me who held the keys to the prison. Was there any chance that the person who hurt [his sister] could get out and hurt him? I had to reassure him that there was no chance of that happening. We wanted justice for our daughter, and that day has come.'

Every parent told a story of the destruction which Lucy Letby had wrought on their lives. The full ripple effect was impossible to quantify, but they'd captured its essence, in heart-rending detail which left many in the room spinning. Each family listened quietly to the trauma that the other families had endured. They had gained strength from each other during the long weeks of the trial, but must have struggled with the collective experience too. Hearing so many distressing accounts, one after another, had the effect of amplifying the testimony. No one could be in any doubt as to the scale of the suffering they'd gone through.

In his chair high up above the well of the court, Mr Justice Goss had absorbed all the detail which was so starkly laid out over the course of nearly two hours. It had been directed at the nurse, but it was also meant for his ears, to inform his sentencing decisions.

The judge took a breath and looked at the courtroom before him. The atmosphere hung heavy as many were struggling to compute the enormity of what they'd been listening to. He suggested a break and adjourned the court for a badly needed half hour of fresh air. When the hearing resumed, he'd be ready to make his own address, and this time it would be televised so the world at large could see what was happening inside courtroom number seven.

Directing his comments towards the seat which Lucy Letby would have occupied, had she been prepared to listen to him, Mr Justice Goss told her:

> You acted in a way that was completely contrary to the normal human instincts of nurturing and caring for babies and in gross breach of the trust that all citizens place in those who work in the medical and caring professions.
>
> You have caused deep psychological trauma, brought enduring grief and feelings of guilt, caused strains in relationships and disruption to the lives of all the families of all your victims.
>
> There was a deep malevolence bordering on sadism in your actions. During the course of this trial, you have coldly denied any responsibility for your wrongdoing and sought to attribute some fault to others. You have shown no remorse. There are no mitigating factors.

Lucy Letby, on each of the seven offences of murder and the seven offences of attempted murder I sentence you to imprisonment for life. Because the seriousness of your offences is exceptionally high, I direct that the early release provisions do not apply. The order of the court, therefore, is a whole life order on each and every offence and you will spend the rest of your life in prison.[26]

There was no instruction to the dock officers to take Lucy Letby down to the cells, because she was already there. Above ground, Letby's guilt had become accepted fact – but from her cell below the court, Letby maintained quiet resistance. She maintained her innocence, refusing to take part in what she clearly saw as the ritual of condemnation playing out in the world above her. All the guards could do was to put her back in the secure van again and return her to prison, leaving a trail of grief, distress and fury in her wake.

Who knows if she ever did watch the judge's comments on video catch-up, or whether she has read his sentencing remarks. What are the chances of her having looked at the parents' statements, which we know she was provided with? She would certainly have plenty of time to do so. The legal reality of her guilt and the inevitable sentence that followed mean that the little girl from Hereford who liked sleepovers and teddy bears was now condemned to die in prison. What did she think that night as the door clanged shut on her cell? Did she comprehend what life imprisonment meant? Deep down, did she accept that justice had been done? Or was Lucy Letby's truth different from the terrible truth established by the system that had convicted her?

Chapter 8

Following the Science

Friday, 18 August 2023 was a day for the tabloids. 'EVIL IN CUFFS . . . monster nurse' read the headline in the *Sun*.[1] 'Evil baby killer,' blared the *Standard*.[2] 'Lucy Letby joins the list of Britain's worst female murderers,' blasted the *Express*.[3] Opinion writers mused on the incomprehensibility of Letby's depravity. 'Lucy Letby's cruelty is unfathomable,' said one writer in the *Telegraph*.[4] For once, the *Guardian* agreed: 'Faced with evil like Lucy Letby's, we yearn for a rational explanation. Sometimes there is none.'[5]

Following her conviction, Lucy Letby became a mascot for evil. To the world, she was little more than a grim police mugshot and the author of unspeakable crimes. Criminologists and their students added Lucy Letby to their seminars and research projects. Journalists and true crime buffs now talked about her in the same breath as Fred and Rosemary West, Charles Cullen and Harold Shipman. Even Letby's old friend Dawn concedes that someone guilty of the crimes for which Letby was convicted would be a terrible person whom the public would understandably hate. The widespread acceptance that Lucy Letby was indeed a monster reflected more than a ghoulish tabloid press and the public's revulsion for baby killers. It revealed an acceptance that after a ten-month trial, the truth about Lucy Letby had been settled. She was guilty of the crimes of which she was accused. It was now an agreed fact: Lucy Letby is Britain's worst child serial killer in modern times.

But not everyone has accepted Lucy Letby's conviction or the process that led to it. Although Letby's parents have shunned the media, it is plain to anyone who observed them during the trial that they continue to believe in their daughter's innocence. Her mother's outburst when the first verdicts came through left little doubt. Several months later, Jonathan spoke to Letby's parents on their doorstep in Hereford. They looked frail, grief-stricken and powerless. Even now, with their daughter languishing in prison, they still didn't want to talk. But there was no mistaking their feelings. Their precious Lucy was innocent – a victim of an unjust system.

Letby's old pal Dawn remains steadfast too. Before the verdicts, she told us that if her friend was convicted, it would be a miscarriage of justice. Dawn says she speaks for the rest of Letby's small gang of friends in Hereford.

Even on the neonatal ward where she worked, not everyone has accepted that Letby is a killer. We know of four or five nurses from her old unit who believe she's been wrongly convicted. Others remain unsure. 'I still don't know,' one of Letby's former nursing colleagues told us. 'I still sit on the fence and even at home with my husband, he's like, "What do you think?" And I'm like, "I don't know. I really don't know. I can't 100 per cent, hands on heart, say that she's guilty and I can't say that she's innocent either."'

Such unease isn't confined to people who knew Letby personally. In September 2023, the *Mail on Sunday* columnist Peter Hitchens wrote a piece under the headline: 'I wish someone else would ask this: What if Lucy Letby is not guilty?'[6] '[O]ur justice system is not as good as we like to think,' he wrote. '[Letby's] friends say she is not guilty. Listen to them. They may just be right. [I]f, ten years hence, she stands under the TV lights in front of a courthouse, unrecognisable after years in prison, but free at last, I would rather be among those who had kept such an open mind, than among those who did not.'

Hitchens was drawing on more than a general mistrust of the criminal justice system. Even before Letby's trial was over, an online community had formed voicing concerns about the case against her. Like all such communities, this one has its fair share of know-it-alls and trolls. But some professed to speak for science, data and statistics. Some statisticians, for example, criticised the prosecution's reliance on circumstantial evidence that showed that Lucy Letby was always present when babies collapsed or died.

An understanding of statistics, they argued, shows that such correlations may have perfectly innocent explanations. The fact that Letby appeared to be always on duty when things went wrong says nothing about her guilt or innocence.

There were challenges to the medical science in the case too. In California, a biotech consultant called Sarrita Adams led the early charge through a website devoted to challenging bad science in court cases.[7] The website, fittingly called Science on Trial, features detailed scientific propositions purporting to challenge every major scientific argument in the prosecution case, most notably the evidence on insulin evidence and air embolism.[8]

Initially, most of these challenges were confined to niche corners of the internet. Peter Hitchens seemed to be the only mainstream journalist to question Letby's guilt. But in May 2024, that changed when an American journalist called Rachel Aviv penned a lengthy article for *The New Yorker*: 'A British Nurse Was Found Guilty of Killing Seven Babies. Did She Do It?' Aviv's piece had clearly taken months of detailed research. 'I drew from more than seven thousand pages of court transcripts, which included police interviews and text messages, and from internal hospital records that were leaked to me,' she said. The result was a 13,000-word dissection of the prosecution's evidence, questioning whether Letby was really guilt.[9]

At the time of its publication, Aviv's article looked like an outlier – a contrary take from a journalist on the other side of the Atlantic. But we'd heard of other similarly questioning articles being prepared by respected UK journalists as well. The only reason they hadn't been published was that Letby was facing further proceedings – a retrial of one of the cases on which the original jury had failed to reach a verdict. UK reporting rules allow journalists to report what happens in court but not much more until court proceedings are finished, so British journalists were muted. But in July 2024, those reporting restrictions were finally lifted and a slew of detailed sceptical articles by UK journalists made headlines. On 9 July 2024, the *Guardian* published an investigative piece by Felicity Lawrence entitled 'Lucy Letby: killer or coincidence? Why some experts question the evidence.' Like Rachel Aviv, Lawrence had spent months dissecting the evidence and speaking to 'dozens' of experts, as she explained:

> While few of the experts the Guardian spoke to went as far as to say they believed Letby was innocent, the questions about the evidence called into doubt, they said, the safety of the convictions . . . Those raising concerns include several leading consultant neonatologists, some with current or recent leadership roles, and several senior neonatal nurses. Others are public health professionals, GPs, biochemists, a leading government microbiologist, and lawyers.'[10]

On the same day that Lawrence's *Guardian* article landed, a team of four journalists at the *Telegraph*, including the newspaper's Science Editor, published an even longer critique of the prosecution evidence. 'Lucy Letby: Serial killer or a miscarriage of justice?' read the headline.[11]

Other journalists have followed a similar course, including the respected medical journalist Phil Hammond. Documentary-makers are getting in on the story too. On 5 August, Channel 5 aired an hour-long film entitled *Lucy Letby: Did She Really Do It?*. Further documentaries like this one are sure to follow. Legally, Lucy Letby's case is settled, but outside of the courtroom, scepticism about the evidence in her case has entered the mainstream, championed by a small but significant community of investigative journalists and medical experts.

Unsurprisingly, our own editors at the BBC wanted to know what we thought. After all, we'd led the BBC's coverage of the case. Could the sceptics be right? It was a question that couldn't be avoided. But nor was it one that we hadn't already been investigating ourselves. Our own process of interrogating the prosecution's scientific evidence began even before Letby's trial had concluded in August 2023. At that point, we could see that a deeper understanding of the science was needed and much of our time since then has been spent in this endeavour.

The lead lawyer for the CPS, Pascale Jones, described the case as a 'constellation' of evidence.[12] If by that, she meant tallying the evidence was a bit like counting stars, she was right. But to sceptical ears, a constellation of evidence might sound like a fancy way of saying there was no smoking gun. And the truth is there wasn't. A handful of witnesses believe that they saw Letby just before or after she'd harmed a baby. But no one ever saw her in the act. There was no CCTV or DNA evidence to prove the case either.

In the background of these sceptical concerns and arguments is the case of another nurse who, like Letby, was convicted of murdering and attempting to murder her patients. In 2003, a paediatric nurse in the Netherlands called Lucia de Berk was sentenced to life in prison for four murders and three attempted murders. Between September 2000 and September 2001, nine infants died or required resuscitation while de Berk had been on duty. Suspicious deaths were identified at other hospitals where de Berk had worked previously. No one saw her harming any patients, but the prosecution in her case argued that, statistically, the chances of mere coincidence were very unlikely – 1 in 342 million.

De Berk's diary also played a role in her conviction. On the day one of her patients died, she wrote that she'd 'given in to [her] compulsion'. She also wrote that she had a 'very great secret'. De Berk claimed that her secret compulsion was tarot cards. But the court was unconvinced and she was convicted.

De Berk appealed, but to her dismay, prosecutors used the opportunity to add more convictions to her record. Blood tests appeared to show that two of de Berk's victims had been poisoned. It wasn't until April 2010 – six and a half years after her original conviction – that another court quashed de Berk's convictions. According to the judges in the case, there was in fact no evidence that de Berk had committed a crime. The prosecution's science and the statistical arguments concerning her presence for deaths and resuscitations was flawed. The use of her diaries as evidence of her guilt was also flawed. In a TV interview, de Berk's daughter claimed her mother's stranger diary entries were notes for a thriller that she had wanted to write. De Berk's exoneration was a shocking indictment of the justice system that had convicted her, and her case remains one of the greatest miscarriages of justice cases in Dutch history. In a retrospective on the case, the scientific journal *Science* noted: 'Tunnel vision, bad statistics, and poor human intuitions about coincidence had marred the investigation.'

The apparent parallels between the de Berk case and the Letby case are chilling. So is Lucy Letby Britain's Lucia de Berk? It would certainly help explain Letby's continued insistence that she is innocent, not to mention our frustrated search for signs of darkness in Letby's background. Could it be that the reason we can't find the 'killer' lurking in Lucy Letby's backstory is that it doesn't exist?

It's a hazardous question. For years, parents of babies who died at the Countess of Chester Hospital had to deal with the unverified possibility that their babies had been murdered.[13] Letby's trial and conviction brought a kind of closure to this question. To revisit it risks grave insensitivity to their pain. At the same time, a nurse has been condemned to die in prison, and a significant number of mainstream journalists and experts have now raised sceptical challenges about the evidence in her case. Any journalist worth their salt would be remiss to ignore the questions posed by these sceptics, and so here we confront them head on. We don't pretend to answer all of them. Some questions will be left unresolved. In some cases, only Letby herself will have the answers. But we have a duty to consider the arguments of the sceptics – to probe as much as we can, dispel misinformation or misunderstanding, and present the truth as far as we know it.

The most basic worry about the Lucy Letby case is that the deaths and collapses for which she was convicted may have simply been a tragic coincidence – an unfortunate 'spike' in incidents for which no one person was to blame. Nothing to do with foul play.

Various facts and figures have been used to advance this idea. For example, it's been pointed out that the babies on the neonatal unit where Letby worked were all premature, which meant that they were already vulnerable. Then there's the fact that several of the babies whom Letby was convicted of harming were twins – six in total – and two more were triplets. Some sceptical journalists have pointed out that twins are three and a half times more likely to die than single newborns, and triplets are five times more likely compared with single births.[14] In other words, the fact that several of the babies in the Letby case were twins or triplets placed them at increased risk of dying. Low birth weight may also increase a baby's health risk.

These observations point to one obvious question: is it possible that the deaths and the collapses of the babies in the Letby case were due to the increased health risks that they were already facing because of factors such as their prematurity, their weight, and whether they were twins or triplets?

Then there's the claim that Lucy Letby was 'always there' when things went wrong. In the early days of the trial, the prosecution presented the jury with what looked like bang-to-rights circum-stantial evidence: a chart listing twenty-four 'suspicious events' involving babies on the neonatal unit, including seven deaths, and a damning column of 'X's showing that the only nurse on duty for all of them was Lucy Letby. When you first see this grid, it almost looks like proof of guilt: twenty-four individual incidents are listed and, by a very large margin, Letby is the only common presence.

But according to several statistics experts, this chart was at best a visual stunt by the prosecution and at worst a self-serving selective presentation of the data. The main problem, they say, is what the grid doesn't tell us. How many other deaths and 'suspicious events' occurred during the thirteen-month period reflected in the grid? Would Lucy Letby look so 'guilty' if these other incidents were included too? Could you not construct a similar grid for any other nurse on the unit? All you'd have to do is pick the same number of incidents when that nurse was on duty and something went wrong. In short, the grid tells us nothing – and in fact offers a distorted view. That's the sceptical view.

Add to that the fact that the grid features only nurses. What about the doctors? How would the stats have looked if their names had been included on the grid? Were there other staff – cleaners or IT people perhaps – whose names were also omitted?

Even if Lucy Letby was on duty for a disproportionate number of incidents, would that really be so surprising? We know that

Letby volunteered for extra shifts. She was single with few domestic commitments – and she was saving to buy a house. She was also one of very few nurses on the unit who had specialist training. So of course she was going to be there for more incidents than many of the other nurses.

Put all of these arguments together and you get two basic objections to the idea that Lucy Letby must be guilty: first, statistically speaking, the babies in the Letby case were already at risk of dying or collapsing; and second, the grid showing that Lucy Letby was 'always there' when things went wrong is not a complete representation of incidents and staff – and therefore tells us nothing conclusive.

These arguments seem straightforward and forceful, but are they as strong as they appear? Imagine for an unpalatable moment that for each of the twenty-four incidents on the police grid for which Lucy Letby was on duty, a baby was found with knife injuries and a bloodied knife was found at the scene. Would we still be talking about the statistical likelihood of a natural spike in baby deaths to explain these injuries? Would we be pointing to the fact that twins are three and a half times more likely to die than newborns? Would we be suggesting that for every other nurse on the unit we could find a similar list of twenty-four stabbing incidents? Of course not. These statistical arguments would be irrelevant. Why? Because the evidence would indicate overwhelmingly that we weren't dealing with natural baby deaths and injuries. The recurring evidence of stab wounds and a bloodied knife at the scene would tell us instantly that we were dealing with foul play. All those statistical arguments about the possibility of a natural spike in baby deaths, or the elevated probability of twins dying, and so on would instantly become dismissible. We would know we were dealing with murders and attempted murders, not a spike in natural deaths and collapses.

What this imaginary scenario tells us is that the most important question, at least at the outset, is how sure can we be that the twenty-four individual incidents on the prosecution's incident chart – for which Letby was the only common presence – were in fact deliberate attempts to harm babies, in some cases fatally? Were they definitely foul play in the way that our imaginary stabbing incidents were? If they were, Letby's presence for all of these incidents *is* a serious piece of evidence. It may not be the whole story, but someone who is present for twenty-four clear-cut cases of deliberate harm, including multiple murders, is a legitimate suspect.

The problem in the Letby case is that determining whether the incidents that feature in the Letby case were foul play isn't as easy as deciding what to make of a scene involving a bloodied knife and a victim with knife wounds. Had someone seen babies being harmed on each of these twenty-five occasions, the answer would be clear. But no one did. So were the incidents that Letby was blamed for definitely foul play? Or could they have been natural causes, or causes to do with the state of the unit more generally? This is the central question in the Letby case, and to answer it the prosecution turned not to statistics but to science – in particular, the medical and scientific facts of each incident.

Delving into the science of the case is no small undertaking. In fact, it's rather daunting.

The Letby case was one of the longest-running murder trials in British legal history – and for good reason. Because in reality, although there was just one woman in the dock, this wasn't just one case. Letby was accused of harming seventeen babies, and faced no fewer than seven individual counts of murder and fifteen of attempted murder – twenty-two allegations in total. Each one was a court case in its own right with vast, sometimes dizzying, bundles of medical and scientific evidence.

We spent months immersing ourselves in the science – sifting it, weighing it, sometimes arguing about it. At times, the deeper we went, the less clear it all seemed. Letby was accused of using a variety of methods to harm babies – injecting air into their circulations, pumping air into their stomachs, overfeeding them with milk, poisoning them with insulin, and even physically assaulting them.

No one saw Letby doing any of these things. No one saw her sneaking into the fridge to steal insulin or injecting air into babies' tubes. No one saw her touch a baby roughly, let alone cause a baby to bleed or suffer internal injuries, as was alleged. The scientific proof that babies had been harmed came almost entirely from the opinions of the prosecution's experts.

Dewi Evans was the first expert that the police had turned to. They sent him the records for around thirty babies in the autumn of 2017 – three years before Letby was charged and five years before she went on trial. Evans then prepared a report on each baby, assessing whether the baby had been harmed. The other prosecution experts in the case came on board later and offered their opinions, but only after reading Dewi Evans' reports. In an important sense, Dewi Evans effectively authored the first draft of the prosecution's scientific case against Lucy Letby.

We've seen extracts from Dewi Evans' original 2017 reports. Several things strike you when you read them. The first is that they bear a pretty close resemblance to what Letby was tried for and convicted of. For example, Evans' reports identified five cases as being consistent with the injection of air into babies' circulations – in other words, air embolism. Letby was prosecuted – and convicted – in all five cases. In the case of another baby, Evans concluded the evidence was 'consistent with some action where [the baby] was given an excessive volume of milk via her [feeding] tube'. Here again, Letby was charged and convicted. In one case, Evans concluded that the baby had been given a large quantity of insulin. This allegation turned out to be a key component of the case against Letby. Indeed, of all the allegations in the case, this was one of the first on which the jury reached a guilty verdict – unanimously.

So in many ways, Letby's trial was a vindication of Dewi Evans' original 2017 reports. But these same reports also show how the science in the Letby case was frequently a matter of judgement rather than absolute certainty. Scientists may well point out that there are no absolutes – and they are right. But some scientific truths are so stable and enduring that we speak of them as facts. Gravity, the composition of water, and the proposition that the earth isn't flat are all settled scientific facts. We don't say that gravity *may* apply or that the composition of water may be H2O, or that the earth *may* be round. We know these things to be true and we feel no need to mince our words when we speak about them. The language in Dewi Evans' 2017 reports, however, was different.

On some matters, he seemed definitive. Of one case, he said: 'In my opinion [this baby] was treated inappropriately . . . the action was carried out with intent to harm.' In another case, he concluded: 'In my opinion [this baby] was subjected to some form of action . . . that an individual trained to look after small babies would know would place the baby in harm's way, i.e. it was done with intent.' In the insulin case, Evans pointed to 'conclusive evidence consistent with the infant having received insulin from an external source, i.e. someone gave [the baby] an insulin injection'.

However, many of the cases where Evans identified harm were couched in much more cautious language. In several of the cases where Evans pointed to air embolism – in other words, the injection of air into the circulation – he merely said that the evidence was 'consistent with' air embolism. That's not the same as saying it's proof. In other cases, Evans said that the baby 'may' have been harmed without saying so categorically. Evans told us that experts use cautious language like this to avoid being emotive or encroaching on the jury's task to make the final determination of what happened. However, several of Evans' opinions – at least as presented in his early 2017 reports – were far from categorical. That's not a criticism. In fact, it indicates a healthy degree of caution. But it tells us that, to begin with at least, explaining what had happened to the babies in the Letby case wasn't always black and white.

Evans also went on to revise some of his initial opinions. In one of his 2017 reports, he said one may never know the cause of the baby's collapse. Five years later, Evans' position had changed: the baby had been deliberately and fatally harmed.

Letby's barrister did put Evans on the spot about such changes in his opinions and Evans was unapologetic. Since preparing his 2017 reports, he said, he received new information about the cases – principally evidence from other witnesses – and as any good scientist should, he adjusted his analysis in light of this new information. Evans told us: 'I was working with the least amount of evidence at the beginning, because I only had evidence from the documents, from the clinical records. But having listened to the local nurses' evidence and the local paediatricians' evidence, plus the other independent reports, I felt comfortable in amending my opinion and I'm quite comfortable with that.'

Evans is right: medics should adjust their analyses in light of new information, but the fact that in one of the seven murder cases, Evans' view effectively changed from 'difficult to explain' to 'murder' shows how dynamic and open to revision some of the science in the case was.

One allegation in the Letby case proved to be especially contentious. For no fewer than nine of the seventeen babies, Letby was accused of injecting air into the venous systems of nine babies, leading to an air bubble in the circulation and ultimately collapse or death. As we've noted previously, it's known as an 'air embolism.'[15] This one allegation dominated courtroom debates and much of the controversy that followed, and the rest of this chapter is focused on it. It's complex but it's impossible to understand the Letby case without grappling with the science underlying the air embolism allegations. Six of the seven murder cases were alleged to have involved air embolism. And Letby was convicted of all of them.

As we saw in Chapter 5, Dewi Evans had first identified air embolism as the cause of several of the baby deaths right at the beginning of the police investigation in 2017. In court, he said he had been 'on the ball from the start'. 'The first person to use air embolus, as far as I was concerned, was me.' After the trial, we had lengthy discussions with Evans about the case. He told us the air embolism explanation had actually been quite straightforward to identify. He was also unflinching in his certainty. We quizzed him about each of the babies and how they had died. Baby A, for example, was the first baby to die. Dr Evans said he had died as a result of air embolism, but how sure was he? 'One hundred per cent,' he said. No hesitation. As for the idea that Letby could be innocent – it's not a thought that Evans even entertains.

Dewi Evans and Sandie Bohin weren't the only expert witnesses who helped the prosecution make the case that babies had died because of air embolism. An expert radiologist, Owen Arthurs, highlighted areas of gas in post-mortem X-rays of some of the babies that he said were 'consistent' or 'compatible' with air embolism. The prosecution's expert pathologist, Dr Andreas Marnerides, also identified post-mortem gas that he said fitted with air embolism. But neither Professor Arthurs nor Dr Marnerides claimed to be able to diagnose air embolism on their own. Each of them offered observations that fitted with air embolism, but the core reasoning for the air embolism diagnosis came from the two clinical experts: Dewi Evans and Sandie Bohin.

But despite their confidence, the air embolism theory turned out to be one of the most controversial aspects of the entire Letby case. Letby's lawyers argued that it was so shaky that they even asked the judge to exclude it from the trial altogether. According to Letby's barrister Ben Myers, '[t]he expert medical evidence is so poor it's inherently unreliable'. Had this argument succeeded, all of the air embolism allegations in the case would have been thrown out. The jury wouldn't even have been asked to consider them – and the outcome of the Letby trial would have been very different. Fortunately for the prosecution, the judge held firm. He rejected the efforts of Letby's defence to get the air embolism evidence thrown out. Nonetheless, this aspect of the trial is an indication of just how controversial the air embolism evidence was. And that controversy didn't end with Letby's conviction. Debates about the air embolism evidence are ongoing – and they'll probably continue at some level for as long as Lucy Letby is in jail.

Previous chapters have charted how the police built their investigation and the drama of the trial that followed, but so far, we haven't dived into the nitty-gritty of the science – in particular the air embolism evidence. It certainly doesn't make for easy reading. But for anyone who wants to understand Lucy Letby and her journey from childhood sleepovers and TV dinners with her friends to a prison cell, these debates are unavoidable. For anyone struggling to accept that 'nice Lucy' from Hereford could really be a baby killer, the arguments about the air embolism science are part of the answer. Letby is where she is today because of these arguments. She will die in prison because of them, and our understanding of her as a serial killer of babies is based, in part, on the understanding that the air embolism evidence stacks up – that babies did collapse and die because Letby deliberately injected air into their blood. And so, if we want to understand not just the Lucy Letby case but Lucy Letby herself and whether this plain young woman is the killer that the jury found her to be, we have to ask: how solid was the air embolism evidence that helped define her as a killer and send her to jail?

Had someone actually seen Letby picking up a syringe and injecting air into a baby's circulation, the air embolism argument would be all but proven. But, as we've noted already, no one saw any such thing. No one on the neonatal unit saw anyone carrying or picking up a syringe in a way that looked suspicious or inappropriate. And there were no suspicious-looking discarded syringes. Syringes in hospitals are a bit like drinks straws in McDonald's. No one keeps count of how many are used. And once they've served their purpose, they're thrown away and incinerated. As a murder weapon, they are ideal – virtually untraceable. What all of this means is that the allegation that babies were harmed by air injection – in some cases murdered – depends almost entirely on the medical, scientific evidence. And that science was controversial – or so argued Letby's defence.

Despite the complex debates that followed, the prosecution's air embolism argument was actually quite straightforward. Ultimately, it boiled down to a kind of 'checklist' of around half a dozen 'features' that indicated that a baby had suffered an air embolism. First, the baby was stable with no warning signs that a serious collapse was about to occur. Second, the collapse was sudden rather than gradual. Dewi Evans spelled this out in court: 'By collapse, I mean change of colour, stops breathing . . . reduced heart rate, and death,' he said. 'This occurs all of a sudden.' Third, the baby didn't respond to resuscitation as expected. And fourth, other potential causes of death were excluded.[16] There were other indicators too. Skin discoloration, such as a 'rash-like' appearance of pink against a blue background, was a significant one. Relentless and unusual crying was another – a pain response to air in the baby's circulation, according to the prosecution's experts. Finally, there might be air in the great blood vessels entering and exiting the baby's heart. This could be observed on post-mortem X-rays and was further evidence, according to the prosecution experts, that the baby had suffered an air embolism.

So the prosecution 'checklist' for identifying air embolism was simple – at least in its basic outline. It was also flexible. In court, Dewi Evans was careful to point out that 'you don't get all the features [of air embolism] in all the cases'. Just because a baby hadn't cried relentlessly, for example, didn't mean that the baby hadn't suffered an air embolism.

But where did the checklist or theory for identifying air embolism come from? Everyone in the trial acknowledged that the scientific research on air embolism in newborn babies was extremely limited. Dewi Evans himself captured the point succinctly. There is 'not a great deal of research' on air embolism in babies, he said.[17] 'You cannot do clinical research' on the effects of injecting air into babies and 'that is not going to change anytime soon'.[18] Occasionally, medics in a neonatal unit somewhere in the world encounter a case of air embolism in a baby and record their observations. Evans came close to one such tragic event at his old hospital in Swansea when an anaesthetist accidentally injected air into a baby's circulation. But historically speaking, documented reports of air embolism in babies are disparate and extremely rare – sometimes little more than medical anecdotes.

In 1989, however, two Canadian researchers decided to collect and analyse all of the reported cases from all over the world – fifty-three in total. They presented their findings in a single four-page paper. 'Pulmonary vascular air embolism in the newborn' was the catchy title. Even today, this 1989 research paper is considered by many to be the most significant study of air embolism in babies. Unsurprisingly therefore, it featured heavily in the Letby case. Throughout the trial, it was referred to as the 'Lee and Tanswell paper' – after the names of its two authors. Part of the paper lists 'clinical signs' of air embolism, and this is the bit that attracted most attention during Letby's trial. It's full of medical jargon, but it's important. Here is an extract:

The presenting signs of pulmonary vascular air embolism were usually sudden and dramatic. The most common signs included sudden collapse with either pallor or cyanosis, hypotension, bizarre electrocardiogram irregularities varying from tachycardia to bradycardia, with the latter being more common . . . Blanching and migrating areas of cutaneous pallor were noted in several cases and, in one of our own cases we noted bright pink vessels against a generally cyanosed cutaneous background . . . A radiograph is diagnostic, and free air may be seen in both the arterial and venous systems, as well as in the heart . . . migrating pallor in small vessels [is] suggestive . . . Only four of the fifty-three infants in this review survived the immediate event.[19]

It sounds complicated, but once translated into everyday language, the jargon is actually quite simple. 'Cutaneous' means 'related to the skin', 'pallor' means paleness, and 'cyanosis' means blueness. So, in simple terms, typical signs of air embolism include sudden and dramatic collapse by the baby, changes in the baby's skin colour, and X-rays showing air in the baby's circulation. The specific changes in skin colour include paleness, blueness and pink vessels against a blue background.

You can see immediately the importance of the Lee and Tanswell paper in underpinning the prosecution's checklist for air embolism. And in many ways, the air embolism cases in the Letby trial seemed to fit with what Lee and Tanswell described – so much so that Letby's former colleague-turned-accuser, Ravi Jayaram, reported feeling a shiver down his spine when he first read the paper.

Baby A, for instance, was the first death in the Letby case, and the first example of the prosecution's air embolism 'checklist' in action. Baby A had died suddenly on the evening of 8 June 2015. According to Dr Evans, the baby boy had been 'perfectly satisfactory'[20] before his collapse. The collapse was sudden and unexpected, and the baby failed to respond to resuscitation. Some of the medics who had treated Baby A recalled seeing unusual skin discoloration on Baby A's body. One described 'patches of blue/purple colour, patches of red and of white that didn't fit'.[21] Another – Ravi Jayaram – described 'pink patches, mainly on the torso, which seemed to appear and disappear and flit around'.[22] A pathologist's report from the time recorded the cause of Baby A's death as 'unascertained'.[23] Of course, that was before Baby A's case became a police investigation. Dr Evans and Dr Bohin concluded that all other possible causes of Baby A's death could be excluded. The only plausible explanation was air embolism.[24]

This same reasoning, or 'checklist', was applied to the cases of the other babies that the prosecution believed had died because of air embolism. Baby C, for example, was the second baby to die unexpectedly – less than a week after the death of Baby A. Just like Baby A, Baby C had reportedly been making good progress and was 'handling well'[25] before his sudden collapse. As the baby fought for his life, one of the nurses recalled that he looked 'mottled'.[26] One of the consultants has a similar recollection – 'pale and mottled' was how he described the baby's skin. After reviewing the evidence, Dewi Evans suggested three possible causes of death for Baby C. Two involved air embolism.

Baby D was the third baby to die in that harrowing two-week period in June 2015. Once again, the baby had been 'stable' before her collapse,[27] according to the prosecution. The collapse was sudden and was reportedly accompanied by skin discoloration. One medic described seeing 'a deep red brown' while others observed that the baby's skin was 'extremely mottled'.

According to the prosecution, a further three babies died of air embolism: Baby E, Baby I and Baby O (although in each of these cases, other contributory causes were offered too). As in the cases of Babies A to D, the prosecution applied its air embolism 'checklist', starting with the unexpectedness of the collapses. Baby E, for example, had been 'incredibly stable', according to Dr Sandie Bohin.[28] Baby I had been in a 'virtually perfect clinical scenario'[29] before she collapsed, while Baby O was 'following a healthy path'[30] with medics reporting no concerns.[31]

In all cases, the babies failed to respond to resuscitation as expected, and there was unusual skin discoloration too. One doctor recalled seeing 'purple patches' on Baby E,[32] while another reported seeing 'a mottled blue appearance of the trunk and peripheries' of Baby I.[33] Baby O's father gave a particularly graphic account of his baby's appearance before he died. 'You could see his veins,' he told police. 'All bright blue, changing colour . . . You could see something oozing through his veins.'[34] In most of the cases, medical staff – some with more than twenty years' experience – said they had never seen this kind of skin discoloration on a baby before.

It all seems to line up – the prosecution's air embolism 'checklist', the findings in the Lee and Tanswell paper, and the medical reports on the babies in the Letby case. So what's the issue? Why was the air embolism science in the Letby case so controversial? One clue was that the two main prosecution experts – Dewi Evans and Sandie Bohin – didn't completely agree between themselves on which babies in the Letby case had suffered as a consequence of air embolism. They agreed that five of the seven baby deaths had been caused wholly or partly by air embolism. But their opinions diverged on other cases – notably, the cases of Baby C and Baby N.

On 3 June 2016, Baby N was heard screaming. He survived, but Letby was convicted of attempting to murder him. Dr Evans suggested air embolism as an explanation for the baby's screaming. Dr Bohin agreed that the baby had been harmed, but she didn't identify air embolism as the cause – as Dr Evans had done. The case of Baby C was even more striking. According to Dr Bohin, Baby C died after having air injected into his stomach, not into his bloodstream.[35] The air had caused the baby's stomach to swell up and stop the diaphragm from working properly – known as 'splinting the diaphragm'. So in Dr Bohin's view, Baby C *was* harmed, but the cause of his death was splinting of the diaphragm, not air embolism. Dewi Evans was more cautious in his view – at least to begin with. In his initial report on Baby C, Dr Evans wrote: 'One may never know the cause of [Baby C's] collapse. He was at great risk of unexpected collapse.'[36] Dr Evans produced no fewer than eight reports on Baby C – and none of them positively identified splinting of the diaphragm as a cause of death. But by the time Dr Evans got into the witness box, his view had evolved – he says after receiving additional information.[37] Dr Evans now agreed with Dr Bohin's assessment – that Baby C had died from splinting of the diaphragm after having air injected into his stomach. Two experts saying the same thing ought to have been good news for the prosecution, but the fact that Dr Evans hadn't said this in any of his reports looked bad. The real surprise, though, came when Evans was being questioned by Letby's barrister.

During a particularly tense cross-examination, Dr Evans' view appeared to shift yet again. Baby C, he told the court, may have died from an air embolism.[38] It caught everyone by surprise – including the prosecution. Crucially, it invited the accusation from Letby's defence lawyers that Evans was theorising on the hoof and reaching for scientific explanations simply because they fitted with the prosecution narrative that Letby was guilty.[39] Of course, Evans denies this. His view, he says, evolved in response to new information. But by introducing air embolism – seemingly in the heat of the moment – as a possible cause of Baby C's death, Evans gave the impression that identifying air embolism wasn't straightforward. After all, if the science of air embolism was clear, why didn't he identify it in his reports on Baby C? And why was there any disagreement between the two prosecution experts about which cases involved air embolism? Did this not suggest that, at the very least, the air embolism science was open to interpretation – and disagreement? It is actually possible to diagnose air embolism with certainty in some circumstances. The 1989 research paper by Lee and Tanswell made a passing reference to some of these methods. 'A radiograph [or X-ray],' the authors wrote, 'is diagnostic.' In other words, an X-ray can settle the question whether a baby has suffered an air embolism. Where this is the case, 'free air may be seen in both the arterial and venous systems, as well as in the heart.'[40] The problem with the Letby case, however, is that, although the case as a whole featured numerous X-rays taken while babies were alive, those X-rays that were specifically used to support the air embolism allegations were all taken after babies had died,[41] and Lee and Tanswell are much more cautious about relying on X-rays taken after death: 'Post-mortem radiographs,' they say, 'need to be interpreted with caution as intravascular air may appear as early as 25 minutes after death.'[42]

There are other recognised methods for identifying air embolism. For example, Lee and Tanswell note that '[t]he most distinctive sign of pulmonary vascular air embolism is the finding of free air when blood is withdrawn from the umbilical arterial catheter. Columns of air, or a frothy mixture of blood and air, were often obtained.' Post-mortem examination of the baby's heart under water can also be used to confirm air embolism.[43] However, in the Letby case, no one suspected air embolism at the time, and so – understandably – these recognised tests weren't carried out. What we have is retrospective analysis – months or even years after the events – of medical records and eye witness testimony. And that analysis boiled down to interpretative *judgements* made by the prosecution's experts. So in many ways, the reliability of the air embolism evidence against Lucy Letby was ultimately a question about the reliability of the prosecution's expert witnesses – in particular, the two paediatric experts Dewi Evans and Sandie Bohin.

Narrow disagreements among experts – even experts who are on the same side in a court case – aren't terribly surprising. But what if you could show that those experts aren't really experts – that in fact they don't really have the expertise to back up their opinions? And what if you could also show that the way that those experts arrived at their opinions wasn't independent either? That's certainly one way to undermine an expert's evidence, and, as we saw in Chapter 6, Letby's barrister Ben Myers adopted this approach to argue that the prosecution's air embolism evidence lacked the necessary expert authority or reliability to be persuasive. Dewi Evans was given an especially rough time. Evans was out of his depth, Myers argued. He wasn't a specialist in neonatal care – what medics call a 'neonatologist'. He'd been out of clinical practice for years. And he had no expertise in air embolism. It was stinging criticism for a man like Evans, who had spent more than three decades looking after babies and had designed and led a neonatal unit in Swansea.[44] But Myers had harsher things still to say. He highlighted a case from 2021 in which Evans had provided an expert report. The judge in that case was scathing about Evans' report. It was, he said, 'worthless' and contained 'partisan expressions of opinion'. The judge also said Dr Evans made 'no effort to give a balanced opinion'.

Unsurprisingly, Evans was indignant. He'd given expert evidence in numerous cases. This one that had been unearthed by Letby's defence was a 'one-off'. It was, he said, the 'only judgement that went against me in a family court in thirty years'.[45] But the suggestion that Evans wasn't balanced or impartial was made repeatedly throughout the Letby trial. Letby's barrister pointed to the circumstances in which Dewi Evans had become involved in the Letby case – an email to a friendly contact at the National Crime Agency. 'I've read about the high death rate for babies in Chester and that the police are investigating,' Evans had written. 'If the Chester police had no one in mind I'd be interested to help. Sounds like my kind of case.' Myers used the email to accuse Evans of 'touting' for work and went on to argue that Evans' close working relationship with the police during their investigation made him a biased investigator rather than an impartial expert. There was even a suggestion that the police had been the ones who planted the thought of air embolism in Evans' head. We asked Evans himself. Evans rejects Ben Myers' insinuations. It did sound like his kind of case, he told us. He was interested in helping. That didn't mean he wasn't impartial on the evidence. The same goes for his close working relationship with the police. They needed expertise: he provided it. That doesn't mean his advice wasn't impartial. On the question of whether the police had been the ones to introduce the idea of air embolism, Evans couldn't have been more forthright: Cheshire Police didn't mention air embolism to him. As far as he was concerned, he was the first person to mention it to them.

True as that may be, the same cannot be said for Sandie Bohin or the other prosecution experts in the case. They were all given copies of Dewi Evans' reports before they prepared their own. Would Sandie Bohin have arrived at the air embolism theory had she not seen Dewi Evans' reports first? She says she would. 'It was as though I was doing it from scratch,' she told the court.[46] But Letby's barrister tried to suggest otherwise. Did he have a point?

Before Sandie Bohin joined the case, Cheshire Police commissioned another expert, the Newcastle-based paediatrician Martin Ward Platt, to 'peer review' Dewi Evans' work. A fatal illness prevented Dr Ward Platt from continuing with the case, but we've seen Martin Ward Platt's report in which he set out what he understood his role to be. He clearly says that his role is not to prepare new reports from scratch: 'Peer review is explicitly not about revisiting every detail of each case or in effect writing a second report on every case.' Dr Bohin's brief was more wide-ranging. Although her job was to peer review Dr Evans' reports, this included providing 'a robust clinical review of Dr Evans' opinions, setting out whether she agreed or disagreed with him and, as appropriate, to provide an alternative causation for the collapse.' Bohin interpreted this instruction broadly. Rather than simply commenting on Dr Evans' work, she prepared her own reports 'from scratch'. She knew that a less comprehensive approach would invite the accusation that she was simply rubber-stamping her fellow expert's work. And, as we've seen already, there are some notable differences between Dr Evans' and Dr Bohin's reports. But on the big questions, they generally agreed and it is a matter of fact that Dr Bohin prepared her reports after reading the reports of Dr Evans. That meant that, however conscientiously Dr Bohin approached her task of arriving at independent opinions, the air embolism theory in the Letby trial could not be said to be a product of expert opinions arrived at in perfect separation from each other. Dewi Evans had introduced the theory and his fellow experts had then largely endorsed it.

These criticisms are significant, but they focus on the experts and their methods rather than the substance of what these experts actually said and argued. It's true that Dewi Evans was criticised by a judge in a different case. It's also true that Sandie Bohin read Dewi Evans' reports before writing her own. These facts don't mean that Evans' and Bohin's air embolism 'checklist' was wrong – or that the prosecution experts were wrong to conclude that babies in the Letby case were harmed by air embolism. But worries about the air embolism evidence in Letby's trial aren't confined to the question of whether the prosecution experts were impartial or suitably qualified, or whether their methods were as good as they should have been. There are further criticisms that go to the heart of the prosecution's air embolism science. This is the real battleground between those who are sure that Letby is guilty and those who argue that the science used to convict her was flawed.

In preparation for her trial, Letby's defence team commissioned two clinical experts of their own to critically examine the medical evidence of the prosecution. One was a paediatrician from Harrogate called Dr Shakeel Rahman. The other was Dr Mike Hall, a Southampton-based academic in neonatology and retired consultant neonatologist. Both doctors prepared reports on the evidence, and in August 2022, two months before Letby's trial was due to start, Dr Hall and Dr Rahman met with the prosecution experts, including Dr Evans and Dr Bohin, to discuss their findings. It was a formal meeting – part of the pre-trial process – to see what areas of agreement and common ground there might be between the prosecution and the defence experts. But there was little meeting of minds.

From what we have gleaned of the meeting, Dr Rahman's real contribution was limited. He prepared reports and was vocal about his views, but he was a strange choice of expert for Letby's defence. He was undoubtedly a respected paediatrician, but his expertise in the care of premature babies wasn't on a par with that of the other experts, and it's hard to escape the impression that he was outside his comfort zone. His analysis played little or no role in Letby's defence and he effectively disappeared from the case. Mike Hall, on the other hand, embraced his assignment with gusto and prepared painstaking dissections of Dewi Evans' and Sandie Bohin's reports, including their assessments concerning air embolism. At virtually every turn, Hall contested Evans' and Bohin's arguments, setting the stage for a courtroom debate over the scientific validity of the air embolism allegations against Letby.

In a trial that would be largely determined by the science, Mike Hall was arguably Lucy Letby's best hope. Her lawyers – as skilled as they were – weren't medical specialists. And despite Letby's own medical training, she was no match for the combined expertise of Dewi Evans, Sandie Bohin and the others. Mike Hall was the only medical expert who could potentially keep her out of jail. But there was an important difference between Hall and the other experts in the case. Unlike Dewi Evans, Sandie Bohin and the other prosecution experts, Dr Hall didn't testify. He advised Letby's lawyers behind the scenes, but he attended court as a silent observer – almost like any other member of the public. To the extent that Letby's lawyers managed to mount a challenge to the prosecution's science, it was almost certainly thanks to Hall's input. But throughout the trial, Hall himself was like a ghost – there but not there, unspeaking – an unknown quantity. Maybe Letby's barrister Ben Myers KC had said everything that there was to be said about the science. Or perhaps Hall was unwilling to testify. Maybe he didn't want to be seen to be defending a serial killer. So many questions. The only way to answer them was to try to speak to Hall himself.

A few months after the trial finished, as Letby's life of permanent captivity was just beginning, Jonathan emailed Mike Hall to see if he might be willing to speak. Our pitch was cautious – a conversation about some general scientific matters related to the case. Hall was equally cautious in response, but he seemed like he had things he wanted to say. Ten days later, we met in a nondescript room in the vicinity of University Hospital Southampton where Hall teaches. It was another breakthrough moment in a story where secrecy and fear of the media seemed to be the norm. We were about to hear from the man who, despite his silence during Letby's trial, was one of the most important influences on her defence.

Mike Hall seemed formidable: polite but serious and somewhat austere. He chose his words carefully and had the bearing of a pedagogue from another era – exacting and not easily impressed. But despite his formal manner, you could tell that the Letby case had consumed him. Our first meeting was a bit like being back at university. For nearly three hours, Dr Hall spoke while Jonathan scribbled, noting as much as he could understand. Hall had brought slides to illustrate his points – X-rays of newborn babies (none from the Letby case), medical diagrams showing veins, arteries and the heart, photographs of intravenous lines and other medical equipment, and selected excerpts from that all-important 1989 Lee and Tanswell paper. But by the end of the lecture, we had barely scratched the surface of the seven murder allegations in the Letby case, not to mention the further allegations of attempted murder. Understanding Hall's perspective was clearly going to take time. But it was necessary. Letby was destined to die in prison. We had to know if the science that had put her there was robust.

In Hall's view, it wasn't. Part of the problem in his view was the 'checklist' for identifying air embolism used by the prosecution experts. According to Hall, there wasn't enough scientific research to support it. Even the 1989 Lee and Tanswell paper, a key piece of research used to support the prosecution's air embolism case, had limited value. The first problem, as Hall saw it, was that the circumstances of the Lee and Tanswell babies were different to those of the babies in the Letby case. For a start, the gas being pumped into the Lee and Tanswell babies was 90 per cent oxygen. That's not quite the same thing as air, which is what Letby is accused of injecting. Air is only 21 per cent oxygen. The rest is virtually all nitrogen, and nitrogen behaves differently to oxygen inside the body. The babies in the Lee and Tanswell paper were also all on ventilators and were being pumped with oxygen at extremely high pressures – pressures that would never have been used at the hospital where Letby worked. The way in which gas entered the babies' circulations was also distinctive in the Lee and Tanswell cases – more or less directly into the heart, according to Hall. In his view, these differences meant that Lee and Tanswell's findings might not necessarily apply to the babies in the Letby case.

But there was a bigger problem with the Lee and Tanswell paper as far as Mike Hall was concerned. The paper had identified various changes in skin colour associated with air embolism. There was 'migrating' paleness, or blueness, or 'bright pink vessels' against a blueish background. However, all of these cases of changing skin colour added up to just 11 per cent of the fifty-three cases examined in the Lee and Tanswell paper.[47] With such a small proportion of cases involving skin colour changes in a sample of just fifty-three cases, could the prosecution experts really rely on skin discoloration as a reliable indicator of air embolism? Even if they could, what type of skin discoloration? Letby's defence barrister described one particular type – the appearance of 'bright pink vessels' against a blueish background – as the 'starting point' for the prosecution's theory of skin discoloration associated with air embolism. But this particular change in skin colour was seen in just one out of fifty-three cases in the Lee and Tanswell study. Could the appearance of bright pink vessels against a blueish background in babies in the Letby case really be taken as a reliable indicator of air embolism?

Even if it could, that isn't what all of the eyewitnesses in the Letby case described seeing. Between them, the medics who worked with Letby gave varying descriptions of the skin discoloration they observed. In some cases, there were different descriptions for the same baby. Baby A reportedly had patches of 'blue, purple, red and white'. For Baby D, one witness observed a 'mosaic, a mottling colour of blotchiness'. Another noted 'a deep red brown – different from mottling', while a third medic noted 'dark brown/black' across Baby D's trunk. 'Strange kind of purple patches' were reported for Baby E, 'mottling' for Baby I, and a 'rash which looks like small spots of blood on skin' for Baby O.

Not all of these descriptions were noted at the time either. In the case of Baby A, for example, both the registrar David Harkness and consultant Ravi Jayaram described seeing changes to the baby's skin colour. However, neither doctor included this in their medical notes for Baby A. Indeed, with the exception of a passing reference to 'mottling' by Lucy Letby herself, there are no contemporaneous notes of skin discoloration for Baby A. It's a similar story with Baby E. Dr Harkness did note skin discoloration on Baby E at the time, but Letby's defence noted that the descriptions he later gave to the police were much more detailed.

Of course, skin discoloration was just one item on the prosecution's 'checklist' for identifying air embolism. What about the others? Did they stack up? Take the first one – unexpected collapse in a baby who had previously been stable. Mike Hall acknowledged that this was uncommon, but it wasn't unheard of. Babies, he said, do sometimes collapse suddenly. Air found in the great vessels after death was another item on the 'checklist', but again Hall argued that it didn't establish that the baby had suffered an air embolism. Air embolism might be one explanation of air in the great vessels after death, but there could be others, and the prosecution's own X-ray specialist Professor Owen Arthurs acknowledged this. Even the observation of relentless crying by some babies wasn't, in Hall's assessment, evidence of air embolism. There was, Hall argued, nothing in the medical research literature that identified this as an indicator of air embolism. In summary, Hall's view was that the prosecution's air embolism 'checklist' was weak and therefore couldn't be used to prove the air embolism allegations. If that doesn't sound stark enough, Hall spelled it out like this: 'I don't think there is irrefutable evidence that there was air in the system before death in any of [the cases].'

For most people, dense scientific arguments like these don't make for easy reading. They're not quite the stuff of the average thriller or true crime box set. But in the Letby case, proving air embolism for the prosecution was the equivalent of finding a gun-shot wound. It was the evidence the prosecution needed to prove that babies had been murdered. And so this evidence is, at least in part, the difference between seeing Lucy Letby as her friends and family see her – the victim of a miscarriage of justice – and Lucy Letby as most other people now see her: a callous serial killer who murdered babies and then lied about it. Testing the air embolism evidence is essential to making our minds up about her, and this science becomes more tangible, if more unsettling, the more one considers the precise mechanics of harm that it implies.

Mike Hall, Letby's silent expert, took a keen interest in these mechanics. The prosecution had alleged that Letby had injected air into babies. Hall wanted to know exactly how *much* air she had injected. This wasn't a macabre curiosity. All of the experts in the case generally agreed that the effects of an air embolism would be quick. Early on in the trial, Dr Bohin told the court that 3–5ml of air per kilogram of baby's body weight 'could be fatal'. The reason that was interesting to Mike Hall was that not all of the babies that Letby was accused of injecting with air had died. Baby B, for example, was said to have had air injected into her circulation and she survived. The prosecution also submitted that Baby D was injected with air three times over a three-and-a-half-hour period. She died only after the third attack. If Dr Bohin was right – that 3–5ml of air per kilogram could be fatal – then the prosecution's position was that Letby was injecting some babies with much smaller doses of air. It's certainly possible to imagine. But one case appeared to put this theory under strain.

Baby M was one of two twins born on 8 April 2016. A day later, he collapsed and almost died. The prosecution experts blamed air embolism. The difficulty, though, was that Letby had had no known contact with Baby M at any point in the fifteen-minute period before he collapsed – and that raised a tricky question: if the effects of injecting a baby with air were supposed to be virtually immediate, how could Baby M's collapse be explained by air injection? The last opportunity that anyone would have had to inject air into his system was fifteen minutes before his collapse.

The prosecution experts did have an answer to this problem, but it wasn't straightforward. They pointed to the baby's intravenous tubing – the visible tubing connecting the baby to the drip. This bit of tubing was known as the 'dead space' and the prosecution experts worked out that this dead space had a volume of 0.4ml. That meant that the dead space could hold a small amount of air – 0.4ml – before it entered the baby. In other words, it was possible that a small amount of air was injected into the dead space of Baby M's tubing, and that this air then took fifteen minutes to move from the dead space into Baby M's bloodstream. In fact, the prosecution experts calculated that, given the rate at which fluids were being infused into Baby M, this is how long it would have taken for 0.4ml of air to move from the dead space into Baby M's circulation and take effect. But that invites two further questions. Could such a small amount of air be enough to almost kill a baby – as it did in the case of Baby M? Yes, said the prosecution. But even if that is true, would a murderer really go to the trouble of injecting micro-doses of air like this?

Letby's expert, Mike Hall, was sceptical. Indeed, this scepticism seemed to permeate all aspects of his work on the Letby case. Hall argued that even if air embolism could be shown to be to blame for some of the baby deaths, it is possible that air got into the babies' systems accidentally. One possible route, he suggested, is where a catheter enters a vein – between the catheter and the wall of the vein. The process of resuscitating a baby is a second way in which air might enter the circulation accidentally, according to Hall. Post-mortem accumulation of gas was a third. Hall admits that these are merely theoretical possibilities, but he points to documented cases of accidental air embolism in adults as well as the fact that all trainee medics are warned about the hazard of accidental air embolism and the precautions that need to be taken in order to prevent it. Hall takes this as an indication that such accidents can happen. There's even evidence from the Letby case that Hall believes demonstrates uncontroversially that accidental air embolism is possible. Baby G was the seventh baby in the Letby case. She was born in Arrowe Park Hospital on 31 May 2015 before being moved to the Countess of Chester Hospital. While at Arrowe Park, air entered Baby G's liver. There was no suggestion that this was deliberate. Hall's point is that it was technically a case of air embolism – accidental air embolism.

Hall acknowledges that these arguments about the possibility of accidental air embolism are theoretical. Indeed, the prosecution experts saw them as a 'dead end'. But Hall had further criticisms to make of the prosecution experts, in particular, their assessments of the medical conditions of the babies in the case. A key element of the prosecution's air embolism argument was that the babies had been stable before their collapses. Their collapses were unexpected and all other possible causes for collapse were ruled out. Air embolism was the only explanation. Hall disagreed. In his view, the picture that the prosecution experts gave the jury of the babies' conditions before their collapse was flawed to the point of being misleading. We put this criticism to Dewi Evans and Sandie Bohin. Both responded emphatically. Dr Evans told us: 'those suggestions are completely flawed and indicate either that the people making them have not seen the clinical evidence or that they are unaware of what constitutes well-being in a premature baby.'

Dr Bohin said Dr Hall had 'launched what can only be described as a campaign against Dewi and me.' She said:

I still maintain that *none* of these babies were unwell enough that a sudden unresuscitatable collapse was imminent. [Mike Hall] may not agree with me but that does not mean I misled the jury. I did not and this is an outrageous accusation to make of someone giving evidence under oath. [Mike Hall] was not called to give evidence – that was not my decision but a decision from the defence team. It just does not stack up that because he didn't give his version of events the jury were misled.

The strength of feeling and conviction in these statements is clear. And yet Hall remains dogged in his view: each of the babies had medical complications that pointed to other possible explanations for their collapse or death.

Detailing the medical histories of the babies in the Letby case would be a separate book in itself – and a pretty hard read – but here's a flavour of what Hall is getting at. In the case of Baby A, for example, the prosecution experts said the baby was stable before his collapse. 'Perfectly satisfactory' was how Dewi Evans described him.[48] A 'stable baby' was Sandie Bohin's description. And in most respects, he was. He didn't need extra oxygen, his heart rate was normal, and his blood gases – another measure of a baby's health – were normal too. But his breathing rate wasn't. In fact, the baby's medical notes show that his breathing rate was abnormally high during the twenty-four-hour period before his collapse. In Hall's view, this was potentially significant. There were other factors too that, in Hall's view, may indicate that Baby A was compromised. For example, the medical notes also show that his heart rate was normal – a good thing in most circumstances. But Hall says the fact that Baby A was breathing unusually quickly suggests he was having to work hard to get the oxygen he needed. Normally, the heart would work harder to help with this, and yet Baby A's heart rate remained normal. Was this a sign of a weakened heart? It's a question that Hall believes goes against the claim that Baby A was 'perfectly satisfactory' before his collapse. Hall also notes that Baby A didn't receive any intravenous fluids, including sugar, for at least four hours in the period before he collapsed.

Baby C was also compromised, according to Hall. He was the baby whose death highlighted differences of opinion between the two main prosecution experts. During cross-examination in court, Dewi Evans suggested that air embolism may have caused Baby C's death. However, his initial view in 2017 had been much more circumspect: '(One) may never know the cause of [Baby C's] collapse. He was at great risk of unexpected collapse.'[49] This initial view of Evans' is certainly closer to Hall's own. Hall notes that Baby C was very premature and had pneumonia when he died. A few hours before he died, Baby C had sepsis – a complication of infection. Hall also argues there was evidence to suggest he had a bowel obstruction and that this may have contributed to his death.

Baby D was the third baby death in the Letby case – and the third of the three deaths in that shocking two-week period in June 2015. In Sandie Bohin's view, Baby D was 'stable' before her collapse, and although she had pneumonia she was 'improving'. Hall's assessment was less optimistic. He noted that she needed breathing support and the circumstances of her birth had left her at an increased risk of infection. Hall also notes that the original post-mortem identified pneumonia as the cause of her death. Hall makes similar arguments for other babies in the Letby case. In almost all of the cases, he argues that the babies were compromised and that there are other possible causes of death. The argument for air embolism is, he believes, not made out.

So what does all of this mean? Does Mike Hall think Lucy Letby is innocent? 'No,' he told us. 'I don't and can't know whether or not Ms Letby is guilty or innocent – I just don't know. However, I don't think that the evidence was strong enough to reach the threshold of beyond all reasonable doubt.' Hall puts his point even more starkly: 'From a medical perspective,' he says, 'I don't think

[Lucy Letby] got a fair trial.' It's a troubling view – far beyond what you would expect to hear from a regular expert witness whose job was to critique the prosecution's science. From the hours we spent talking to Hall, it's clear that these concerns are not merely academic. Hall is genuinely worried that the air embolism science is weak, and that the prosecution experts overstated their case.

If Hall is right, we should all be worried about Lucy Letby's conviction. If the air embolism theory is wrong and babies died of other causes, then the premise of the Letby case – that there was a murderer on the neonatal unit at the Countess of Chester Hospital – could be wrong. Is it possible that in fact there was no baby killer and the case against Lucy Letby was hollow? Faulty science has led to numerous miscarriages of justice. Those words of Peter Hitchens should ring in our ears: 'our justice system is not as good as we like to think . . . [If], ten years hence, [Lucy Letby] stands under the TV lights in front of a courthouse, unrecognisable after years in prison, but free at last, I would rather be among those who had kept such an open mind, than among those who did not.'[50]

Dewi Evans and Sandie Bohin were both familiar with Dr Hall's arguments. They'd met with him before the trial had even begun. They'd studied his reports and spent months in a Manchester courtroom jousting with Letby's barrister as he channelled Mike Hall's criticisms. And yet, none of these criticisms persuaded either Evans or Bohin that they were wrong. They defended their positions throughout the trial, and today – despite the criticisms of the sceptics – they appear to remain as confident in their air embolism evidence as Hall is sceptical.

Ideally, the Lucy Letby case – at least the expert part of it – would have nothing to do with personalities. Ideally, it would be all about the truth – cold, objective, scientific truth. But it was hard not to notice the contrast in character between Hall on the one hand, and Evans and Bohin on the other. Hall was formal in manner and intensely analytical. He didn't seem to care too much for small talk or idle chatter. Intellectually, he was sceptical. You could tell he had an aversion to over-reaching or over-confidence in expert evidence – a trait that made him an ideal adviser to Letby's defence. In Hall's world, scientific certainty is rare and hard won – and as he sees it, only certainty will do when a young woman's life and liberty are on the line.

Evans and Bohin, by contrast, were chatty, 'down to earth', informal. While we were writing this book, Jonathan went to meet Evans at his flat in Cardiff. 'Will have something for us to eat,' Evans texted. The menu was M&S pizzas and chocolate mousse. Evans likes to chat. Politics in particular seems to animate him – and he leaves you in no doubt where he stands on the big issues of the day. With both Evans and Bohin, you get a sense that the truth is actually not that complicated. Barristers may try to make it complicated, but to medics who've spent their lives caring for babies and making life-and-death calls, finding and speaking the truth, plain and simple, is part of the job. When we finally settled down to talk about the Letby case, Evans shook his head and muttered in his Welsh brogue: 'She bloody murdered those babies.' Evans' certainty is almost infectious, but was he right? Sometimes we left our conversations with him unable to decide whether he was a medical genius with a natural intuition for the truth honed by long experience, or a dogmatist whose many years as a sought-after expert witness had left him with slightly too much bullish self-belief. Probably neither of these extremes captures the reality fairly.

But it's important to note that Evans and Bohin both believe they have strong arguments that show that Mike Hall's worries about the air embolism evidence are misplaced. Evans in particular doesn't pull his punches. Hall's expert reports, he told us, were 'convoluted'. Evans goes as far as to argue that Hall misunderstood his role in the case – opting to play the role of Letby's advocate rather than an impartial expert. It's a striking claim from someone whose own impartiality was subject to repeated challenge by Letby's defence. It's also a charge to which Mike Hall has a simple response: he was asked to appraise – or 'referee' – the prosecution experts' evidence and that's what he did. But Evans' belief in his own position – and the weakness of Hall's – is unshakeable. Some of Hall's arguments, Evans says, are 'ridiculous'. One example was Hall's claim that air might have entered babies' circulations by accident. Of course, this *could* happen. Theoretically, air could enter a baby's circulation accidentally. Hall had outlined three ways this could happen: (1) between the vein wall and a catheter, (2) during resuscitation, or (3) the accumulation of gas in the body after death. But in Evans' and Bohin's view, none of these was plausible. Bohin explained as follows. In normal neonatal practice, any potential gap between a vein and a catheter – the first route for accidental air entry identified by Mike Hall – is sealed with a piece of cord and stitched to close the gap and stop air getting in. In addition to this, any blood around the gap sticks, effectively forming another seal – so much so that the blood has to be soaked before the tube can be removed. Bohin was similarly dismissive of Hall's other two theories for accidental air embolism. It is true, she says, that air can enter the bloodstream via the lungs when pumped into a baby at very high pressure – in other words, during high-pressure resuscitation. However, this doesn't explain why it is that the babies collapsed so suddenly and unexpectedly in the first place. Also, the pressure needed to force air into the bloodstream via the lungs was greater than the pressure involved in a resuscitation at the Countess of Chester Hospital. As for the idea that air might have accumulated in the blood vessels post-mortem: as Dr Bohin noted, the only way this could occur to any significant extent would be through putrefaction of the body. And yet, most of the babies' post-mortems were carried out within a day or two of death. In other words, the extent of possible putrefaction would be limited. Moreover, it wouldn't explain why babies collapsed and died and showed signs that seemed to fit with the prosecution's air embolism 'checklist'.

Evans and Bohin also rejected Hall's repeated argument that the babies in the Letby case were not as well or as stable as the prosecution had claimed, and that there were other possible causes for their collapses. In the case of Baby A, for example, Hall had pointed to the fact that the baby's breathing rate was abnormally high during the twenty-four-hour period before his collapse. The fact that Baby

A's heart rate was normal, rather than being reassuring, was a further cause for concern, given how rapidly the baby was breathing. But Hall and Bohin disagreed. Evans listed nine 'markers' that he had used to assess Baby A's health and stability. He concedes that Baby A's breathing was not 'in the normal range', but he says all eight of Baby A's other 'markers' were normal. Bohin agrees with Evans. She also disputes Hall's argument that Baby A's normal heart rate might suggest that his heart was weak given that his breathing rate was abnormally high. Baby A had a mild respiratory illness, she says, but the baby was stable which is why his heart rate was normal. On top of this, the prosecution radiologist Dr Arthurs identified an explained 'line of gas' in front of Baby A's spine and an air bubble was found in Baby A's brain. Neither of these observations was proof, but the prosecution's expert pathologist Dr Andreas Marnerides said air bubbles in Baby A's brain and lungs were 'highly suggestive' of air embolus.

Arguments like these about the stability of the babies before their collapse were slugged out in the courtroom during Letby's trial. But to the jury, the two sides of the debate can't have looked evenly matched. For a start, Hall himself didn't go into the witness box, so the jury never got to hear his arguments from the mouth of an expert witness. Would it have helped Letby? Or might cross-examination of Hall by the prosecution have made her case appear even weaker? We can only wonder. But even if Hall had testified, he would have had another body of medical opinions to contend with, namely the medics who worked on the neonatal unit alongside Letby. Time and again, medics from Letby's unit stood up in court and declared that, as far as they were concerned, a particular baby was stable or improving or, at the very least, not at obvious risk of collapse. Baby A was 'clinically stable'. There were 'no concerns for him at all'. Baby B was 'doing relatively well' with 'no obvious signs that caused any concern'. Baby C was 'a stable baby', according to one of the nurses who looked after him. And so on. Around the time of Letby's conviction, our BBC colleague Michael Buchanan interviewed the woman who took charge of the Countess of Chester Hospital after Letby was arrested. Susan

Gilby is an anaesthetist and intensive care doctor by training and she backed up the assessments and reasoning of the medics on Letby's unit, as well as Dewi Evans and Sandie Bohin. 'There were deaths and near deaths, which could not be explained, and were unexpected,' she said. 'And that just does not happen on a neonatal unit.' Mike Hall would no doubt disagree. He would also point out that Susan Gilby isn't a neonatologist. But she seemed to speak for many of the medical staff on Letby's unit.

For the consultants at the Countess of Chester Hospital, the tipping point in that traumatic year of baby deaths was in June 2016 – the deaths of two of three triplets. During the trial, the two babies became known as Baby O and Baby P. These two deaths are especially difficult to explain – and they pose a real challenge for anyone who might wish to defend Letby. Even Mike Hall conceded as much: 'I think the two that are probably most difficult to explain are [Baby O and Baby P],' he said. And it's not hard to see why. Both triplets died within twenty-four hours of each other – leaving medics shocked and stunned. According to Dr Brearey, all three triplets were born in good condition and were 'following a healthy path'. The third triplet – the only one of the three whom Lucy Letby didn't look after – had no issues and survived without difficulty. Nothing in medicine is certain, but it's clear from this that whatever killed Baby O and Baby P, it wasn't genetic. In the case of Baby O, the prosecution's expert witnesses identified air embolism as one cause of death. Even if they were wrong about this, it was clear that something wasn't right about the sudden and unexpected death of Baby O and his triplet brother.

Dr Hall is right. Babies do collapse suddenly – but very rarely. The probability of multiple babies on a small neonatal unit collapsing suddenly and unexpectedly and then failing to respond as expected to trusted and reliable resuscitation techniques has to be vanishingly low.

What about the prosecution's checklist for identifying 'air embolism' – the theoretical basis underpinning all of the air embolism evidence? Hall argued – with some force – that this was a theory without the necessary scientific knowledge and research to support it. He cited the prosecution's reliance – untenable reliance as he saw it – on the 1989 Lee and Tanswell paper. He also highlighted the fact that the descriptions of skin discoloration on the babies' bodies were so varied – in some cases noted long after the fact – that they proved nothing.

There's no denying it – Hall's critique is a powerful one. The Lee and Tanswell evidence appears thin. Add to this the fact that the prosecution applied their checklist 'flexibly' to each of the babies in the Letby case. But Evans and Bohin argue that they weren't relying solely on the Lee and Tanswell paper. In 2019, three years before Letby went on trial, Dewi Evans prepared his own 6,000-word survey of existing reports on air embolism in babies. Some of these reports had presumably been examined by Lee and Tanswell themselves in their 1989 paper, but Evans spelled out the descriptive detail from these reports. He included reports from after 1989 as well. Evans' survey wasn't a peer-reviewed piece of academic research, but the accounts of air embolism that it contains are striking – and more detailed than Lee and Tanswell's four-page overview. 'The baby screamed, turned blue, arrested and died,' noted one. 'The baby became cyanotic with grunting, had a mottled skin and unmeasurable blood pressure,' noted another. 'The baby's cries had turned into screams; he then coughed or gasped loudly; his back arched and his arms stiffened. He lost consciousness . . .' Reading this survey by Evans and its descriptive accounts of air embolism, it's not hard to see why he feels so confident in his position. Sandie Bohin also cited research other than the Lee and Tanswell paper in her evidence.

Evans and Bohin didn't just apply their air embolism 'checklist'. They offered physiological accounts that seemed to explain why the checklist and the evidence from eyewitnesses in the case made sense. The variations in descriptions of skin discoloration is a good example. According to Evans and Bohin, an air bubble could end up in a range of places in a baby's circulation – and in each case the visible effects could be different. An air bubble might, for example, end up in the heart, forming an airlock which stops blood from entering and exiting the heart. If this happens, the baby would lose colour. Alternatively, an air bubble might be dispersed around the body, ending up in one of the organs, such as the liver or the kidneys. It could end up in the skin too, and if it did, that could cause a fleeting rash-like appearance. According to Evans and Bohin, these different possibilities partly explain why the descriptions of skin discoloration from the medics on Letby's unit were so varied. Mike Hall argues that these explanations of skin colour changes by Evans and Bohin are fine theories, but they lack evidence. For Evans and Bohin, they are almost physiological common sense. If you know how a baby's physiology and circulation work, the various skin colour changes reported in the Letby case all fit with the air embolism theory. Bohin also notes that people's descriptions of the same rash are rarely the same: 'I've given lots of talks to medics and clinicians,' she told us. 'I have showed them a rash and asked them to describe it. And everybody describes it slightly differently.'

Ultimately, Evans and Bohin argued that, while no single feature or indicator on their air embolism checklist is on its own proof of air embolism, combinations of these features can be. Both Evans and Bohin – perhaps not coincidentally – used the same term that the CPS lawyer had used: constellation. The evidence for air embolism – like the rest of the evidence in the Letby case – was a constellation. It had to be taken together, holistically.

So where does all of this leave us with the air embolism evidence? Is it solid? In Dewi Evans' view, the evidence for air embolism is so strong, it's a fact. To argue against it is to argue against facts. Mike Hall, by contrast, thinks the evidence for air embolism is so weak it doesn't meet the threshold of beyond reasonable doubt. After ten months of painstaking courtroom detail and argument, the jury decided that Dewi Evans' and Sandie Bohin's arguments were convincing enough to find Lucy Letby guilty beyond all reasonable doubt.

But there is one other fundamental concern that left some people worried at the end of the Letby trial. Although most of Mike Hall's arguments were presented in court by Letby's barrister Ben Myers KC, Hall himself did not give evidence. Why? It was, perhaps, the biggest question for those of us who watched Letby's trial closely. The prosecution had an army of expert witnesses: two paediatricians, a radiologist, a pathologist, a blood expert and an expert in insulin testing. Surely it was obvious that without her own expert witness giving evidence in open court, Letby's hopes of securing a not guilty verdict would be impossibly weak. Had Mike Hall refused to testify? Had Lucy Letby been unjustly deprived of an expert witness? If she had, her trial can't have been a fair one.

We asked Mike Hall if he had been willing to testify in court in Lucy Letby's defence – and he confirmed that he had indeed been willing. Hall had spent six months preparing reports for Letby's side and he was more than happy to go into the witness box and present his arguments against the prosecution experts. In fact, Hall wasn't merely willing. He was adamant that he should be called to testify. For him, it was a matter of justice. 'Although I had been primed [that medical witnesses may not be called for the defence], I didn't really believe that that would be the case,' he told us. 'And I was admittedly, I think, indignant that that did not serve the cause of natural justice if [Lucy Letby] didn't have people providing reasonable counter-evidence to that which was provided by the prosecution.' Hall believes that if he had been called, the jury may have seen a slightly different evidential picture. Sure, Letby's barrister ensured that the jury heard most of Hall's arguments. But even the most skilled barrister is not a substitute for a medical expert.

Dewi Evans has his own view about why Mike Hall wasn't called as a witness. Evans believes that Hall's arguments were so weak, they wouldn't have withstood cross-examination. And so, on balance, it was better for Letby to keep Hall out of the witness box. But talk to Hall and you get the opposite perspective. He is as confident in his critical views as Evans and Bohin are in theirs. He believes Evans and Bohin overstated their case and the scientific basis for it. He even goes as far as to argue that they misrepresented the evidence and in so doing misled the jury. It's a serious charge. It's also part of what makes the Letby case so confounding: so much rests on expert opinion, and although Mike Hall is in the minority, his views create deep disagreement among respected experts involved in the case.

Even if Evans and Bohin are right – that Hall's arguments are so weak that they would have been taken apart by the prosecution – it's still hard to understand how it can have been better for Letby to have no expert medic testifying in her defence. In a trial that was always going to be fought and won on the basis of expert opinion, Letby surely needed expert witnesses if she wanted to win the case. Had the jury heard an expert neonatologist arguing in Letby's defence against the air embolism theory, would they have been so ready to convict her?

We will never know the answer to this question. However, the decision not to call Mike Hall to testify was ultimately down to one person – Letby herself. Lucy Letby was the one who decided not to call Dr Hall to testify in her defence. Why she reached that decision we don't know.

We don't know if her legal team cautioned against calling Dr Hall and she complied with their view; or whether they advised her that he should testify and she went against their advice. What we do know is that she had the final say. Her team were bound by her instructions, as any legal team is by the instructions of its client.

And that fact alone reveals something about Letby and her view of her own defence case. Ever since her conviction, some people have argued that Lucy Letby didn't have a fair trial. Many of these same people – 'Letby defenders' for want of a better term – have argued that the science used to convict her was not robust, or at the very least it wasn't robustly tested in court. But if these defenders are right and the air embolism theory wasn't properly challenged in court through defence expert testimony, Letby herself is directly re-sponsible – and the question has to be asked: why did she not want Mike Hall to testify in her defence? Could it be that she wanted to maintain the pretence of arguing she was innocent – perhaps for the sake of her parents – without actually wanting to win the case? Or did she simply know that the game was up? Could it be that her team felt that Hall's arguments ultimately stood little chance against prosecution cross-examination? Whatever her reason, Let-by's decision not to call as a witness the only expert who was on her side suggested a lack of faith in her own defence. It's hard not to wonder whether it also signalled a lack of belief in her own innocence.

The debates about the air embolism science are heavy-going. But there are some further details from Lucy Letby's own testimony that are also relevant to the question of whether the prosecution experts were over-reaching or landing on the truth. Just two weeks before Baby A died – of air embolism according to the prosecution – Lucy Letby completed a training course on administering medicine using intravenous lines. As part of the course, the dangers of air embolism were explicitly highlighted. This proves nothing, but it raises an obvious question that the prosecution eagerly pointed out: did Lucy Letby use her new training and heightened awareness of the dangers of air embolism to murder babies?

When she was questioned by police, Letby said all nursing staff would be aware of the dangers of an air embolus [the air bubble itself], but she claimed she didn't know much beyond this. She said 'I don't know exactly what [an air embolism] is. When we were taught about lines, we were taught about clearing lines because that's what it would lead to.' She also told police she was only aware of air embolisms in adults. However, in July 2016, less than two weeks after the death of Baby O, Letby had a text exchange with one of her nursing friends in which the two discussed inadequacies in Baby O's care before he died. It seems that his catheter hadn't been changed and a 'port' in the catheter had been left open. Letby was quick – and specific – in her criticism: 'it's a massive infection risk,' she wrote, 'and risk of air embolism.'

These details about Letby's awareness of air embolism can be read in more than one way. Her supporters will argue that they add further evidence to the picture of poor care on the unit and a specific risk of accidental air embolism in the case of Baby O – something that Mike Hall also argued was a possibility. Letby spotted an error that her colleagues had apparently missed. Now she was being blamed. That's what the sceptics will say. Looked at another way, it is unsettling to see in black and white Lucy Letby talking about air embolism after the death of a baby she would later be accused of murdering by this very method. As far as we know, air embolism was not a routine discussion point on the neonatal unit. Of course, medics took precautions to prevent air getting into babies' circulations. That was drummed into them. But in the accounts and conversations we've seen, the first discussion of air embolism was among the consultants at the end of June 2016 – after the death of Baby O. Apart from this private discussion, Letby was the only one to mention air embolism explicitly as a potential factor in the case of a baby who died. It also makes it harder to understand why Letby told police that she was only aware of air embolisms in adults when she clearly knew the risk to newborn babies. For the prosecution experts, these details will only give them further confidence in their interpretations. Neither Dewi Evans nor Sandie Bohin had seen Letby's text messages or knew about the training course she had attended when they first presented their air embolism theory. If their theory was wrong, it was a remarkable coincidence.

Chapter 9

The Search for the Smoking Gun

Throughout her trial, home for Lucy Letby was HMP New Hall, a women's prison in West Yorkshire, just south of Leeds. This is where she reflected and ruminated after each day's evidence in court. One of her fellow inmates was the serial killer Rose West. West is one of just four women ever to be sentenced by a UK court to spend the rest of their lives in prison. Letby is one of the others. It's astonishing to think of 'nice Lucy' from Hereford in such reviled company.

We spoke to a former inmate of New Hall. 'Jo' – not her real name – left the prison before Letby arrived, but she knows what life for Letby would have been like there.

'I don't know if you watch typical [TV] programmes [in a] prison setting,' said Jo. 'It's just like that basically – high ceilings, two storeys with cells all around the edges.' 'The walls weren't very clean,' she recalls. There were 'signs of excrement and lots of graffiti.' Outside, the exercise yard '[looks] a bit like a tennis court with high wire'.

Inmates are woken at 7 a.m. each day. Mornings and afternoons are spent 'working' – sewing, cleaning and the like – or attending classes. Most inmates share a cell – or a 'pad' – and sleep on bunk beds, but the most serious offenders have their own cells – for their protection. They're also housed away from the rest of the inmates in a quasi-medical wing of the prison called 'Rivendell'. Rose West is housed there. Jo believes Letby would have been housed there too. If she was, she would almost certainly have met West.

Not all of the inmates in New Hall are serious criminals, but the prison has its fair share of cold-blooded killers.

'There was a woman who was [due] to take the gym class. She'd murdered her partner,' Jo recalled. 'She stabbed him. They just had an argument and she'd stabbed him in the stomach. Another woman had murdered somebody that she'd been preying on and watching for a while. I remember she had alopecia and she walked with a stick. Little woman with glasses. Can't remember her name.'

According to Jo, the gritty TV depictions of prison life are accurate – including the ever-present threat of violence. While Jo was at New Hall, a prison officer was 'kettled' with boiling water laced with sugar. Jo herself was told by another friendly prison officer to watch her back and keep busy.

High-security prisoners like Rose West have extra security to escort them round the prison. 'You'd be sat in sewing and there might be sixty people sat at sewing machines or cutting materials or whatever, and occasionally you see somebody like Rose West being escorted with five or six prison officers,' Jo recalled. '[Otherwise] she would be attacked.'

Letby, too, would almost certainly have been a target for violence. 'Those inside hate anybody that does anything to children,' Jo said. 'She'll have to watch her back all the time. And the prison officers will have to watch her like a hawk for her safety.'

After her trial, Letby was moved out of New Hall – first to Low Newton jail in Durham and then to HMP Bronzefield in Surrey – Europe's largest female prison. By all accounts, Bronzefield is more comfortable than the other two prisons – which didn't go down too well with the tabloids. Following Letby's relocation, the *Sun* splashed a story under the headline: 'Fury as evil baby killer Lucy Letby serves sentence in cushy private jail with en suite shower and 24-hour protection.' According to the story, Letby 'has her own cell with en suite shower, a desk, phone and telly. She has dyed her hair brown, gets round-the-clock protection and does not have a prison job.' A source reportedly told the paper: 'Letby seems happy as Larry. She is in a nice cell and on her own. The facilities at Bronzefield are much nicer than most jails, because it's privately run.'[1] But even if Letby's current accommodation is a step up from what it was before, she will never be able to stop looking over her shoulder for as long as she is inside.

It's possible that Letby is secretly resigned to a life behind bars. It's difficult to tell from her blank demeanour in court. But when we heard the news that she wanted to appeal against her convictions, we weren't surprised. She'd argued her innocence for seven years. Why would she stop now? And what did she have to lose?

After Lucy Letby was found guilty, her legal team applied for permission to appeal, which is the first step in the criminal appeal process. A single judge looked at the papers and ruled against her. But there was no public hearing, and we journalists were left none the wiser about Letby's grounds for appeal and the judge's reasons for denying her request. However, Letby wasn't completely out of options. The system allowed her to make one last attempt. This time, her appeal bid would be before three judges in the Court of Appeal in London – and the hearing would be public. Finally, we would get to hear Letby's arguments. We might even get to see Letby herself. It would be our first sighting of her since she refused to enter the dock at the end of her trial.

On the morning of 22 April 2024, barristers, journalists and interested members of the public shuffled into Court 4 in the Royal Courts of Justice. It was a far cry from the 1970s sterility of Manchester Crown Court. The Royal Courts are what many people imagine when they think of a criminal trial. It's the stuff of TV courtroom dramas – dark wooden panelling, benches, carvings, high ceilings, deep-red curtains, and an imposing coat of arms above the judicial bench. Outside, a small group had gathered around a banner: JUSTICE FOR LUCY LETBY. We spotted a few of the online sceptics inside the courtroom too.

Of course Letby's legal team was present, headed up by Ben Myers KC. The prosecution was there in some number – led by Nick Johnson KC, accompanied by a phalanx of lawyers and police officers who filled the benches behind him. It felt like a rematch was on the cards. Many of those who'd played a part in the original trial were also involved – but weren't in the court itself. They'd chosen to observe proceedings remotely via a secure video link.

Some were anonymised – appearing simply as numbers: Number 1, Number 2, Number 3, and so on. We guessed these were the parents of the babies. Letby's parents were also on the link, invisible but clearly identified: 'John Letby and Susan Letby'. Everyone had their cameras and microphones off but it was all strangely intimate nonetheless.

When Letby herself appeared, we didn't want to blink – in case we missed something. For those in the courtroom, she appeared as a small figure on a faraway screen – beamed in remotely from an anonymous room in HMP Bronzefield. But there was no hiding for Letby from those of us watching on the video link. Her camera remained on and offered a perfect unblinking full-frontal mid-shot of her face and upper body. Our view of her was so clear, we might as well have been sitting opposite her in the same room. At any moment, we could see the action in the courtroom and Letby herself. If she moved in her chair, we could see it. If she blinked or even swallowed, we could see that too. It was as if she was on display.

The room they'd put her in was small but modern-looking and impressively sterile: spotless grey walls, a white table, and two chrome-framed chairs arranged side by side with blue fabric and sleek armrests. Letby sat on one. The other remained empty. Behind her right shoulder was a door with a small square of opaque glass at the top. Occasionally you could see the dark blob of someone's head as they walked past, but no more. On the wall beside the door was what looked like a poster of a royal crest – a nod to the legal reality that the room she was sitting in was now a virtual extension of the court. Other than that, the room was empty – zero clutter, no stray objects that might tell a story.

Yet again, the most striking thing about Letby was her plainness. She wore a dark cardigan-like business jacket over a black round-neck top with small white dots on it. Dark trousers. She looked like a provincial office worker. Her hair had grown a bit and was a slightly darker shade of brown than it was all those months ago. It looked freshly washed and straightened. Judith noted that Letby had put on a bit of weight, but her face was essentially the same as the face in her police mugshot – less pasty and shocked-looking perhaps, but she had those same gloom-filled eyes and that strangely large down-turned mouth. She looked exposed. Maybe it was the lack of make-up and the bright lighting. Ignoring the sterile surroundings and the cheap business attire, Letby looked like one of those plain, unmistakably English-looking women you see in depictions of old witch trials.

She knew we were all looking at her. Maybe that's why she hardly moved. She seemed to avoid looking at the camera – the way people on the metro try to avoid eye contact with the strangers sitting opposite them. Occasionally she fixed her hair. At one point, she got up to check that the door in her room was closed. She appeared to be alone. In preparation for the arrival of the three judges, the court clerk addressed Letby through a microphone, asking her to confirm that she could hear him. She could. It was just a few words, but her tone was interesting. There was no fear. Letby didn't sound timid or squeaky. Her voice didn't crack. She sounded assured. There was something steely about her.

The same reporting restrictions that had governed the original trial were still in place. We couldn't name the babies or their families, for example. Some of the medics from the hospital still had their identities protected – the married doctor among them. In case anyone was in any doubt, the court clerk read out the full list of names, starting with the babies. Would Letby's face give anything away? As the babies' names were read out, she lowered her eyes. She blinked a lot – a clue perhaps that she wasn't at ease. But apart from this, there was no visible reaction to the names of the babies she had been convicted of harming. Mention of the married doctor's name didn't provoke a reaction either. This time, there were no tears or signs of emotion. Letby remained poker-still, poker-faced. And this is how she would stay as this next phase of her courtroom drama unfolded.

Legally, Letby's options were limited. She couldn't simply pick the best of the sceptical arguments against her convictions and effectively rerun her trial in front of three judges instead of a jury. That's not the way the appeals system works. Criminal appeals are not, as lawyers sometimes put it, 'a second bite of the cherry'. The only way Letby would be allowed to appeal against her convictions was if she could show that the judge in her original trial had made a legal mistake, or there was new evidence that, had it been available at the time, might have led the jury to different verdicts. These are very specific and narrow options – and Letby's barrister tried both.

The trial judge, he argued, had made several mistakes. One concerned a surreal episode involving one of the jurors. In August 2023, Letby's trial was still running and had entered its tenth month. All the evidence had been heard and the jury was still deliberating when a member of the public contacted the police to complain that they'd overheard one of the jurors talking about the case in a local café. If true, it was a grave breach of jury rules. The Court of Appeal heard that the juror's partner had worked there and had had a dispute with the café owner over a mobile phone. The café owner ended up assaulting the juror's partner and the police were called. No charges were brought, but a few hours after the incident, the café owner's partner contacted the court and alleged that she'd overheard the juror talking about the case in public and saying the jury had 'already made up their minds about [the] case from the start'. It was a serious allegation and potentially grounds for the judge to dismiss the juror from the case. But after questioning the juror and looking at the details surrounding the allegation, the judge decided that it was unreliable and the jury should remain intact. Even Letby's barrister Ben Myers didn't accept the suggestion that the jurors had made up their mind at the start of the case. This can't have been right, he said, because of the way the verdicts were returned. However, Ben Myers did argue that the judge should have questioned the person who'd made the allegation as well as the juror. His decision not to was, Myers argued, a mistake. Only after questioning the source of the allegation could the judge decide if it amounted to anything. If it did, the juror would almost certainly have been dismissed and the entire outcome of Letby's trial might have been different – or so argued Letby's barrister.

It was a surreal, technical argument – nothing at all to do with the question of Letby's guilt or innocence. It also smacked of a certain desperation. But Letby's request for permission to appeal rested on further, more substantial arguments too. And interestingly, these further arguments concerned the evidence on air embolism. During Letby's trial, her barrister Ben Myers had tried to persuade the trial judge that the evidence of Dewi Evans should be excluded. According to Myers, Dr Evans was biased and unqualified to identify air embolism. Later in the trial, Myers asked the judge to exclude all of the air embolism evidence from the case altogether on the grounds that there wasn't enough scientific knowledge or research to support it. The trial judge rejected both of these requests. And that was why Letby was back in court now. According to her barrister, the judge had decided wrongly: Dewi Evans' evidence and the air embolism evidence more generally *should* have been excluded from Letby's trial. Had that happened, Myers argued, the entire case against Letby would have fallen apart.

Standing back from the procedural complexities of the criminal appeal process, one thing was apparent: Letby – or her barrister Ben Myers – clearly saw the air embolism evidence and the way it featured in Letby's original trial as the weak spot in her convictions. And Myers didn't just argue that the judge at Letby's original trial had made mistakes in how he had handled this evidence. Myers also argued that there was *additional* evidence on air embolism, not heard during Letby's trial, that could show that Letby's conviction was 'unsafe'. It was a drum-roll moment. What could this new evidence be? If it was significant, Myers might be right – the entire case against Letby would be vulnerable.

As Myers delivered his orations, Letby watched in silence from her colourless room in Bronzefield prison. She'd brought a black overcoat with her, which she'd pulled over her knees and hands like a blanket. As she did so, we caught a flash of a white Fitbit-style watch on her wrist. She had a notebook and pen with her, but she made no use of them. She remained passive and motionless. One of the journalists present remarked wryly that he thought the screen had frozen. Her facial expression barely changed, but doesn't every face tell a story of some kind? What story did hers tell? Was it guilt, dissociation, resignation perhaps? She certainly looked downcast, but it was hard to see anything in her demeanour that looked like an innocent person desperate to be freed. As we watched and analysed, we scribbled impressions in our notebooks: 'She doesn't look like she wants us to feel for her,' read one jotting. 'Poker face! No attempt to connect with us. [Surely] we [journalists and observers] would be a lifeline for an innocent person.' This is probably what stood out most about Letby's appearance. She'd spent eight months in jail as a convicted criminal, and two years in custody before that. The court hearing we were witnessing now was her first opportunity to connect with the wider world – to send a message even if it wasn't verbal. From an innocent person, you might expect to see signs of hope or fear, perhaps hints of anger and frustration – at the very least, a desire to be noticed. 'Help me! I'm innocent!' Isn't that what you'd expect an innocent person to project – somehow? But Letby was the opposite. She looked like she didn't want to be seen. She avoided the camera's gaze. Her expression communicated nothing. Did she look guilty? She didn't look innocent.

Back in the courtroom, Letby's barrister was making up for the lack of fighting spirit in his client. He had 'new evidence' that he wanted to present on her behalf, and when he announced where it had come from, it sounded pretty strong. Letby's defence team had managed to track down Dr Shoo Lee, one of the two authors of the seminal 1989 Lee and Tanswell paper. The prosecution had cited this paper in their case for air embolism. Now one of the authors of that paper was going to appear – in Letby's defence. His credentials were impeccable. He was a neonatologist, founding president of the Canadian Neonatal Foundation, professor emeritus at the University of Toronto, and honorary staff physician at the Mount Sinai Hospital. In short, he looked like a star witness.

For the three judges sitting on the bench, a key legal question was whether Dr Lee's testimony should be admitted as evidence at all. It had to be new and there had to be good reason to explain why it wasn't available during Letby's trial. But before making their decision, the judges agreed to hear what Dr Lee had to say. At 2 p.m. on Tuesday, 23 April, Dr Lee made his appearance by video link from his wood-panelled study in Canada. The courtroom was hushed. Was the man who had co-authored the Lee and Tanswell paper about to puncture the prosecution's case?

Dr Lee's job wasn't to offer a complete assessment of all the prosecution's evidence. That would have amounted to a rerun of Letby's trial. Instead, Letby's defence wanted him to answer one narrow question: what type of skin colour change in babies is 'diagnostic of' – in other words, proof of – air embolism? In his 1989 paper, Dr Lee and his co-author A. K. Tanswell had identified various changes in skin colour associated with some cases of air embolism in babies. Paleness, blueness or bright pink vessels against a blue background were the main three. But which, of any of these, was *proof* of air embolism? Dr Lee's answer was revealing. Babies sometimes suffer circulation failure – known as a 'circulatory collapse'. When they do, they will experience skin discoloration. This skin discoloration might be paleness or blueness. Air embolism is one possible cause of circulatory collapse, but there are others. That means that when you see skin discolorations such as paleness or blueness on a baby, you can be sure the baby has suffered a circulatory collapse, but there's no way to be sure, without other evidence, whether that circulatory collapse was caused by air embolism or something else entirely. In other words, paleness or blueness are not proof of air embolism.

There is, however, according to Dr Lee, one kind of skin discoloration that is a sure sign of air embolism, and that is pink vessels against a blue background. If you see this, he said, you can be sure that the baby has suffered an air embolism. It was a different argument to the one that Letby's original defence expert Dr Mike Hall had made. Hall had argued that the evidence supporting the claim that skin discoloration is a sign of air embolism is weak. Dr Lee broadly agreed with one narrow exception, namely, where bright pink vessels against a blue background are observed. This allowed for a new argument to be made in Letby's defence. Witness after witness in Lucy Letby's trial had come forward with descriptions of unusual skin discoloration. One had described a 'mosaic, a mottling colour of blotchiness'. Another noted 'a deep red brown – different from mottling', while another medic had noted 'dark brown/black' across a baby's trunk. According to Letby's barrister, none of these descriptions proved anything. Dr Lee had been clear: pink vessels against a blue background was the only type of skin discoloration that was proof of air embolism, and none of the eyewitness descriptions in the Letby case matched this description exactly. There was therefore only one conclusion: the prosecution's evidence for air embolism was fundamentally flawed and this additional evidence from Dr Lee proved it.

You can see why Letby's defence thought Dr Lee's evidence would help their cause. But as we listened to him, we began to wonder if he was really the secret weapon that the defence seemed to think he was. The main problem was that neither of the prosecution's main expert witnesses, Dewi Evans and Sandie Bohin, had claimed that any particular skin discoloration, on its own, was proof of air embolism. Their case was a holistic one. In their view, proof of air embolism rested on a combination of features from their air embolism 'checklist'. Skin discoloration was one. Sudden and unexpected collapse and failure to respond to resuscitation were others – and so on. Dr Lee's evidence did nothing to undermine this. Indeed, his own 1989 research paper confirmed that various kinds of skin discoloration were consistent with air embolism, even if they weren't proof of it on their own. In other words, the fact that eyewitnesses on Letby's unit had reported seeing a variety of skin colour changes other than 'bright pink vessels against a blue background' didn't mean those babies hadn't suffered air embolism. It simply meant that these skin colour changes, on their own, weren't proof – a claim that no one on the prosecution side had made.

But there was a second point that weighed even more heavily in the prosecution's favour. Some of the eyewitness descriptions of skin discoloration in the Letby case did appear to satisfy Dr Lee's requirements for proving air embolism on the basis of observable skin changes. Dr Ravi Jayaram, for example, reported seeing 'bright pinkness of patches against a bluey/grey background' in Baby A.[2] He described seeing something 'very similar' on Baby M: 'patches of very bright pink on his torso that flittered around. They would appear and disappear.' According to prosecuting barrister Nick

Johnson KC, these descriptions were the 'bullseye'. If Dr Lee's evidence was that the only skin discoloration that proved air embolism was bright pink vessels against a blue background, Ravi Jayaram's eyewitness testimony was that proof.

Of course, Letby's defence denied this. They argued that Ravi Jayaram hadn't made any note of skin discoloration of any kind at the time of the incidents, and that his vivid descriptions of these skin changes were given after he had read the Lee and Tanswell paper. The implication was that Dr Jayaram's evidence was at best unreliable and at worst fabricated – something Jayaram vehemently rejected during Letby's trial, and which the Court of Appeal judges would also dismiss when they came to give their judgement. Dr Lee also took the view that Dr Jayaram's descriptions didn't quite amount to 'pink vessels against a blue background'. To lay ears sitting in the courtroom, however, Lee appeared to be splitting hairs – quibbling over the specific words that Dr Jayaram had used rather than their meaning. The truth is that Dr Lee's evidence, far from strengthening the defence case, had probably backfired. He hadn't disputed that a variety of skin discolorations may be observed in cases of air embolism. Moreover, his new evidence gave the prosecution a new means of proving some of their allegations that they hadn't had before: according to Dr Lee, one particular type of skin discoloration – bright pink vessels against a blue background – was proof of air embolism: finally, a way to prove air embolism beyond doubt. And despite Dr Lee's quibbles over words, Ravi Jayaram's descriptions of what he saw in the cases of Baby A and Baby M – if they were true – seemed to be that proof.

At this point, it looked like Dr Lee's evidence was an unintended victory for the prosecution, and perhaps a form of closure on a long-running and tortured debate about the air embolism evidence. But there were further bombshells in Dr Lee's evidence that left the door open for more uncertainty. During his questioning of Dr Lee, Letby's barrister Ben Myers asked whether a combination of 'a [skin] lesion, a collapse, and a requirement for resuscitation' would be enough to exclude other possible causes and prove air embolism. Dr Lee's answer was blunt and categorical: 'Definitely not,' he answered. What this showed was that, in Dr Lee's view, even a certain combination of features from the prosecution's air embolism 'checklist' wasn't enough to prove that air embolism had in fact occurred. That left an obvious question: what combination of these features, if any at all, would amount to proof? Indeed, what did Dr Lee make of the prosecution's air embolism 'checklist' in general? Could it be used to prove air embolism? Sadly these questions were never asked. We could only guess what Dr Lee's answers might have been. But towards the end of his court appearance, Dr Lee made one further statement that potentially threw the air embolism debate wide open once again.

In correspondence, Letby's solicitor Richard Thomas had sent Dr Lee summaries of the cases of alleged air embolism that had featured in Letby's trial. Neither Letby's barrister nor the prosecution barrister Nick Johnson KC asked Dr Lee in court for his overall assessment of these summaries – that would have been outside the scope of the proceedings – but Dr Lee volunteered his assessment anyway: 'Based on the symptoms that were described in the [case] summaries,' he said, 'I could not diagnose air embolism.' The formalities of the criminal appeal procedure meant that no one on either side – defence or prosecution – followed up on this bombshell statement, but for the non-lawyers like us, observing proceedings from the sidelines, it was a remarkable development. In Dr Lee's view, he saw no conclusive evidence of air embolism in the Letby case. It's important to point out that we don't know what information Letby's team supplied to Dr Lee. We know they sent him 'summaries', but we don't know what these contained or how brief they were. He certainly didn't have anything approaching the thousands of pages of original medical notes that the prosecution experts Dewi Evans and Sandie Bohin had studied. He confirmed to the court that he had not been sent any of the eyewitness accounts of skin discolouration, or any of the babies' medical records. But his statement was troubling nonetheless. At the very least, it suggested that – even after all this time spent discussing and arguing about it – the evidence for air embolism is still open to debate.

For now though, those debates are relegated to beyond the

courtroom. On 24 May 2024, the Court of Appeal announced that it had denied Lucy Letby's request for permission to appeal. Five weeks later, the three judges published their reasoning. They concluded that the judge in Letby's original trial had 'handled the trial with exemplary skill and patience'. Letby's barrister Ben Myers had tried to argue that Dewi Evans' evidence should have been excluded on the grounds that Dr Evans wasn't sufficiently qualified. Myers had also argued that the level of scientific knowledge generally wasn't reliable enough to allow instances of air embolism to be identified in the case. The Court of Appeal judges rejected both of these arguments. They concluded that the judge in Letby's original trial had been right not to exclude Dewi Evans' evidence. They also had this to say on the state of scientific knowledge on air embolism:

> We do not accept that the level of scientific knowledge concerning air embolism is so limited that no reliable expert evidence at all can be given about it. Air embolus as a cause of collapse or death in a neonate is not a 'bogus' medical theory. The fact that air embolus can occur in neonates is not in dispute. Research is necessarily limited, and the number of observed cases is fortunately small; and there are therefore limits to the extent of scientific knowledge of the topic. But it does not follow that there can be no expert evidence as to whether an air embolus did or did not occur in a particular case.

There were validatory remarks about Dewi Evans too. According to the judges, 'it is unarguably the case that Dr Evans was suitably qualified – or to put it another way, it is not arguable that he lacked the necessary expertise – to give evidence . . . He certainly had sufficient knowledge to render his opinion of value; he had expertise that was capable of assisting the jury and was unarguably able to provide evidence with regard to neonates on matters within his expertise, but outwith the experience of the jury.' As to Dr Evans' impartiality, the judges remarked:

[W]e agree . . . that the judge was fully entitled to conclude that the approach of Dr Evans to his task was reasonable and did not amount to partiality or lack of independence, nor was it unreasonable for Dr Evans thereafter to provide some direction and structure in relation to identified cases. To the extent that he was acting as an investigator or director of the investigation, he was not doing so in a way that precluded him from being an expert witness in the case.

What about the new evidence of Dr Shoo Lee about skin discolouration and which type of skin discolouration is proof of air embolism? Letby's barrister Ben Myers had argued that this evidence had become available to the defence since the trial and that it showed that the prosecution's experts Dr Evans and Dr Bohin wrongly used skin discolouration as a means of diagnosing air embolus. But the three judges in the Court of Appeal disagreed. 'We are not persuaded by Mr Myers' submission that the applicant could not reasonably have been expected to seek evidence from Dr Lee before or during the trial,' they remarked. They also concluded that Dr Lee's evidence didn't undermine the prosecution case because 'there was no prosecution expert evidence diagnosing air embolus solely on the basis of skin discolouration.' Furthermore, 'air embolus may be associated with a variety of skin discolouration. In short, the prosecution witnesses did not fall into the error which the proposed fresh evidence seeks to assert they made. The proposed evidence is therefore irrelevant and inadmissible.'

It's important to be clear on what the Court of Appeal was and wasn't saying in its judgement. Its job was not to decide if the air embolism evidence was true. Nor was its job to decide whether the jury in Letby's original trial had reached the right verdicts. The Court of Appeal's job was to answer the much narrower question of whether Letby should be allowed to appeal on the grounds that the *process* of her original trial was flawed or incomplete, and they decided that it wasn't. Legally, for now at least, the case is closed. But outside the courtroom, the debates about the quality of the air embolism evidence in Letby's case look set only to intensify further.

But what about the other scientific evidence in the case? After all, the prosecution didn't hang solely on the air embolism evidence. Other methods of harm were part of the case too. It was argued that several babies collapsed after having air and milk forced into their stomachs via their nasogastric tubes (or NG tubes). Others were said to have had their breathing tubes moved or their alarms switched off and three showed signs of trauma. Two were alleged to have been poisoned with insulin. Proving any one of these alleged methods of attack would establish once and for all that someone on the neonatal unit at the Countess of Chester Hospital was harming babies. And yet, once again, there was no direct evidence. No one on the unit saw Lucy Letby – or anyone else – doing any of these things. So how strong was the evidence of these other forms of harm?

Lucy Letby's efforts to appeal against her convictions made no reference to these other allegations and the scientific evidence used by the prosecution to support them. That in itself is significant. We understand that her legal team initially planned to make a challenge concerning the insulin evidence but then withdrew it. But that doesn't mean that these other areas of scientific evidence are uncontroversial. Since Letby's conviction, all of them have been subject to sustained critique by sceptical journalists and their expert sources. The *Guardian*, the *Telegraph*, the *New Yorker*, Channel 5, and others have all challenged the full range of scientific evidence in the Letby case. The Conservative MP Sir David Davis has thrown his weight behind the sceptical cause too, saying he may be prepared to meet Lucy Letby in prison and raising questions about a possible miscarriage of justice. The view that 'dodgy' science has caused Lucy Letby to be wrongly imprisoned is now part of mainstream conversation about her case and the very suggestion should worry anyone who cares about justice. So what are we to make of this concern?

One sceptical suggestion is that staffing shortages on the neonatal unit may be what caused so many babies to collapse and die, not Lucy Letby. During her trial, Letby's barrister Ben Myers tried the same argument. The neonatal unit was 'understaffed and overstretched', he said, and this was partly to blame for the rise in unexpected baby deaths and collapses. Myers wasn't the only one to highlight the issue of inadequate staffing. The Royal College of Paediatrics and Child Health (RCPCH) observed '[t]here are . . . significant gaps in both medical and nursing rotas . . . Nurse staffing levels are frequently less than the recommended levels' Even the Care Quality Commission in its 2016 report – a piece of work that was far from curious or probing – highlighted low staffing levels as a 'high-risk' area of concern. If anything, these dry reports and Letby's own barrister underplayed the staffing pressures on the unit in 2015–16. One of the nurses from the unit who spoke to us was vivid in her recollection of that time. Those years were 'horrendously busy', the worst she could remember since 1986. Staff were 'absolutely stretched to the limit', 'run ragged' – so much so that she warned her manager that 'something awful' was going to happen.

There were similar warnings from doctors. Some were working twenty-hour shifts or more. In late 2015, one of the consultants emailed the hospital's CEO Tony Chambers, warning him that staff were 'chronically overworked'. At times, she said, the unit was so busy that it was running out of vital equipment. Her message to senior management couldn't have been starker: 'Over the past few weeks I have seen several medical and nursing colleagues in tears . . . This is now our normal working pattern and it is not safe. Things are stretched thinner and thinner and are at breaking point. When things snap, the casualties will either be children's lives or the mental and physical health of our staff.'

It's alarming stuff. And by virtue of her training, Letby was in the eye of the storm. Unlike many of her colleagues, she had specialist training in intensive care. Naturally, therefore, she was often the one to be looking after the sickest babies. So is it possible that there wasn't actually a bad actor on the neonatal unit at the Countess of Chester Hospital? Was the search for a culprit based on a faulty premise? Could all those baby deaths and collapses have innocent explanations?

There's no doubt that the staffing shortages in Letby's unit were real and acute. But as bad as things were, staffing shortages aren't a persuasive answer to the question why so many babies collapsed and died between June 2015 and June 2016. Strains on staffing might well cause more incidents to occur, but it would be relatively straightforward to figure out medically what had caused those incidents. The situation at the Countess of Chester Hospital was very different: babies were collapsing unexpectedly and were unresponsive to resuscitation, and the staff, with all their combined expertise, couldn't figure out why.

Another suggestion – discussed outside the courtroom more than inside it – was the theory that a seasonal virus known as an 'enterovirus' was to blame for the rise in baby deaths at the hospital. Enteroviruses affect the intestine and are especially common in the summer months. Six out of the seven babies who died in the Letby case died during the summer. During Letby's trial, a plumber who worked at the hospital testified that 'foul water' had come up from a washbasin in one of the nurseries in the neonatal unit at some point in 2015 or 2016 – although not at the time of any of the incidents in the case. So could an enterovirus explain the baby deaths? Letby's defence expert Mike Hall says that enteroviruses were not specifically tested for at the Countess of Chester Hospital, so the enterovirus theory is a hypothesis that can neither be proved nor disproved, although he thinks, with the exception of one case, that it's unlikely.

Another consultant neonatologist we spoke to was even more sceptical. He points out that the babies in the neonatal unit at the Countess of Chester Hospital were in an environment where enteroviruses are relatively much less likely to develop. More importantly, the babies there were being closely and continually monitored. The assumption is that staff would have picked up on the symptoms and warning signs of viral infection. In other words, the spate of sudden and unexpected collapses and deaths in 2015–16 doesn't fit with the enterovirus theory.

What about bacterial infection? It's been reported that harmful bacteria were found on some of the taps in the unit in 2015. However, we understand that all babies who had post mortems – six out of seven in the case – would have been tested for evidence of infection, and those tests revealed no evidence of bacterial infection.

But however unsubstantiated these alternative theories of staffing shortages and infection may have been, the prosecution's own allegations of harm were far from straightforward or easy to prove. The allegations concerning air embolism show this, and there were challenges with some of the other allegations in the case too. Some of them were strikingly vague. The case of Baby H was a good example. Baby H collapsed unexpectedly on two consecutive nights in September 2015 while Lucy Letby was on duty. The prosecution alleged that the collapses were due to 'sabotage' by Letby. It was suggested that she may have moved Baby H's breathing tube but this was more speculation than allegation. The precise method of alleged 'sabotage' was never conclusively specified. As it happens, the jury failed to reach a verdict on this count and it's not hard to see why.

Other allegations in the case seemed obviously strained or weak. Baby N, for example, suffered a deterioration at 1 a.m. on 15 June 2016. Letby had been the baby's designated nurse that day. However, she had finished her shift at 8 p.m. – five hours earlier. Was Letby really to blame? The prosecution argued she was.

Perhaps the weakest allegation against Letby involved one of three counts of attempted murder relating to Baby G. According to the prosecution, Letby deliberately switched off Baby G's monitor. During the trial, however, one of Letby's nursing colleagues came forward to say that two of the doctors, not Letby, had been responsible for leaving the monitor switched off, and that they had actually apologised to her for doing so. The jury found Letby not guilty on this count, but it was a sobering indication of how shaky at least this part of the prosecution case against Letby could be.

Of course, these were just a fraction of the twenty-two allegations of murder and attempted murder that Letby faced, but there were other allegations in the case that presented a more basic, perhaps more human, challenge for the jury – and that was the sheer level of violence that they implied. 'Could this bland, innocuous-looking girl, Lucy Letby, really be capable of *that*?' was the uncomfortable question they invited. It's not so difficult to imagine the mechanics of picking up a syringe and injecting air into an intravenous line or a tube going into a baby's stomach. As heinous as these actions are, the violence they involve is subtle and invisible. But Letby faced other more visceral allegations too. In the case of Baby E, for example, she was accused of inflicting an injury somewhere in the baby's upper gastrointestinal tract using a wire-like object, causing the baby to bleed copiously through his mouth. In the case of Baby O, Letby was accused of causing such damage to his liver that it was comparable to the kind of injury only seen in road traffic accidents or assaults by parents or carers. The sheer horror of these allegations forces us to consider what it would have meant for Lucy Letby to have done these things. How must they have played out practically for her – minute by minute, second by second. Could she really have done these things?

There was no direct proof of any of it. Some witnesses saw what the prosecution said was the immediate aftermath of an attack. The most shocking and vivid example comes from the mother of Baby E who recalls hearing her baby screaming and seeing blood around his mouth. But there was no CCTV and there were no eyewitnesses who actually saw Letby harming any baby and so once again, science and expert evidence were key to proving that these horrific allegations were true. If the prosecution's science was correct, it had helped to unmask Lucy Letby and expose her as a killer, but how reliable was it? We've seen the complexity of the air embolism evidence. What about the rest of the science in the case – would it be any clearer? Bluntly put: did this science reveal a smoking gun?

One of the most prominent allegations in the case – in addition to the air embolism evidence – was the claim that Letby had injected air into babies' stomachs. Several babies had been attacked in this way, according to the prosecution. In some cases, the quantity of air had allegedly blown up the baby's stomach so much that it squashed the baby's diaphragm, which meant that the baby couldn't breathe. In medical jargon, it was referred to as 'splinting the diaphragm'.

In some ways, these 'stomach air' cases were less complicated than the air embolism cases. X-rays and other evidence clearly showed there was air in the babies' stomachs. The question was how it got there – and whether it was the result of deliberate harm. The prosecution experts concluded it was, and for all but one of the babies the jury agreed.

The prosecution evidence in each case was compelling. Baby C, for example, was the first baby in the case who the prosecution alleged had been murdered by having air pumped into his stomach. On the day he died, Baby C's nurse checked to see if his stomach had any air in it. She found none. She then left the room after which Baby C's alarm went off. The prosecution's pathologist Dr Andreas Marnerides reviewed the case and noted 'massive' swelling of Baby C's stomach. His conclusion was that air must have been 'injected into the nasogastric tube', splinting Baby C's diaphragm and fatally compromising his breathing.

Baby I suffered multiple collapses, two of which were blamed on air being pumped into her stomach. An X-ray after her first collapse on 30 September 2015 revealed 'a massive amount of gas in her stomach and bowels and her lungs appeared "squashed" and of small volume'. Another X-ray from 14 October showed 'widespread gaseous distention sufficient to splint the diaphragm and prevent Baby I breathing properly'.

Baby O also suffered 'profound gastric and intestinal distention', while his triplet brother Baby P was found to have air in his bowel. In both of these latter cases, Marnerides concluded that air had been injected into the babies' stomachs – a conclusion shared by the two paediatric experts, Dr Evans and Dr Bohin.

During Letby's trial, there were arguments about whether various forms of breathing support could have caused the babies' stomachs to fill with air, but these arguments were ultimately rejected by the jury. So do the 'stomach air' cases amount to a smoking gun? Dewi Evans and Sandie Bohin believe they do. Unsurprisingly perhaps, Letby's defence expert-in-waiting Mike Hall disagrees. The consensus of opinion among the prosecution experts, he believes, is incorrect. He didn't quite say it, but you could tell he thought expert groupthink was a factor. In the case of Baby C, for example, Hall believes that the reason the baby's stomach filled with air may have been that the baby had suffered an obstruction of the bowel, not the deliberate administration of air into the baby's stomach. Hall is also sceptical of the allegation that air in babies' stomachs is what killed them. Air in the stomach could certainly cause a baby to collapse, he says, but removing excess air should in most cases be straightforward, as should resuscitation. Stomach air doesn't explain why babies died, he says.

Hall's bowel obstruction theory for Baby C was categorically rejected by the prosecution expert's pathologist Dr Marnerides. According to him, a bowel obstruction would have been detectable from the post-mortem evidence and it wasn't. However, we spoke to another pathologist who played no role in the Letby case but who has seen the post-mortem report for Baby C. That pathologist says there are several kinds of bowel obstruction that would be identifiable at post-mortem. However, this doesn't apply to all varieties of bowel obstruction, so it's difficult for a pathologist to say categorically that Baby C did not have a bowel obstruction of some kind. If our pathologist is right, Hall's bowel obstruction theory might well be possible too.[3]

What about Hall's more general scepticism towards the prosecution claim that babies died because of excessive air in their stomachs? In July 2024, the *Guardian*'s Felicity Lawrence wrote an article questioning various aspects of the scientific evidence in the Letby case, including the basic allegation in the 'stomach air' cases:

> [T]he idea that injecting air into the stomach via a nasogastric tube could cause collapse leading to death was described as nonsensical or 'rubbish', 'ridiculous', 'implausible' and 'fantastical', by eight separate expert clinicians who spoke to the *Guardian*, seven of them specialising in neonatology. Several said it was not practically feasible. Nasogastric tubes are tiny; it would take several refills using the 10ml syringes on neonatal units to inject a significant quantity of air. Furthermore, it would leak out or the baby would burp or vomit it up, or pass it as wind, they said.[4]

It sounds troubling, so we asked Sandie Bohin, one of the two prosecution experts behind the stomach air theory. Dr Bohin told us that while it might be possible to remove air from the baby's stomach, once that air enters the baby's gut – as it did in some of the babies – it cannot be removed and the consequences can be fatal. We spoke to another respected consultant neonatologist with knowledge of the Letby case who added to Sandie Bohin's view. The consultant noted that 'everyone will recognise that you can get gaseous distension [i.e. swelling] of the stomach' and this could be done deliberately by injecting air down a baby's nasogastric tube. This could squash the diaphragm from below, and if the baby's respiratory system is already compromised, this could be enough to cause collapse and ultimately death. The consultant agreed that it might take several refills of a syringe – perhaps four or five refills of a 10ml syringe – to blow up a baby's stomach so much that it would squash the baby's diaphragm. But it would be perfectly doable – and would take less than a minute. 'It's entirely plausible,' the consultant told us 'that somebody, if they have malicious intent, could inject any volume of air you wanted to, and the fact it's a small syringe isn't a limiting factor. If somebody was in the mindset to do that, it's certainly possible to inject air down the nasogastric tube.' We also spoke to a paediatric pathologist who agreed: it is possible to blow up a baby's stomach with air and for this air to be trapped and squash the baby's diaphragm.

It appears, therefore, that the prosecution's 'stomach air' allegations are at least physically and physiologically possible. Whether they meet the standard of beyond reasonable doubt is another question – and one on which experts will disagree. There were, however, points in the trial where the prosecution's experts appeared to undermine their own case that Lucy Letby injected air into babies' stomachs. One was in the case of Baby I. On 23 August 2015, Baby I suffered 'abdominal distention'. The prosecution experts agreed this was 'consistent of harm'. The problem was that Lucy Letby wasn't on duty that day, according to the rota. A similar problem arose in the case of Baby C. The last X-ray for Baby C while he was alive was taken on 12 June 2015 – two days before he died.

The X-ray showed gas in the stomach and the prosecution's experts agreed it was suspicious. The expert radiologist also appeared to agree, noting that the gas observed in the X-ray was 'consistent with air administration via the NGT'. But according to the staffing rota, Lucy Letby wasn't on duty on the day that the X-ray was taken. She hadn't been on duty for the previous two days either. It meant that either the prosecution experts had misinterpreted two 'stomach air' events as 'suspicious' when in fact they were innocent, or alternatively, someone other than Letby was pumping air into babies' stomachs.

These incongruities are just a part of the prosecution's evidence in the trial – evidence which, taken as a whole, the jury found compelling and convincing. But they are important. At the very least, they highlight the fact that the evidence isn't clear-cut and is subject to expert judgement. They also add to questions about the strength of scientific evidence implicating Letby. Finally, the fact that there are experts who doubt the plausibility of the stomach air allegations – whatever the counter-arguments may be – suggests that the 'stomach air' cases, like the air embolism cases, are not a smoking gun.

Shifts in the experts' positions during the years-long police investigation didn't help either. The case of Baby C, detailed in the previous chapter, is the clearest example. Here, Dr Dewi Evans initially concluded: 'One may never know the cause of [Baby C's] collapse. He was at great risk of unexpected collapse.' But by the time he got into the witness box, Dr Evans' view on Baby C's death changed. He told the court that Baby C's diaphragm had been splinted following the administration of air into his stomach before going on to introduce the possibility that Baby C had had air forced into his bloodstream. It was a striking shift. And there were other cases like this.

Baby E was one of the shocking cases of alleged trauma. Letby was accused of causing an injury to the baby, which resulted in significant blood loss and blood around the baby's mouth. She was also accused of injecting air into Baby E's bloodstream. In his 2017 report, however, Dr Evans made no mention of air embolism. On the question of Baby E's bleeding, Dr Evans' 2017 report observed that '[Baby E's] sudden demise is the result of an acute gastro-intestinal haemorrhage'. However, Evans went on to say: 'I'm at a loss to explain the cause of his haemorrhage . . . In the absence of a post-mortem it's not possible to say whether [Baby E] sustained trauma to his upper gastrointestinal system.'

In court, Dr Evans robustly defended evolutions in his position. 'In virtually all of the cases, I have benefited from additional information since then,' he said. 'As a clinician, if I receive additional information that allows me to change or modify my opinion, that is what we do as clinicians.' In a particularly testy exchange with Letby's barrister, Evans said: 'The idea that I could get it all perfectly right from looking at all the notes is simply unrealistic. I was not able to speak to any member of the local staff. I was never going to get everything 100 per cent correct.' This is undoubtedly true, but the shifts in some of Evans' positions show the extent to which some of the science in the case was open to revision – and not just minor revisions: revisions that could turn the dial on a particular allegation against Letby from not guilty to guilty. Which begs the question: was any of the science in the Letby case beyond debate?

What about the allegation that Letby had overfed some of the babies with milk in an attempt to kill them? How straightforward was that? In many ways, this looked indisputable. Baby G was one of the babies Letby was accused of overfeeding. In the early hours of the morning of 7 September 2015, the baby was receiving 45mls of milk every three hours. The milk entered her stomach gently under gravity, and before each feed, Baby G's stomach was 'aspirated' – in other words, contents from the stomach were sucked out to check that there was no undigested milk before the new feed was started. Medical staff were therefore shocked when Baby G projectile-vomited. What shocked them more was that even after the vomits, she still had 45mls of milk in her stomach. The only conclusion seemed to be that she had been overfed sometime before her collapse but after her nurse had confirmed that her stomach was empty. The same thing happened again two weeks later.

For the prosecution, this was an open-and-shut case, but even here Mike Hall disagreed. He argued that although Baby G's nurses had checked to see if her stomach was empty before continuing her feeds, the method they used wasn't necessarily reliable. This method involved measuring the acidity rather than the volume of the baby's stomach contents. If these contents were acidic, that was taken as a sure sign that the stomach was empty and didn't contain undigested milk. Hall's contention was that this was unreliable and he made his point by referring to a different baby in the Letby case – Baby O. Baby O's stomach contents were even more acidic than Baby G's had been. However, despite this, the prosecution experts had accepted that Baby O's stomach had milk in it. In other words, high acidity wasn't proof that the stomach was empty. Hall's point was that Baby G's projectile-vomits might have been the result of undigested milk in her stomach that the acidity test didn't identify, not overfeeding. Of course, the prosecution disagreed, but how could we tell who was right?

For us non-scientists, much of the science in the Lucy Letby case felt like a fog. Were we giving Mike Hall's sceptical arguments too much weight? Or were we doing what journalists should do – questioning group consensus among experts? It was sometimes hard to tell.

Herein lies part of the agony of trying to assess the scientific evidence in the Letby case. Almost all of it came down to individual expert opinions and judgements. Did babies die from air embolism? Were babies overfed with milk? Did they have air forced into their stomachs, causing their diaphragms to stop working properly? These questions were answered by individual experts weighing the evidence – principally Dewi Evans and Sandie Bohin. Experts are chosen because they know – or are supposed to know – more than the rest of us. But experts are also fallible. And they disagree. At the time of the baby deaths, none of the local pathologists identified foul play. One of those local pathologists was Dr George Kokai. Dr Kokai is now retired, but we've spoken to two paediatric pathologists in different parts of the country who both vouch for his experience and skill. Of course, Dr Kokai and his colleagues weren't working on the basis of a theory of foul play, but if it was obvious, wouldn't they have spotted it? Whatever the answer to this question, it's safe to say that expert opinions, however esteemed, often disagree and they're never absolute.

That said, it's important to be clear on just how much expert opinion went against Lucy Letby during her trial. We know about the two main prosecution experts – Dewi Evans and Sandie Bohin. Then there were Letby's medical colleagues at the Countess of Chester Hospital. Their testimonies and medical assessments weighed powerfully in support of the prosecution case. There were other experts in the case too – the pathologist Dr Andreas Marnerides, the radiologist Professor Owen Arthurs, a blood expert, and an insulin expert. Although Dewi Evans and Sandie Bohin did most of the heavy lifting in the prosecution's scientific arguments, these other experts made their own contributions to specific parts of the prosecution case. That raises an obvious question: why did Letby's defence not call their own army of experts – their own pathologist, their own radiologist, their own insulin expert, and so on? Did her defence team fail to seek out their own experts? Or – as in the case of Mike Hall – did Letby herself choose not to call any experts, and if she didn't why didn't she?

We spoke to several people with inside knowledge of the case and what we discovered is revealing. Letby's defence team did approach their own pathologist, their own radiologist and their own insulin expert. But in each case, these experts largely concurred with the assessments of their counterparts on the prosecution side. For example, Letby's team approached an eminent radiologist in the hope that she would find flaws in the evidence of the prosecution's expert radiologist Owen Arthurs. But she didn't – or at least she didn't find anything that would make a substantial difference to Letby's defence. Likewise, we understand that the pathologist that Letby's lawyers spoke to basically agreed with the findings of the prosecution's pathologist Andreas Marnerides. In the end, Mike Hall was the only expert in her corner, which makes Letby's decision not to call him even more difficult to comprehend. What should we conclude from this?

The obvious conclusion is that on questions of pathology, radiology, and the insulin evidence, there were no serious defence arguments to be made. The science – in these areas at least – was settled. But was it? There are alternative possibilities. Maybe the experts that Letby's defence team approached weren't critical enough. Or maybe they weren't sufficiently thorough or independent-minded. Were they at the top of their fields? And if they were, can we be sure that they approached their task with the conscientiousness that it required? Did they have any natural biases or temperamental qualities that meant they weren't inclined to go against what the prosecution experts were saying? Groupthink can afflict experts in the same way it does everyone else. Was this a factor in the expert opinions commissioned by Letby's defence team?

We don't know. Nor do we know how effective Letby's legal team was at seeking out the best defence opinion – but there are reasons to wonder. Letby's solicitor is a local Chester-based brief called Richard Thomas. Thomas was the solicitor called in to represent Letby when she was first arrested. We understand that some of Letby's friends expected her to hire a more specialist lawyer. The fact that she didn't has left some people wondering if the outcome would have been different with another team. That's not a question for us to answer. What we can consider, however, is whether there were significant arguments that were available to Lucy Letby's defence and that weren't presented in court. Mike Hall did his best to advise Letby's defence team on the clinical evidence. But what about other areas of scientific evidence in the trial – like the pathology and insulin evidence?

Of all the prosecution expert judgements in the Letby case, one leaps out for its simplicity, force and pure shock value. It's separate to the air embolism and stomach air allegations and it came not from Dewi Evans or Sandie Bohin, but from the prosecution's expert pathologist Andreas Marnerides.

On 23 June 2016, Baby O died. He was the penultimate baby to die before Lucy Letby was removed from the unit. Marnerides gave this account of Baby O's death: 'In my view, the cause of death was inflicted traumatic injury to the liver, profound gastric and intestinal distension following acute excessive injection/infusion of air via a naso-gastric tube and air embolism due to administration into a venous line.' So three causes of death: air embolism, air injected into the stomach through the NG tube, and impact-style trauma.

We've already outlined the disagreements over air embolism and air in the stomach, but what are we to make of Dr Marnerides' conclusion about traumatic injury?

Letby's defence argued that Baby O's liver injury could have been caused by CPR, in particular, squeezing applied to Baby O by medics in their efforts to resuscitate him. But Marnerides rejected this interpretation. Here's part of his exchange with the prosecution barrister Nick Johnson:

NJ: How does that injury come to be in a child of [Baby O's] age?'
AM: The distribution, the pattern and the appearance of the bruis-
    ing indicates towards impact-type injury. I'm fairly confident
    this is impact-type injury.

According to Dr Marnerides, the evidence showed 'extensive haem-orrhaging into the liver' of a kind he had only seen in road traffic collisions and assaults from parents or carers.

Letby's barrister Ben Myers also had a chance to question Dr Marnerides and that exchange was equally interesting. 'I have never seen this type of injury in the context of CPR,' Marnerides said. 'I would say the force required would be of the magnitude of that generated by a baby jumping on a trampoline and falling.' Could rigorous chest compressions be the cause of Baby O's internal bruising? 'I don't think so, no,' Marnerides replied. 'This is a huge area of bruising for a liver of this size. This is not something you see in CPR.'

It was a shocking finding. So what weight should we attach to Dr Marnerides' expert opinion? Marnerides leads the forensic children's pathology service at Guy's and St Thomas' Hospital in London – a prestigious position by any measure. And Letby's de-fence team didn't manage to produce a pathologist of their own to dispute Dr Marnerides' findings. But does that mean that his opin-ion is correct? Dr Marnerides is known for his role as a prosecution expert witness in a number of major court cases. Is this relevant? Readers can form their own view. But what should we make of Dr Marnerides' assessment of Baby O's liver injury?

The first thing to say is that Baby O's liver damage is indisputable. Baby O suffered what are called subcapsular haematomas. A haematoma is simply a collection of blood. A subcapsular liver haematoma is a collection of blood below the 'capsule' or outer covering of the liver. In Baby O's case, there were several subcapsular liver haematomas, some of which had burst or ruptured. The question is what caused these haematomas.

After Baby O's death in 2016, a post-mortem was carried out by an experienced local pathologist George Kokai. Dr Kokai concluded that Baby O's death was natural. He found that Baby O died as 'a consequence of intra-abdominal bleeding from ruptured subcapsular liver [haematoma . . .] of the liver.' But what caused the haematomas? From what we know of Dr Kokai's post-mortem report on Baby O, it's clear he was at a loss to explain the cause of the liver haematoma that he believed killed Baby O. He concluded that the most likely cause of the haematoma was 'hypoxia', a technical term for insufficient oxygen. But it was little more than a theory. Ultimately, Dr Kokai classified Baby O's death as 'Sudden Unexpected Postnatal Collapse', which, as one pathologist told us, effectively means: 'we've looked and we can't figure out why he died.' Importantly though, Dr Kokai didn't conclude that Baby O's liver injury was the result of inflicted trauma similar to a road traffic accident – and yet this is what Dr Marnerides concluded. Both pathologists were looking at the same information – although it's important to note that Dr Kokai conducted the physical examination of Baby O's body, whereas Dr Marnerides was looking solely at Dr Kokai's reports and photos. So why the difference of opinion between Dr Kokai and Dr Marnerides? And whose opinion is more reliable?

We spoke to one paediatric pathologist who did not play a role in the Letby case but who has seen Baby O's post-mortem report. The pathologist, who we will call 'P', spoke to us on condition of anonymity. 'P''s assessment was that it wasn't possible for a pathologist to confirm that Baby O's death was due to natural causes.

'P' also agrees with the prosecution assessment that Baby O's clinical history shows that he was doing well and his liver injury and death have no obvious explanation. However, 'P' is not convinced by Dr Marnerides' conclusion that Baby O's liver injury was caused by inflicted trauma similar to a road traffic accident. According to 'P', inflicted trauma would likely produce 'one massive injury' on the liver rather than multiple haematomas, as were seen in Baby O's liver. Also, 'P' says that if the liver injury had been the result of inflicted trauma, you would also expect to see injury to the bowel – and yet Baby O's bowel showed no signs of injury. 'Given the relatively small size of an infant's abdomen, I think it would be very unusual to get localised damage,' 'P' told us. 'It wouldn't be unusual to get no bruises on the skin, but you'd expect more of a diffuse injury to the intra-abdominal organs if you've had enough force to cause that amount of haemorrhage.' 'P' isn't arguing that Baby O wasn't killed or that his liver injury wasn't caused by foul play. 'P' believes that if Baby O's stomach was blown up with air, this pressure might conceivably explain the haematomas in his liver. 'P''s point is that we don't know, and we certainly can't be sure, that Dr Marnerides' theory of inflicted trauma is correct. In short, for 'P', Marnerides' theory isn't established beyond reasonable doubt. In 'P''s view, there are no absolutes in pathology. 'Always' and 'never' are not part of the pathologist's lexicon. So where does this leave us?

It is very likely that the science in the Lucy Letby case will continue to be debated for many years. What is clear is that eminent experts looking at the same evidence in the case disagree. Mike Hall disagrees with Sandie Bohin and Dewi Evans. Dr Shoo Lee in Canada probably has a different view still to Drs Hall, Bohin and Evans. Dr Marnerides disagrees with Dr Kokai, and our own expert pathologist 'P' has an alternative view to both Dr Marnerides and Dr Kokai. All of this invites some rather obvious questions: what if the police had asked Mike Hall to be their expert paediatrician instead of Dewi Evans? Or what if they had turned to 'P' instead of Dr Marnerides? We – and Lucy Letby – might be in a very different world. And therein lies one of the central difficulties of the Letby case: the expert evidence is open to debate and dispute, and yet the consequences of Lucy Letby's trial are more or less final.

There is a further worry about expert evidence in criminal trials more generally that our pathologist 'P' summed up as follows:

> Courts want people who are more absolute and whose evidence doesn't give rise to more questions, and that means we've ended up with the same people appearing in case after case, and everyone knows who the hawks are and who the doves are. Depending on your preferred outcome, you know whom to engage for prosecution or defence. And people who genuinely change their position or ask questions end up in trouble.

But there is one further pillar of scientific evidence in the Letby case that is much less reliant on individual expert opinion – and should therefore be harder to argue against. It's the prosecution's evidence of insulin poisoning. According to the prosecution, Baby F and Baby L were both poisoned with insulin. Unlike the other allegations in the Letby case, these insulin cases were based on laboratory tests. These tests looked so solid that there was no scientific challenge to the prosecution's science – not even from Mike Hall. Neither of the two babies involved died. The charges were attempted murder, not murder. But evidentially, they formed the cornerstone of the rest of the prosecution case because they appeared to prove the most basic allegation of all – that someone on the unit was harming babies. As the prosecution put it, they proved that 'a poisoner [was] at work' in Letby's unit. Once that premise is established, it becomes much easier to accept the other allegations in the case. It's little wonder that one of the police officers who investigated Letby described the insulin cases as a 'milestone in the investigation'. So can we trust the prosecution's insulin evidence or is it – like so much of the other science in the case – open to debate?

Once again, the example of the Dutch nurse Lucia de Berk is a cautionary tale. De Berk had been wrongly convicted of several things – poisoning patients among them. And there was another case, closer to home, that has echoes of the de Berk case. In 2008, a nurse called Colin Norris was convicted of injecting patients with insulin in hospitals in Leeds. In the years since, our own *Panorama* colleague Mark Daly has made several programmes questioning the scientific evidence in the case. Norris is still in jail, but the debate about the science that convicted him is still raging. Letby herself was first questioned about the insulin cases after her first arrest in July 2018. Police believed someone had contaminated the nutrition bags that were used to give intravenous feed to Babies F and L. At the end of her interview, Letby had a question of her own for the police: did they have the nutrition bag? According to the prosecution barrister Nick Johnson, Letby asked this question 'repeatedly'. She 'taunted the police' with it, Johnson claimed, because Letby knew that the bag had been disposed of. The police didn't have it. So how could they prove that babies had been poisoned? 'She thought the fact they didn't have the bag would give her a free pass,' Johnson told the court.

But the police didn't need the nutrition bags to make their case. In the course of trawling through medical notes, Dewi Evans and consultant Steve Brearey – completely independently of each other – discovered the results of lab tests carried out on blood samples taken from the babies. The results indicated that someone had given the two boys dangerous quantities of insulin. Whatever else is said about Dr Evans and Dr Brearey, this discovery was probably the most significant breakthrough in the case. The basic science was outlined in previous chapters, but it's worth recapping here. Where there is insulin that has been naturally produced by the body, you will also find a substance called C-peptide. Conversely, if you find insulin without corresponding C-peptide, that indicates that the insulin is not natural and has instead been administered. Babies F and L were found to have high levels of insulin in their blood with no corresponding C-peptide. Neither baby had been prescribed insulin and the possibility that they had been given it accidentally was ruled out.

The evidence looked bulletproof. Even Letby herself agreed in evidence that the insulin found in the babies' blood could not have been administered accidentally.[5] She just said she wasn't responsible. However, some of Letby's supporters have argued that she was wrong to concede so easily. For a start, she's not an insulin expert or an expert in the testing method that was used to establish that insulin had been given to the babies. They point out that she may have agreed with what the police were telling her, but that didn't prove anything one way or another. Imagine the police telling an innocent person they had found his DNA at a crime scene. The innocent person might hear 'DNA' and assume that the police's evidence was indisputable, but even if he said so, it wouldn't mean he was guilty.

But there have been more direct challenges to the science involved in the insulin evidence. These arguments are complex, but they're so important to the question of whether Lucy Letby is guilty or not that we've decided to tackle them in some detail. To help us, we've spoken to several experts on insulin, hypoglycaemia and the laboratory test used in the Letby case. Some of these experts didn't want to be named, but their expertise has informed our understanding.

The first thing to say is that you don't have to be a Lucy Letby supporter to question the insulin results. One of the hospital's own consultants who missed the significance of the insulin / C-peptide results told us that they thought the results must be a mistake at the time. They said: 'It is relatively common for samples to give inaccurate results as the blood cells are broken down (haemolysis) or clotted together.' Could this be a reason to doubt the insulin / C-peptide results in the Letby case?

It is true that blood samples can become unsuitable for testing because of cell destruction or clotting. However, had this been true of the blood samples in the Letby case, the lab would almost certainly have rejected them. The lab would not have performed an insulin / C-peptide test on an unsuitable sample, so this is one concern we don't need to worry about.

Some sceptics have tried a different argument. They've pointed out that Baby F was found to have had an insulin concentration in his blood of 4,657 picomoles per litre – abbreviated as pmol/l.

This is huge and would be enough to cause death or severe brain damage. And yet Baby F survived. So does this not suggest that the 4,657pmol/l reading was unreliable? Again, there's an obvious counterargument. Insulin itself doesn't kill or harm. It's the effect of insulin on the body's glucose levels that does the damage. Left untreated, 4,657pmol/l of insulin would indeed stop the body releasing glucose, leading to a very harmful drop in blood sugar. However, the medics on the neonatal unit at the Countess of Chester Hospital were on the case. They could see that Baby F's blood sugar was plummeting so they were pumping him with glucose to counteract the harm. Had they not done so, Baby F may well not have survived. As it turned out, Baby F does suffer from acute learning and other difficulties, and his parents have told us that they are in no doubt that this is the result of the insulin poisoning.

Another sceptical worry concerns the blood samples that were sent to the lab and whether they could have been compromised before they reached the lab, causing misleading results. The obvious worry here is degradation. A significant delay in a sample reaching the lab could lead to the sample degrading, and we know there was a delay in getting Baby L's blood sample to the lab. But once again, there's nothing in the Letby case to suggest that any of the blood samples had degraded by the time they reached the lab. And even if they had, the insulin and the C-peptide would both have degraded. Degradation would not lead to a sky-high insulin reading and a very low or zero reading for C-peptide.

All of these sceptical questions are pretty easy to deal with. But there is a more fundamental worry about the lab test that goes to the heart of its reliability: could it be that the results showing high levels of non-natural insulin were flawed? More precisely, could it be that either the high insulin readings or the low C-peptide readings were somehow false? Let's start with the low C-peptide readings first. Take the case of Baby F. The lab test on a blood sample from Baby F showed that he had 4,657pmol/l of insulin in his blood. That is a lot of insulin. If this insulin had been natural, you would expect to see C-peptide as well – and in even greater concentration than the insulin. That's because the body clears insulin 5–10 times more quickly than it clears C-peptide. That means that you would expect to find at least 5–10 times as much C-peptide as insulin in a blood sample if the insulin in the blood sample is natural. In the case of Baby F, however, the lab was unable to detect any C-peptide in the baby's blood. There seemed to be only one conclusion: the insulin had to be medical insulin administered from an external source – often called exogenous insulin. But is it possible the lab test simply failed to detect C-peptide – even though C-peptide was actually there in the blood sample?

There is a phenomenon in laboratory testing known as the 'Hook effect'. The Hook effect occurs when a testing procedure becomes overwhelmed and incorrectly records a zero for the substance it's trying to quantify. Could this have happened in the lab tests for Baby F and Baby L? Modern laboratory testing methods are generally designed to prevent Hook effect distortions, and there is no reason to doubt that these methods were used in the Letby case. However, some people have tried to argue that the C-peptide results in the cases of Baby F and Baby L may still have been distorted by a Hook effect. This argument presupposes that the high levels of insulin found in Baby F's and Baby L's blood were produced naturally, and that in the case of newborn babies, the C-peptide level in the blood can be as much as twenty times the level of naturally produced insulin. If this is true, the C-peptide value could have been as high as 93,000pmol/l, which is twenty times the amount of insulin found in Baby F's blood. According to some sceptics, this quantity of C-peptide would likely lead to a Hook effect – in other words, an erroneous reading of zero – giving the false impression that the insulin in the babies' blood wasn't natural.

This looks like a serious argument – but it isn't for one simple reason. Baby F had an insulin level of 4,657pmol/l, while Baby L's blood insulin was 1,099pmol/l or more. According to the experts we've spoken to, no baby could produce these levels of insulin naturally. It's not physiologically possible. What that means is that the C-peptide produced by a newborn baby would never reach the level that could supposedly lead to a Hook effect and a false reading of zero. Indeed the insulin levels for Baby F and Baby L are so high that you don't even need to know what their C-peptide readings were to know that the insulin in their blood can't have been natural. It was simply far too high.

What about the high insulin values in the blood samples of Baby F and Baby L? Is it possible that these were somehow the result of an error in the lab test – a 'false positive' as scientists sometimes call it? If it was, that would change everything. Those high insulin values are the key evidence for the allegation that babies were poisoned, confirmed by the low C-peptide values. So what are the chances that the high insulin values for Baby F and Baby L that came back from the lab were wrong? This is one of the questions that the *New Yorker* journalist Rachel Aviv tackled in her explosive May 2024 article about the Letby case. Aviv claimed that the Liverpool-based lab where the insulin test was carried out featured a warning on its website that its insulin test was 'not suitable for the investigation' of whether synthetic insulin had been administered. Aviv also cited an expert based in Sweden who said that the testing method provided by the Liverpool lab was 'not sufficient for use as evidence in a criminal prosecution'.[6] Aviv added that 'a biochemist' at the Liverpool lab 'had called the Countess [of Chester Hospital] to recommend that the sample be verified by a more specialized lab', but this didn't happen.

Unsurprisingly, sceptics latched on to these claims and quickly concluded that the insulin evidence against Letby was flawed. Were they right? The lab where the insulin tests were carried out is at the Royal Liverpool Hospital. We spoke to the lab and they provided us with some clarifications that appear to show that the Rachel Aviv article is, at least in part, slightly misleading. The first issue is Aviv's claim that the lab's website featured a warning that its insulin test was 'not suitable for the investigation' of whether synthetic insulin had been administered. That's technically true, but according to the lab, the point of the warning was that measuring insulin *on its own* is not enough to determine whether the insulin is synthetic. You need to measure C-peptide as well. But that's exactly what the lab did in the Letby cases. They measured both insulin and C-peptide. Indeed, it was the fact that the C-peptide was low compared to the insulin level that told investigators that the insulin was synthetic.

Other experts have noted that labs like the one in Liverpool often add a further disclaimer about their insulin test. The test is not guaranteed in all circumstances to detect every variety of synthetic insulin. Some synthetic insulin might go undetected. This is a significant limitation if it applies to the Liverpool lab test, but it's important to be clear on what it would mean for the Letby case. If a baby had been poisoned with exogenous insulin, it is theoretically possible that the lab test might not detect that synthetic insulin. In that event, the lab result would simply show that no exogenous insulin had been administered to the baby. What the test wouldn't do is give a false positive: the test would not falsely identify synthetic insulin where there was none. If anything, this limitation would work in favour of a poisoner.

Rachel Aviv's claim that a biochemist at the Royal Liverpool Hospital 'called the Countess [of Chester Hospital] to recommend that the sample be verified by a more specialized lab' is also – according to what the lab told us – not a faithful account of what happened. It is true that there is an alternative method for measuring insulin that is even more reliable than the method used by the Royal Liverpool Hospital. It is also true that the lab made the Countess of Chester aware of this alternative method. But according to the lab, there was no 'recommendation' that the hospital make use of this further testing method, nor was there any implication that the Royal Liverpool Hospital's own testing method was inadequate.

But what about the expert based in Sweden cited by Rachel Aviv who said that the testing method provided by the Liverpool lab was 'not sufficient for use as evidence in a criminal prosecution'? Is this true? We spoke to Aviv's expert – a respected forensic toxicologist called Alan Wayne Jones. Jones points out that the most reliable method for measuring insulin in a blood sample is a technique called mass spectrometry. In Jones' view, mass spectrometry is the only suitable method for measuring insulin for a criminal trial. The problem with the Letby evidence, in Jones' view, is that it relied on a different, less reliable method known as the immunoassay technique. In many ways, this is the key question in assessing the insulin evidence in the Letby case: could the immunoassay method used in the Letby evidence be flawed, and if so, does this invalidate the prosecution's insulin evidence?

In order to answer this question, you need to know what the immunoassay method is. First, some jargon: insulin is a hormone. Like most other labs, the Royal Liverpool Hospital where the Letby insulin tests were carried out employs the immunoassay technique, which uses antibodies to measure insulin. Many people will have a dim memory of learning about antibodies in biology lessons in school. Antibodies are produced by the immune system to tackle and eliminate substances that the body regards as harmful. But antibodies are also used in immunoassays to detect substances, including insulin. The immunoassay method used by the Royal Liverpool Hospital works by using antibodies to 'latch on to' insulin. Those antibodies then generate a 'signal' that can be measured. The greater the signal from the antibodies, the more insulin there is. The problem is that there are circumstances where the antibodies in the immunoassay might 'mistake' another substance for insulin. Where this happens, it's known as 'interference', and where there's interference, the test could give a misleadingly high insulin value – a false positive. In other words, it could give the impression that there is lots of insulin in a particular blood sample when in fact there isn't. Many of the sceptics looking at the Letby case have pointed out that because the lab used the immunoassay method and because immunoassays can in some cases give false positives because of interference, the high insulin values cited as evidence in the Letby case aren't reliable.

Mass spectrometry – the alternative method for measuring insulin recommended by Dr Jones in Sweden – doesn't suffer from this vulnerability. It's as close to infallible as it is possible for such a test to get. And that's the sceptics' point: the insulin evidence in the Letby case used the fallible immunoassay method and not the gold-standard mass spectrometry method. Therefore it can't be trusted. But is this argument as worrying as it appears?

One claim that has been made by some is that immunoassays might mistake 'proinsulin' for insulin. Proinsulin is a molecule produced in the pancreas that gets broken down into insulin and C-peptide. If the immunoassay method mistook proinsulin for insulin, that could give a falsely high insulin value. We checked with several experts and they all agreed that the immunoassay used by the lab in the Letby case would not have mistaken proinsulin for insulin: proinsulin would not 'interfere' with the immunoassay.

There is, however, another substance that can 'interfere' with immunoassays. Some people's bodies produce antibodies that the lab-produced antibodies in the immunoassay test mistake for insulin. Where this happens, it's possible that a lab test on a sample of their blood might mistake those bodily antibodies as insulin and potentially give a misleadingly high insulin reading. This is sometimes seen in people who've been receiving exogenous insulin for a long time. People suffering from Type 1 diabetes are a good example. It may also be seen, albeit rarely, in people who have developed antibodies in response to animals in their environment – for example, rodents in their home. Newborn babies in a hospital neonatal unit clearly don't fit into any of these categories. They haven't been receiving medical insulin for a long time and they haven't been exposed to animals. However, it's theoretically possible that they might have received antibodies from their mother that could interfere with an immunoassay test. Could this have happened in the Letby case?

From what we can tell, the likelihood that the high insulin values in the Letby case are false positives caused by interference with the immunoassay is low. Here's why. First, although the immunoassay method is not infallible, it is still very reliable. As one expert put it to us, 'immunoassay can pick up things with great precision and accuracy'. There is, however, an additional factor that Rachel Aviv and many of the other sceptics overlook and that is the clinical condition of Baby F and Baby L. If the high insulin values for Baby F and Baby L were false positives and were simply the result of interference by antibodies in their system, it is unlikely that these babies would have shown symptoms associated with excessive insulin. But the reality is that both babies did show such symptoms. They were severely hypoglycaemic. Their blood glucose level was very low and the only reason it wasn't fatally low was that medical staff were pumping them with glucose. This is further compelling evidence that there was indeed excessive insulin in their systems, as opposed to antibodies masquerading as insulin. There are other indicators of excessive insulin too. We've seen the medical data for Baby L. This data shows that as well as showing a high insulin value and a low C-peptide value, Baby L had a low potassium value. A low potassium value is further evidence of there being too much insulin in the system. These clinical facts about Baby F and Baby L are strong evidence that the high insulin values recorded by the Royal Liverpool Hospital lab were not false positives but were in fact correct.

There is one further question raised by Rachel Aviv that is also worth considering. In her *New Yorker* article she cited the case of Baby L. A lab test on a blood sample from Baby L showed an insulin level of 1,099pmol/l or more and a C-peptide level of 264pmol/l. Aviv didn't cite these figures, but she did offer the following cautionary assessment of Baby L's case:

> According to Joseph Wolfsdorf, a professor at Harvard Medical School who specializes in paediatric hypoglycaemia, the baby's C-peptide level suggested the possibility of a testing irregularity, because, if insulin had been administered, the child's C-peptide level should have been extremely low or undetectable, but it wasn't.[7]

The reasoning here appears to be that if Baby L had indeed been poisoned with synthetic insulin, his body's natural insulin production would have switched off, which means that his C-peptide level would have been significantly lower than 264pmol/l. The fact that his C-peptide level was 264pmol/l raises the question whether something had gone wrong with the lab test.

We spoke to Professor Wolfsdorf ourselves. We were also able to provide him with more information about Baby L than Rachel Aviv appeared to have, including the baby's blood glucose level and other results from his blood test. Professor Wolfsdorf said he couldn't explain the C-peptide reading in Baby L's blood, although he did note it was low. Other experts we spoke to agreed that it was surprising, although they offered some possible explanations. One noted that C-peptide is broken down and removed from the body more slowly than insulin, which means there will often be C-peptide in the blood even after the body has stopped producing insulin. Another expert raised the possibility that Baby L may have had an impaired renal function, which meant that it took longer for him to clear C-peptide from his system. Another possibility was that, although Baby L was experiencing hypoglycaemia, the glucose that medics were giving him to raise his blood sugar levels might have briefly 'reactivated' his natural insulin production. Another possibility still is that Baby L's natural insulin production was 'dysregulated', causing him to continue producing some insulin naturally even though his blood glucose level was dangerously low. This would never explain the extremely high insulin level found in Baby L's blood, but it might explain the C-peptide level.

With the exception of Dr Jones in Sweden, none of the experts we spoke to – including Professor Wolfsdorf – argued that Baby L's puzzling C-peptide result indicates that the insulin / C-peptide test result is incorrect. Professor Wolfsdorf told us: 'You put your weight on the things that make the most sense in the context, so if you've got a baby whose blood glucose is extremely low and you're having to pump that baby full of glucose in order to correct the low blood sugar and you obtain a blood insulin level that's off the charts high, that's where I'll put my emphasis . . . All I can confidently state,' he said, 'is the insulin: C-peptide molar ratio . . . is consistent with factitious hypoglycaemia.' 'Factitious hypo-glycaemia' means deliberately induced hypoglycaemia. In other words, the surest conclusion we can draw from Baby L's test result is that he was poisoned with insulin. We spoke to two other experts and they agreed. It's also worth noting that in the case of Baby F, the C-peptide value was so low that it was unmeasurable. In other words, even if we discount the case of Baby L, Baby F remains a compelling case of apparent insulin poisoning.

This is not to dismiss the sceptics. It is puzzling that at no point in Letby's trial did Letby's defence team present any of the sceptical arguments outlined above. Letby's lawyers didn't highlight the difference between mass spectrometry and immunoassays and the theoretical possibility that the immunoassay method might produce false positives. Nor did they raise the question: why did Baby L still appear to be producing insulin naturally – indicated by his C-peptide level – if his system had been poisoned with an overdose of exogenous insulin? These arguments have been raised in the pages of the *New Yorker* and other British newspapers. Sceptics are right to ask why these arguments weren't presented to the jury in Letby's trial. Our understanding is that Letby's defence team did consult with an insulin expert, but that these arguments were either not presented to them in this way or were dismissed as too weak to help Letby's case.

Would these arguments have made a difference? When we step back from all of the complex detail, accounting for the sceptics' concerns, how does the prosecution's insulin evidence look? It can certainly be argued that it's not perfect. The lab that provided the results used the immunoassay technique, rather than the gold-standard mass spectrometry technique, which means that we can't completely exclude the possibility that the high insulin results were the result of the immunoassay mistaking antibodies as insulin, however unlikely. Repeat testing would also have been preferable. However, while the immunoassay method is not infallible, it is widely considered to be very reliable. Moreover – and this is crucial: the clinical information on the babies in the case – Babies F and L – supports the conclusion that both babies were suffering as a result of dangerously high insulin levels. They both had hypoglycaemia – strong evidence that the high insulin levels recorded by the lab were not false positives. This clinical information about Babies F and L has been overlooked in many of the sceptical arguments against the insulin evidence in the Letby case. Does this mean we can have absolute certainty about the insulin evidence used to convict Lucy Letby? No. The insulin evidence is imperfect. But it is very persuasive – and by far the best evidence in the Letby case as a whole. It does appear, despite its imperfections, to show that someone at the Countess of Chester Hospital was harming babies. What it doesn't answer is who.

Chapter 10

But How Do We Know It Was Lucy?

Sometimes it's science that identifies a killer. A strand of hair or a fingerprint can be enough to say whodunnit. But we know that's not what happened in the Letby case – despite the vast quantity of scientific evidence involved. Not only was there no CCTV or direct eyewitness evidence – there was no DNA or other forensic evidence to identify her as a killer. So what was it that singled Letby out?

During her trial, the prosecution highlighted the fact that she had done multiple online searches for the parents of several of the babies who had died. The parents of Babies E and F were one such case. Letby searched for them on many occasions after the death of Baby E and the near-death of Baby F. She even searched for them on Christmas Day. Some of Letby's searches were done years after the events. Baby K, for example, spent just a few hours on the neonatal unit in February 2016, and yet two years later, in April 2018, Letby searched for the family online. The prosecution also referred to the fact that Letby had taken medical notes for some of the babies in the case home with her: 257 'handover sheets' with babies' details were found at her home.

But presented in context, these facts may not be as sinister as they seem. According to her defence barrister, Letby made no fewer than 2,318 Facebook searches. Just 31 of these related to parents in the case. And of the 257 handover sheets that were found at her home, 21 related to babies in the case. The fact that Letby held on to these handover sheets, despite knowing that the police were investigating her, confuses the picture further. If these hospital documents had been genuinely incriminating, wouldn't she have disposed of them? The case for considering Lucy Letby as a prime suspect would require clearer evidence than this.

For this, the prosecution relied heavily on a completely different set of data, namely hospital records of which staff were on duty at key points in time and what those individual staff members were doing at those times. So they used expert science to identify deliberate occasions when babies at the Countess of Chester Hospital were harmed. Then they used Lucy Letby's attendance data to argue that she was the only common presence for all of these 'harm events'. Conclusion: Lucy Letby harmed babies.

Officially, there were twenty-two such harm events: seven murders and fifteen attempted murders. But in the course of presenting their evidence, the prosecution identified further incidents that they also attributed to Letby. The most visually arresting presentation of the totality of these incidents was the presence grid prepared by Cheshire Police showing twenty-four separate incidents and a damning column of 'X's next to Lucy Letby's name. According to the grid, a few of the nurses had been there for as many as seven incidents. Another document showed that a senior doctor had been there for ten. But none of the staff listed got close to Letby's twenty-four incidents. If this was indeed a comprehensive list of all the potential 'harm events' on the neonatal unit, Lucy Letby was the standout suspect. The list would have to be radically incorrect for the finger of suspicion to point to anyone else.

But it's not too difficult to see how this argument might unravel. What if there was a major mistake in the prosecution's identification of harm events? What if a large number of the incidents in the prosecution case weren't actually harm events at all? Given what we know now about the science, it may not be so hard to imagine. Suppose that the air embolism theory or the theory that someone deliberately pumped air into babies' stomachs turned out to be wrong. We'd end up with a very different – and much shorter – list of harm events. Lucy Letby would still be a suspect but there would almost certainly be others joining her in the frame.

Here's another 'what if': what if there were other incidents that the prosecution's experts didn't pick up on and that Lucy Letby *wasn't* present for? As we pointed out in the previous chapter, the prosecution experts identified two suspicious incidents involving air in babies' stomachs where it turned out Lucy Letby wasn't actually present – one for Baby C on 12 June 2015 and one for Baby I on 23 August 2015. Neither of these incidents were part of the prosecution's case. Were there any others like these? If there were, the 'true' list of harm events might point to a different suspect – other than Lucy Letby.

Unfortunately, we don't have to go too far back in history to find other cases where medical crimes have been blamed on the wrong person. Rebecca Leighton was a twenty-something-year-old nurse like Lucy Letby. She worked at Stepping Hill Hospital in Stockport, just an hour's drive from the Countess of Chester Hospital. In 2011, police found evidence that bags of intravenous fluid at the hospital had been contaminated. Leighton had been caught stealing prescription drugs from the hospital and she quickly became the police's prime suspect for the poisoning offence. In the same year, Leighton was charged with six counts of 'causing damage with intent to endanger life or being reckless to whether life is being endangered'.[1] Leighton was denied bail and spent six weeks in prison awaiting trial before the case against her was discontinued for lack of evidence, and she was released. Nazir Afzal was the senior prosecutor who dropped the case. He told us: 'With that particular person [Rebecca Leighton], the police had alleged offences and they made a significant leap. They said: "Well, if she was responsible for the theft of medication, if she was present during the time that people were being harmed, somehow she might be responsible." They saw correlation when there was just coincidence.'

Years later, in a rare interview with the *Manchester Evening News*, Leighton described how she narrowly avoided attacks by other inmates by changing her name and appearance. But the police and the CPS had got the wrong person. Another nurse at the same hospital called Victorino Chua had sailed quietly under their radar. The evidence ultimately pointed to him, not Leighton, and Chua was eventually convicted in 2015 for murdering two patients and poisoning nineteen with insulin, and attempting to poison a further seven, in the summer of 2011 and January 2012. He was sentenced to life in prison with a minimum term of thirty-five years. Rebecca Leighton was cleared, but her life and reputation were destroyed. 'It has affected my life deeply,' she said. 'I went from being this bubbly, happy-go-lucky, hard-working girl to my life being taken totally out of my control. It was such a horrific time. I was wrongly caught up in it, chewed up and spat out. I'll never be able to put this behind me fully.'[2] Could Letby have been wrongly accused like Rebecca Leighton was?

The possibility that prosecution experts overlooked harm events that might have pointed to a suspect *other* than Lucy Letby isn't the only remaining question we might ask. Another 'what if' is whether some or all of the events that the prosecution said involved deliberate harm should simply have been classified as unexplained. Some people might argue that even so, one nurse being on duty for lots of unexplained baby deaths and deteriorations is a pretty clear indication of guilt. But the reasons to be cautious are strong. Remember the case of Lucia de Berk. De Berk was damned by attendance data and faulty reasoning about the statistical probability that one member of staff could be present for so many suspicious events. A legal scholar had argued in de Berk's trial that the chances of coincidence between her presence and a string of baby deaths where she worked was 1 in 342 million. It looked like proof. And yet, it wasn't. In fact, it pointed to a very different truth, namely that freak events do happen. Clusters of suspicious-looking incidents do come along that turn out to have perfectly innocent explanations. As numerous statisticians have pointed out, convicting someone simply because they were there is shoddy statistics and a recipe for shoddy justice. It's also been highlighted that Letby was trained to care for the sicker babies – and so tended to be in their vicinity more often.

There are lots of possible 'what ifs' about the list of harm incidents that the prosecution selected as the basis of its case. What if *all* of the science in the Letby case was wrong? It sounds like a crazy question and it probably is, but it's worth imagining: what if the prosecution experts all got it wrong and no harm events occurred at the Countess of Chester Hospital? In this fantastical scenario, all of the deteriorations and deaths would be simply down to natural causes or systemic failures at the hospital. If that were true, the entire Letby case would collapse. It would be based on a false premise that babies had been deliberately harmed and there was a baby killer to be caught. The point in posing these 'what if' questions isn't to say that the prosecution's science *is* wrong. It's simply to show how much in the case against Lucy Letby hinges on this science being correct – in particular the opinions of the prosecution experts – and how different the picture could be if even some of these opinions turned out to be wrong or incomplete, or both.

And there are more questions still about how the prosecution arrived at its list of incidents that so neatly mapped on to Lucy Letby's shifts. When the prosecution experts joined the case, they were given a pre-selected set of medical notes to review by Cheshire Police. Dr Dewi Evans told us he asked the police to send him medical records for *all* deaths and deteriorations on the neonatal unit in 2015 and 2016 – around thirty to begin with. He then told the police which ones he thought were suspicious. But did Dr Evans get to see the full set of 'incidents' that had occurred at the Countess of Chester Hospital? There was no mistaking the deaths and we know he got to review all of these. But what about the deteriorations? What counted as a deterioration and who decided? Were all of the deteriorations sent to Dr Evans or just the ones judged to be suspicious? Evans had asked for all of them, but did he receive them?

Here's what we know. In May 2017, when Steve Brearey and his colleagues first sat down with Cheshire Police, they presented officers with a document entitled 'Reasons for concerns regarding a possible criminal cause for increased neonatal mortality at the Countess of Chester Hospital NHS Foundation Trust, June 2015 – July 2016'. The document highlighted twenty-one incidents that they thought were suspicious. Lucy Letby was on duty for almost all of them.

Our understanding is that these cases made up about two thirds of the roughly thirty cases that were initially sent to Dewi Evans to review. It's not clear where the remaining cases came from – probably police interviews with other hospital staff and witnesses – and we don't know how many of those Lucy Letby was on duty for. But what's relatively clear is that most of the thirty or so cases that were initially sent to Dewi Evans by Cheshire Police were first identified by the consultants. It's not hard to anticipate what the sceptics will say to that: not only is the prosecution's science open to debate, but the initial list of suspicious incidents that formed the basis of the case was shaped by the consultants, whose views on Lucy Letby by that point were decidedly hostile.

There's one further point about the prosecution's claim that Lucy Letby was always on duty when things went wrong. Establishing that Lucy Letby was on duty somewhere in the neonatal unit when a suspicious event occurred doesn't come close to establishing that she was responsible. For a start, it doesn't specify where exactly she was or what she was doing. What if she was in a different room or on a break when the event occurred?

You can see the challenge here in a case such as Baby M's. Letby was accused of injecting air into Baby M's bloodstream on 9 April 2016. Experts agreed that the effects would be more or less immediate. But the circumstantial evidence showed that the last time that Letby would have had an opportunity to harm Baby M was fifteen minutes before his collapse. We've seen previously how the prosecution dealt with this. They argued that Letby injected only a very small amount of air, which then took fifteen minutes to pass through the external tubing into Baby M's system. It was an ingenious argument by the prosecution but it seemed strained.

At the beginning of Chapter 8, we suggested that if the incidents in the Letby case were obvious instances of harm – like a series of crime scenes, each one with a victim with stab wounds and a bloodied knife – the case wouldn't be so complicated. The problem with the Letby case is that the list of incidents that that prosecution identified as attacks on babies are not as straightforward. Significant parts of the science are debatable. On top of that, we don't have the full picture about other incidents that may have taken place at the Countess of Chester Hospital and, without that full picture, we can't comprehensively assess Lucy Letby's record and how it compares to those of her colleagues.

The circumstantial case against Lucy Letby isn't just complicated by the fact of incomplete or inconclusive information. Some of the evidence that the prosecution presented about the movements of staff in and out of the neonatal unit was demonstrably incorrect.

During Letby's trial, the prosecution made reference to 'door swipe data', which it said gave precise timings for individual staff members entering and exiting the unit. However, this data was flawed. The door swipe data doesn't actually show when staff left the unit. It records only those points in time where staff entered. So the swipe data that the prosecution said showed staff leaving was wrong. This data was in fact a record of staff entering the unit.

The Crown Prosecution Service said it is confident that the error 'had no meaningful impact on the prosecution – which used multiple, more significant, strands of evidence to prove guilt.' But in a case built on evidence about who was in the neonatal unit at key points in time, an error in the swipe data seems highly significant and unsurprisingly it has added fuel to the argument that Letby's trial was unfair. So how significant could the error be?

It's clearly alarming. At the most basic level it raises the obvious question: 'what else did they get wrong?' The period of time concerned is also significant. The CPS told us that the 'mislabelling' of door swipe data applied to the period 14 April 2015 to 26 April 2016. Bear in mind that the incidents for which Letby was convicted occurred between June 2015 and June 2016, so the mislabelling of door swipe data coincided with eleven out of the thirteen months in the Letby case. It looks like the kind of thing that could cause a prosecution case to unravel.

And yet, as far as we have been able to understand, the erroneous door swipe data is unlikely to impact fundamentally on the circumstantial case against Letby – for several reasons. First, according to the CPS, the error relates to one door in the neonatal unit. We understand there were five doors between the unit and the rest of the hospital. Four of these five doors required swipe access, and the erroneous data applied to only one of these doors. The error also appears to have no bearing on movements within the unit itself, as internal doors didn't require swipe access. More importantly, door swipe data played very little role on its own in placing Letby at the scene of suspicious incidents. For the most part, the recollections of Letby's colleagues were the key basis for placing her at key places in the unit at particular points in time. Could the police have used erroneous door swipe data to 'jog' the recollections of witnesses in police interviews? If so, these recollections might be contaminated. This is a legitimate question, but at the time of writing we have no reason to doubt witnesses' recollections of Letby and her where-abouts at key points in time. Letby's own clinical notes and those of her colleagues were also evidentially important in tracking her whereabouts and activities. The nursing rota showing which staff were on duty – and which staff were designated to care for which babies – was another important piece of the jigsaw, and this too was independent of the door swipe data.

The CPS told us that a 'comprehensive review' of the misla-belling error was conducted after it was discovered. This review concluded that the error had 'a material impact' on just one out of the twenty-two counts in the original trial. This was a count on which the jury failed to reach a verdict, namely, the alleged attempted murder of Baby K. If true, that means that the door swipe data error had no material impact on any of the counts for which Letby was convicted in her original trial.

Sceptics might say, 'Well, the CPS would say that, wouldn't they?' However, the CPS also told us that they notified Lucy Letby's defence team about the mislabelled door swipe data six-and-a-half weeks before Letby appeared at the Court of Appeal in April 2024 to request permission to appeal her conviction. Had the swipe data had a material impact on Letby's convictions, her defence team would surely have raised it as a point of appeal. They didn't – a point that the CPS noted in correspondence with us. They said: '[Letby's] defence did not deem the issue significant enough to include it in Letby's unsuccessful appeal'.

You get a better sense of the force of the prosecution's circumstantial evidence when you look at the detail of some of the individual incidents and what Letby was doing at key points in time. Baby A, for example, suffered a fatal collapse at 8.26 p.m. on 8 June 2015. That was just half an hour after Letby came on shift. Letby was Baby A's designated nurse and in the moments surrounding the infant's collapse, she was with him. According to the prosecution's Nick Johnson KC, Letby was 'literally standing over [Baby A]' at the time of the collapse. This timing is especially significant for this and other cases where Letby is accused of injecting air into the baby's bloodstream. We know that the effect of intravenous air injection is virtually immediate. So if the prosecution experts are right to conclude that Baby A died because air was injected into his bloodstream, Letby was the only person at the scene when the crime was committed.

Letby was also on her own with Baby C when he collapsed at around 11.30 p.m. on 13 June 2015. The prosecution experts agreed that air had been injected into his stomach, although Dewi Evans ultimately concluded that air may also have been injected into Baby C's bloodstream.

In several of the cases where Letby wasn't the baby's designated nurse, colleagues reported stepping away from a baby who seemed to be doing well only to be called back – sometimes by Letby herself – to find that same baby fighting for their life. Baby I, for example, died after collapsing in the early hours of 23 October 2015. Shortly after 1 a.m., Baby I's designated nurse Ashleigh Hudson stepped away from the baby's nursery. Baby I seemed stable so there appeared to be little to worry about. However, while the nurse was away, the monitor alarms sounded. When the nurse returned, Letby – who wasn't Baby I's designated nurse – was by her incubator.

It wasn't the only incident witnessed by Ashleigh Hudson involving Letby and Baby I. Ten days earlier, Hudson left Baby I to help a colleague in one of the other nurseries. Shortly after her return, Letby appeared at the doorway and remarked that Baby I looked pale. The observation would have been unremarkable had it not been for the fact that the lights in the room were low and Baby I was covered with a blanket and a 'cot canopy'. When Hudson went over to Baby I, she was shocked to find the baby girl gasping for breath and seemingly at the point of dying. Hudson was adamant that it would have been impossible to see that Baby I was pale from the doorway where Letby was standing in such low light. The implication was clear: Letby knew Baby I was in trouble because she had harmed her. Under cross-examination, Letby was asked how she'd been able to see that the baby was pale despite being partially obscured and in low light. She answered: 'I knew what I was looking for,' before quickly correcting herself to say: 'looking *at*.'[3] This change from 'looking for' to 'looking at' may sound like a tiny detail, but for the prosecution, it was a revealing slip-up. 'Looking *for*' implied that Letby already had the notion in her head that Baby I was pale and in trouble. How would she know or expect this unless she had been responsible?

As we saw in Chapter 6 – and as we'll revisit later – Ravi Jayaram says he experienced something similar. Shortly after 3.30 a.m. on 17 February 2016, Baby K's designated nurse left the nursery. Letby was the only one in the room. When Dr Jayaram walked in to check everything was OK, he says he found Baby K's breathing tube had been dislodged and her chest wasn't moving. Her alarm hadn't sounded either. Despite all of this, Jayaram says Letby was doing nothing to help. When he asked Letby if anything had happened, she said: 'She's just started deteriorating now.'

A few hours later, something similar happened again. An X-ray, believed to have been taken at around 6.20 a.m., confirmed that Baby K's breathing tube was correctly positioned, but within a few minutes, the tube had become dislodged. The reason that's suspicious is that Baby K was just a few hours old, very premature and sedated with morphine. It was therefore hard to see how she could have dislodged her own breathing tube. Lucy Letby had been looking after a baby in another nursery, but she'd gone into Baby K's nursery sometime after 6.10 a.m. to return some medical notes – right around the time that Baby K's breathing tube became dislodged. Even to a sceptical observer, this sequence of events must count as suspicious. Baby K survived that traumatic night, but sadly she died a few days later.

The case of Baby E is also particularly difficult for sceptics or defenders of Letby. This is the baby whose mother walked down to the neonatal unit at around 9 p.m. on 3 August 2015 and heard her baby screaming from the corridor. When she entered the nursery, Letby – who was her baby's designated nurse – was 'faffing about', trying to 'look busy' according to the mother's recollection. Her son, meanwhile, had blood around his mouth. When the mother asked Letby what had caused the bleeding, Letby told her it must be the nasogastric tube irritating the baby's throat. She then told the mother to go back to the ward.

This incident is troubling for several reasons. First, Letby's notes omitted all reference to the baby's bleeding or his mother's visit at 9 p.m. that evening. And yet we know that the mother is correct in her timings. We know this not because of police work or clever cross-examination by the prosecution. Rather, the baby's mother asked her mobile phone company for records of her phone calls that evening. She knows she called her husband shortly after her visit to the neonatal unit, and her phone records show exactly when she called him: at 9.11 p.m. In other words, her visit to the unit must have been shortly before 9.11 p.m.

The woman's recollection of what she heard and saw when she visited the unit are also troubling. Her baby was screaming and bleeding, and yet Letby appeared to be doing nothing to help. Letby was also alone with the baby at the time. In her police interviews, Letby herself expressed surprise when it was put to her that she had told the mother that the blood around her baby's mouth had been caused by the nasogastric tube irritating the throat. 'I don't know why I would have said that,' Letby told police, apparently agreeing that a feeding tube wouldn't cause the bleeding witnessed by the baby's mother. The plastic in the feeding tubes used in the Countess of Chester neonatal unit was of the softest variety. According to Dewi Evans, it was so soft 'it wouldn't have broken the skin on a rice pudding'. It couldn't have been the cause of Baby E's bleeding. Something else caused it. And yet Letby seemed uncurious. During the nurse's trial, the prosecuting barrister described Baby E's mother as 'a very, very important' witness. He was right.

These incidents are a compelling constellation of circumstantial evidence placing Letby at the scene of medical emergencies that caught everyone around her by surprise. And there are plenty more like them. But are they enough to make the case against her decisive? Letby's defenders will point out that the mother of Baby E didn't challenge Letby when she saw her 'faffing about' while her son was in distress. The mother told us that she was worried enough to race to phone her husband, but she trusted Lucy Letby as a nurse and didn't suspect her personally that night. Indeed, it wasn't until she learned of Letby's arrest three years later that the pieces of the prosecutorial jigsaw fell into place for the family. Likewise, Letby's nursing colleague Ashleigh Hudson said nothing at the time of the incidents she witnessed – at least none that we're aware of – that indicates that she found Letby's behaviour suspicious. Ravi Jayaram says he did have his suspicions about Letby – that's why he went to check up on her while she was alone with Baby K. But his suspicions weren't sufficient for him to challenge Letby or her manager or make a note of what he had seen. The question is obvious: were these witnesses now making sense of past events with the benefit of hindsight, or were they misinterpreting these past events in light of what they were now thinking and hearing from the police about Letby?

Even if the circumstantial evidence linking Lucy Letby to suspicious events is compelling, is it enough to prove that the events involved deliberate harm? That's where the science comes in, but we've seen how complicated that can be. This feeling of going round in circles is a familiar experience for anyone who takes a deep dive into the Letby case. At one moment, the science promises to explain a suspicious-looking incident. Then, when the science starts to look debatable, we find ourselves being redirected to the inherent 'suspiciousness' of the incident and the apparent volume of other similarly suspicious incidents. It never quite feels evidentially satisfying or grounded.

One way of escaping this circularity is to focus on the cases where the science is strongest – and then look at what Lucy Letby was doing in those cases. The obvious candidates are the two insulin cases of Babies F and L – and interestingly these were two of just three charges in the Letby trial where the jury reached unanimous verdicts of guilt. So how strong is the circumstantial evidence tying Letby to these two insulin cases, and is she the only one in the frame?

According to the prosecution, the two insulin cases singled Lucy Letby and only Lucy Letby out for blame. Letby was on duty when both babies – Baby F and Baby L – experienced hypoglycaemia as a result of insulin poisoning. Only two other people were also on duty for both. One was a nursery nurse who the prosecution said wouldn't have been in the same room as the babies who were harmed, and the other was a nurse called Belinda Simcock. There's no evidence to suggest that Nurse Simcock poisoned any babies with insulin and Letby herself never accused her of doing so. These two cases look like the next best thing to catching Letby red-handed. But were they?

The case of Baby L clearly puts Letby in the frame. Professor Peter Hindmarsh of University College London Hospital analysed Baby L's case and, with his help, the prosecution pinpointed two windows of time when Baby L was poisoned with insulin. The first was between midnight and 9.36 a.m. on 9 April 2016. The second was sometime after 4.30 p.m. that same day. Letby was on the day shift that day from approximately 7.30 a.m. to 8 p.m., so her hours clearly overlap with both of the time frames identified by the prosecution on the basis of expert analysis from Professor Hindmarsh: she was on duty for two hours before 9.36 a.m. on 9 April 2016 and she was also on duty for three and a half hours after 4.30 p.m.

However, Letby isn't the only one whose shift overlaps with both of these time periods. Her other colleagues on the day shift are also theoretically in the frame. And then there are those colleagues who were working on the night shifts before and after Letby's day shift. According to the prosecution, the first of Baby L's nutrition bags could have been contaminated at any point between midnight and 9.36 a.m. Letby didn't come on duty until 7.30 a.m. and the night shift didn't officially end until 8 a.m. That leaves eight hours when the night shift team was on duty. As for the second bag: it was spiked after 4.30 p.m. Letby didn't finish her shift until 8 p.m. so she had three and a half hours to spike that bag. But the bag could also have been spiked after Letby finished for the day. We know that Baby L was still experiencing low blood sugar in the early hours of 10 April 2016. In other words, the range of possible suspects for the insulin poisoning of Baby L includes everyone on the day shift on 9 April 2016 and everyone who was working both night shifts before and after the day shift. We don't have the complete staffing list, although we do know that the married doctor with whom Letby became close was working on the night shift of 10 April 2016. No one has suggested any wrongdoing or professional impropriety on the doctor's part and nor do we, although his presence may be relevant to analysing Letby's actions.

Placing Letby at the scene of the other insulin case – the case of Baby F – also has its challenges. She's in the picture, for sure, but that picture isn't entirely clear-cut. Baby F experienced symptoms of insulin poisoning – low blood sugar or hypoglycaemia – in the early hours of 5 August 2015. Letby was on duty at the time. In fact, the symptoms started directly after she and another nurse hung a bag of intravenous feed for Baby F. Judging from the medical records, it's apparent that Baby F was suffering from an excess of insulin: medics were pumping him with glucose and yet he remained hypoglycaemic. However, the blood sample from Baby F that was sent to the lab for insulin / C-peptide testing wasn't taken until 5.56 p.m. on 5 August 2015. Lucy Letby had finished her shift at 8 a.m. that morning – in other words, ten hours earlier. Moreover, a new bag of intravenous feed had been hung for Baby F at midday – four hours after she had gone home. So the lab test showing that Baby F had been given exogenous insulin was based on a blood sample taken while Letby wasn't on duty and suggested that Baby F had been poisoned by means of a nutrition bag that was hung four hours after she had gone home. The prosecution argued that Letby had contaminated the bag sometime before going home. But the truth is, there is nothing to indicate when or how any bags of nutrition were contaminated with insulin. Theoretically, they could have been contaminated by someone else when Letby was off duty. As in the other insulin case involving Baby L, the circumstantial evidence singling out Letby in the case of Baby F isn't nearly as neat as the prosecution claimed.

Are there any other incidents in the prosecution where the science is, if not clear, at least compelling? For us, the case of Baby O stands out – and interestingly, this was the third of three cases in which the jurors agreed unanimously that Letby was guilty. Baby O was one of the two triplets who died on consecutive days in June 2016. His brother was Baby P. One of the most memorable pieces of expert evidence about Baby O's case came from the prosecution's expert pathologist Dr Marnerides. He said that Baby O had suffered an impact-type liver trauma that he had only ever seen in cases such as road traffic accidents, and it's more than possible that this is what convinced everyone on the jury. And yet in Chapter 9 we heard from another pathologist, 'P', who took a different view to Dr Marnerides. 'P''s view was that if Baby O's liver injury had been the result of inflicted trauma, you would also expect to see 'more of a diffuse injury to the intra-abdominal organs', not just injuries to the liver. So why is Baby O's case scientifically compelling?

One reason is the strength of feeling among the medics on the neonatal unit that there was nothing that suggested that Baby O or his brother were in danger. Medically, both babies were doing well – and in a way that even Letby's defenders find it difficult to argue with. Letby's defence expert Mike Hall conceded that of all the deaths in the Letby case, the deaths of Babies O and P were the most difficult to explain. The original pathologist couldn't explain Baby O's death either. That's why he recorded it as 'Sudden Unexpected Postnatal Collapse'.

Baby O's liver injury is also troubling, even if you accept that Dr Marnerides' explanation may not be correct. The original pathologist Dr Kokai ventured that 'hypoxia' (or oxygen deficiency) was the 'most likely' cause for the liver injury, but that was just a theory. Our pathologist 'P' offered another tentative theory:

perhaps Baby O's stomach was blown up with so much air that the pressure caused the injuries in his liver. We can't be sure.

At Letby's trial, the prosecution argued that three things killed Baby O: inflicted trauma to the liver, air embolism, and air being pumped into his stomach. We've already seen the arguments and debates arising from all of these theories. But even if none of these theories is quite right – even if we don't quite know precisely what caused Baby O to die – what we can say with some confidence is that his death is very difficult to explain in terms of natural causes. It looks suspicious.

So where was Lucy Letby when Baby O got into trouble? On the day that Baby O died, he and his triplet brother Baby P were both in the same nursery along with a third unrelated baby. Letby was the designated nurse for all three babies and she was the only nurse working in their nursery. That morning, Baby O was examined by one of the doctors on the unit called Dr Cooke. The Court of Appeal summarised this examination as follows: 'Baby O was breathing normally. Dr Cooke undertook an abdominal examination which revealed that the abdomen was full but not distended and was soft and not tender. This examination effectively established that no liver damage was present at the time of this examination.' So no liver injury at the start of Letby's shift – assuming that Dr Cooke's examination was thorough. In court, Letby herself accepted that Baby O's liver injury occurred at some point during her shift. She also accepted Dr Marnerides' analysis of an impact-type injury of the kind seen in road traffic accidents. Is this enough to prove that Letby murdered Baby O? No, it isn't. But it should make uncomfortable reading for Letby's supporters.

The two insulin cases – Babies F and L – and the case of Baby O are the strongest evidence of foul play in the Letby case as a whole. If these babies were indeed harmed, can we be sure that Letby harmed them? Again, the answer is no. We can't be sure whether there was anyone other than Letby who would have had the opportunity to harm these babies. But from the incomplete staffing information for the days in question released by Cheshire Police, Letby does look like the prime suspect.

One under-appreciated feature of the Letby case is how much the jury's verdicts on the other babies might have depended on these three strongest cases – the cases of Babies F, L and O. We know this because of what the judge said as he sent the jury out to deliberate. The jury, he said, did not have to 'resolve every conflict in the evidence', nor were they expected to reach their verdicts by examining each piece of evidence separately. The prosecution case, the judge noted, relied 'substantially, but not wholly' on circumstantial evidence – in other words: 'pieces of evidence relating to different facts, none of which on their own directly prove that the defendant is guilty, but which taken together, lead . . . [according to the prosecution] to the inevitable and irresistible conclusion that the only explanation for them is that the defendant is guilty of the offences upon which she is charged.' In other words, the prosecution's case rested on the full combination – or 'constellation' – of evidence, rather than individual pieces of evidence on their own.

But the judge had further directions for the jury on how to navigate the minefield of evidence in the case. If jurors satisfied themselves that Letby had indeed harmed a particular baby, they were then entitled to assess the credibility and probability of other allegations in the case in light of this. The judge didn't spell it out, but here's one possible reading of what he was getting at: if, for example, the jury was satisfied that Lucy Letby had poisoned Babies F and L with insulin, and that she had murdered Baby O, then they were entitled to rely on this to help them decide on the more contentious allegations in the case. Maybe the air embolism evidence wasn't clear-cut on its own, but if it was established that Letby was a baby killer, the jury was entitled to factor this into the equation when weighing up the evidence on air embolism. Some might disagree with this idea. How, they might ask, does evidential certainty on the insulin cases tell us anything about the quality of the evidence on air embolism? The two are entirely distinct. Indeed, Letby's barrister made this very point in the course of his efforts to secure permission for Letby to appeal her conviction. He was unsuccessful.

But although science and circumstantial evidence were the key pillars in the case against Lucy Letby, it's important to remember that they aren't the only evidence we have to go on to help us answer the question whether the jury that consigned Lucy Letby to a life behind bars got it right. Lucy Letby's testimony during her police interviews and during her trial was another window onto the truth for the jury and everyone else who was watching.

In many ways, Letby was a model of co-operation and candour during her interrogations. In the words of lead detective Paul Hughes, '[Letby] was comfortable,' in her police interviews. 'She'd go through medical notes, she would talk to us, she was co-operative, she engaged.' But there are points in her testimony where, even on a sympathetic view, she appears to be lying.

When police asked her about Baby D, for example, Letby said she couldn't remember her. Baby D was one of the babies who died – at that point still a relatively rare event on the Countess of Chester neonatal unit. After Baby D's death, Letby texted a colleague: 'We lost [Baby D] . . . So upsetting for everyone. Parents absolutely distraught, dad screaming . . . Dad is beside himself. They only saw her briefly but don't want her to be moved out of 1 . . . '

It sounds extreme – a dad screaming after the death of his daughter. And Letby was in the thick of it. She was looking after two babies in the same room as Baby D that night. She was present around the time of Baby D's collapse. It's difficult to believe that she would have no memory of Baby D.

Letby's memory also seemed to fail her when she was asked why she had searched for some of the parents in the case, including the mother of the twins Baby E and Baby F. By her own account, Letby had developed a good relationship with the mother. She even bathed Baby E in front of his parents after he had died. Letby searched for the couple numerous times – two days after Baby E's death, then again every month until the end of that year. She even searched for them on Christmas Day. And yet, when asked by police, she said she couldn't remember why.

Letby's statements about air embolism are also intriguing. Remember what she told the police: she said all nursing staff would be aware of the dangers of an 'air embolus', but she claimed to have little knowledge besides that. 'I don't know exactly what [an air embolism] is,' she said. 'When we were taught about lines, we were taught about clearing lines because that's what it would lead to.' She also told police she was only aware of air embolisms in adults. And yet less than two weeks after the death of Baby O in late June 2016, Letby texted one of her pals to criticise the way her colleagues had looked after the baby boy. His catheter, she said, posed a 'risk of air embolism'. It's an interesting observation – and one that few observers of Letby's case have picked up on. After Baby O's death, the consultants began to consider air embolism among themselves as a possible explanation for some of the unexplained events, but other than this, no one else on the unit that we know of had mentioned air embolism at any point in the preceding twelve months.

Then there are the 'mistakes' and omissions in Letby's medical notes. Throughout Letby's trial, the prosecution barrister Nick Johnson alleged that Letby had falsified or fabricated medical notes on numerous occasions. Letby's defence rejected this, but one case offers compelling proof that Letby's notes were alarmingly at odds with the facts. Once again, it's the case of Baby E – the baby whose mother found him with blood around his mouth.

Baby E's mother knows when exactly on the evening of 3 August 2015 she visited her baby – at around 9 p.m. She also knows what she heard and saw. She heard screaming from the corridor and saw blood around her baby's mouth – like a 'goatee beard'. But neither of these details were reflected in Letby's notes. It was as if they hadn't happened. Letby noted that Baby E's mother had visited at around 8 p.m. and then again at 10 p.m. – not 9 p.m. There was no record of the mother's concern, nor was there any record of Baby's bleeding at 9 p.m. Instead, Letby notes '16ml mucky aspirate' for 9 p.m. We asked Letby's dogged defender Mike Hall an obvious question: 'Is mucky aspirate very different from fresh blood?' Yes, he said. The description 'mucky aspirate' would be interpreted quite differently from the description of 'bloody aspirate'. If we take that as a given, it is not plausible that Lucy Letby would have mistaken fresh blood for mucky aspirate.

Then there is Letby's answer when Baby E's mother asked her

about the bleeding. 'It must be the NG tube rubbing the back of his throat,' she said. But we know this is untrue. Remember what the prosecution's expert witness Dewi Evans said: the plastic on the NG tubes used in the Countess of Chester Hospital was simply too soft to inflict such an injury. Indeed, Letby herself agreed when she was asked about it in police interview. So why did she say it to Baby E's mother?

Letby's notes for that evening also record that a feed for Baby E had been 'omitted'. This is something that would have been agreed with a doctor. But the doctor concerned has no recollection of agreeing to any such thing. Letby also notes that the mother of Baby E and the registrar on duty that evening had a conversation that neither the mother nor the doctor recalls. In other words, Letby's notes for the evening of 3 August are inaccurate.

Devil's advocates might argue that these are just innocent mistakes. But we have to bear in mind what we know about Lucy Letby. Even when she was at school, Letby was known for her rigorous note-keeping. It was her forte on those geography field trips and on the weather-monitoring project she took part in. Remember what one of Letby's old friends told us: Letby had been a teacher's pet at school and she was 'someone who did not tend to make mistakes'.

In May 2016, the neonatal unit manager said: 'I have found LL to be diligent and have excellent standards within the clinical area.' It feels safe to conclude that the spike in baby deaths at the Countess of Chester Hospital wasn't down to incompetence on Lucy Letby's part. Even if she did somehow harm babies through error, the incompetence would almost certainly have been straightforward to identify and rectify. Incompetence does not explain thirteen months of unexpected and unexplained deaths and collapses.

Perhaps the most fascinating pieces of evidence of the whole trial were Letby's handwritten notes. As mystifying as these are, in some sense they probably contain the keys to the entire case. In these notes, Letby is talking to herself. She's not pretending. She's not wearing a mask. 'NOT GOOD ENOUGH,' she writes. And then further down, that shocking sentence: 'I killed them on purpose because I'm not good enough to care for them.' Letby's barrister argued strenuously that this wasn't a confession. It was simply an outpouring of anguish. The criminologist Professor David Wilson agreed that this was one possible meaning when we showed him the note. Letby, he argued, might have been articulating the allegations that were being made against her rather than confessing to them. On this reading, what she meant was this: '*It is alleged that* I killed them on purpose . . .' etc. Is this convincing? When she was asked about it by police, Letby said she wrote the note 'when I'd not long found out I'd been removed from the unit and they were telling me my practice might be wrong.'

With this in mind, it is possible to follow David Wilson's 'innocent' reading. Letby's practice was being questioned. She was deemed unfit to be on the unit. Maybe she was simply catastrophising on paper. Maybe what she was really saying was: 'I'm being accused of murdering these babies because my best efforts as a nurse weren't good enough to save them.' That's one reading and there are reasons to consider it carefully. It's been reported that Letby was encouraged by her GP and the Countess of Chester's head of occupational health to 'write down her feelings as a way of coping with extreme stress' – although it's notable that neither Letby herself nor her defence made reference to this advice during her trial.[1] One might also wonder whether a murderer would keep a note like this lying around when she knew that the police were investigating.

But for those who favour this innocent reading, the timing of the note cuts the other way too. Letby said she wrote it not long after she'd been removed from the neonatal unit. That was in July 2016 – nearly a year before the police became involved and two years before she was arrested on suspicion of murder. At this stage, no one had formally accused her of murder. She still had the backing of her nursing managers, and the hospital bosses were nowhere near getting the police involved. Of course Letby will have known about the consultants' suspicions of her, but the fact remains that she was writing about herself as a murderer of babies long before any murder allegations or police involvement had become a reality.

These facts about the note's timing don't resolve the question of how we should read it, but they do challenge the 'outpouring of anguish' interpretation – not to mention the fact that, taken at face value, the note looks like a confession. All of this evidence was laid out for everyone to see and hear during Letby's trial, and readers will form their own conclusions on what it all adds up to. But there is a new set of information that we have uncovered that wasn't included in Letby's trial and that might bring more clarity to the question of whether she is guilty or innocent. Much of this information has never been made public.

Two questions that have animated some of Letby's supporters concern the other deaths on the neonatal unit that didn't feature in Letby's trial and for which she wasn't charged: how many of these other deaths were there, and is there anything about these deaths that might strengthen or weaken the case against Letby? Part of the challenge in answering this question is getting accurate death statistics for the Countess of Chester neonatal unit. It's easy to see where confusion comes from. Following Letby's arrest in July 2018, then Detective Inspector Paul Hughes of Cheshire Police said that the investigation into Letby had widened to include the deaths of seventeen babies between March 2015 and July 2016.[4] A Freedom of Information request from September 2018 suggested something similar. It identified eight 'early neonatal deaths' at the Countess of Chester Hospital in 2015 and a further seven in 2016. It also identified one 'late neonatal death' in each year.[5] So fifteen 'early neonatal deaths' and two 'late neonatal deaths' in 2015 and 2016. So where is the confusion?

The best source for baby death statistics are the neonatal unit's own internal documents, some of which we've seen. In March 2016, the neonatal unit manager Eirian Powell emailed the lead consultant Steve Brearey with the mortality figures for the previous six years. She listed '8' deaths for 2015. Internal documents from the neonatal unit also record a further seven baby deaths between January and July 2016 – the month that Letby was moved off the unit. So it appears there were fifteen deaths on the unit between January 2015 and July 2016.

It seems that two out of these fifteen deaths were generally agreed to have innocent explanations. When a team from the Royal College of Paediatrics and Child Health came to visit the hospital's neonatal unit in September 2017, they noted a 'cluster of 13–15 deaths', but their report concentrated on a subset of thirteen deaths on the unit. In October 2016, the London-based neonatologist Jane Hawdon produced a separate review of deaths on the unit for the hospital's medical director Ian Harvey. She too analysed thirteen deaths. Internal hospital emails between the consultants on the unit also refer to thirteen deaths, and during our own investigations we obtained an anonymised list of these deaths and the dates on which they occurred. There were thirteen. So that's the number: there were thirteen baby deaths in total and they all occurred between June 2015 and June 2016 – the period covered in the Letby case.

It's little wonder that Steve Brearey and his fellow consultants were worried. In her March 2016 email to Steve Brearey, Eirian Powell listed the annual mortality figures for each year from 2010 to 2014. The number in each case was either two or three. So the thirteen deaths between June 2015 and June 2016 were five times the annual average.

Letby was tried and convicted of murdering seven of these thirteen babies. But what about the remaining six deaths? Some of Letby's supporters might argue that these six deaths undermine the prosecution's narrative. The deaths, they might say, show that something else must have been going on at the Countess of Chester Hospital – independently of Letby. When you consider that there were thirteen deaths in total, Letby's association with seven of them looks less damning. Is that a fair point?

So far, very little information on these deaths has made its way into the public domain. They weren't discussed in Letby's trial and for obvious reasons, the identities of the babies and their families remain protected. When Dr Jane Hawdon conducted her case-note review of the thirteen baby deaths, she singled out four that in her view warranted further investigation. By implication, nine of the deaths, from what she could see, were not suspicious. A few months later, in February 2017, one of the most senior neonatal consultants in the North West, Nim Subhedar, also took a look at the evidence. He concluded that eight, not four, of the thirteen deaths should be investigated. At the time, Steve Brearey probably agreed. But today, he fears that as many as twelve of these thirteen deaths are due to foul play. And therein lies a clue.

According to Brearey, Lucy Letby was on duty for no fewer than twelve of the thirteen baby deaths that occurred on the neonatal unit between June 2015 and June 2016. We don't know if Steve Brearey's fears about all of these deaths are right. What we can say is that the additional baby deaths at the Countess of Chester Hospital from 2015–2016 that weren't included in Lucy Letby's trial don't help her case. Indeed, they appear to undermine it.

What about the death rate since Letby's departure from the neonatal unit in July 2016? In our *Panorama*, we asked Steve Brearey that very question. His answer was stark. 'One,' he said. One death in seven years.

Some sceptics have questioned the truth of this. They've pointed to figures compiled by the research organisation MBRRACE which show three neonatal deaths at the Countess of Chester Hospital in 2017 and a further three deaths in each of the years 2019 and 2021. Sceptics have also pointed to figures released by the Countess of Chester Hospital itself in response to a Freedom of Information request in 2018. According to those figures, there were two 'early neonatal deaths' and two 'late neonatal deaths' in 2017 and a further two 'early neonatal deaths' in 2018. So who's right? Brearey? MBRRACE? Or the Countess of Chester Hospital?

We asked Steve Brearey about the MBRRACE figures and he offered this simple explanation: the MBRRACE figures define 'neonatal death' very broadly so as to include babies who died in the hospital's delivery suite and therefore didn't make it as far as the neonatal unit – which is where Letby worked. They also include babies who were born at the Countess of Chester Hospital but died at a different hospital within twenty-eight days. Neither of these categories is relevant to the question how many babies died *on the neonatal unit.*

What about those 2018 figures from the Countess of Chester Hospital noting several neonatal deaths in 2017 and 2018? We asked the Countess of Chester Hospital and they told us that their 2018 Freedom of Information figures were incorrect. They explained that the data used to compile these figures sat across various platforms and that a manual check conducted in 2023 confirmed that the 2018 figures were wrong. There were, they told us, 'no neonatal deaths from 1 July 2016 to 31 December 2018'. That is consistent with what Steve Brearey told us: starting in July 2016 and including the years after 2018, there has been just one death on the neonatal unit.

Of course, context is important, and there's one important bit of context that shouldn't be overlooked. In the same month that Letby was removed from neonatal duties, the unit at the hospital was downgraded, which meant that it no longer cared for high-risk babies in the way that it had done previously. So you would expect the death rate to fall. But even so, a decrease from thirteen deaths in a thirteen-month period to one death in seven years? No doubt, the statisticians among Letby's supporters will argue against jumping to conclusions on that evidence alone – and they would be right. They will also remind us that Letby was specially trained to work with the sickest babies. Again – true and relevant. But the numbers are striking nonetheless: the average death rate on the neonatal unit was two to three per year. Thirteen babies died between June 2015 and June 2016. Letby was on duty for twelve of them. And there's been only one death since her removal from the unit. These further revelations don't confirm Letby's guilt but they certainly point in that direction.

What about other baby collapses or incidents on the neonatal unit that didn't feature in Letby's trial or that the experts didn't get to see? Recall that shortly after Dewi Evans started working on the case in 2017, officers sent him the medical notes of around thirty babies to look at, most of which had been flagged by the consultants. One worry from Letby's supporters is that these individual cases might have been selected by the consultants in a way that was biased against Letby. Is this valid? Well, we can now account for thirteen of those thirty-odd cases. Thirteen were deaths – and deaths are black and white, so there's no possibility of selection bias there.

That leaves around seventeen cases of baby deteriorations, at least eight of which were highlighted by the consultants. The worry from Letby supporters is that there may be other cases of baby deteriorations that were excluded from this set of seventeen that mightn't have pointed so neatly to her. How do we know, for example, that there wasn't a series of unexplained or suspicious incidents involving another nurse – or doctor – that weren't selected by the consultants for the police and then shared with Dewi Evans and the other experts? If such cases existed, they might undermine the prosecution's neat fit between harm events and Letby's presence.

We don't know the full story here, and it's quite possible that no one does – not even the consultants at the Countess of Chester Hospital. To compile a comprehensive list of all baby deteriorations on the neonatal unit, you'd probably need a panel of independent experts with limitless time and resources to examine every page of medical notes of every baby who had spent time there and identify every event that they thought was a deterioration. Even that wouldn't be enough. You'd also need to interview every staff member who had worked there to get further information that wasn't in the notes. Such a comprehensive survey would be ideal, but is it necessary to reach a view on whether Lucy Letby was on duty for the most suspicious events? At some point, we have to rely, at least provisionally, on what the staff on the unit told police about which events they considered to be suspicious – even if some of these suspicions were formed retrospectively.

But there may be more to go on than this. We've learned that although Dewi Evans initially examined around thirty cases, the total number of cases that he examined was many more. By early 2018, the number of cases he had looked at had increased to thirty-four – and that was just the start. When Cheshire Police first arrested Lucy Letby in July 2018 and her name became public, it was inevitable that other families whose babies had spent time at the Countess of Chester Hospital would wonder whether their babies had also been targeted by the nurse – assuming she was guilty.

Unsurprisingly, worried parents started calling the hospital. Any one of these calls could potentially be another line of enquiry for the police. So Cheshire Police asked Evans to take a look at each new case to see if there was anything that looked suspicious. Evans examined a further forty-eight cases and of these he concluded that several looked worrying.

During 2020 and 2021, Evans recorded his concerns about these new cases in a series of reports, which he sent to Cheshire Police. However, none of these new cases featured in Letby's trial. Why? Did the police feel they had enough on their plate with the cases they were already looking at? Had they perhaps begun to lose faith in their lead expert? Or could it be that the cases that Evans had identified didn't put Letby in the frame and therefore didn't fit the prosecution narrative?

During Letby's trial, relations between Evans and the prosecution team he was working with weren't always harmonious. Some of Evans' changes of opinion during the trial, particularly with regard to Baby C, were a source of friction and it seems that Cheshire Police had begun to give him the cold shoulder too. A month after Letby's conviction in August 2023, Evans wrote to Cheshire Police to remind them of the additional cases that he had highlighted back in 2021 and to offer his latest view. Here's what he said:

> I reviewed another 48 cases, following various concerns from families, staff, or following my review of reports prepared by my fellow paediatrician Dr Sandie Bohin. I have reviewed all 48 cases over the past couple of weeks. I have noted 18 cases that in my opinion require more careful scrutiny. Some are probably not particularly concerning if one had access to a properly paginated set of records . . . Several are very concerning indeed.

We don't know if Lucy Letby was on duty for all of these additional eighteen incidents highlighted by Evans. Nor does he. His job was simply to highlight incidents he thought were suspicious. Linking these incidents to staff was the job of the police. He did, however, review five of the eighteen cases for us to see if Lucy Letby's name appears on the medical notes around the time of the incidents in question, and in each case it did. In one case from June 2014, a baby under Letby's care experienced 'large vomits' only to recover when Letby went off shift. A further two cases from September 2014 suggest the dislodgement of two babies' breathing tubes – both while Lucy Letby was on duty. That's according to Dr Evans.

Evans has also gone over some of the cases he was initially sent by Cheshire Police and has since concluded that a further seven of these are concerning. He mentioned these too in his letter to the police. He's heard nothing back. Even before the end of Letby's first trial, Cheshire Police told us they were following new leads in the Lucy Letby case. Insiders call it 'Operation Hummingbird Phase 2'. Whatever that involves, it appears that Dewi Evans won't be part of it.

So what are we to make of this new information from Dewi Evans? It all depends on the weight and reliability of his opinion. Is he a great medical expert to whom we can and should defer or not? Those who are convinced of Lucy Letby's guilt will draw further support from Evans' findings. Evans, they will point out, spotted the all-important insulin evidence. (So too did Steve Brearey, as it happens.) And Evans' analysis shaped the entire prosecution case. The Court of Appeal also affirmed Evans' status as an expert witness. According to the judges, 'it is unarguably the case that Dr Evans was suitably qualified – or to put it another way, it is not arguable that he lacked the necessary expertise – to give evidence . . . He certainly had sufficient knowledge to render his opinion of value; he had expertise that was capable of assisting the jury and was unarguably able to provide evidence with regard to neonates on matters within his expertise, but outwith the experience of the jury.' There is an additional point that bears on the question of how we should view Dewi Evans' suggestion that there are other cases of harm involving Lucy Letby. If Letby did murder and attempt to murder babies between June 2015 and June 2016, she probably didn't start then. If Letby was indeed a killer, wouldn't we expect to see evidence of her harming or attempting to kill babies before the first suspicious death in June 2015? What we know of Dewi Evans' additional evidence offers a story that fits with this intuition. He told us, 'I think that there was a pattern of breathing tubes being displaced when Lucy Letby was on call going back twelve months or possibly more before the first fatality. I think that she could well have started her off by displacing breathing tubes. I think she then moved on to injecting stomachs with lots of milk and air.'

Critics of Evans, on the other hand, will argue that his scientific opinions during the trial were flawed, or at least contested, hypotheses, and that his concerns about additional cases are likely to follow that pattern. Some may also wonder whether, as Evans' involvement in the case progressed, he had perhaps become biased in favour of finding foul play in the evidence he was examining. Evans would robustly deny this. A final and obvious objection is that, given the fact that the additional cases that Evans examined came to him after Lucy Letby was arrested and her name was publicised, it was to be expected that fresh concerns from parents and staff would be focused on her. If you tell the world a particular nurse might have been serially harming babies, it's inevitable that new suspicions and allegations will be skewed towards her, whatever the truth may be.

But Dewi Evans isn't the only one who has been examining Lucy Letby's medical footprint. Letby had worked at the Countess of Chester Hospital ever since she finished university in 2011. But remember – she'd also spent time at another hospital as well. In 2012, she spent six weeks on a professional induction programme at Liverpool Women's Hospital, and in 2015, she returned to Liverpool Women's to complete specialist training in intensive care. So far, Letby hasn't been formally accused of harming any babies while she was at Liverpool Women's Hospital, but the police say they are investigating her time there.

The police have been tight-lipped about their enquiries concerning Letby's time in Liverpool, but we've done some digging of our own. We understand that Letby did about twenty shifts while she was there in 2012 and another twenty in 2015. We spoke to someone familiar with the investigation who told us there were 'incidents that I was concerned about'. Moreover, 'the number of events is ridiculously high compared to what you would expect', although it's unclear how many of these coincided with Letby being on duty. There were no suspected murders and the number of incidents was fewer than one per shift. There was also no smoking gun pointing to Letby. However, our source told us they were 'convinced that something was going on in Letby's early period at Liverpool Women's Hospital'. In other words, the suspicion is that Letby was harming babies as early as 2012. If our source is right, then the murders and attempted murders for which Letby has been convicted could be just a fraction of the overall number.

We have spoken to one highly respected consultant neonatologist who played no role in Letby's trial but who has been asked to examine a number of further incidents at the Countess of Chester Hospital involving babies whom Lucy Letby was caring for. The consultant identified 'more than one case where there were unexplained clinical deteriorations in an infant's condition which correlated with Lucy Letby's involvement in their care'. At least one of the incidents predates those in Letby's trial and, according to the consultant, appeared to involve one of the methods of harm identified by Dewi Evans in his initial set of reports. From what we understand of these cases, the correlation between Lucy Letby's involvement with the babies and their unexplained and rapid decline is both stark and highly irregular.

It's an important and alarming account, and one that we consider to be highly credible. At the same time, we haven't seen the detail and it's just one expert's opinion. But there is a second individual incident that, although it didn't feature in Letby's trial, presents one of the most serious challenges to her defenders. It's another case of apparent insulin poisoning.

As we know, Letby's trial featured two cases of insulin poisoning – the cases of Baby F and Baby L. What neither the jury nor the general public knew was that a third insulin case was discovered during the police investigation. We also understand that the prosecution's original expert witness Dewi Evans discovered it. On 3

November 2015, the male doctor who became Letby's confidant recorded observations for a baby whom we'll call Baby Y. The observations were cause for concern – so much so that that a sample of the baby's blood was sent off to the laboratory at Royal Liverpool University Hospital for insulin-C-peptide analysis. Two days later, the results arrived. They showed a large quantity of insulin in the baby's blood – 'greater than 1,000' – and a low C-peptide level – '220'. We haven't seen the original lab documentation – just a doctor's note – and the unit of measurement for the insulin and the C-peptide isn't specified in the note. But the standard unit of measurement is pmol/l and there is no reason to think it was different in this case. It appeared that the baby had been given dangerous levels of exogenous insulin. Moreover, Lucy Letby had been on duty.

We've seen medical records that show the precise sequence of events – and who was present. The picture is troubling. Baby Y was born on 2 November 2015. Early on the morning of 3 November, he was transferred to the hospital's neonatal unit where his blood glucose level was measured. A blood test timed at 6.56 a.m. confirmed that Baby Y's blood glucose level was normal. Anything between 3 and 7mmol/l is considered normal. Baby Y's blood glucose was 3mmol/l.

Lucy Letby was on the day shift, which means she probably came on duty shortly before 8 a.m. – an hour after Baby Y's blood glucose was recorded as normal. Within hours of Letby's arrival, Baby Y's blood glucose level plummeted. A blood test timed at 13.54 showed that his blood glucose had fallen to 1mmol/l. Baby Y was now hypoglycaemic.

Baby Y's blood glucose level remained low for most of the day. We understand that at some point during the day, a blood sample was taken from Baby Y and sent to the laboratory for insulin / C-peptide analysis. A note that day from a doctor records 'hypo screen obtained', and a separate note from another medic timed at 7.45 p.m. on 3 November says: 'A/W [await] insulin / C-peptide levels'. Two days later, the lab results came back. They showed that Baby Y had been given dangerous levels of insulin.

Lucy Letby likely finished her shift at 8 p.m. on 3 November. By 11.30 p.m. that night, Baby Y's blood glucose levels had returned to normal. It looks like one of the clearest pieces of circumstantial evidence against Letby: within hours of her arrival on the unit on the morning of 3 November 2015, Baby Y's blood glucose level dropped and remained low throughout the day, having been normal before Letby arrived. A lab test on a blood sample taken that day appeared to confirm that Baby Y had been given dangerous levels of insulin. Letby finished her shift at 8 p.m. that evening, and a few hours later Baby Y recovered.

The married doctor was also on duty that day. Indeed, he wrote many of the observational notes for Baby Y. He also appears to have been the one who oversaw and helped obtain the insulin / C-peptide results. Indeed, he was the one who jotted these results down in Baby Y's medical notes. He made no comment on what the results indicated.

Baby Y's medical records show that a reviewing consultant also missed the significance of the insulin / C-peptide results. In a note dated 5 November 2015, consultant John Gibbs wrote: 'Blood insulin indicates neonatal hyperinsulinemia' – in other words, elevated insulin levels in Baby Y's blood. A few hours later, Dr Gibbs wrote: 'Investigations likely to be arranged to see if a localised part of pancreas is producing too much insulin.' Dr Gibbs' hypothesis appears to have been that the reason there was so much insulin in Baby Y's blood was that Baby Y's body might be producing too much insulin naturally – and there was cause to consider this possibility. We understand that Baby Y suffered from congenital hyperinsulinism – a condition (distinct from hyperinsulinaemia) where the body produces too much insulin naturally. Indeed, medics on the neonatal unit had to continue treating Baby Y to ensure his blood sugar remained normal. But the insulin / C-peptide results indicated that was not what had caused Baby Y's blood sugar to plummet when Lucy Letby was on duty on 3 November 2015. These results pointed clearly to exogenous insulin – poisoning. Why wasn't this picked up, we might wonder? We know Dr Gibbs saw the insulin / C-peptide results because his own note is written directly below them. It was another missed opportunity by the Countess of Chester Hospital's senior medics. Three months earlier, doctors had missed the significance of Baby F's insulin-C-peptide results. Now, pretty much the same thing had happened again.

We wrote to Dr Gibbs and put it to him that he should have spotted – with expert help if needed – that Baby Y's blood test indicated that he had been given exogenous insulin. Dr Gibbs responded quickly – and he didn't try to dodge the issue. '[I]n those babies in whom it is likely insulin was administered,' he said, 'the blood results were not interpreted properly and the likelihood that the insulin measured was largely exogenous (hence had been administered), was regrettably overlooked.' He added: 'The views of those who work in the specialist laboratories that measure blood insulin levels would be helpful in determining how reliably exogenous insulin can be recognised from the insulin and C-peptide blood levels and also how best these results should be reported to clinicians to hopefully avoid in future overlooking a result indicating insulin was likely to have been administered.'

In any event, the case of Baby Y looked just like the other two insulin cases that were brought to trial. So why was it not included in the case against Letby? We can only speculate, but it's possible that the lawyers in the Crown Prosecution Service thought the fact that Baby Y suffered from congenital hyperinsulinism might open up an unhelpful scientific debate about whether Baby Y's high insulin levels were a result of poisoning or natural overproduction. The prosecution already had two strong, clear-cut insulin cases. They didn't need a third to prove their point – although the parents of Baby Y may well take a different view. In any event, however, this third insulin case looks like further evidence that someone was poisoning babies in the Countess of Chester neonatal unit. It also places Letby at the scene at the time of the crisis.

So where does all of this new information take us? Are we so dazed and confused by the blizzard of evidence that we don't know what to think? Or has a clear picture emerged from the constellation? That depends partly on what question we're asking. For many people – understandably – the pressing question is whether Lucy Letby had a fair trial. Did she get the best possible defence? Did the jury get to hear the evidence they needed to hear to reach informed verdicts?

For others, the question is whether the evidence against Lucy Letby meets the criminal standard of proof – beyond reasonable doubt. For the jury, it did.

And yet, the last few chapters show that there are reasons to question whether Lucy Letby had a satisfactory trial. There are also reasons to question whether all of the evidence against her meets the threshold of beyond reasonable doubt. Everyone will have their own view on what this threshold is. For some, the fact that the science was contested and the evidence was circumstantial is neither here nor there. The case for Letby's guilt is overwhelming. For others, there are too many uncertainties in the case to be sure. Even if we are persuaded that someone at the Countess of Chester Hospital was harming babies, can we be certain it was Lucy Letby? Could there be another bad actor who has so far managed to remain undiscovered? Remember the case of Rebecca Leighton – wrongly accused of the crimes of one of her colleagues. Could this have happened to Lucy Letby? These are legitimate and necessary questions.

But there is another question that we can ask that is different to whether Lucy Letby is definitely guilty and it's this: can it be said that she is *innocent*? You may believe that Letby's trial was unfair. You may feel the case was not proven beyond reasonable doubt. But that isn't the same thing as being sure that she is innocent. So is she? Many will say that this question is irrelevant. The onus is simply on Letby's accusers to prove that she is guilty, and as a matter of law, of course they are right. But outside of the courtroom, it's fair to ask: how strong is the case for Letby's innocence?

For Letby's most loyal supporters – her parents and Dawn – Letby *is* innocent and nothing less than a full confession from her will persuade them otherwise. Even if she did confess, there would doubtless be some people who would refuse to believe her. Our view is based on the evidence that we have seen. What we can say is this: for all the imperfections of her prosecution and her trial, the case for Lucy Letby's innocence is not an easy one to make. If it's unclear for some that she is definitely guilty, it's far from clear that she is innocent.

Chapter 11

The Retrial

June 2024. Officially it was summer, but no one had told Manchester yet. Office workers huddled against the elements in raincoats, and though the city centre bars did their best to look bright with sunset drinks promotions and Wimbledon-themed décor, it was a tall order.

The Crown Court, however, wasn't such an incongruous sight. Its grey concrete edifice merged miserably with the leaden sky, and camera crews shivered as they lined up in their well-worn spot at the bottom of the front steps. It was eight months since they'd last congregated here to film the reaction to Lucy Letby's sentencing. Now her retrial was about to get under way, and the media circus was back in town.

The old gaffer tape that the TV companies used to mark their pavement territory was still stuck in position, but though the court backdrop hadn't changed the second time around, the atmosphere surrounding the new trial was palpably different.

Since the verdicts, the Letby case seemed to have taken on a life of its own. Heavy reporting restrictions to protect the retrial meant that there was minimal media coverage for many months. But the online court of public opinion paid scant regard to those rules, and the debate had continued to rage on blogs, forums and websites. Was Lucy Letby a monstrous serial baby killer or a victim of Britain's worst miscarriage of justice? That was the debate – and everyone seemed to have an answer. A scroll through social media was an invitation to disappear down a rabbit hole of posts ranging from the thoughtful to the screechingly abusive.

Lucy Letby's failure to win permission for an appeal had provided fresh outrage for those on the sceptical side of the argument, and there was a newly charged mood surrounding the retrial. Letby was back in court to face one count of attempted murder that the original jury was unable to decide. It was the charge that she'd tried to kill Baby K in February 2016 by moving a breathing tube. This was the 'he-said-she-said' allegation that rested on the word of Dr Ravi Jayaram, who was claimed to have walked in after the attack.

The hospital consultants had been acclaimed in the wake of the verdicts. As they told the story of their struggle to get managers to listen to their concerns about Letby, they were celebrated for their persistence and bravery. But the scepticism in some quarters about her convictions meant that the seeds of another narrative stood to be sown, and the second trial was limbering up to be a rematch between the nurse and the consultants.

The jeopardy for both was clear. If the jury accepted Ravi Jayaram's word, it would mean further validation for the doctors, another life sentence for Lucy Letby, and a rebuke to the sceptics. But what if the jury chose to believe the nurse's version of events over that of Dr Jayaram? What would that do for the consultants' credibility? At first glance, given the weight of Letby's previous convictions, the case might have looked like a foregone conclusion, but the stakes underlying it meant it was anything but.

Day one of the retrial was an exercise in déjà vu. 'Back again?' asked the court security guards, ready with their metal detector wands once more. There was no need to ask the way – courtroom seven had been reallocated to the Letby case and Neil, the court clerk, was back in his familiar seat just below the judge's bench. The same lawyers carried their files into the room, though each side had reduced its arsenal of barristers from three down to two. With this trial focusing only on one baby, it would be a far shorter affair, and the legal benches were slightly emptier as a result.

There were others whose absence we quickly noticed too. Sue and John Letby, who'd faithfully trudged into court nearly every day for the entire ten months of the first trial, were nowhere to be seen. Perhaps this shouldn't have been a huge surprise. The couple had been there to support their daughter right up until the point when she was no longer prepared to turn up herself. Once it became apparent that Lucy Letby was boycotting the verdict and sentencing hearings, her parents followed suit and vacated their seats.

Now the retrial was about to begin, and the defendant was brought back into the dock. Though her mum and dad must have told her that they wouldn't be there, she looked across to where they used to sit. She was rewarded with the sight of a row of journalists who'd been given their seats. Judith was amongst them. The defendant caught her eye and the two locked each other in a stare. That had never happened before. At the first trial, Letby had always avoided eye contact. Did this signal a change of some kind – perhaps a new confidence? Or was she channelling some darker feeling – perhaps towards the media and our coverage of her case? Judith wasn't sure what to make of it, and waited for Letby to look away first.

The Letbys' absence might have looked like a cooling in support for their daughter, but that was unlikely. The retrial was available to observe remotely, via a secure video link. Following the evidence from the comfort of their front room was doubtless a far more appealing prospect than coming along in person – which would have involved travelling from Hereford to Manchester, only to run the gauntlet of cameras in front of court each day.

So, no parents. But that didn't mean there was no support for Lucy Letby inside courtroom seven. The nurse's faithful friend Janet Cox was back – now the lone member of the inner circle – promoted to the status of 'family' by court staff who allowed her to enter the room each day before the media and public.

And what of the public? That was the most notable difference, second time around. At the first trial, just a handful of regulars would turn up to watch the proceedings. They were retired or studying or otherwise able to dedicate the long hours needed to keep up with the evidence. A few of them told us that they'd never followed a trial before. Richard, a student, said, 'I thought, "Is it a bit weird that I'm wanting to go and watch a court case? Especially one like this, given the nature of it?" But what struck me was the amount of detail that's been presented. It's immense. And to really understand the case, I think you have to be there to listen to it and absorb as much of it as you can.'

Leah, a young mum, started coming along after reading news coverage of the opening of the prosecution. She said, 'The headlines that were coming out – it was like, "I won't believe it till I see it. There must be some other explanation." I'd never been in a court in my life, and I just had to see her for myself.'

This group of 'court watchers' became familiar to those of us covering the first trial. They sat quietly in the overflow seating area, following the action for their own reasons, but never becoming involved in it, and respecting the solemnity of the setting. Richard said, 'I think it's a very privileged position to be in. There are flaws with the courts, but the fact is that a member of the public can go in and observe a trial of this gravity and seriousness, and be present for the verdicts, and I think that's a good thing about the system.'

It was no surprise to see the same group back again for the retrial. But this time, the ranks of onlookers had swollen. Many of the new arrivals were there to support Lucy Letby – and they made their presence felt. Yes, they had come to observe. But there was a simmering sense of protest and anger too.

One of the previous regulars, Katie, picked up on it immediately. 'People came with more of an open mind last time,' she said. 'This time they had an agenda. They were coming up to me saying, "What's your view? This is mine." They were handing out email addresses and flyers for websites, so it was obvious who they were supporting.'

Some of the throng had also travelled to London for the appeal hearing, where they stood outside the Royal Courts of Justice with a 'Justice for Lucy Letby' banner. They stopped short of repeating the demonstration in Manchester.

On the first morning, a queue started forming sometime before the courtroom doors opened. The corridor quickly filled up, and the trickle of spectators jostling for position grew into a crowd. The court ushers corralled them into two halves, parting the waves so that Baby K's parents could get through the throng and into the room. The couple looked ashen as they took their seats for this second take. They'd already been through the anguish of one trial without a verdict to show for it. Now here they were again – steeling themselves for a rerun of that ordeal. Last time, they'd had the company of the families of the other babies. This time – other than the police officers who were there in support – they were going it alone. As a result, there was a lot more space in the public gallery, and it was soon filled by some of those who'd queued up for 'pole position' seats. It meant that people who'd travelled to show their support for Lucy Letby were sitting right up alongside the family of the baby she was accused of trying to kill. The arrangement looked like it had pyrotechnic potential, but the clerk rapped on the door, and the room hushed as Judge Goss swept in.

Seconds earlier, we'd seen Letby sharing a laugh with the prison officers behind the glass of the dock. It was just a fleeting moment, but it felt like a glimpse of another Lucy Letby – the old Letby perhaps. Maybe she could sense her small army of supporters in the courtroom. But as soon as the judge appeared, her expression became sullen.

'Are you Lucy Letby?' asked Neil the clerk, out of formal necessity rather than extraordinary ignorance.

'Yes,' the defendant confirmed, playing along with the script.

She was invited to sit. Over on the press bench, we were ready to start reporting the case. But the court wasn't moving at quite the same pace. First there was the matter of selecting the jury. Forty-three people were brought into the room, carrying bags and coats, as though on a day trip. They stood nervously, crammed into a space meant for far fewer people, and some of them, unable to help themselves, glanced across at the woman in the dock. As if he was reading their thoughts, the judge verified that they were indeed looking at Lucy Letby, and that any of them could end up on the eventual jury of twelve who'd try her case. 'There has been a previous trial of which you will be aware,' he added simply. Then he told them it would be the next day before the jury would be chosen because there was legal business to deal with. He sent them home with a warning shot. 'Don't speak to anyone about the fact you're potentially serving on a trial about this case,' he said. 'You're bound to be asked whether you're sitting on a case. Say you aren't. Don't communicate on social media. Don't conduct any research over the internet. You can get a lot of information and misinformation there. Simply block this out of your minds until tomorrow. I can't impress the seriousness of this upon you enough. Any breach of these obligations is a contempt of court. You can go to prison.'

Suitably cowed, the potential jurors shuffled out of the room, and Lucy Letby's defence barrister got up. The court might have looked trial-ready, with every seat full, the defendant present and jurors on standby. But now here was Ben Myers KC, with the aim of stopping the case before it could begin.

'My Lord, I am making an application to stay the indictment as an abuse of process,' he said in fluent legalese.

The meaning? Myers was arguing that the trial should be abandoned because his client couldn't hope to have a fair hearing. He blamed the volume of media coverage after the end of the previous trial. He slated the police and CPS for making 'highly prejudicial and emotive statements' after the verdicts, including an hour-long promotional film produced by Cheshire Police's press office that featured officers talking about how they had cracked the case.

He offered up a 39-page dossier filled with examples of reporting about the case.

'That must have been very time-consuming to create,' said the judge.

'It was,' Letby's barrister agreed.

But it wasn't just the media that Myers had in his sights. That very weekend several tabloid papers had run a story about the prosecution's star witness at the retrial, Dr Ravi Jayaram. He was reported to be helping develop a TV drama about the case with star actresses in the running to play the nurse, and *Line of Duty* creator Jed Mercurio at the helm. There was no mention of who might be lined up to play Letby's silver-haired barrister – but that wasn't what had incensed Myers. 'It's extraordinary for a prosecution witness to be behaving in this way,' he said, 'in the context of waiting to give evidence . . . peddling his own narrative and taking a starring role!'

There followed a sideshow scrap between the barristers about whether there was any truth in the articles, and whether Jayaram should be questioned about it. The prosecution dismissed the reports as 'show-business gossip'. It all felt a long way from the issue at the heart of the case – the allegation that Lucy Letby had attempted to murder another baby – but for Letby's defence, it spoke of Ravi Jayaram's calibre as a witness.

Nicholas Johnson KC was leading the charge for the prosecution, just as he had at the first trial. He rose to argue that it was entirely possible for a fair trial to be held. 'The crimes committed by Lucy Letby, and which have been proved against her, were appalling. They are without precedent . . . and to indicate the point, I'd like to read out part of what Your Lordship said in sentencing,' he said. 'What followed in the media was nothing more than a fair reflection of that.'

Letby shuffled uncomfortably in her seat. There had been a lot of publicity about the fact that she'd refused to turn up to the sentencing hearing – a decision that prompted criticism after the trial from many quarters including the Prime Minister. It meant that she'd avoided having to listen to the judge's remarks. Now, here was Nick Johnson, about to reprise them.

'You acted in a way that was completely contrary to the normal human instincts of nurturing and caring for babies, and in gross breach of the trust that all citizens place in those who work in the medical and caring professions,' he read.

Letby showed no reaction as the barrister ran through her criminal curriculum vitae, detailing its impact. 'Loving parents have been robbed of their cherished children and others have to live with the physical and mental consequences of your actions.'

The defendant looked down at her lap. She was flanked by three female officers, whose job it was to escort her from prison each day. Two of them bowed their heads. It didn't make for easy listening for anyone.

The barrister got to the end of the judge's comments and added his own assessment. 'We submit that nothing has been said (by the media) about Lucy Letby that comes close to eclipsing the truly dreadful catalogue of murder and attempted murder for which she is responsible,' he concluded. 'All the publicity was entirely legitimate.'

Was it really possible for Lucy Letby to have a fair hearing after everything that had gone before? Judge Goss concluded that it was. 'I've listened very carefully,' he pronounced, 'and I'm satisfied that the defendant can have a fair trial.' Ben Myers' application to stop the case was refused. And there was more bad news to come for Letby and her legal team. Myers had argued that the jurors should be told about two counts from the previous trial on which the jury had found Letby not guilty.

He'd contended that it was only fair, given that they were going to hear about the convictions. Judge Goss turned him down, later explaining that the acquittals weren't relevant to the baby who was the subject of the retrial.[1]

The defence team bristled – but there was nothing more they could do to fight their client's corner before the jury was sworn in and the case against Letby got under way.

The next morning, Nicholas Johnson KC was ready with his opening speech. He started by addressing the point that the jurors would already have heard of the woman on trial. 'We have already proved that Lucy Letby was a murderer,' he said, before explaining that the nurse was convicted of attacking thirteen children, and the baby they were concerned with – Baby K – was number fourteen.

'You should not convict her because of what she's done in other cases, but it gives you significant evidence as to what her intention was at the time that we allege she did something to Baby K,' he declared.

'In a nutshell, we say that her status as a multiple murderer and attempted murderer is an important piece of evidence that you should take into account when you are considering whether we have proved that she was trying to kill her.'

Nick Johnson read out a roll call of all of the babies Lucy Letby had been convicted of murdering or attempting to murder. He was headlining his campaign with it, but he still had to prove the new case. Just because the first jury had found Letby guilty of harming different babies, didn't mean this jury would accept that she'd attempted to murder Baby K. We were only there at all because the original jurors couldn't agree about the charge, and there was no guarantee that this set would find it any easier to reach a conclusion.

The barrister explained the context of the case. He told them that Baby K was a very premature girl, born at just twenty-five weeks' gestation. Her mother had gone to the Countess of Chester Hospital as it was nearest to home, when she was worried by symptoms that turned out to be early labour. Medics wanted to move her to a hospital that was better equipped to care for such a premature birth, but the nearest such bed was over sixty miles away in Preston and would have involved more than an hour in an ambulance. It was deemed too risky to attempt the transfer as it was clear the labour was advancing quickly.

Baby K was born in the very early hours of the morning on 17 February 2016, and Nick Johnson told the jury that she 'did remarkably well for such a premature baby'. She was taken through to the neonatal unit where Lucy Letby was on a night shift and transferred into an incubator in the intensive care room – Nursery One.

The prosecution case was that Letby tried to murder Baby K less than two hours after she was born.

The allegation was that the nurse had moved the endotracheal tube, which was the baby's means of breathing by ventilator. No one had seen her doing it, and there was no CCTV or other direct evidence. Instead, the claim was built on the word of the paediatric consultant Ravi Jayaram, who was said to have walked into the nursery shortly after the tube was dislodged, to find the baby's blood oxygen levels plummeting, and Letby right there, doing nothing to intervene. The monitor alarm hadn't gone off, and the prosecution suggested that she'd purposely silenced it. The doctor said he'd given rescue breaths to the baby to stabilise her.

Johnson couldn't shy away from the fact that the case would rest on the word of the consultant against that of the nurse. He said, 'Ultimately this may all come down to whether you believe

Dr Jayaram. Are you sure he is telling the truth about what he saw, and if you do accept what he says, what is it that you think Lucy Letby was intending to do?'

When Ben Myers made his opening speech a few minutes later, he landed on the very same point. 'On this, the prosecution and defence are in agreement,' he said. 'It comes down to the evidence of Dr Jayaram. If his account is not truthful or accurate, then there is no safe basis for convicting Lucy Letby on this charge.'

What about the nurse's word? Myers laid it out for the jury. 'Miss Letby does not remember specifically the events of that night,' he told them. 'Some people may raise their eyebrows and wonder "well, why not?" Given the hundreds of babies that she may have cared for in a year it's hardly surprising. She doesn't agree that she interfered with the tubing at any point, or that she did anything to harm Baby K.'

The barrister knew that he'd also have to tackle his client's substantial criminal record, head on. 'Miss Letby has maintained she's guilty of nothing,' he said. 'Well, you have those convictions, and you'll consider them, and they're potentially a powerful and emotive part of this case. It's important to emphasise the convictions don't prove this allegation. But convictions like that in a trial like this may make it easier to convict someone of something they haven't done.'

The battle lines had been laid out. It wouldn't just be the King against Lucy Letby. It would also be Ravi Jayaram against Lucy Letby.

Baby K's parents were sitting at the back of the courtroom, holding hands. They'd had to relive their painful story many times over the years, recounting it to detectives, and listening to it in court. Now they readied themselves to hear it once more. The baby's mother had prepared a written statement which was read out by a junior barrister. He spoke slowly and with little intonation, but the dryness of his delivery didn't mask the emotion that clearly lay behind the words the woman had chosen. She described how thrilled she and her husband had been to learn they were expecting a baby, and how the pregnancy had progressed normally at first.

Then, the worry of waking up with aches and pains one morning, and the trip to hospital where she was told labour had begun. The drama of the emergency alarm being pressed, and the room filling with people as the baby was coming. And the anxiety of the delivery, as the tiny girl – weighing just a pound and a half – was surrounded by staff who coaxed her into life, getting her breathing and keeping her warm.

You could sense the couple's bewilderment and sense of powerlessness in that moment. The baby's dad had gone over to see his daughter but came away again as he didn't want to get in the way. A consultant explained that the baby would be cared for on the neonatal unit, and the new parents went to rest for a couple of hours.

The charge was that Letby attempted to murder the baby at around 3.45 a.m., and the woman's statement reached that point in the night's chronology. Had she or her husband seen anything? Did they have any memory of it?

It seemed not. The mother didn't give any detail from the parents' perspective about what was alleged to have happened at that time. Her account moved straight on to events at 4.30 a.m. when she'd been helped into a wheelchair and taken to visit her daughter, and time-stamped pictures were taken of the new family of three by a female nurse who she remembered had blonde hair.

Whatever had or hadn't happened to Baby K at 3.45 a.m., the infant's parents weren't going to be able to shed any light on the picture, but their story didn't end there. Later that morning the tiny girl had been transferred by ambulance to another hospital, which was better equipped to care for such premature babies. Her parents had followed and were staying in family accommodation there three nights later, when the mother had a sudden sensation. She said, 'I had the strangest feeling that I can't possibly describe.' The couple went to see their daughter and found that she was in a really bad way. They were told that she'd been fighting for survival all night, and things were looking bleak.

At the back of courtroom seven, the baby's parents held each other as their gut-wrenching account was relayed to the jury. 'She had been poked and prodded from the moment she was born. Her tiny little delicate body had swollen up so much and we didn't want her to be suffering any more,' the mother had written. 'We made the decision together to switch off the machines and let her go. It was by far the hardest decision of my life.'[2]

The baby girl was wrapped in a blanket and placed into her father's arms. The doctors told her parents, 'We can do this whenever you're ready,' and when the signal was given they removed the infant's breathing tube and stepped away. The couple was told that the infant would have about twenty minutes of life left, and her daddy cradled her until she took her last breath.

Baby K was pronounced dead at three days old. Eight years had elapsed since that day, and it was clear that her parents' pain was undimmed. Husband and wife now wept together as if their mutual wound had been reopened.

Less than five metres from them, Lucy Letby's expression betrayed no emotion. She hadn't been there when the baby died, and she wasn't charged with her murder. The Crown wasn't alleging that her actions had led to the little girl's death – only that she'd attempted to murder her three nights before she died. The prosecution had originally charged Letby with the murder of Baby K, but the charge was changed to attempted murder before the first trial got under way. No post-mortem examination had been carried out, and the cause of death was certified as 'extreme prematurity and severe respiratory distress syndrome'.[3] The prosecution described the baby as 'the epitome of fragility'.[4]

It was a case with some layered complexities to work through. Letby was accused of interfering with the tube but not murdering the baby; she was also said to have done it three times – but only to have intended murder once. The other two occasions, later on the same shift, were said to have been her effort to cover her tracks and create the impression that Baby K had a habit of displacing her own tube.

It was a lot for the jurors to get their heads around, and the intense atmosphere in court wasn't helped by the temperamental air conditioning unit that oscillated between Baltic and tropical.

At one point, Judge Goss asked if the jury needed to get some air. 'It's very hot in here,' he observed, 'and you don't have to wear horsehair on your heads like I do.' The jurors smiled, but turned down the offer of a break, and the judge had to keep going too. The court was ready to hear from the star witness for the prosecution.

Dr Ravi Jayaram entered the courtroom. It was familiar territory for him, having been in and out of the witness box several times at the first trial. He's a confident man – at ease in public, and happy touring TV studios as a medical pundit. But there was no swagger as he took up his position to give evidence. He seemed wearier than he had at the first trial.

'Do you remember Baby K?' Nick Johnson asked him.

'I have a memory of certain events from that night, yes,' answered the consultant.

It was nothing that Lucy Letby hadn't heard before, but over in the dock she started to cry, and one of the dock officers handed her a tissue. She dabbed her eyes as Dr Jayaram began to give his account.

He'd been on call overnight when the woman had gone into labour, and he was in charge at the birth. After Baby K was taken through to the neonatal unit, he was in the process of arranging her move to another hospital when he was interrupted. The nurse who'd been assigned to care for the baby came to tell the consultant that she was going to the postnatal ward to update the parents, and Lucy Letby was looking after her instead.

Dr Jayaram said that had made him feel uncomfortable because by that point there had been a number of unusual incidents with babies, and he and his colleagues had noticed that the nurse was always present. He took the jury through the same narrative as last time, explaining that he'd gone into the nursery to satisfy himself that things were OK, but had found the baby in trouble with blood oxygen levels plummeting and Letby standing idly by. The monitor alarm wasn't sounding and he asked the nurse what was happening, to which she replied, 'Oh, it looks like she's desaturating.' The breathing tube was dislodged, he said, and he'd had to resuscitate the infant with manual ventilation equipment.

348

Dr Jayaram was confident in his telling of the story. He'd been through it repeatedly over the years – and he was standing by it. No other witnesses had been inside the nursery at the time, and there was only the nurse to contradict it.

Ben Myers KC got up now, to ask questions on Letby's behalf. At the first trial, there was a palpable tension between the barrister and the consultant. That atmosphere quickly re-established itself again. Myers accused Jayaram of exaggerating some of the detail. Jayaram told Myers he was 'struggling to understand' the lawyer's rationale.

Myers told the doctor, 'I'm going to suggest that whatever happened with Baby K, you didn't find it suspicious at the time. Whatever did or didn't happen, you've added details to make it sound suspicious. You may or may not agree.'

Ravi Jayaram did not agree, but Ben Myers wasn't going to let it go. He referred to the TV interview, broadcast after Letby's first trial, in which Dr Jayaram recounted those events from February 2016. 'That night is etched on my memory,' the doctor had said. '[It] will be in my nightmares forever.' It was a memorable line, and one that Jayaram repeated in court. But it raised several questions – all presented in the course of the first trial but now reprised for the benefit of a different jury: if Dr Jayaram honestly thought he'd interrupted Lucy Letby attempting to murder a baby, why had he not called the police? Would he not at least have made a note of what he had seen, or challenged Letby or her manager?

For Ben Myers, Dr Jayaram's not calling the police merited special interrogation.

'You'd got her, hadn't you?' he said. 'You'd caught her as good as red-handed!'

Dr Jayaram maintained that it wasn't that simple. In part, he said, it was because the consultants had started to think the un-thinkable about Lucy Letby but didn't want to believe it. He also cited the response that the consultants predicted such a phone call would receive. He said, 'There's a culture in the NHS of clinicians who raise concerns – there was a strategy to keep us quiet. I can tell you what would have happened if we'd called the police. They'd have spoken to the medical director and the chief executive, who'd have said, "Just ignore them, they're a bunch of complaining pae-diatricians." We don't have any training about how to handle these situations.'5

'To ring the police doesn't take training, Dr Jayaram!' exclaimed Myers. 'You didn't call the police because it didn't happen!'

'Well, how are you proposing it did happen, Mr Myers?' Jayar-am thrust back. 'I'd like your hypothesis of how you think it did happen!'

Ravi Jayaram gave as good as he got. But for those of us who had studied the timeline of events at the Countess of Chester Hospital, some of his explanations for not calling the police were puzzling.

'Why were you prepared to potentially allow this nurse to go on killing?' Ben Myers asked.

Dr Jayaram responded: 'None of us were prepared to do that at all but we were in uncharted territory . . . We were meeting big resistance from people at the top.'

This is true. The consultants did encounter big resistance from senior management – but was this a fair reflection of what was happening in February 2016 when the events relating to Baby K occurred? By that point, Lucy Letby's association with baby deaths had been fed up the managerial chain and a meeting with senior management had been requested. Hospital bosses were silent, in-active, apparently uncurious, but there is little evidence that there was 'big resistance' from them at this time. That would come later – in the summer of 2016.

Elsewhere in his cross-examination, Ben Myers put it to Ravi Jayaram that he hadn't called the police because he hadn't seen anything worthy of calling them about. The doctor replied, 'In sub-sequent weeks and months we were told it would be inappropriate to call the police. We were being advised from the start that the police would be the wrong route.' Is this fair? Again, it's true that senior hospital managers argued against calling the police – but as far as we understand, the first such discussion about it didn't take place until June 2016, three months after the events involving Baby K. At the time of that incident, and in the twelve weeks following it, no hospital managers that we know of had voiced any position about calling the police. As far as we know, the question hadn't been put to them.

The paediatrician said it was a matter of infinite regret that he hadn't handled things differently. He also accepted that he hadn't recorded the tube dislodgement in the clinical notes. But he stuck to his guns when it came to the allegation he was making.

The prosecution was counting on that certainty to help to persuade the jury that it was the doctor, rather than the nurse, who was telling the truth.

That left the matter of hearing Letby's side of the story. Whether or not she was going to was up to her, but it was also a matter of strategy for both sets of barristers. The defence team didn't have to show its hand on that front while the prosecution case was still under way. Letby was under no obligation to give evidence. The prosecutors, for their part, had to plan for the possibility of her choosing to stay quiet. They felt the defendant had done herself no favours when testifying at the first trial and were assuming she'd elect to stay out of the witness box this time around. But, given their dim view of Letby's performance under questioning, they wanted to make sure that the jury had the chance to hear her speaking.

The answer, they decided, was to play the court some of the video interviews that detectives had conducted with Lucy Letby each time she was arrested. These videos had never been played in open court before. It promised to be a fascinating watch.

The TV screens flashed into life, and a six-year-old image appeared. The opening interview was from July 2018, recorded a couple of days after the police came knocking at Letby's door for the first time. She sat, subdued in grey police-issued sweatshirt, sipping from a Styrofoam cup as two detectives identified themselves for the tape. Letby's solicitor, Richard Thomas, was there too, with his hallmark mop of curly hair, looking much younger than he seemed now, on the back row of the courtroom. The case had clearly aged him.

The officers read Lucy Letby her rights and told her that they were going to discuss Baby K, asking her what contact she'd had with the infant.

'I don't recall why I was in the nursery with Baby K,' Letby began. 'I would have to look back to see if I had other babies that I was caring for in the room, and that's why I was there. Or whether I was covering for somebody who was on a break. I don't recall why I was in the nursery or what I was doing with Baby K, if anything.'

When they interviewed her again the following year, the police put Ravi Jayaram's account to Letby. 'Explain to me what you were doing, Lucy, when Dr Jayaram walked into the nursery?'

'I don't recall.'

'Is there a reason why Dr Jayaram might be mistaken, Lucy?'

'I don't know. He obviously seems to remember it quite specifically in terms of timing. I don't. And, you know, it's a shame that, if he felt uncomfortable with me being in the room, that he didn't raise that sooner, or with me personally, if he had a problem with my work prior to that.'

'Dr Jayaram clearly puts you there, at her cot-side at the time. Do you agree with that?'

'On what Dr Jayaram has said, yes.'

The third video was a flashback to the Covid era. The nurse and her solicitor were there at the police station again, she in a visor, he in a mask. Social distancing was only just about possible in the small interview suite. This time the detectives asked Lucy Letby why she'd searched on Facebook for Baby K's surname in April 2018 – more than two years after she'd last crossed paths with the family. The nurse agreed that she had made the search but said she couldn't remember doing it.

The videos were a useful guide to the arc of what Letby had to say about Baby K over the two years between her first arrest and the point when she was charged in 2020.

Critically, she hadn't disputed being next to the baby's incubator when Dr Jayaram entered the room. The question was whether these videos were going to be her only word on the matter or not. The prosecutors wrapped up their case, fully expecting the nurse to reserve her right to silence.

Ben Myers got up. 'On Monday, I will open the case for the defence,' he announced. 'And I will call Miss Letby to give evidence.'

The prosecution lawyers did their best to conceal their surprise, having assumed she'd do the opposite. But Lucy Letby was clearly adamant about protesting her innocence – and confident enough to stand up to further interrogation. There was also good reason for Ben Myers to want her to give evidence – he had some work to do to undo the damage Letby had done herself in the police videos.

Before she was interviewed by detectives, the nurse had been given the standard warning – 'It may harm your defence if you do not mention when questioned something which you later rely on in court.'

The problem that Ben Myers now had to deal with was that Lucy Letby had never mentioned to the police that she had no memory of being in the room with Baby K.

In 2018 she'd told them that she didn't remember *why* she was in the room and in 2019 she agreed with Ravi Jayaram that she'd been at the cot-side. Now her defence case was that she didn't agree she was in the room after all because she couldn't remember the night. The barrister knew he'd have to confront the difference in those accounts.

On Monday morning, the crowd at the courtroom door had swollen again. It seemed that a record number of people wanted to get inside, but the entrance was locked. Lucy Letby was being brought up from the cells in handcuffs and escorted to the witness box. Once she was in place, with cuffs off, and prison officers in position, the doors opened.

The defendant sat with her back to the public gallery as the crowd entered and the seats behind her filled up. She rocked gently from side to side as if to steady herself for the experience to come. She'd chosen a black trouser suit for the occasion – dour, professional, serious. From the front, she looked ready for business. But underneath the desktop of the witness box we could see that she was clutching a fluffy ball, pinching and squeezing it like a stress toy.

Ben Myers looked at her kindly. 'I'll start by asking you this,' he began. 'Did you attempt to kill Baby K?'

'No,' Letby said firmly.

'The jury has the list of convictions from previous proceedings. Do you accept you've ever intended to hurt any baby in your care?'

'No,' she said again.

The barrister moved on to the events involving Baby K.

'Do you have any recollection of Ravi Jayaram coming into the room when you were there yourself?'

'No.'

'Do you recall being there at all at that time in those circumstances?'

'No.'

'Do you accept that it happened?'

'No.'

This quick back and forth was an efficient way for the nurse and her defender to set out their stall. But Ben Myers still had to tackle the issue of why his client had said one thing to the police and was saying something else now. He asked her why she'd agreed with part of Ravi Jayaram's evidence.

'I took Dr Jayaram's word to be the truth,' she answered.

Myers asked Letby if she'd ever agreed that she'd been standing there without reacting while the baby's oxygen levels dropped. She said that she hadn't.

'Why did you say that to the police?' he enquired.

'I was trying to be helpful. At the time they were asking me questions that I believed to be factually correct.'

Myers took Letby to easier territory, asking her a run of questions about nursing practice and feeding procedures and getting her to explain technical abbreviations. He spoke slowly, respectfully. She was always 'Miss Letby' – never 'Lucy'. The nurse responded in kind, speaking clearly and confidently – keen to assist. It was only her eyes that betrayed the possibility that she might be finding things difficult. They darted and flickered as she blinked constantly – the movement a contrast to her ramrod-still posture.

Myers asked Letby if she'd been trying to cover her tracks by moving the baby's breathing tube three times. 'No,' she said, looking fed up. There were no more questions from the defence.

'Would you like a break now?' suggested Judge Goss.

'If I could, please,' Letby replied meekly. She knew that the real test was about to begin.

A few minutes later, Nick Johnson KC got up and the dynamic changed immediately.

'What Dr Jayaram says cannot be right. Is that your case?'

'Yes,' said Lucy Letby. 'I did not dislodge any tube.'

'Are you saying he's not telling the truth?' Johnson queried.

Letby gave what could be viewed as a politician's answer. 'I don't think I can comment on whether he's not telling the truth,' she said. Then added, 'I just know that did not happen.'

'You thought Dr Jayaram was out to get you . . .' suggested the prosecutor.

'Yes,' agreed the nurse.

Johnson brought Letby back to the explanation that she'd just given her own barrister – her suggestion that she'd been trying to help the police.

'To be helpful, you were prepared to go along with a doctor that you said had it in for you?'

'I don't think I've ever accepted his account.'

'How were you being helpful then?'

'The police kept asking me and asking me,' Letby explained. 'It's very intimidating when you're in a police interview and I was trying to help.'

'Who were you helping?' Johnson asked.

'I don't know,' Letby replied, adding ruefully, 'not me.'

The prosecutor wanted to exploit discrepancies between the different things Letby had said about the allegation at different times. He brought up the defence statement that she'd made with her lawyers, in preparation for the trial.

'Where does it say I wouldn't have hurt Baby K because I don't do that kind of thing?'

'It doesn't,' she accepted, adding, 'but I've made it quite clear that I did nothing to hurt Baby K.'

'Where does it say that you don't agree with what Dr Jayaram says?'

'It doesn't appear in those words.'

Letby was being lawyered, but she held her nerve. 'I think we're going round in circles,' she parried at one point.

After her arrest in 2019, Lucy Letby had told the police that she might have been standing next to Baby K doing nothing because she was waiting to see if the baby's declining oxygen levels 'self-corrected'. She'd added, 'We don't normally intervene straight away if [the levels] weren't dangerously low.'[6]

Now Nick Johnson highlighted a statement that had been given by a nursing adviser called Elizabeth Morgan. She'd said that in her professional opinion, when it came to babies as premature as Baby K, it was not 'normal practice' to wait before acting. Letby and her lawyers had concurred with this statement before the trial began, and it had been read to the jury as agreed evidence.

'Do you agree with this agreed evidence?' Johnson now asked Lucy Letby.

'No,' she said.

'You're lying, aren't you?' pushed the prosecutor.

'No,' insisted the defendant.

'And you're lying because you know you were caught cold by Dr Jayaram.'

'No,' said Letby, again.

At the first trial, Letby spent fourteen days in the witness box. At the retrial, her evidence was completed in a little over a day. She returned to the glass dock as the barristers made their closing speeches.

Nick Johnson KC went first. 'Lucy Letby is an extraordinary person,' he declared, before clarifying, 'but not in a good way.' He had a 'terrible list' to recite, he said, before reading the name of every baby Letby had been convicted of attacking. 'Baby A, murdered on the day he was born. Baby C, murdered when he was four days old. Baby D, murdered at two days of age . . .' and so on, up until babies O and P.

'From the first murder to the last was one year, two weeks and three days,' the barrister said. 'Now you have to consider whether she also attempted to murder Baby K.'

Though Nick Johnson wasn't generally given to courtroom

theatrics, there was a degree of showmanship to his closing speech. He praised the skill of the hospital staff while gesticulating towards Letby, exclaiming, 'The one notable exception to that is sitting in the dock!' He pointed at the courtroom clock and performatively counted the seconds up to thirty, to show how long it would have taken Baby K's oxygen levels to drop after her tube was moved. He told the jurors Letby had given them an 'extraordinary performance as she tiptoed through the minefield that is her police interviews'.

But if Johnson was animated, Ben Myers was positively histrionic – and he directed his energy straight at the jury.

'There's a reason why you are here, ladies and gentlemen!' he proclaimed. 'You are not spectators! You decide whether guilt has been proved. Not the state! Not the prosecution, or the Crown, or whatever they call themselves! You!'

Fully warmed up, he started to shout. 'If anyone thinks this is a done deal then they are wrong! This is not a done deal! This is a trial!'

Myers accused the prosecution of calculating that the previous convictions would guarantee another guilty verdict. 'Because who's going to care?' he reasoned. 'Well, if we're just here to rubber-stamp a conviction, it's not going to be a fair trial! You must not use those convictions as a shortcut to guilt!

'We say Baby K was a fragile, unwell baby right from the start. She was at the margins of viability . . .' Myers paused. The baby's parents were sitting in court, listening to his oration. 'I'm not being insensitive,' he said. 'I do understand the dynamics in this courtroom and how sensitive this is.'

The barrister turned his attention to the consultant whose allegation the whole case was built upon. 'Do you believe what Dr Jayaram says he saw? That's why we're here!' Myers was scathing about the doctor's evidence. 'Pathetic blustering! Utter rubbish!' He banged on the desk. 'If he saw what he says he saw, it would have been his excuse to go to management and say he'd caught her red-handed. It's unbelievable!'

The speech reached its crescendo. 'Whatever Lucy Letby has been convicted of elsewhere, the only safe verdict on this count is

357

not guilty, and that is the verdict we ask you to return.'

Ben Myers sat down again. Judith looked across at Letby to see what she'd made of the declamation. Once again, the nurse stared back, holding her gaze. What was she thinking? Her expression was neutral. It had been the last word in her defence. It was up to judge and jury now.

Judge Goss told the jurors to respect each other's opinions as he readied them to start their deliberations. 'You are under no pressure of time,' he said, before sending them out.

The court emptied. Letby was taken down to the cells, everyone else spilling out into the corridor like last time. Lawyers went to their backroom offices. Letby's friend Janet Cox sat by the court-room door, a bag of nerves and worry. Journalists took up their familiar perches, ready for an open-ended wait. No one expected this jury to take long – they only had one charge to consider. At the first trial this particular allegation of attempted murder had been one of the hardest counts to decide though, and we were only here again because that jury had been unable to reach a verdict. We prepared ourselves to settle down for the duration. But there had barely been time for lunch when Neil the court clerk hove into view. It wasn't unusual for him to stretch his legs and pass the time of day, so Judith joked, 'Hello, Neil, are you just out for a wander or have you got white smoke coming out of your ears?'

'I wouldn't go anywhere, if I were you,' he replied, as he picked up his pace, scanning the hallway for barristers.

This was court code for 'verdict is imminent'.

By any measure, this was quick. The jury had been sent out to start work at 11.30 a.m. and they were back with a result before 3 p.m. Whatever they'd decided, it was clear that they were both certain, and unanimous.

We filed back into court. Neil rose and addressed the jury fore-man. 'Of the attempted murder of Baby K in February 2016, how do you find the defendant – guilty or not guilty?'

'Guilty'.

There was a sob from the back of the room. The baby's parents, who'd suffered through seven years of police investigation and two trials, finally had some resolution. The infant's father held his head in his hands while his wife cried as years of pent-up emotion found their release.

In the dock, Letby's face betrayed no expression. No reaction to the news that she was now convicted of another attempted murder. No inkling either as to whether her parents were watching from their living room in Hereford, and if so, how they'd responded.

The jury's decision had served as further legal vindication for Dr Ravi Jayaram and the consultant body – but if he was buoyed by it, there was no public celebration. He was back on the ward at the Countess of Chester Hospital, and though he was no stranger to TV cameras, he kept his reaction to himself.

The sentencing was fixed for two days later. It was the morning after the UK general election, and the country was waking up to a new Prime Minister and a change of government. Journalists arriving at court looked bleary-eyed, having covered the political beat through the night. The sentencing of Lucy Letby for her fifteenth crime was unlikely to make headline news, given the rolling political coverage, but there was keen interest in seeing whether she would turn up to the hearing, or boycott it like before.

We looked across at the dock, and the rear door opened. Lucy Letby was brought in and she took her seat, with prison officers either side. Baby K's mother steeled herself. She'd written a statement to read aloud, without knowing if the woman who'd tried to kill her daughter would be present to hear it. She was determined to get through it without emotion getting the better of her, and her voice just about held as she fought the urge to cry.

She spoke about the impact that had been made on her family – 'Like ripples in the water, layer by layer, every aspect of your life is touched.' She revealed that she and her husband had gone on to have three more children – 'One day we will have to sit our children down and explain what happened to their big sister, and that is the biggest task to overcome.' She talked about the experience of a retrial: 'Learning we were doing it over again was heart-wrenching, but our baby girl needs a voice. We too had no choice.'

Then the baby's mother looked across at the dock, where Letby was listening impassively. Her last words were carefully chosen and delivered directly at the nurse. 'You, Lucy Letby, will never hurt another child or have the privilege and joy that children give. Our time and effort that you have absorbed over the years will stop today, and our focus will remain on our beautiful children and building the most exciting and love-filled life that we possibly can.'

Letby was told to stand. Judge Goss looked at her. 'Only you know the reason or reasons for your murderous campaign . . . Baby K was another of your victims in what was a campaign of murder spanning almost thirteen months . . . The impact of your crimes has been immense . . .'

Lucy Letby bowed her head slightly as though physically taking the brunt of the judge's ire.

'During the course of this trial, as you did in the last trial, you have coldly denied any responsibility . . . You have no remorse . . .'

Letby started to shake her head, just slightly, from side to side.

'For this further offence of attempted murder, I sentence you to imprisonment for life . . . You will spend the rest of your life in prison.'

The dock officers were ordered to take Lucy Letby down to the cells. They began to move her towards the exit. As they did, the nurse turned and looked directly at the judge. She opened her arms, in an almost-shrug, and said just two parting words. 'I'm innocent!'

Chapter 12

Behind the Mask

'I'm innocent!' What did the judge think as Letby uttered those words? What about the police officers and the numerous other functionaries of the justice system – each one no more than a cog in a machine, but a machine with the power to condemn and incarcerate? We know what Lucy Letby's supporters thought as she spoke. What about the rest of us – especially those wrestling between two competing narratives of guilt and innocence?

Do guilty people say they're innocent? Yes. All the time. Even serial killers whose guilt is not in question. Dr Harold Shipman, the GP who murdered up to 260 of his patients, maintained he was innocent until he took his own life in 2004. Rose West continues to claim she's innocent. The prisons are full of offenders who deny their crimes.

But what about Lucy Letby? Let's also not forget that at the end of her first trial – a trial that resulted in fourteen convictions for murder and attempted murder – she said nothing. No protestation of innocence. Those words were confined to the retrial of the attempted murder of Baby K. Was Letby drawing a distinction here?

Within these questions lies the torment of the Letby case. The arguments for guilt and innocence are both compelling. Her supporters say that there is nothing in her personality or background – at least nothing that anyone has found out about – that fits with her being a killer, and it's true that neither we, nor anyone else, have been able to unearth a secret darkness or dysfunction in her past. The more one learns about Lucy Letby, the more difficult the case is to understand. Her consistent protestations of innocence and the fact that there was no direct evidence against her only reinforce this feeling. Then there's the science that convicted her

– controversial and almost entirely dependent on the judgements of a small group of experts. The emergence of contrary expert views in recent months raises legitimate questions about whether the jury in Letby's trial heard enough about the science to be able to reach an informed view.

The 'miscarriage of justice' narrative is a forceful one. But so too is the case for guilt. Thirteen babies died in the space of thirteen months in a unit that generally experienced no more than three deaths a year. Lucy Letby was on duty for twelve of these thirteen deaths. Death followed her. When she was moved from nights to days, the incidents followed her. When she went on holiday, the incidents stopped. When she left the unit, the deaths stopped. For the medics on the unit, the seven deaths for which Letby was convicted were completely out of the ordinary – sudden, unexpected, inexplicable. Much of the science in the Letby case was subject to expert argument and debate, but the insulin evidence is compelling. It may not be perfect, but taking everything into account – the lab test, the hypoglycaemia of the babies, and so on – the conclusion that there was a baby poisoner on the unit is hard to avoid. The third insulin case reinforces this. Letby might not be the only person in the frame for these incidents – but she's in the frame. Then there are the handwritten notes. Do innocent people write lines like: 'I killed them on purpose because I wasn't good enough to care for them?' – years before being formally accused of murder? We know that Letby was a meticulous note-taker and a conscientious nurse. And yet her medical notes contained convenient inaccuracies and her explanations for suspicious events were, even by her own admission, untenable. (Blaming Baby E's bleeding on his feeding tube is a standout example.) She claimed to forget incidents and parents whom she had clearly obsessed about. And finally, Letby's performance in the witness box: passionless, evasive, robotic, and sometimes demonstrably dishonest. Parts of the media are salivating for a good 'miscarriage of justice' story. An online army of supporters – from scientists to statisticians – has formed to support Letby. And yet she – and her family and defence team – have avoided them all. Why?

The question of who Lucy Letby is must depend on which narrative is true. To some people, the answer will be obvious, but not to us. In the course of writing this book, we have wrestled with these questions daily. We have disagreed too. Not profoundly, but in emphasis. Even today, our individual views are not completely aligned. Jonathan's worry that Letby could be innocent trumps all others. For Judith, seeing Letby in the witness box felt like confirmation of the prosecution's case. And yet we both agree that Letby's trial had flaws and that the science is open to further debate. We also agree that, although the case is not clear, we aren't able to say that Lucy Letby is innocent. Only she can answer that question.

Should these issues and uncertainties keep us from probing more deeply into Lucy Letby's psyche? After all, if there's debate surrounding her guilt, how fair is it to ask questions that are predicated on it? Some say it's a redundant exercise. It's a reasonable objection.

At the same time, there are those for whom the verdicts did offer certainty, and a legal absolute. Those readers may also resist analysis of Lucy Letby for a different reason. At the end of the trial, the headlines reduced Letby's multi-layered complexity to a tabloid caricature. The convictions were secured without the jury hearing any explanation of psychology or motive. For some, the music has stopped on guilty and there's little reason to dig deeper now.

Regardless of your point of view, it is still valid to ask: is it theoretically explainable for someone like Lucy Letby – at least the Letby that we have come to know – to be a baby killer? Do the fields of psychiatry and psychology offer any answers to this question, and what further insight can we draw from our own observations of her and those who know her?

It's the question Judith gets asked most often, having sat in the courtroom throughout both trials. No matter what their view about the verdicts, people want to know one thing: what was Lucy Letby like?

It's no surprise that there is such interest in the woman at the centre of this most controversial of cases. There's also frustration that the months in court did little to expand the public under-standing of Letby's psychological profile.

From the outset, though they were leading the charge against her, the prosecuting lawyers were wary of being drawn into the-ories about motive. The solicitor who led the case for the Crown Prosecution Service, Pascale Jones, said she hoped the jury hadn't pondered too much on the reasons why Letby murdered. She ex-plained, 'That is not an aspect that we've got to visit. We don't have to prove a motive. They're entirely personal to the perpetrator, so we just stay clear of that. What we've got to prove is the criminal intent.

'We don't really want to know what the motive was. I certainly don't want to get into her mindset, even though having a window into her mind, like the messages on her phone, was important. It helped our understanding of why her colleagues thought she was incapable of wrongdoing, because she'd been reassuring them time and time again. But reading into her mind is speculative, it's not rational.'

Other prominent lawyers take an equally sceptical view of the need to get inside an offender's head. Twenty-five years ago, Sir Richard Henriques prosecuted Dr Harold Shipman. Now a retired High Court Judge, Henriques says, 'Motive is a very odd thing and I often think about middle-class shoplifters. I mean there's nothing rational at all about shoplifting when you don't need the goods be-cause you can perfectly well afford to pay for them. There's nothing rational at all about deciding deliberately to commit a crime.'

Former Chief Crown Prosecutor for North West England, Nazir Afzal, also believes there's no need to establish a motive – but says that finding one is the 'icing on the cake' when searching to make sense of a case.

Lawyers prosecuting criminals for actions that they can't explain – isn't this a cause for concern? After all, if you can't figure out why someone committed a crime, might that not be a reason to question whether they actually did it? It's a fair question, but it's not just prosecutors who believe that the question of motive can be a red herring in our practical response to terrible crimes. During the making of our *Panorama*, we spoke to celebrated criminologist Professor David Wilson. Wilson has spent forty years studying serial killers. For him, motivation can be a distraction: 'I say to my friends who are FBI profilers: "It doesn't matter what's motivating the killer. I can, if you really want, get inside the head of the killer, but what good does that do?" Because their motivation for why they're killing is going to be banal, or at the other extreme, is going to be extraordinary. But none of that helps you to overcome the circumstances in which killers are able to target repeatedly, to murder time after time after time.'

That's a criminologist's view – and one based on long experience. But not everyone feels the same. For others at the heart of the case, who are in no doubt of Letby's guilt, the 'why' of it all has been left painfully unresolved.

The mother of twin boys E and F told us: 'You start thinking, "Did we do something? Did we offend her? Did we tell a joke that really wasn't funny? Was there something about us that she just didn't like, and she thought she'd hurt us, and hurt our children?"'[1] It was a measure of both the desperation for answers and the lack of them.

The need to make sense of the senseless is an entirely under-standable impulse, and one which isn't restricted to the parents of the babies. In a case of this prominence involving seven dead children and others with severe injuries – and a young woman condemned to die in prison – we crave answers. For some people, accepting Lucy Letby's guilt is too difficult without some kind of explanation.

Given the horror of the crimes Lucy Letby has been convicted of, it's natural that some have speculated that she may be mentally ill or questioned whether there's a psychiatric 'box' or category that we can put her into that might help us to comprehend her better. They wonder what lies behind the mask that we see in that infamous police mugshot and look for parallels with other cases – particularly those involving women, who are so rarely convicted of serial murder.

The names Rosemary West and Myra Hindley spring to mind,

or that of Joanna Dennehy, who murdered three men near Peter-borough in 2013. But Lucy Letby's character and interests seem strikingly different to theirs.

Rosemary West, who murdered at least ten women and girls with her husband Fred, had been sexually abused by her father. The crimes that she and her husband committed between 1967 and 1987 were defined by torture, rape and sexual depravity. After the Wests were arrested, their house became known as the 'house of horrors'.

Myra Hindley was also part of a depraved duo. Between 1963 and 1965, she and her lover Ian Brady murdered five children and buried them on the moors near Manchester. But for anyone who had been watching closely, the signs of Hindley's moral decline were there to see. Ian Brady was obsessed with Nazi philosophy and pornography, and Hindley followed his lead.

Joanna Dennehy had a history of self-harm and substance abuse and was a sadomasochistic sexual deviant.

Letby displayed no such dysfunction. Quite the opposite. Her neat little house, with its privet hedge and subdued décor looked as prim as its owner – certainly no 'house of horrors'. She doesn't seem to have had relationships, other than the flirtation with the married doctor – which she denied was romantic and he later described as 'unrequited'. She had no visible vices either. Her social media photos show her enjoying nights out with friends, but they're markedly tame – the outward epitome of middle-of-the-road normality.

What about her line of work? That's prompted comparison with one female serial killer in particular. Beverley Allitt was another British nurse found to have murdered babies and children on a hospital ward. Allitt injected air, insulin and other drugs into young patients at Grantham Hospital in Lincolnshire in 1991. Just as in Chester, the children collapsed suddenly and unexpectedly, and the nurse killed four and harmed another nine before she was stopped. It sounds eerily close to the Letby case. But there are important differences.

A government-commissioned inquiry into the crimes of Beverley Allitt noted that she showed signs of Munchausen syndrome – a psychological condition named after the German aristocrat Baron Munchausen, who was known for telling wild and unbelievable tales. Sufferers of Munchausen syndrome pretend to be ill, or induce symptoms in themselves, so that they become the centre of attention. Allitt induced illness in herself to gain attention. She also had a history of frequent self-inflicted minor injuries which could be traced back to her schooldays. She took significant sick absence from college, and often showed her injuries to teachers. Her appendix was removed but found to be normal, and she was suspected of interfering with the wound.

Over time, Allitt's medical history became 'more florid and bizarre', according to the inquiry team. On one occasion she reportedly injected herself with water.'[2] The inquiry concluded that Allitt's crimes 'must be rooted in some form of mental instability'.[3] The nurse has been detained at the secure Rampton Hospital rather than within the prison estate. At a sentence review in 2007, High Court judge Mr Justice Stanley Burnton said he was satisfied that she was suffering from an 'abnormality of mind' when she committed the offences.[4] In 2023 she was denied permission to be moved to a mainstream prison.[5]

As helpful as this might be in making sense of Beverley Allitt, none of it sounds like Lucy Letby, who has no known history of self-harm, substance abuse or self-inflicted illness.

The Letby case is so unusual that even criminologists find it difficult to find a template for it in their case files. Professor David Wilson has studied every subspecies of serial killer, including serial killers who are healthcare workers. We asked him: Does Lucy Letby fit the profile of a healthcare serial killer? 'No, she doesn't,' he answered. 'She is very social, she has friendship groups, she has people in the hospital who befriended her, mentored her. She is somebody that's not seen suspiciously. There's no evidence that's she's fascinated by serial killers.' The list went on.

It would seem that, if there is such a thing as an identikit female serial killer, Lucy Letby doesn't fit the formula. Nor is she suffering from any psychiatric disorder – at least not one that would have rendered her unable to participate in the prosecution process. Some defendants don't have the mental capacity to understand the difference between 'guilty' and 'not guilty'. They're too disordered to understand the function of a judge and jury, and as a consequence of being unable to take part in a full criminal trial they're dealt with differently. That didn't apply here. Letby was assessed as fit enough both to be questioned by police[6] and to stand trial. Then, once at court, she didn't offer a defence of diminished responsibility (she'd have to have admitted the crimes for such a defence to be available to her). Once she was convicted, her barrister offered no mental health argument in mitigation, and she was sent to a mainstream prison – not to a secure hospital. In other words, her entire journey through the system – from the point of arrest until the moment of sentencing – was predicated on her having full mental capacity.

Those convinced of her innocence will find no surprise in any of this and point to it as further evidence that she isn't guilty of the offences she stands convicted of. To others, it's not that straightforward. The prison system is full of offenders with psychiatric disorders which don't meet the bar for hospitalisation. Could Letby be suffering from one of these?

Psychopathy is the one that most people will think of. In law, Letby is Britain's most prolific child killer of the modern era. Surely someone fitting that bill must be a psychopath. After all, what other name would you give to someone who has murdered a string of babies?

We spoke to a consultant forensic psychiatrist who has assessed and treated mentally disordered offenders in the North of England, including several who have been convicted of murder and manslaughter. Dr Michael Crawford hasn't been involved in the Lucy Letby case, and without being able to assess her in person he is unable to make a clinical diagnosis. However, like anybody else, Dr Crawford has been able to look at the information which is in the public domain, including Letby's text messages and other material from the trial.

There's a common assumption that serial killers are psychopaths – manipulative, lacking in empathy, and with no regard to the consequences of their actions. But Dr Crawford believes that doesn't ring true here. He says, 'She doesn't seem psychopathic to me. She appears more like an inadequate woman who's living a very empty life that has this real need for fulfilment.'

Professor Mark Freestone agrees that Lucy Letby doesn't display symptoms of psychopathy. An expert on forensic mental health, he's worked in prisons and the NHS with some of the UK's most notorious and high-risk criminals and was a series consultant on the TV drama *Killing Eve*, advising on the portrayal of the fictional psychopathic female protagonist Villanelle. He points out that psychopathy is not as well understood in women as it is in men but says the associated antisocial behaviours 'are things that just don't occur in women with anything like the same kind of frequency'.

In Professor Freestone's view, Letby doesn't fit the psychopathic bill. He says, 'There are lots of red lines she just doesn't cross. Psychopaths are inherently quite chaotic. They don't do "normal". They don't make bedrooms look nice so they can live there, they're probably people who have clothes all over the floor. Everything is temporary, they're usually quite promiscuous sexually. They're pathological liars who don't lie constructively. There's pretty good evidence that there is a neurological problem in people with a diagnostic psychopathy . . . I just don't get any of that from Letby at all.'

Not all psychopaths are criminals, and not all serial killers are psychopaths. But if psychopathy isn't at play, mustn't there be another psychiatric explanation for serial murder? Not always. It's hard to get much further without considering another famous case involving a medical serial killer.

Dr Harold Shipman is the most prolific British serial killer of our times – murdering hundreds of his patients in Hyde near Manchester. Sir Richard Henriques, who prosecuted him, remembers that psychiatry didn't feature in that case as part of the evidence on either side. He says, 'One thing is plain. Shipman had no form of psychiatric disorder at all. He was very capable, and an interesting feature is that when he wasn't killing people, he was a very good GP. Had he tried to run a psychiatric defence, that would have been one of the strengths of the prosecution case – we'd have said, "You were extremely able as a GP, patients would come in, you were making the right decisions on them. You knew what you were doing, one hundred per cent. You absolutely knew what you were doing.'''

Dame Janet Smith, who chaired the government-commissioned Shipman Inquiry, produced six reports into the doctor's crimes. She asked four forensic psychiatrists to offer their opinions and advice on his likely state of mind. Unable to examine him in person, they made their assessments based on documentary evidence, including his medical and prison records. Dame Janet reported that: 'They did their best to consider possible explanations for Shipman's conduct but, with the materials available, were unable to reach any conclusions. I am grateful for the assistance they have given me but, in the end, I have been unable to attempt any detailed explanation of the psychological factors underlying Shipman's conduct. All I can do is draw attention to features of his behaviour which might throw some light on his personality and motivation.'[7]

The Lucy Letby case seems to take us to much the same place: multiple convictions for heinous crimes and no obvious psychiatric theory to explain them. And yet, that doesn't mean there isn't such an explanation.

Borderline personality disorder, or BPD, is another theory that's been floated to make sense of Lucy Letby's mental condition. BPD is a disorder of mood and how a person interacts with others. Emotionless reactions are one red flag for the condition.

This does chime with what we witnessed of Letby in court over the course of both trials. In total she was on view through the glass display case of the dock for nearly a year, and she spent the best part of sixteen days giving evidence. During that time, her demeanour was studiedly blank. Although she may have had little choice in the matter when it came to being there in the first place, she could at least control the impression that she created – and that seemed designed to give nothing away. Her frumpy clothes in muted colours, drab hair and blank expression all seemed designed to deflect interest and say nothing. But even that can tell a story, and no one knows this better than the court artists who sketch the proceedings which aren't televised.

Julia Quenzler and Elizabeth Cook each have more than thirty years' experience of drawing some of the most famous trials – and infamous defendants – in British legal history, including Ian Huntley, Fred West and Rolf Harris. They both drew Harold Shipman and Rose West, and Julia also sketched Beverley Allitt. They were in court when Lucy Letby first entered the dock, and their practised eyes bore into her, absorbing every detail.

Julia remembers that Allitt had been animated, chatting with the dock officers, and Shipman folded his arms in arrogant defiance, but Letby's body language was entirely different: 'I can remember on day one when she was brought in, she just looked somewhat vacant and sat very still. It was difficult to read anything from her – I don't recall seeing anyone quite like that before. Usually when defendants first come into court, they'll be looking around checking out who's there, out of curiosity, but with her there was none of that. You'd almost have thought that perhaps she was on some sort of medication. She sat bolt upright and looked straight ahead. I didn't take my eyes off her for that first fifteen minutes – I didn't see any reaction, movement or any expression. In some respects, she was easy to draw, but usually you're looking for some sort of expression to capture and there was none. It was just vacant.'

Elizabeth Cook had much the same impression. She'd seen the pictures of Lucy Letby in nursing scrubs, grinning for the camera, and expected her to look very different in court. She remembers: 'I took my seat on the press bench, and I knew that this time I wouldn't be seeing a smiling, animated face like in the photographs because by then she'd been in custody for two years.

'My role is to note the small details and to convey a moment in time, and I'm looking for the angle of the head, the set of the mouth, whether the eyes are downcast or forward focused. Letby didn't turn her head at all from side to side. She stared straight in front of her, and her eyes were dull. Her face was a bit thinner than the photographs and there was no smile this time. She was noticeably still, and I drew all that.'

It wasn't the first time that Elizabeth had observed a female murder suspect looking so blank. She remarks, 'The only other person who was like that was [serial killer] Rosemary West. She sat expressionless and still the whole time too. Very similar.' Letby's rigidity was almost trance-like, as if moving her body might break whatever spell she was under. But at the end of the session, she had to get up to be taken out again. Elizabeth Cook observed the nurse glance fleetingly across the crowded courtroom to look for her parents. She says, 'She just did it with her eyes, she didn't animate her body, and she didn't look at the babies' parents – not ever.'

As the months rolled by, Lucy Letby followed the proceedings closely, looking at her iPad and sending notes to her lawyers. But while she was in the dock, with a couple of rare exceptions, she never showed any reaction to what she was hearing or engaged with the room at large. It was as if she was trying to divorce herself from the experience.

Occasionally Letby's inanimation left us with the impression that, mentally, she'd checked out of the court. On one occasion, when she was in the witness box being questioned by her own barrister, she seemed to lose her concentration, and Ben Myers had to bring her back into focus. On other occasions, her body remained stock-still but her eyes blinked and darted around as if she was distracted by something else.

Some people will legitimately point out that a courtroom is the last place that someone's true personality and feelings will be shown – particularly someone with a tendency to be reserved when outside of her comfort zone. They may also point out that by the time of her trial, Letby had been in custody for two years. Her world had imploded. She was the country's most reviled murder suspect. What is 'normal' behaviour for someone like that?

It's also worth remembering that Letby wasn't completely emo-tionless during her trial. She did crack, albeit only a handful of times, which made each one very noticeable. There was the moment she burst into tears on hearing the married doctor give his name, and there were occasions when she was in the witness box, and the questioning hit a nerve. Court artist Elizabeth Cook remembers thinking that by the time Letby began her evidence seven months into the trial, her appearance had changed. The artist was watching the nurse on a TV monitor as the hearing was being transmitted by video to an overspill annexe. She was able to watch her in extreme close-up as the camera was trained fully on Letby's features, and she recalls, 'Her face seemed longer and thinner and her eyes were puffy and dark underneath. Her barrister, Ben Myers, wanted to get her to express her feelings, and she broke down momentarily, telling the court that she was devastated and had only ever done her best, and she reached for a tissue and her face crumpled, and I drew that moment.'

Elizabeth kept watching Letby when she came under questioning from the prosecutor. She says, 'I thought her demeanour when she was questioned by her own counsel was mostly calm, and her answers were short, but things seemed to change when Nick Johnson began his cross-examination. Her face was set, she stared ahead – she refused to look at him . . . her head rarely moved, she blinked a lot, but her eyes were lacklustre, and she mostly stared into space in the middle of the court. She looked pale, tired and her mouth was turned down.'

We put it to one of Letby's old friends that she looked blank and poker-stiff in court. The friend reacted with exasperation: 'She was clearly petrified!' they told us.

And yet there was something unrelatable about Letby's demeanour in court. With the exception of a few memorable moments, she was devoid of emotion – incomprehensibly so. So could the borderline personality theory be right? Could this fit with Lucy Letby as a serial killer?

Letby's performance in court isn't the only basis for entertaining such a theory. Lucy Letby has been widely observed as passive and devoid of emotion. On the ward, this came across as businesslike and efficient – or as she once described herself to her doctor-crush, 'serious Lucy'. She could be brusque – remarking, 'He's not leaving here alive, is he?' after Baby P collapsed.[8] She was often shown to have misjudged the mood around vulnerable families – or at least seemed to put her own needs ahead of theirs – hovering around the parents of Baby D as they willed her to give them some privacy,[9] and upsetting the parents of Baby I by chattering brightly at them while they bathed the body of their dead daughter.[10]

She was also noted to be particularly calm during resuscitations. This ought to have been a good thing, but in Letby's case more than one colleague observed that she was almost too calm – unnervingly so, as if she was in her comfort zone.

Professor of Mental Health Mark Freestone says, 'Lack of affect in situations like this is weird. It's not normal. It doesn't show somebody who is normal, it shows somebody who's blank, and blank is not what we expect.'

It was this behaviour which alarmed consultant Stephen Brearey when he observed Letby in the debrief meeting after the two triplets had died in June 2016, and saw that – while other staff were in pieces – she seemed to be unaffected by the trauma they'd all experienced. Her breezy refusal of his offer to take time off, and her determination to work through the weekend, struck him as totally different to the way the rest of the team had responded to the two deaths.

Dr Brearey couldn't help but contrast it with his impression of the nurse a year earlier. He remembers that in June 2015, when he was made aware that Letby was present at each of the first three deaths, he thought, 'Oh no, not nice Lucy!' considering her benign and wholesome. She wasn't dynamic – she didn't attract attention – there was nothing about her personality that caught the imagination. 'Nice' was the word that came first to his mind, capturing the banality of her character.

A year on, that blandness translated differently to Dr Brearey. Now, as the rest of the staff seemed to be crumbling, her neutrality and breeziness came across to him as unfeeling and odd.

The detectives who arrested Lucy Letby say they observed something similar when they got her back to the police station for questioning. Paul Hughes, now a detective superintendent, was the senior investigating officer in charge of the police investigation. He remembers: 'She was very emotionless. She didn't respond in a typical human way that I would have expected. We didn't see any sadness, or any passion, or anything more – like an innocent person banging on the table demanding that we should go and find the proper killer. There was nothing from her that appeared to be affected by what was going on around her.

'It was about herself rather than the babies. It appeared to be more about how she was. She was just very clinical in her answers. She was comfortable – she'd go through medical notes and talk to us. She was co-operative, she engaged, but she didn't respond with any empathy. There was no sympathy with what had gone on at all.'

Prosecutor Nick Johnson KC latched on to the same point in court when he started his cross-examination of the nurse by asking her why she only cried when talking about herself, and not when mentioning the babies. Letby denied it, but the barrister was only voicing a question that we'd all been wondering for weeks ourselves, having witnessed it first hand.

But as with almost everything in the Letby case, there is an alternative way of looking at the evidence. One of Letby's former classmates had told us Letby could appear 'stony and cold'. Letby's old friend Dawn said something similar: 'Outside of our group she would present as shy, reserved, serious, you know, level-headed.' According to Dawn, that was just Letby's nature. Nothing serious or sinister. If Dawn is right, it is perhaps to be expected that Letby would be quiet or awkward around senior consultants and at her most reserved and introverted in a courtroom.

We also know that Letby did become emotional around people she trusted. After she was removed from her position on the neonatal unit in July 2016, the Lead Nurse for Urgent Care Karen Rees became one of Letby's most trusted confidantes. Rees later said: 'I witnessed her in complete distress, crying and swearing her innocence.' In a separate TV interview, Rees said: 'If I think back to all the times when I have seen her really, really upset – I wouldn't say hysterical, but really upset – and I would think that how can somebody continually present themselves in that way on a near weekly basis for two years? I find that really difficult and I think, "Oh my gosh! Would she have been that good at acting?"'

This proves nothing, but it does show that Letby wasn't always stony and reserved in her efforts to defend herself.

Debates over whether Lucy Letby's emotional responses are suggestive of borderline personality disorder have no easy resolution. But whether she does have such a condition or not, for the lay person, such speculative diagnoses will be unsatisfying. The question that we really want an answer to is this: given what we know about Lucy Letby, can we find a possible motive or 'reason' for her to murder babies? The difficulty of this question was captured powerfully by the mother of Babies E and F: 'She had everything going for her and then starts killing babies. What happened?'

The lawyers prosecuting Letby made a point of saying that their case didn't depend on offering a motive – and for the most part, they avoided the motive question. But not entirely. One theme that emerged in the prosecution's depiction of Letby's behaviour was control.

For Nicholas Johnson KC, who led the team of three prosecution barristers, this is one feature of Lucy Letby's behaviour which particularly stands out. In his closing speech at the first trial, he told the jury, 'She was controlling things. She was enjoying what was going on and happily predicting something she knew was going to happen. She, in effect, was playing God.'

CPS solicitor Pascale Jones agreed, saying, 'It's all about control. I've rarely come across a personality who is as self-centred as she was, all about herself, and the power she was granting herself of life and death over all the babies at her mercy. Mercy? She didn't show any.'

Criminologist David Wilson has seen this impulse to control in many of the serial killers he has studied. 'I've worked with so many serial killers in my career and all of them liked having the power to be able to decide who would live and who would die. Because of course that's the ultimate power for God. [It's] a God complex, a desire to have power and control in their professional life which is often missing in their personal lives.'

Prosecutors in the Letby case pointed to the way she behaved in the wake of the deaths – staying involved with the families in the immediate aftermath, bathing the babies' bodies, taking footprints and photographs. Letby also sent one family a bereavement card, and searched for many others on Facebook, keeping them in mind for many months.

Forensic psychiatrist Dr Michael Crawford interpreted this as her looking to see how the parents had responded to the death of their child. He said, 'Maybe it gave her a sense of agency – that "people are experiencing this because of me". It says something about agency and power over the way others see her.'

Dr Harold Shipman stayed in the orbit of his victims after their deaths. He made sure their bodies were sent to an undertaker rather than hospital and persuaded the families not to have post-mortem examinations carried out. Dame Janet Smith, who wrote the official inquiry reports on Shipman, said, 'I have the impression that after a death, when the relatives had assembled, he would enjoy acting as "master of ceremonies". He would be the centre of attention and would take control.'[11]

If you want to, you can see much of Letby's behaviour through this lens of 'control'. Her text messages, for example, showed that she was trying to control which nursery room she worked in – asking to be placed in intensive care. It can also be argued that Letby tried to control the narrative in her texts about why babies had died. In June 2015 four babies collapsed, and only one of them survived. Afterwards, the nurse texted a colleague and posed the question, 'How do such sick babies get through & others just die so suddenly & unexpectedly? Guess it's how it's meant to be. I think there is an element of fate involved. There is a reason for everything.'

And yet, if you look at exactly the same evidence but assume Letby is innocent, does any of it really look that unusual? Being involved with bereaved families – isn't this what an attentive nurse would do? As for Letby's text messages: on their own, are they any different from those of her colleagues? Even if the idea of 'control' could fit with the idea of Letby as a serial killer, what need in her might this have fulfilled? Why would the need to control have resulted in her killing babies? Was it a God complex as some have suggested?

The mother of twin boys E and F felt that Letby's efforts to control events continued into the courtroom. We asked her if the process of going to court to give evidence had been personally cathartic or helpful, and she said, 'No, not really . . . I feel that this whole trial has been about fulfilling a need within her. We've all had to go over things and give evidence in court. We had to relive that time in front of all those people, and be questioned on it . . . I feel that this whole situation – I think she's feeding off it. I think she feeds off other people's pain.'[12]

The twins' mother added that she sees the lack of a known motive as part of the same picture. She said, 'I think it's something we'll never know, and I think as a family we need to make our peace with that. It's part of the power and control that she has, and I think she'll keep hold of that because it's all she's got left.'

At the sentencing hearing, the twins' mother nodded towards the empty dock, where the nurse should have been, and said, 'Even in these final days of the trial she has tried to control things. We have attended court day in and day out, yet she decides she has had enough and stays in her cell – just one final act of wickedness from a coward.' Whatever the nurse's motive had been, whatever her psychology was, this was a moment of release. 'Lucy no longer has control over our lives,' she said firmly. 'She holds no power or relevance in anybody's life. She is nothing.'

Dr Michael Crawford agrees that the nurse's refusal to sit in the dock for her first sentencing was part of a power impulse. He explains, 'It's a little bit of control when she'll have no control for the rest of her life.' But Dr Crawford can also see an alternative explanation for the boycott. He says, 'If she really believes she's not guilty, it's almost a way of saying, "No, I'm not part of this."'

Having spent months researching Letby and trying to figure her out, we had some potential theories of our own that we thought might fit with Letby as a killer. One was that she killed because she was bored. This was mooted by the prosecution during Letby's trial. Nicholas Johnson KC put it to her that she was especially bored during the shifts when she was not allocated to the intensive care nursery. Letby denied this, replying 'I've never been bored at work. I've never described my work as boring.'[13] He also suggested to her that she got a buzz from watching parents in the aftermath of a baby's death. He told her, 'You were getting a thrill out of the grief and despair that you were watching in that room weren't you?'

'Absolutely not,' she answered.[14]

In this scenario, the suggestion is that harming babies and watching the ensuing crises provided the nurse with a thrill or sense of excitement that the rest of her life lacked. Sure, she went to salsa and hula-hoop and the odd pub quiz, but none of it set the pulse racing. Forensic psychiatrist Michael Crawford wonders, 'Those things look quite normal, and might well meet the social needs of most people in their twenties. But maybe they weren't meeting what she needed. Maybe she needed to be in really quite extreme situations to feel anything, to feel satisfied or content – what we call sensation-seeking. Very few of us do BASE jumping, but for some of us, if we're not BASE jumping life feels empty.'

Once again, the case of the murdering GP Harold Shipman comes to mind. The man who prosecuted him, Sir Richard Henriques, spent a lot of time looking at what prompted Shipman to kill repeatedly, and he thinks there's merit in the argument that part of it was about thrill-seeking. He says, 'Shipman had no real outside interests. He had time to fill in between morning and afternoon surgeries. He had no [GP] partners, and there was no surgery chit-chat. Nearly all his murders were committed in that [afternoon] gap . . . and I think it was this kind of tightrope walking – the thrill that persuades people to do thoroughly dangerous things.'

Henriques wonders if there is some similarity here between Shipman and Letby. He says:

> The fascinating thing is, what was it that persuaded them to do it time and again? I've come to the conclusion that the first time was possibly the difficult one, but they obviously – certainly in Shipman's case – did it so often that the experience must have been enjoyable. You don't do the same thing a hundred times if you don't enjoy it. Or four hundred, possibly. So what was it that caused Letby and Shipman to

repeat it? The actual physical act of injecting air or diamor-
phine – there's nothing particularly satisfying or enjoyable
about that. But I think it was the whole experience thereafter,
and the adrenaline . . . The getting away with it, equivalent
to walking out of the shop with the goods having avoided
payment and arrest. The sheer buzz, the thrill of that, and in
possibly rather a repetitive, mundane life.

It's easy to see the draw of this theory. But once again, it doesn't
quite fit with what we know about Lucy Letby. There are few
indications in her background or behaviour that suggest she was
an adrenaline junkie. She was never a thrill-seeker, and although
her life may have been bland or lacking in variety, she never suggested that she wanted it to be otherwise. She seemed comfortable
with the mundanity and as more than one person who knew her
observed, she didn't seem to get her kicks from breaking rules or
taboos. She just wasn't that kind of person. Killing babies for the
transgressive thrill of it doesn't fit with what we know of her wider
behaviour.

There is another theory that occurred to us that wasn't suggested during Letby's trial. Could it be that Letby killed babies
because she was jealous? Many of her nursing colleagues had
families and children – something we know Letby dreamed of
for herself. And yet, she was persistently single, working endless
night shifts while her colleagues were at home with their families.
If this could explain Letby's motivation, what must she have felt
towards those happy mothers and fathers whose babies were on
the neonatal unit, waiting for the all-clear to go home and begin
their lives? Maybe each happy couple and their beautiful babies
were a painful reminder to Letby of her loneliness and failure to
find love.

This theory is compelling, but it doesn't stand up against what
we know of Letby's personality and background. As one of Letby's
former school friends pointed out to us, Letby was only twenty-five
when she supposedly committed her crimes. Her window of opportunity to find a husband and have a family of her own was a

long way from closing. Sure, she may have been jealous of others around her, but it's doubtful that such jealousy had hardened into the kind of bitterness that might have driven her to kill. Letby hadn't yet found love, but she still had time on her side.

There is, however, a further theory of motivation that might fit with what we know about Letby. In considering it, we're not drawing any final conclusions about her guilt. The question we're grappling with is a theoretical one: given everything we know and have seen of her, is there any explanation or model that might explain how someone like Lucy Letby could be a baby killer? Is such an explanation possible?

According to this theory, Letby deliberately pushed babies to collapse so that she could demonstrate how skilful and cool-headed she was in a medical crisis. If a baby collapsed, Letby would be there to call for help before anyone else. Where a baby survived, it would be thanks to Letby's quick acting and nursing proficiency. You might call it a kind of 'saviour complex'. Whenever a baby died, Letby would be there to comfort and support the grieving parents. This was Letby showing everyone what a great nurse she was – feeling needed, noticed and valued. If this theory does explain her actions, it's not hard to imagine where the married doctor with whom Letby had developed an attachment might come into it. Letby wanted his validation and admiration, and what better way than to show him just how good she was in a crisis. It might even bring them closer together.

From our conversations with people who knew and worked with Letby, this 'saviour complex' is plausible. That's not to say it's correct, but it fits. Securing the respect and validation of her colleagues and superiors mattered deeply to Letby.

This is certainly in line with the picture of the young Lucy Letby that we heard about. Was Letby passionate about her schoolwork, we asked one of her former classmates? The answer was revealing: 'I would say she was more passionate about being good at the things that she was doing than actually passionate about the subjects themselves.' What about mistakes? Was she prone to blunders – practical or otherwise? No, the former classmate told us. 'This is somebody who does not tend to make mistakes.'

Letby wanted to be good at whatever she was doing. Colleagues thought of her as diligent and she was critical of others who fell short of her standards. In November 2015, Letby was at a salsa class when she got a call from a nurse at the unit. It seemed the nurse didn't know how to give a baby intravenous immunoglobulin treatment and needed Letby's advice. Afterwards, Letby texted one of her pals from the unit.

'Just can't believe that some people were in a position when they don't know how to give something, what equipment to use and not being supported by manager,' she wrote scathingly.

But her text exchanges also suggest a need for validation from her superiors and colleagues even after catastrophic events – confirmation, almost, that she had been the steady pair of hands. Like this one from August 2015, sent after the death of Baby E and the near-death of his twin brother:

'[The babies' parents] both cried & hugged me saying that they will never be able to thank me for the love & care I gave to (the older twin) & for the precious memories I've given them. It's heartbreaking.'

Her colleague texted back: 'It is heartbreaking, but you've done your job to the highest standard with compassion and professionalism. You should feel very proud of yourself.'

If Letby was searching for approval or attention, it was often forthcoming.

The following month, Letby's manager Eirian Powell sent her a supportive text: 'I just want to commend you for all your hard work these last few nights. You composed yourself very well during a stressful situation. It's nice to see your confidence grow as you advance through your career x.'

'You're a star,' texted another nurse. 'You've done yourself proud. You've given positive memories to the family whatever the outcome. Let's hope they can tease her in a few yrs about her 'attention-seeking' ways. Sleep well. Xx.'

Following the death of another baby on the unit, one of the female registrars offered her comfort. 'Try to think of all the babies you've saved and have gone home happily with their parents,' she texted. 'You're a fab nurse.'

The messaging reached its apogee at the same time as the number of babies collapsing surged in June 2016. The nurse had started chatting on Facebook Messenger with the married doctor earlier that month, and he was quickly ready to offer her constant attention, reassurance and empathy.

After a third baby collapsed in as many days, Lucy Letby ventured, 'Just worry I haven't done enough . . . We've lost 2 babies I was caring for and now this has happened today, makes you think "am I missing something / good enough".'

The sympathy from the doctor came in spades: 'Lucy, if anyone knows how hard you've worked over the last three days it's me.'

'Thanks, really appreciate you saying that. So relieved that it's you who has been there throughout,' she wrote back – underlining the fact that this doctor had been called to help with each resuscitation and had been caught up in the same dramas as she had, working alongside her in the heat of the emergencies.

In a comment he now doubtless wishes he could wipe off the internet forever, the medic replied, 'You are one of a few nurses across the region . . . that I would trust with my own children.'

This idea of attention-seeking was also advanced by the prosecution during Letby's trial, with a particular focus on this doctor who had become a significant part of Letby's life.

When cross-examining Lucy Letby, Nick Johnson KC asked her if she had enjoyed working with the married doctor. She confirmed that she had, and that she'd called him over when the first triplet collapsed.

'Did you want to get his attention?' he asked.

'No,' she replied.

'Is that the reason you sabotaged Baby O?'

'No,' she said again.[15]

In his closing speech, Mr Johnson advanced the same theme, telling the jury, 'For some reason she enjoyed these situations, and he [the doctor] was there.'

The idea that Letby harmed babies to get attention does have precedents or parallels in other cases, most notably the case of nurse Beverley Allitt, who was convicted of murdering four babies and attempting to murder three more. As we mentioned earlier, Allitt was said to have had Munchausen syndrome – a condition whereby the sufferer pretends to be ill or induces symptoms in themselves so that they become the centre of attention. But in addition to Munchausen syndrome itself, Allitt was also thought to have been suffering from an allied condition called Munchausen syndrome by proxy – a form of abuse where an adult exaggerates or deliberately causes illness in a child. The Allitt trial brought the syndrome to wide attention and seemed to satisfy something of the public thirst to understand her behaviour, although the idea of the condition itself was contentious.

The concept of Munchausen syndrome by proxy was first suggested in 1977 by paediatrician Sir Roy Meadow in the medical journal *The Lancet*. Meadow's subsequent career as an expert witness was later mired in controversy due to his use of statistics, when he gave evidence in three high-profile infanticide trials which were later exposed as miscarriages of justice. His work relating to Munchausen syndrome by proxy also came under fire, with debates over the credibility of the idea. One member of the House of Lords called it a 'theory without science'. The government-backed inquiry into Allitt was similarly scathing about its relevance to her offending.

However, the theory of Munchausen syndrome by proxy is still recognised, albeit in a different guise. It's now listed as 'Factitious Disorder Imposed on Another' by the World Health Organization,[16] and in the UK the National Health Service has rebadged it 'Fabricated or Induced Illness (FII)', defining it as 'a rare form of child abuse. It happens when a parent or carer exaggerates or deliberately causes symptoms of illness in the child.'[17] Could Letby have been suffering from what used to be known as Munchausen syndrome by proxy?

Medical labels can be unhelpful – particularly when dealing with a case as disturbing as Letby's. They risk trying to categorise something that is beyond categorisation. But the underlying idea that

Lucy Letby was so motivated to demonstrate her nursing abilities in crisis situations that she generated crises by harming babies is for us the most plausible theory to explain Letby's actions – assuming she is indeed guilty.

This is an elaborate theory and one that we simply offer as a possibility. But if this theory seems convincing or at least plausible, there is one further question that anyone who believes Letby is guilty must also grapple with: is it possible that she could maintain a lie for so long? Letby has always maintained her innocence. From the moment suspicions against her first emerged in 2016, Letby has denied everything – to the point of putting thirteen families, and her own parents, through the hell of a ten-month trial. Is this really the behaviour of a guilty woman? Could Letby really deceive everyone for so long?

When we asked her school pal Dawn if she'd entertain the idea that her friend had fooled everyone around her, she was adamant that Lucy wasn't capable of it. She sighed deeply and said:

> If she's fooled everyone – I just don't think it's possible. The only way I'd ever believe she's guilty is if she told me that she's guilty. I don't think there's any way that she could have presented herself the way she has and be guilty of these crimes. I think she's a very honest person. She's transparent almost. She always says what she thinks, and she's very level-headed and calm. She couldn't have acted this part for so long if it wasn't the truth.[18]

However, another of Letby's childhood friends gave us a different perspective, saying, 'I don't think maintaining a lie like this would be as difficult for Lucy as it might be for somebody else.'

It's a striking claim and it's based on Letby's relationship with her parents. Letby craved validation and approval from her school-teachers, her colleagues and her managers, but most especially from her mum and dad. To admit guilt would be to shatter her parents' faith and belief in her. This alone would be enough to allow Letby to maintain the lie of her innocence so consistently and for so long.

From everything we've seen and heard from people who know Letby, our view is that, if she is guilty, she is unlikely to admit her guilt while her parents are alive.

It seems, then, that the theory that Letby killed for attention and validation of her ability to handle medical crises is at least possible. Whether it is likely is another question. Letby's supporters will note that our search for a theory to explain Letby as a serial killer is a difficult and contorted one. The reason for that, they will argue, is that the entire effort is misconceived: there is no crime to explain; Letby is not the devious wolf in sheep's clothing that her accusers have portrayed her to be; the difficulty of finding a theory to explain her crimes is further evidence that she's innocent. Whatever we may think of this perspective, the steadfast belief in Letby among those of her supporters who know her cannot be set aside lightly.

Recall Dawn's words, which she said reflected the view of Letby's other Hereford friends: 'We know she couldn't have done anything that she's accused of, so without a doubt we stand by her. I've grown up with Lucy, and not a single thing that I've ever seen or witnessed of Lucy would let me for a moment believe that she was capable of the things she was being accused of. Unless Lucy turned around, and said, "I'm guilty," I will never believe that she's guilty.'

Then there was Letby's close friend from university who told us: 'Lucy was my closest friend at uni. She was a wonderful student nurse and I firmly believe she is innocent of all the charges against her.'

Another university associate of Letby's told us something similar: 'My gut instinct is rarely wrong. I am a reasonable judge of people and I can't believe she's a murderer based on my experience of her.'

Writing about the case, the journalist Peter Hitchens offered these cautionary words: 'The close family of someone in this position have little choice but to be loyal. Friends, faced with a jury verdict of this kind, could be excused if they resorted to saying, "Well, I would not have thought it of her, but . . ." These friends say she is not guilty. Listen to them. They may just be right.'

And then there are the nurses who worked with Letby and who believe she is innocent. Janet Cox is one, but there are others.

The view of the married doctor is interesting too. He testified in court and before the trial we heard that he had been the object of unrequited affection from Letby. However, we know the two of them went to London together in June 2017 – a full year after she had been removed from the neonatal unit. It would appear that until that point at least, he too still believed in her.

Eirian Powell, Letby's old unit manager, defended Letby against the suspicions of the consultants. Even after thirteen deaths in thirteen months – twelve of which Letby had been on duty for – Powell still believed in the young nurse: 'Lucy Letby does everything by the book,' Powell said in June 2016. 'She follows policy and procedure to the letter.' Even after Letby was removed from the neonatal unit, Powell seemed determined that she would return.

Karen Rees, another manager at the Countess of Chester Hospital, also believed in Letby.

'Prior to the trial, I had thought that she was innocent,' Rees said later.

Can so many people be wrong? Everyone we spoke to from Letby's schooldays has wrestled with the Lucy Letby they believed they knew and the killer nurse they have heard about on the news. 'They seem like two entirely separate people,' said one former classmate. 'I find it difficult to comprehend. I keep thinking I'm going to wake up tomorrow and it's going to be a miscarriage of justice.'

The seeming incongruity of Lucy Letby and the crimes for which she's been convicted is magnified by what we've seen of her background. As far as anyone can make out, Letby's backstory is innocent and wholesome, characterised by sleepovers and *The X Factor*, pizza and trips to the cinema. Could the girl who enjoyed her mum's cooking and nights in with friends watching *The X Factor* really have it in her to kill babies?

Her existence in Chester seemed to be a continuation of her childhood. From the outside, she had a rounded life with cocktails, salsa, pub quizzes and holidays. Even her bedroom – memorably captured in those police photographs taken after her arrest in July 2018 – was a picture of girly innocence.

During Letby's trial, the prosecution made extensive use of her text messages to reinforce their case. But viewed without the lens of guilt, Letby's texts look unremarkable.

We must also presume that, with the important exception of her searches for parents and families of babies, the police found nothing of interest in Letby's search histories or devices. No searches relating to dead babies or methods of murder. In short, outside of the events of the case, Lucy Letby's life looks spotless.

If this were the final word on the story, we might be pressed to conclude that there has been a mistake – that Letby isn't the baby killer that a jury decided she was. And that is the conclusion some people have drawn. But that isn't the end of the story either.

Peter Hitchens is right to say we should listen to those friends of Letby's who believe she is innocent. But as difficult as it may be to comprehend, it is also possible that Letby's friends are wrong. It's worth casting an eye back to the cases of Harold Shipman and Beverley Allitt. There were many people within the orbits of both Shipman and Allitt who also struggled to accept their guilt. The Allitt Inquiry team interviewed the nurse's colleagues and reported that:

> Having listened to nearly all of those who worked alongside Allitt, the overwhelming burden of the evidence was that she did indeed appear to be just like everybody else. She was friendly, willing and efficient, helpful to the student nurses, and well-liked by other staff. Her colleagues knew about her health problems but had no suspicion that they were self-inflicted . . . One or two of the people we have interviewed said that it was no surprise, once they knew that someone was suspected of attacking the children, to find that it was Allitt. On the other hand, a greater number said they could not believe it until after she was convicted, and some did not believe it even then, still thinking there had been a terrible mistake.[19]

When Harold Shipman first came under suspicion, it was hard for many of his patients to accept, and a number felt that he was innocent and being unfairly targeted.[20] Dame Janet Smith wrote in the Shipman Inquiry's first report, 'Shipman had the reputation . . . of being a good and caring doctor. He was held in very high regard by the overwhelming majority of his patients. He was also respected by fellow professionals. His patients appear to have regarded him as the best doctor in [their town].'[21]

Of course, Shipman's popularity and his elevated societal status as a community doctor provided the perfect cover for his crimes. He groomed hundreds of people into believing that he was an affable old-fashioned medic who offered home visits and went the extra mile for his patients. The respect they held him in allowed him to go undetected for years, in much the same way that Jimmy Savile could abuse children in plain sight due to his impeccable public reputation. How can anyone be sure that Lucy Letby is not another unlikely killer like Harold Shipman before her?

Letby's handwritten notes are also challenging. In court we pored over every word, pulling apart the phrases Letby had written in the context of trying to establish if they amounted to a confession – as the prosecution claimed – or anguish at being wrongly suspected – as the defence argued. Less courtroom time was given to analysis of the form the notes took – lines of scrawl crammed together like knitted biro.

Professor Mark Freestone says, 'That sort of writing that's very compressed, with masses of ideas, like a sort of word-vomit . . . It looks to me awfully like a kind of written self-harming.' But reports since Letby's convictions have suggested the opposite – that the notes were a form of therapy. As we noted in an earlier chapter, sources close to Letby have indicated she wrote the notes on the advice of counsellors as a way of dealing with extreme stress – although she made no mention of this advice in court.

Sceptics and supporters of Letby have sought to downplay these notes. The criminologist David Wilson told us: 'I worked on a number of murder cases whereby you get people writing strange notes all the time. It's evidence of there perhaps being underlying stress, mental health problems. It's not necessarily evidence of guilt.'

But are such dismissals too easy? Even if Lucy Letby's notes can be read in more than one way, they show that there was – at least at the times when she wrote them – another, darker Lucy that the rest of the world did not see. 'I AM EVIL.' 'HATE.' 'I killed them on purpose because I'm not good enough to care for them + I am a horrible evil person.' Whatever these words signify, they undermine the idea that Lucy Letby was two-dimensionally nice and normal.

We asked the mother of Babies E and F, who has the perspective of having observed Letby both at the hospital and in court. She says:

> 'It's like they were two different people. I remember a very tactile, quiet, softly spoken person [on the unit]. In the trial she seemed cold, belligerent and awkward. Really, really awkward . . . But then, look at Harold Shipman . . . look at Ted Bundy . . . You know, these people fly under the radar because serial killers are monsters that haven't got horns coming out of their heads. They look like you and me and that's how they get away with it. They can blend in and they can morph into what society wants, and she used her tools to her advantage, she used that blandness, that empathetic voice. For me she's [absolutely] a serial killer.'

What of Letby's relationship with her parents? We know they were close and everything we've seen of their relationship suggests it was warm and loving. But there was a stifling dimension too. Letby herself hinted at this in a text to a colleague: 'My parents worry massively about anything & everything.' Unsurprisingly, Letby's parents supported their daughter when things began to fall apart at work – so much so that her dad John attended meetings with the hospital CEO Tony Chambers to argue his daughter's case. John Letby was even there, staying at his daughter's house, when the police arrested her.

But could there be secrets in Letby's childhood that only she and her parents know about – a health scare or a private tragedy, perhaps, or some other life-changing event? If something seismic did happen during Letby's seemingly stable childhood, it has been well hidden. But that doesn't mean it isn't there. We spoke to the renowned American criminologist Katherine Ramsland. Ramsland is a professor of forensic psychology and spent six years interviewing the American serial killer Dennis Rader in prison.

'There are no distinct signals of a budding serial killer,' she cautioned. 'Any behaviour is interpretable in a benign or malignant manner.' Letby's early and dogged fixation with becoming a neonatal nurse immediately comes to mind. From one angle, it looks sweet. From another, it could appear sinister. So how can you decide?

According to Dr Ramsland, 'It's certainly possible for kids from seemingly normal circumstances to develop violent thoughts and impulses.' Also, 'just because you haven't dug up information about someone's childhood doesn't mean it's not there . . . We have lists of issues and conditions that come up in [serial killers'] backgrounds,' she said. 'But none is a confirmed precursor [for murder] . . . And some of the budding killers keep these things secret. Or lie about them . . . Even if you were to find nothing in Letby's background, that doesn't mean it's genuinely absent. It could mean no one knew how to interpret the signs . . .'

We can't say, but based on our own observations, Lucy Letby does not want to be seen or understood – at least not yet. Although she went through the motions in her two trials, she didn't look or sound like someone who believed she was the victim of a great injustice. Maybe we shouldn't read too much into such impressions. But let's also remember that she decided not to call the one expert witness who just might have made a difference to her case. Was she following bad advice or did she not truly believe in her own case?

Letby's silence and resistance to help is another factor that makes her case strange. During her trial, she asked her friends to stay away. Her parents have shunned the media. Letby herself appears equally resistant. When we asked her solicitor if she would speak to us, he wrote back to say: 'We have spoken to Lucy about your [approach]. She is aware of the request for contact, but does not wish to enter into communication about the case at this time.'

Could that change? Just before this book went to press it was reported that Letby had changed her legal team and was planning a fresh appeal, with hopes of taking her case to the Criminal Cases Review Commission. At the very least, it indicates a change in approach – and possibly a sign that she is ready to play a more active role in the information war that is now raging about her case.

Some people are certain of Lucy Letby's guilt. The consultants who fought to see her tried believe she is guilty. So do the parents who have suffered and lost so much. And so did two trial juries. There are others who are certain that Lucy Letby is innocent, including those who ought to know her best. For the rest of us, our feelings lie somewhere between these extremes. Ultimately, no one but Lucy Letby really knows the truth.

Postscript

Following Lucy Letby's conviction, senior managers at the Countess of Chester Hospital released statements. These are reproduced below.

Tony Chambers, former CEO

All my thoughts are with the children at the heart of this case and their families and loved ones at this incredibly difficult time. I am truly sorry for what all the families have gone through.

The crimes that have been committed are appalling and I am deeply saddened by what has come to light.

The trial, and the lengthy police investigation, have shown the complex nature of the issues raised. I will co-operate fully and openly with any post-trial inquiry.

Ian Harvey, former medical director

At this time, my thoughts are with the babies whose treatment has been the focus of the trial and with their parents and relatives who have been through something unimaginable and I am sorry for all their suffering.

As Medical Director, I was determined to keep the baby unit safe and support our staff. I wanted the reviews and investigations carried out, so that we could tell the parents what had happened to their children.

I believe there should be an inquiry that looks at all events leading up to this trial and I will help it in whatever way I can.

Mr Harvey also noted that, following a complaint against him from four of the consultants at the Countess of Chester Hospital, an investigation was conducted by the General Medical Council (GMC). He says the GMC investigated thoroughly and in May 2022 informed him that the case was closed with no further action.

Stephen Cross, former head of corporate affairs and legal services

My thoughts are and always have been with the families.

I do not wish to . . . make a statement.

I look forward to the Public Inquiry which will give me the opportunity to set out a record of the facts known to me.

Alison Kelly, former head of nursing

It is impossible to imagine the heartache suffered by the families involved and my thoughts are very much with them.

These are truly terrible crimes and I am deeply sorry that this happened to them.

We owe it to the babies and their families to learn lessons and I will fully cooperate with the independent inquiry announced.[1]

—

Karen Rees, former lead nurse for urgent care

On 19 August 2023, a day after Lucy Letby was first convicted, Karen Rees released a written statement to the media:

1 I have not worked at the Countess of Chester Hospital since March 2018 when I retired. I had been Head of Nursing for the Urgent Care Division, one of the two deputies to our Director of Nursing, at the hospital from August 2015. I reported to the executive team, comprising Alison Kelly (Director of Nursing), Ian Harvey (Medical Director) and Karen Townsend (Divisional Director).

2 My role included overseeing the Neonatal unit (NNU) at the hospital. My area of expertise was Cardiology.

3 I had little knowledge of Lucy Letby before 24 June 2016. I was completely unaware of any complaints that had been made about her by the Consultants on the NNU.

4 On 24 June 2016, I was informed by Karen Townsend that during a general review meeting between Karen and Ravi Jayaram (a Consultant, who was Clinical Lead for neonates and paediatrics), he had told her that there were concerns about Lucy Letby's clinical practices, and that he (and Stephen Brearey, who was also a Consultant) thought that she should be removed from the NNU.

5 I immediately went to find Ravi Jayaram and Stephen Brearey in order to obtain more information about the allegations that had been made. I went straightaway as it was a Friday afternoon, and I was conscious that staff would be going home for the weekend. I wanted to find out what the concerns were.

6 I went to the office that Ravi Jayaram and Stephen Brearey shared. Stephen Brearey was not there, but Ravi Jayaram was. I asked Ravi to explain his allegation and to give me more details so that I could understand the concerns. However, Ravi wouldn't give me any information to explain why Lucy Letby should be removed from the unit. He said nothing about air embolus, or over feeding. He did not even mention babies dying and Lucy Letby being present. He just asked for Lucy Letby to be removed from the NNU.

7 As Ravi Jayaram had not given me any information, I asked him where Stephen Brearey was, because I urgently needed to speak with him. He called Stephen Brearey while I was present in his

office. He said that Stephen Brearey was still in the hospital and was in clinic.

8 I then went to the clinic and waited outside to speak with Stephen Brearey. I waited for around 60 minutes. I was not going to leave the hospital until I had spoken with him. I had never spoken with Stephen Brearey before.

9 When he came out of clinic, we went to his office together. Ravi Jayaram had gone home by that time. We then spoke about Lucy Letby. Stephen Brearey was measured throughout. I told him that Ravi Jayaram had told the Divisional Director that there were clinical concerns about Lucy Letby. Although he would have been fully aware of the protocol, I explained to him that I needed more information from him before I could remove a nurse from the NNU. I said that if there were issues, then I needed to know what they were.

10 Despite that, he refused to give me any more information. He said that he had evidence, but he refused to show it to me. He just stated that I needed to remove Lucy Letby, but he would not tell me why. I did not understand (and still don't understand) why he would not provide any further information to me, as he must have known that I needed a reason to effectively suspend someone.

11 At no point did he say that he suspected she had been purposely harming babies. If he had said that there had been 16 deaths, and that she was present for all of them, then my actions may well have differed. If Stephen Brearey had given me whatever evidence he said he had, that may have meant that a further death could potentially have been prevented.

12 I told Dr Brearey that as he was not prepared to provide me with any information, I was going to go to the Executive team to speak with Alison Kelly, the Director of Nursing, who was the most senior nurse in the hospital. I left his room and went immediately to the Executive office. I told Alison Kelly everything that had happened that afternoon. Alison Kelly informed me that she was going to discuss this with Ian Harvey, the Medical Director, and that she would deal with it.

13 Although the issue had been escalated to the Executive team, I wanted to find out as much as I could about any potential issues. I therefore went to see Eirian Lloyd Powell, who was the unit manager of the NNU. I asked her whether she had any concerns about any nurses on the unit. She said that she did not. I then asked her specifically whether she had any clinical concerns about Lucy Letby. She said she had no concerns. She mentioned nothing about any concerns raised by any Consultants.

14 As the Director of Nursing had told me to leave the matter with her, I returned to see Karen Townsend, the Divisional Director, and informed her that I had referred the matter immediately to the Director of Nursing and that she in turn was going to speak with the Medical Director. I told her that I didn't understand why the consultants wouldn't give me the information I had asked for.

15 I then went home, which was after 6 p.m. I received a telephone call from Stephen Brearey when I was at home. He asked me whether I had immediately removed Lucy Letby. I told him that I was not in a position to make that decision, and that I had escalated the situation to the Director of Nursing and that she was going to discuss the matter with the Medical Director.

16 Stephen Brearey then said that he didn't believe that I had been to see Alison Kelly. He effectively accused me of lying. I told him that he needed to speak to the Medical Director and ask him what decisions had been made. I said that I had escalated their concerns as he would not give me the information that I needed to be able to make a decision.

17 I called Alison Kelly shortly after Stephen Brearey's call, and informed her about the content of our conversation that had just taken place on the telephone.

18 I am aware of the statements made by Stephen Brearey concerning that telephone call, which are not true. He has said that he asked me if I 'would take responsibility for anything that might happen to other babies the next day (25 June 2016), and he says that I replied 'yes'. That is simply not true. I have no

recollection of him asking any question like that, and if he had, I would never have said 'Yes', and nor would anyone else in my position.

19 It has also been alleged that Stephen Brearey said words to the effect: 'Would you be happy if something happened to any of the babies tomorrow?' and that I replied: 'Yes'. That is completely untrue, and an outrageous allegation to make. Again, I have no recollection of him asking any question like that, and if he had, I would obviously never have said 'Yes', and nor would anyone else.

20 I am currently taking legal advice about the untrue allegations that Mr Brearey has made about me.'

On 23 August 2023, Karen Rees released a second statement following on from the one she'd issued four days previously:

'I have been asked to comment on my view of Lucy Letby's guilt. I have no doubt at all that she was guilty of these despicable crimes, having seen the reports of the evidence. I did not attend the trial, so I had an incomplete picture until the verdicts were announced, and more detail provided.

Prior to the trial, I had thought that she was innocent, as (1) I had understood that the most life-threatened babies had been placed in her care (as she was one of the most qualified members of the NNU), (2) no performance issues had been raised with me until 24 June 2016, and (3) the NNU manager had assured me that there were no concerns about Nurse Letby.

I also had to have regular meetings with Nurse Letby after her suspension, which was part of my job. I witnessed her in complete distress, crying and swearing her innocence. She was very convincing.

I now know that this was a calculated (and successful) attempt to make me believe her story, and I was deceived, as were so many others.'

Appendix

Operation Hummingbird
Chart 1: Nurses present Summary

Band 4 Staff/ Nursery Nurses/ Registered Nurses

Event Chron	Baby	Date Shift Started	Shift Type	… (staff names redacted)	Lucy LETBY	… (staff names redacted)
1	Child A	08/06/2015	NIGHT		X	
2	Child B	09/06/2015	NIGHT		X	
3	Child C	13/06/2015	NIGHT		X	
4	Child D	21/06/2015	NIGHT		X	
5	Child E	03/08/2015	NIGHT		X	
6	Child F	04/08/2015	NIGHT		X	
7	Child G	06/09/2015	NIGHT		X	
8	Child G	21/09/2015	DAY		X	
9	Child H	25/09/2015	NIGHT		X	
10	Child H	26/09/2015	NIGHT		X	
11	Child I	30/09/2015	DAY		X	
12	Child I	12/10/2015	NIGHT		X	
13	Child I	13/10/2015	NIGHT		X	
14	Child I	22/10/2015	NIGHT		X	
15	Child J	26/11/2015	NIGHT		X	
16	Child K	16/02/2016	NIGHT		X	
17	Child M	09/04/2016	DAY		X	
18	Child L	09/04/2016	DAY		X	
19	Child L	02/06/2016	NIGHT		X	
20	Child N	14/06/2016	NIGHT		X	
21	Child O	23/06/2016	DAY		X	
22	Child O	24/06/2016	DAY		X	
23	Child P	24/06/2016	DAY		X	
24	Child Q	25/06/2016	DAY		X	
			Total	…	24	…

'('X') indicates 'on duty' presence on the shift, where a suspicious event has been identified)

Endnotes

Chapter 1

1 https://www.independent.co.uk/news/uk/crime/baby-murders-nurse-countess-cheshire-hospital-neo-natal-unit-woman-arrest-police-a8428341.html

2 Gabriella Swerling, John Simpson, Chris Smyth, 'Police arrest nurse Lucy Letby over "murder" of eight babies at Countess of Chester Hospital', *The Times* (4 July 2018). https://www.thetimes.co.uk/article/police-arrest-nurse-lucy-letby-over-murder-of-eight-babies-at-countess-of-chester-hospital-735nqnn5s

3 Gabriella Swerling, John Simpson, Chris Smyth, 'Police arrest nurse Lucy Letby over "murder" of eight babies at Countess of Chester Hospital', *The Times* (4 July 2018). https://www.thetimes.co.uk/article/police-arrest-nurse-lucy-letby-over-murder-of-eight-babies-at-countess-of-chester-hospital-735nqnn5s

4 https://www.dailymail.co.uk/news/article-5921303/Police-dig-garden-home-neonatal-nurse-28-arrested-baby-deaths-Chester.html

5 https://www.dailymail.co.uk/news/article-5921303/Police-dig-garden-home-neonatal-nurse-28-arrested-baby-deaths-Chester.html

6 Gabriella Swerling, John Simpson, Chris Smyth, 'Police arrest nurse Lucy Letby over "murder" of eight babies at Countess of Chester Hospital', *The Times* (4 July 2018). https://www.thetimes.co.uk/article/police-arrest-nurse-lucy-letby-over-murder-of-eight-babies-at-countess-of-chester-hospital-735nqnn5s

7 Gabriella Swerling, John Simpson, Chris Smyth, 'Police arrest nurse Lucy Letby over "murder" of eight babies at Countess of Chester Hospital', *The Times* (4 July 2018). https://www.thetimes.co.uk/article/police-arrest-nurse-lucy-letby-over-murder-of-eight-babies-at-countess-of-chester-hospital-735nqnn5s

8 https://www.dailymail.co.uk/news/article-12433159/I-never-believe-

Lucy-Letby-guilty-Childhood-friend-maintains-nurse-innocent-video-emerges-pair-Night-Terror-six-years-day-murderer-tried-kill-set-twins.html

9   https://www.thetimes.co.uk/article/lucy-letby-friends-question-how-kind-and-geeky-nurse-could-be-suspected-child-killer-39fvnjnvq

10   https://www.thetimes.co.uk/article/lucy-letby-friends-question-how-kind-and-geeky-nurse-could-be-suspected-child-killer-39fvnjnvq

11   https://www.herefordtimes.com/announcements/birthdays/birth-day/8762299.lucy-letby/

12   *Hereford Times* (December 2011).
https://www.itv.com/news/central/2023-08-18/the-quiet-cul-de-sac-in-here-ford-where-killer-nurse-lucy-letby-grew-up

13   https://www.mirror.co.uk/news/uk-news/lucy-letby-one-time-hospi-tal-30437423

14   https://www.bbc.co.uk/news/uk-england-merseyside-46448260

15   https://www.coch.nhs.uk/media/74663/chester_standard_babygrow_page_999kb__07.03.2013_.pdf

16   https://www.theguardian.com/uk-news/2023/aug/18/lucy-letby-the-beige-and-average-nurse-who-turned-into-a-baby-killer

17   https://www.coch.nhs.uk/media/74654/chester_standard_babygrow_page_1070kb__28.03.2013_.pdf

18   https://www.cheshire-live.co.uk/news/chester-cheshire-news/update-giv-en-public-inquiry-lucy-29266165
Interestingly, the 2012-13 annual report for the Countess of Chester Hospital is no longer available on the hospital website: https://www.coch.nhs.uk/corporate-information/corporate-documents-and-downloads/annual-reports.aspx

19   https://www.coch.nhs.uk/media/121105/6th-august-2015.PDF

Chapter 2

1   Source: Bliss website, 2021 statistics. The neonatal charity estimates that nearly 58,000 babies are born prematurely in the UK each year and says this means that one in every thirteen UK babies are premature (born before thirty-seven weeks' gestation).

2   From the mother's witness statement read to the court during Lucy Letby trial on 17 October 2022.

3   From the mother's victim personal statement read at sentencing on 21 August 2023.

4   From the mother's witness statement to the court during Lucy Letby trial on 17 October 2022.

5   From the prosecution opening note in Lucy Letby trial.

6   Prosecution opening note and parents' witness statements from Lucy Letby trial.

7   BBC courtroom notes from Lucy Letby trial on 19 October 2022.

8   Medical notes and prosecution opening statement from Lucy Letby trial.

9   Widely referenced, e.g. in prosecution opening statement and medical statements in Lucy Letby trial.

10 Grandmother's witness statement read during Lucy Letby trial on 17 October 2022.

11 Author's courtroom note of grandmother's statement in Lucy Letby trial on 17 October 2022.

12 Prosecution opening note in Lucy Letby trial.

13 According to timings on doctors' notes discussed in Lucy Letby trial.

14 Parents' victim personal statements read on the day of sentencing in Lucy Letby trial on 21 August 2023.

15 Court testimony of Dr David Harkness from Lucy Letby trial on 20 October 2022. https://www.bbc.co.uk/news/uk-england-merseyside-63333684

16 Testimony based on author's courtroom notes, PA and sentencing statements from Lucy Letby trial.

17 Family statements from Lucy Letby trial. Length of time of resuscitation based on medical notes.

18 Evidence from Lucy Letby trial on 20 October 2022.

19 Evidence from Lucy Letby trial on 20 October 2022.

20 Lucy Letby medical notes and text messages from Lucy Letby trial.

21 Mother's witness statement read in court during Lucy Letby trial on 17 October 2022.

22 Victim personal statement read on the day of sentencing in Lucy Letby trial on 21 August 2023.

23 Mother's witness statement read in court during Lucy Letby trial on 17 October 2022.

24 Father's witness statement read in court during Lucy Letby trial on 17 October 2022.

25 Prosecution opening note in Lucy Letby trial.

26 WhatsApp message to [Anon. Medic 1], 9 June 2015 at 18:32:17, and text

message to Melanie Taylor at 18:54:41. Released during Lucy Letby trial.

27 Text message to Melanie Taylor, 9 June 2015 at 18:54:41. Released during Lucy Letby trial.

28 Text message to Melanie Taylor, 9 June 2015 at 19:03:27. Released during Lucy Letby trial.

29 WhatsApp messages from [Anon. Medic 1], 9 June 2015 at 18:38:26 and 18:38:45. Released during Lucy Letby trial.

30 Yvonne Griffiths was the unit's deputy manager in 2015.

31 Text message from Yvonne Griffiths, 9 June 2015 at 21:46:06. Released during Lucy Letby trial.

32 Prosecution opening note in Lucy Letby trial.

33 Prosecution opening note and medical notes in Lucy Letby trial.

34 Mother's witness statement in Lucy Letby trial.

35 Claire Hocknell (Cheshire Police) court evidence in Lucy Letby trial on 18 October 2022.

36 Claire Hocknell (Cheshire Police) court evidence in Lucy Letby trial on 18 October 2022.

37 Prosecution opening note in Lucy Letby trial.

38 This is drawn from the mother's witness statement in Lucy Letby trial. The consultant's own evidence regarding the skin discoloration was given in court on 25 October 2022.

39 Prosecution opening note in Lucy Letby trial.

40 Father's witness statement in Lucy Letby trial.

41 WhatsApp message from 10 June 2015 at 22:45:26, released during Lucy Letby trial.

42 Lucy Letby texts from 10 June 2015. Released during Lucy Letby trial.

43 11 June 2015. Text messages relating to Baby C released during Lucy Letby trial.

44 Prosecution opening note and text messages relating to Baby C released during Lucy Letby trial.

45 13 June 2015. Text messages relating to Baby C released during Lucy Letby trial.

46 Prosecution opening note in Lucy Letby trial.

47 Mother's statement heard in court during Lucy Letby trial on 26 October 2022. https://www.bbc.co.uk/news/uk-england-merseyside-63406551

48 From evidence heard during Lucy Letby trial on 28 October 2022. https://www.chesterstandard.co.uk/news/23084146.recap-lucy-letby-trial-friday-october-28/

49 Mother's statement heard in court during Lucy Letby trial on 26 October 2022.

50 Mother's statement heard in court during Lucy Letby trial on 26 October 2022.

51 Mother's statement heard in court during Lucy Letby trial on 26 October 2022. https://www.bbc.co.uk/news/uk-england-merseyside-63406551 and PA.

52 Text messages from 14 June 2015.

53 Text messages from 14 June 2015.

54 From prosecution opening note and witness evidence given in person to the court by the mother of Baby D during Lucy Letby trial on 3 November 2022.

55 Prosecution opening note in Lucy Letby trial.

56 Evidence of Dr Andrew Brunton in Lucy Letby trial on 7 November 2022. PA and also https://www.bbc.co.uk/news/uk-england-merseyside-63545151

57 Prosecution opening note in Lucy Letby trial.

58 Father's witness statement in Lucy Letby trial on 3 November 2022. https://www.bbc.co.uk/news/uk-england-merseyside-63497920

59 Sentencing statement from mother of Baby D on 21 August 2023.

60 22 June 2015. Text messages released during Lucy Letby trial.

61 Post-mortems referred to in prosecution opening note in Lucy Letby trial.

62 Dr Brearey referred to this meeting (although not the precise date) in court on 14 March 2023.

63 Interview with BBC *Panorama*.

64 Interview with BBC *Panorama*.

65 Interview with BBC *Panorama*.

66 Interview with BBC *Panorama*.

67 BBC *Panorama* interview and court testimony from Lucy Letby trial on 14 November 2022.

68 Court testimony from Lucy Letby trial on 16 November 2022. The consultant (whose identity is protected by reporting restrictions) told the court: 'A cause of death is needed for a death certificate, and anyone who dies unexpectedly. At the time I felt that [Baby E] had NEC [a bowel condition] which led to the deterioration, so I discussed that with the coroner, and we agreed to put that as his cause of death.'

She added: 'The parents were understandably devastated that [Baby E] had died and were not keen on a post-mortem, and I didn't want to make what was a terrible situation any worse so I didn't push which is something I now regret.' Under cross-examination, the consultant apologised to the parents of Baby E and denied 'steering them away' from a post-mortem. She said, 'That's not the case. I don't believe I ever did that and I apologise if anything I said was interpreted as that.'

69 Includes testimony from mother's court evidence during Lucy Letby trial on 14 November 2022.

70 Interview with mother of Babies E and F in 2024.

71 Prosecution opening note, par. 156.

72 Message to anon colleague, 9 August 2015.

73 BBC, 24 November 2022:

Giving evidence at Manchester Crown Court, the paediatric consultant described medical notes made by a colleague following tests made on Child F after his condition deteriorated.

They showed high levels of insulin alongside low levels of a hormone called C-peptide, something she said 'strongly suggests' he had been given insulin as a medicine, rather than it being naturally produced by the body. 'This is something we found very confusing at the time,' she said.

She said Child F had been given a small dose of insulin to help regulate his blood sugar shortly after his birth, but this would have 'long gone' by that time.

Chapter 3

1 Text exchange between Letby and colleague, 4 August 2015. Released during Lucy Letby trial.

2 Courtroom notes from 1 December 2022 and parents' statements from Lucy Letby trial. More here: https://www.bbc.co.uk/news/uk-england-merseyside-63825295

3 Prosecution opening note in Lucy Letby trial.

4 Baby G mother's statement from Lucy Letby trial.

5 Prosecution opening note and BBC reporting from Lucy Letby trial on 6 December 2022.

6 Gestation information re thirty-seven weeks sourced from NHS online – https://www.nhs.uk/pregnancy/week-by-week/28-to-40-plus/37-weeks.

7 Author's courtroom notes and PA reporting from Lucy Letby trial on 1 December 2022.

8 Text exchange between Lucy Letby and colleague, 7 September 2015. Released during Lucy Letby trial.

9 Text exchange between Lucy Letby and deputy unit manager, 26 September 2015.

10 Text exchange between Lucy Letby and colleague, 27 September 2015.

11 Baby H relates to two attempted murder charges on the trial indictment. Letby was acquitted of one (relating to 26/09/15) and the jury was hung on the other (relating to 27/09/15).

12 Detail on this was included in the prosecution opening note in the Lucy Letby trial. It was also addressed extensively during cross-examination of Lucy Letby on 25 May 2023, as documented in author's courtroom notes.

13 Author's courtroom notes from Lucy Letby trial on 2 February 2023.

14 Author's courtroom notes from Lucy Letby trial on 2 February 2023.

15 Mother's witness statement in Lucy Letby trial.

16 Evidence from nurses Christopher Booth and Melanie Taylor during Lucy Letby trial, 2–3 February 2023. See court reports from BBC and PA.

17 Evidence from Melanie Taylor during Lucy Letby trial on 6 February 2023.

18 Mother's witness statement in Lucy Letby trial.

19 Court testimony and exhibit in Lucy Letby trial on 2 February 2023.

20 Email from Eirian Powell, 23 October 2015.

21 'Dr Evans described the collapse [of Child J] at 07:11hrs on the 27th November 2015 as unexpected without any straightforward explanation.' Prosecution opening note, par. 270.

22 CQC, *The Countess of Chester Hospital Quality Report* (2016), p.107.

23 CQC, *The Countess of Chester Hospital Quality Report* (2016), p.41.

24 CQC, *The Countess of Chester Hospital Quality Report* (2016), p.107.

25 Price of house as listed on Rightmove

26 Text message from 8 April 2016. Released during Lucy Letby trial

27 Texts from 9 April 2016. Released during Lucy Letby trial.

28 'Baby M did not respond well to resuscitation. Treatment was about to be withdrawn after the injection of 6 doses of adrenaline over a period of 25 minutes when he suddenly improved. Dr Jayaram could not find any cause for the sudden collapse, but the discoloration he saw caused him to suspect an air embolism.' Prosecution opening note, par. 315.

29 In a court report of the Prosecution Closing Speech, dated 19 June 2023, the *Chester Standard* reported: 'Dr John Gibbs said the low blood sugar level should have meant the level of insulin in Child L was also low. He said it had "never occurred to him" that someone was administering insulin to Child L. He said he had never received the lab results for Child L – they went to junior doctors who "didn't appreciate its significance" at the time.' https://www.chesterstandard.co.uk/news/23597625.recap-lucy-letby-trial-monday-june-19---closing-speeches/

30 'Dr Anna Milan, a consultant clinical scientist at Royal Liverpool Hospital said a blood sample from Child L sent to its lab by the Countess of Chester showed the insulin was 'exogenous'. The readings confirmed it was given to the patient rather than being naturally produced by the pancreas, she told the court. The results were later communicated by phone to the Countess of Chester's biochemistry lab on April 14.' PA court report of Letby trial on 20 February 2023

31 On 19 August 2023, a day after Lucy Letby was first convicted, Karen Rees released a written statement to the media. It is reproduced in full in the Postscript.

32 The seniority of nurses is reflected by 'bands' with higher bands being more senior. As unit manager, Eirian Powell was at a higher band level than Lucy Letby: https://nna.org.uk/career-opportunities-as-neona-tal-nurse/5-neonatal-management-career/

33 Response from Ian Harvey, dated 23 August 2023, to BBC corres-pondence. On 28 February 2023, Dr Jayaram was cross-examined by Lucy Letby's barrister Ben Myers KC in relation to Baby K. Dr Jayaram had said in his testimony that he had walked into the nursery in February 2016 and seen Lucy Letby alone standing next to Baby K's incubator. Baby K's blood oxygen levels were dropping, the alarms were not sounding and Letby was 'doing nothing'. In cross-examination, Ben Myers KC asked Dr Jayaram if he had confronted Lucy Letby at the time of the incident. Dr Jayaram answered: 'No, absolutely not.' Mr Myers then put it to Dr Jayaram that the incident was not documented in medical notes. (See PA court report dated 28 February 2023.) The following is from the *Chester Standard*'s court report of an exchange between Dr Jayaram and Ben Myers KC earlier that day:

'Dr Jayaram says that would not be the sort noted in medical documentation. Mr Myers says there is nothing to say the tube is dislodged. Dr Jayaram says it is obvious from the medical notes. He says, in isolation, the incidents were unusual, and more concerning in a pattern of behaviour. [Dr Jayaram] said: "We, as a group of consultants by this stage, had experience of an unusual event, and there was one particular nurse. All of these events were unusual. Yes, if we put in Datix [incident forms] we could have investigated sooner and been here [in court] sooner." He said he, and his other consultants, wanted to know how this could be investigated, and tried their best to escalate concerns higher up the hospital.'

https://www.chesterstandard.co.uk/news/23351305.recap-lucy-letby-trial-tuesday-february-28/

34 Facebook messages between Lucy Letby and the married doctor began on 2 June 2016. Messages released during Lucy Letby trial.

35 The jury convicted Letby of attempting to murder Baby N on 3 June 2016. The jury was unable to reach a verdict on two further counts of attempted murder relating to the same baby on 15 June 2016.

36 Facebook messages released during Lucy Letby trial.

37 Opening prosecution note in Lucy Letby trial, pars 336–38. The jury convicted Letby of one charge of attempted murder relating to this child but was unable to reach a verdict on a further two charges.

38 Evidence from Lucy Letby trial on 8 June 2023. https://www.bbc.co.uk/news/uk-england-merseyside-65844522

39 Text exchange from 21 June 2016. Released during Lucy Letby's trial. [Baby O.]

40 Text at 14.11 on 22 June 2016. Baby O died at 17.47 on 23 June 2016. Baby P died at 16.00 on 24 June 2016. The prosecution in Letby's trial noted seventy-two hours to include Baby Q too. https://www.bbc.com/news/uk-england-merseyside-65844522

41 Prosecution opening note in Lucy Letby trial.

42 Mum's statement based on author's courtroom notes on 8 March 2023.

43 Grandmother's statement based on author's courtroom notes on 8 March 2023.

44 PA court report from Lucy Letby trial on 9 March 2023.

45 Prosecution opening note in Lucy Letby trial.

46 Evidence from Melanie Taylor during Lucy Letby trial. https://www.bbc.co.uk/news/uk-england-merseyside-64899099

47 Father's statement in Lucy Letby trial on 8 March 2023.

48 Mother's statement in Lucy Letby trial on 8 March 2023.

49 Father's statement in Lucy Letby trial on 8 March 2023.

50 Grandmother's statement in Lucy Letby trial on 8 March 2023.

51 Mother's statement in Lucy Letby trial on 8 March 2023.

52 Father's statement in Lucy Letby trial on 8 March 2023.

53 Text exchange from 23 June 2016. Released during Lucy Letby trial.

54 Text exchange from 24 June 2016

55 Parents' statements from Lucy Letby trial on 8 March 2023.

56 11.30 a.m. desaturation.

57 12.30 p.m. pneumothorax.

58 Grandmother's statement from Lucy Letby trial on 8 March 2023.

59 Text timed at 13.30 on 24 June 2016. Released during Lucy Letby trial.

60 PA court report during Lucy Letby trial on 21 March 2023.

61 The prosecution in the Lucy Letby trial stated that this remark was made just before the transport team arrived. See prosecution opening note in Lucy Letby trial.

62 Parents' statements in Lucy Letby trial on 8 March 2023.

63 Text timed at 18.34 on 24 June 2016.

64 Parents' statements in Lucy Letby trial on 8 March 2023.

65 Steve Brearey court testimony in Lucy Letby trial on 14 March 2023. (Kim Pilling, 'Lucy Letby "tried to murder baby after bid to remove her from duties refused"', PA, 14 March 2023.)

66 For full statement from Karen Rees see Postscript.

67 This relates to Baby Q. The jury was unable to reach a verdict in respect of one charge of attempted murder relating to this baby.

Chapter 4

1 Excerpts from text messages read to the court during Lucy Letby's trial on 6 April 2023.

2 https://www.bliss.org.uk/parents/in-hospital/about-neonatal-care/how-does-neonatal-care-work

3 Response from Tony Chambers, dated 18 August 2023, in response to BBC correspondence.

4 According to Tony Chambers, these measures included:
'– The unit being redesignated to Special Care Unit (SCU) caring for infants from a minimum of 32 weeks gestation.
– A comprehensive review of the Neonatal Unit to include, activity, acuity and staffing levels.
– A review of babies who collapsed unexpectedly (led by Dr John Gibbs)

– Invited review from Royal College of Paediatrics and Child Health (RCPCH)

– Nurse LL [Lucy Letby] redeployed off the unit.'

Response from Tony Chambers, dated 18 August 2023, in response to BBC correspondence.

5   RCPCH report, p.5 (par. 1.1) and p.8 (par. 3.13).

6   'The redactions to the [RCPCH] report were requested by the RCPCH and were purely because they related to HR concerns.' Letter from Tony Chambers to the consultants, dated 30 May 2018.

7   On 23 August 2023, Karen Rees released a short statement following on from a longer statement she'd issued four days previously. This latter statement is reproduced in full in the Postscript.

8   Interview with Karen Rees, ITV (2023).

9   'Prior to the trial, I had thought that she was innocent . . .' Karen Rees public statement, 23 August 2023. See full statement in the Postscript.

10   'I also had to have regular meetings with Nurse Letby after her suspension, which was part of my job. I witnessed her in complete distress, crying and swearing her innocence. She was very convincing. I now know that this was a calculated (and successful) attempt to make me believe her story, and I was deceived, as were so many others.' Karen Rees public statement, 23 August 2023. See full statement in the Postscript.

11   This point was put in written correspondence by the seven consultants to Ian Harvey's senior colleague Tony Chambers. Chambers responded as follows in a letter dated 30 May 2018:

> I've discussed your question with Ian Harvey who describes how time constraints precluded a comprehensive reading and has no recollection that he omitted to mention that further investigation of a small number of cases was recommended, it certainly was not intentional. Ian was progressing this concurrently – the next step seeking permission of the Coroner to speak to the Alder Hey pathologists, then consulting them regarding post-mortem findings. Both Ian and I are sorry if the constrained summary at the meeting is perceived to be derogatory towards you or the paediatric service.

12   Letter from Tony Chambers to consultants, dated 30 May 2018:

> I know how difficult this meeting was for both you and me. I needed to be clear and direct with you and I am sorry for how it made you feel. It is with regret that this was seen as aggressive and threatening,

this was never my intention either at the meeting or at any time subsequently. At the meeting I acknowledged that such events can sometimes lead to unprofessional language, much like that described in 2.7. I also acknowledged that I understood that feelings and emotions can cause this and as such would be happy to 'draw a line' and move on. The drawing of this line was never meant to imply that we had 'drawn a line' under requirements for further investigations. I can now see in the pressure of the meeting how this might have been interpreted and with hindsight I should have asked where you stood on the review and allowed you time to formulate your advice.

13 Statement from Tony Chambers, dated 18 August 2023, in response to BBC correspondence.

14 Ravi Jayaram interview with ITV News, broadcast 18 August 2023. https://www.youtube.com/watch?v=2jnDr5EIpmY

15 In correspondence, Tony Chambers told us: 'The QC input was to help prepare for the police inquiry.' Statement from Tony Chambers, dated 18 August 2023, in response to BBC correspondence.

16 https://www.ddscp.org.uk/cdop/

17 In correspondence, Tony Chambers told us: 'It is wrong to state that the consultants, not the trust, were responsible for getting the police involved. It was a joint decision.' Statement from Tony Chambers, dated 18 August 2023, in response to BBC correspondence.

Chapter 5

1 https://www.dailymail.co.uk/news/article-12421791/Inside-sprawling-Lucy-Letby-investigation-hospital-called-detectives-didnt-expect-discover-killer-nurse-blame-chilling-reality-began-unfold.html

2 Response from Ian Harvey, dated 23 August 2023, to BBC correspondence.

3 This was Paul Hughes' rank at the time. Paul Hughes subsequently became a Detective Superintendent.

4 Cheshire Police PR film about Operation Hummingbird.

5 https://www.dailymail.co.uk/news/article-12421791/Inside-sprawling-Lucy-Letby-investigation-hospital-called-detectives-didnt-expect-discover-killer-nurse-blame-chilling-reality-began-unfold.html

6 See *Chester Standard* court report from Lucy Letby trial, 25 October, https://www.chesterstandard.co.uk/news/23075662.

live-lucy-letby-trial-tuesday-october-25/ The full quotation is: 'I thought I could help, advise review case notes and form an opinion that led to the collapses of [Child A and Child B].'

7 https://adc.bmj.com/content/early/2020/06/30/archdis-child-2020-319326?versioned=true

8 https://www.goldlearning.com/speaker/192/martin-ward-platt

9 See PA court report from Lucy Letby trial on 28 June 2023.

10 See PA court report from Lucy Letby trial on 24 November 2022.

11 Public statement from Karen Rees, 23 August 2023.

12 https://www.chesterstandard.co.uk/news/23493710.recap-lucy-letby-trial-tuesday-may-2---defence-begins/

13 Tony Chambers told us that this was 'an hour-long interview that has been taken out of context'. Statement from Tony Chambers, dated 18 August 2023, in response to BBC correspondence.

14 Interview with author.

15 See PA court report from Lucy Letby trial on 17 April 2023.

16 See PA court report from Lucy Letby trial on 18 May 2023.

17 See PA court report from Lucy Letby trial on 25 April 2023.

18 Interview with author.

19 22 June 2015. Text messages released during Lucy Letby trial.

20 22 June 2015. Text messages released during Lucy Letby trial.

21 22 June 2015. Text messages released during Lucy Letby trial.

22 24 September 2015. Text messages released during Lucy Letby trial.

23 26 September 2016. Text messages relating to Baby H released during Lucy Letby trial.

24 14 June 2016. Text messages relating to Baby H released during Lucy Letby trial.

25 Prosecution opening note in Lucy Letby trial, pars 46, 87 and 112.

26 Prosecution opening note in Lucy Letby trial, par. 140.

27 Prosecution opening note in Lucy Letby trial, par. 368.

28 Prosecution opening note in Lucy Letby trial, par. 64.

29 Author's courtroom notes from Lucy Letby trial on 24 January 2023.

30 Author's courtroom notes from Lucy Letby trial on 24 January 2023.

31 Author's courtroom notes from Lucy Letby trial on 24 January 2023.

32 '[W]e knew that she would write a lot and she did. We've seen it during the first arrest. So we wanted to arrest her and see what she'd been writing about. Maybe in the year that we've been investigating.' Cheshire Police PR film about Operation Hummingbird.

33 Paul Hughes: 'The third arrest, in November 2020, was because we had exhausted sufficient lines of enquiry and that's where we were really. You know, because if we'd got any further, we'd have probably lost the opportunity to interview her the final time. And we wanted to ask some questions, and the Crown Prosecution Service wanted us to ask some questions, but if you get too far and you're already in a position where you know you will charge, then PACE only allows you to clarify some things. It doesn't allow you to investigatively question. So it was that balance where we were almost satisfied, but not quite. And we had conversations with the CPS. It just seemed that the time was right. The stars had aligned in evidential process and we arrested her. And at that third point, we had every intention of arresting her and seeking charge advice and being successful with getting charge advice.' Cheshire Police PR film about Operation Hummingbird.

34 Cheshire Police PR film about Operation Hummingbird.

Chapter 6

1 This was prior to the death of Queen Elizabeth II, so the senior barristers in the case were still QCs.

2 From author's notes of pre-trial hearings on 4 and 6 October 2022.

3 Source: Freedom of Information request – data provided by UK Ministry of Justice. Defence costs paid through Legal Aid reached £1,505,142.42 between arrest and conviction in August 2023. This figure does not include the appeal or retrial, and is therefore expected to rise.

4 Ben Myers and Nicholas Johnson became KCs (previously QCs) a month earlier on the death of Queen Elizabeth II, 8 September 2022.

5 Author's courtroom notes from Lucy Letby trial, 13 October 2022.

6 Evidence heard during Lucy Letby trial on 3 November 2022.

7 Court testimony from the mother of Baby D during Lucy Letby trial on 3 November 2022.

8 Letby's trial featured charges relating to seventeen babies but involved thirteen families (thus twenty-six parents). There were three sets of twins and one set of triplets.

9 This section is largely taken from the author's courtroom notes during Lucy Letby trial on 14 November 2022.

10 BBC *Panorama* interview.

11 BBC *Panorama* interview.

12 Author's courtroom notes during Lucy Letby trial on 14 November 2022.

13 Prosecution closing speech, 21 June 2023.

14 Lucy Letby trial on 1 November 2022.

15 Ruling of Goss, J., 10 January 2023. The ensuing paragraphs are drawn from the same ruling.

16 Ravi Jayaram Twitter bio.

17 Testimony of Ravi Jayaram on 24 October 2022

18 Evidence of Ravi Jayaram in Lucy Letby trial on 25 October 2022.

19 Based on author's courtroom notes from Lucy Letby trial on 28 February 2023.

20 Dr Jayaram set this chronology out in his evidence during the Lucy Letby trial on 28 February 2023.

21 From author's courtroom notes during Lucy Letby trial on 28 February 2023.

22 From author's courtroom notes from Lucy Letby trial on 14 March 2023.

23 Author's courtroom reflections, 22 February 2023.

24 Author's post-trial interview with mother of babies E and F in 2024.

25 From court testimony, 9 June 2023

Chapter 7

1 Source of information on prisoners having TVs and laptops: HM Inspectorate of Prisons report into New Hall Prison, November / December 2022, page 22. This was during Lucy Letby's time on remand at New Hall Prison.

2 Letby's barrister Ben Myers conducted a quick-fire question and answer with Letby twice – at the end of her first day in the witness box on 2 May 2023 and on 17 May 2023.

3 The envisaged six-month timetable was mentioned at several junctures, including at a pre-trial hearing on 4 October 2022.

4 Filmed record of author's courtroom notes, 16 May 2023.

5 Prosecution barrister Nick Johnson KC suggested that Letby had told the court that Dr Ravi Jayaram was a liar but hadn't made that allegation to the police when they interviewed her. Author's courtroom notes from 17 May 2023.

6 Author's courtroom notes, 18 May 2023.

7 Prosecution questions in Lucy Letby trial on 6 June 2023. See also re-examination by the defence on 9 June 2023.

8 Author's note of courtroom exchange between Nick Johnson KC (NJKC) and Lucy Letby (LL) on 18 May 2023:

NJKC: Do you agree that Baby F was poisoned with insulin?

LL: Yes, I agree that he had insulin, yes.

NJKC: Do you agree that somebody gave it to him unlawfully?

LL: Yes.

NJKC: Do you agree that someone was targeting him specifically?

LL: No.

NJKC: So you think it was a random act?

LL: I don't know where the insulin came from.

9 Author's courtroom notes, 19 May 2023.

10 Author's courtroom notes, 25 May 2023.

11 Author's courtroom notes, 7 June 2023.

12 Text exchange from 2 June 2016. Texts released during Lucy Letby trial.

13 Author's courtroom notes, 8 June 2023.

14 End of prosecution cross-examination, 9 June 2023.

15 Lucy Letby spent 14 days in the witness box between 2 May 2023 and 9 June 2023.

16 Nick Johnson KC, closing speech, 19 June 2023.

17 The twelfth juror was discharged on 3 August 23.

18 Verdicts Hearing (1), held on 8 August 2023, at which the jury informed the court that it had reached guilty verdicts on counts 6 and 15.

19 Author's court observation.

20 Verdicts Hearing (2), held on 11 August 2023, at which the jury informed the court that it had reached guilty verdicts on counts 3, 12, 16, 17, 20, and 21.

21 Verdicts Hearing (3), held on 16 August 2023, at which the jury informed the court that it had reached guilty verdicts on counts 1, 2, 4, 5, 7, and 8, and a not guilty verdict on Count 9.

22 Verdicts Hearing (4), held on 17 August 2023, at which the jury informed the court that it had reached a not guilty verdict on count 10.

23 Ben Myers KC, address to judge, 17 August 2023.

24 The cases of Babies H, J, K, N, and Q all resulted in hung verdicts, although Lucy Letby was also convicted on one count of attempted murder against Baby N.

25 The parents of babies whose cases resulted in not guilty or hung

verdicts didn't make statements at the sentencing.
26 Sentencing remarks of Mr Justice Goss, Manchester Crown Court, 21 August 2023.

Chapter 8

1   https://www.thesun.co.uk/news/23533358/moment-lucy-letby-arrested-murder-babies/

2   https://www.standard.co.uk/news/crime/moment-lucy-letby-baby-murder-nurse-caught-video-b1101592.html

3   https://www.express.co.uk/news/uk/1803321/lucy-letby-britain-worst-female-murderers-rose-west-amelia-dyer

4   https://www.telegraph.co.uk/columnists/2023/08/18/lucy-letby-trial-guilty-nhs-betrayal-of-trust/

5   https://www.theguardian.com/commentisfree/2023/aug/18/lucy-letby-rational-explanation-inquiry

6   https://www.dailymail.co.uk/debate/article-12552809/peter-hitchens-lucy-letby-not-guilty.html

7   'Science on Trial, Inc., led by Sarrita Adams, a University of Cambridge educated translational scientist, is a multifaceted, advanced biotechnology and high expertise forensic science consultation company. It aims to address the complex integration of scientific evidence in the criminal justice system, catering to the legal profession's needs.' https://www.scienceontrial.com

8   'Scientifically, the case against Ms Letby has not been proven. The major scientific evidence presented to the jury amounted to two blood tests and x-rays. All the other evidence relies on significant interpretation by expert witnesses, and the reliability of these witnesses is questionable given that they overlook clear pathological symptoms which are reported in the literature. For example, the bruising of the liver, is a widely appreciated phenomena, which is associated with prematurity, and sepsis. Likewise, internal bleeding is not regularly associated with air embolism, yet a number of children exhibited significant signs of internal bleeding. Questions should be asked as to how such minimal medical evidence can be used to convict a person of murder and attempted murder, least of all when the original autopsies performed do not correspond with the alleged cause of death.' https://www.scienceontrial.com/post/the-lucy-letby-case-issues-of-reliability

9 Rachel Aviv, 'A British Nurse Was Found Guilty of Killing Seven Babies. Did She Do It?', *The New Yorker* (13 May 2024). Hereafter cited as 'Rachel Aviv, *The New Yorker*'.

10 https://www.theguardian.com/uk-news/article/2024/jul/09/lucy-letby-evidence-experts-question

11 https://www.telegraph.co.uk/news/2024/07/09/lucy-letby-serial-killer-or-miscarriage-justice-victim/

12 BBC interview with Pascale Jones, CPS lawyer.

13 Letby was first arrested in 2018. She was convicted in 2023.

14 https://www.telegraph.co.uk/news/2024/07/09/lucy-letby-serial-killer-or-miscarriage-justice-victim/

15 The term 'air embolus' refers to the air bubble itself and this term may also be used.

16 'Dr Evans is asked to explain the features of an air embolus. "An air embolus will lead to a sudden and unexpected collapse. A patient, otherwise stable, collapses. And by collapse, I mean change of colour, stops breathing . . . reduced heart rate, and death. This occurs all of a sudden. There are additional features – you don't get all the features in all the cases. The two main associated features are unusual skin discoloration and the presence of air in 'great vessels' – various parts of the body. Those are the compounding features which lead to a diagnosis of air embolus. This occurs when there is no other explanation . . . which fits the collapse, and when resuscitation is unsuccessful."

'He adds the subsequent x-ray and skin discoloration reports had firmed his opinion. [. . .] Dr Evans dismisses alternatives put forward by the defence, including "infection", saying such evidence would appear on a post-mortem examination. He dismisses a suggestion of a "rapidly spreading infection" in the baby as "ridiculous", as he said such evidence would again be found post-mortem by a pathologist. Dr Evans said his conclusion of an air embolus was based on a baby "suddenly crashing" and, "more significantly", followed by "resuscitation which was unsuccessful".' Court report from *Chester Standard*, Tuesday, 25 October 2022.

17 PA court report from Lucy Letby trial, 9 February 2023.

18 BBC court report from Lucy Letby trial, 23 February 2023.

19 S K Lee and A K Tanswell, 'Pulmonary vascular air embolism in the newborn', Archives of Disease in Childhood, 1989, 64, 507-8. Hereafter cited as 'Lee and Tanswell'.

20 Dr Evans said, just before Child A's collapse, he was 'in a stable

condition'. In his report he had described his condition as 'perfectly satisfactory'. PA court report from Lucy Letby trial, 25 October 2022.

21 Dr Harkness said: 'It was incredibly unexpected. This was a completely stable, well baby who had no reason to deteriorate. I was very surprised to be called back . . . There was very unusual patchiness on his skin which I had not seen before. There were patches of blue/purple colour, patches of red and of white that didn't fit . . . This was bright red patches . . . that means you have blood going round your body.' PA court report from Lucy Letby trial, 20 October 2022.

22 Dr Jayaram told the jury of eight women and four men the situation he faced was 'unusual' as the youngster's observations were stable up to the point of collapse. Giving evidence at Manchester Crown Court on Monday, he said: '(Child A) was pale. What I did not give any clinical significance to at the time was unusual patches of discoloration. I didn't actually record it in the notes. 'Pink patches, mainly on the torso, which seemed to appear and disappear and flit around . . . I had never seen anything like it before but my focus at the time was on ABC, airway, breathing, circulation.' PA court report from Lucy Letby trial, 24 October 2022.

23 'The case was referred to the Coroner. A post-mortem examination was carried out by a pathologist at Alder Hey Children's Hospital in Liverpool. The cause of death was recorded as "unascertained" at the time.' Prosecution opening note, par. 37.

24 Dr Evans said he had '"only one" conclusion, that Child A had received an air embolus, "through an IV line"'.

Child A's mother wept in the public gallery as Dr Bohin said she was left with only one 'plausible explanation' for her son's collapse and death which was an air embolism. PA court report from Lucy Letby trial, 25 October 2022.

25 Mr Johnson says Child C, a baby boy, was 'born in good condition' and 'made good progress' and was 'handling well'. Prosecution closing speech. *Chester Standard* court report from Lucy Letby trial, 21 June 2023.

26 *Chester Standard* court report from Lucy Letby trial, 31 October 2022:

> The prosecution asks the nurse about Child C's collapse at 11.15 p.m.
> 'I do not remember where, but I was not in nursery room 1.'
> She recalls 'a shout for help', but does not remember who called it.
> She entered room 1 and saw Melanie Taylor and Sophie Ellis, and a Neopuff device was being administered.

She noticed Child C was not breathing and the heart rate was very low.

The Neopuff gave Child C chest movement, but he did not breathe himself.

Child C had a 'mottled' skin appearance, the nurse recalled.

27 Mr Johnson says there is 'no doubt' Child D and her mother suffered sub-optimal care, but her progress went 'upward' upon her transfer to the neonatal unit. Child D was 'stable' with 'minimal' oxygen support, and 'responding well to treatment'. Prosecution closing speech, as reported by the *Chester Standard*, 21 June 2023.

28 Dr Sandie Bohin said Child E had been 'incredibly stable' prior to the deteriorations. The 16ml aspirate at 9 p.m. 'struck' her as 'really odd' in that context. She was 'at a loss to explain where this had come from'. Prosecution closing speech, as reported by the *Chester Standard*, 21 June 2023.

29 Child I was in a 'virtually perfect' clinical scenario, Mr Johnson says. He says Letby 'got herself involved'. Prosecution closing speech, as reported by the *Chester Standard*, 22 June 2023.

30 Dr Brearey said all triplets had been born in good condition and were 'following a healthy path', and these events were 'exceptionally unusual', and the type of rash was 'something he had never seen before or since'. Prosecution closing speech, as reported by the *Chester Standard*, 20 June 2023.

31 Shift leader Melanie Taylor said there were no concerns for Child O at the start of the shift. 'She did not expect [Child O] to collapse.' Prosecution closing speech, as reported by the *Chester Standard*, 20 June 2023.

32 PA court report of Lucy Letby trial, 17 November 2022: Dr Harkness said: 'There were these strange purple patches over the outside of his tummy, So patches, not one solid purple area.'

33 [Baby I]'s fluid balance chart was noted by Ashleigh Hudson at 23:00hrs. At just before midnight [Baby I] became unsettled. Nurse Hudson and Lucy Letby attended to her but [Baby I] collapsed and required cardiac compressions. Dr Chang, on-call Registrar, attended followed by Dr Gibbs, who was the on-call consultant. He arrived at 00:15 hrs on 23rd October. Dr Gibbs noted that CPR was under way and [Baby I] had a mottled blue appearance of the trunk and peripheries. Prosecution opening note, par. 246.

34 Mr Johnson says Child O's mother gave a description of the rash. The

father said of Child O: 'You could see his veins, all bright blue, changing colour . . . 'You could see something oozing through his veins.' Prosecution closing speech, as reported by the *Chester Standard*, 20 June 2023.

35 Dr Bohin considered that [Baby C's] collapse was concerning and had no clear cause. She conducted a review of all the notes to determine whether or not the NGT had been on free drainage at the time of or before the distension was noted on 12.06.15 [. . .] She found a note in the nursing record of 13.06.15 showing that it was on free drainage and that it was also being aspirated every 3–4 hours yielding only small volumes on each occasion (0.5ml). It follows that any suggestion that the build-up of gas at the time of [Baby C's] collapse was from CPAP or any other breathing assistance is not viable. Therefore, in her view the only feasible mechanism for the excessive air in the gut at the time of [Baby C's] collapse was the deliberate introduction of air via the NGT. In other words – [Baby C] was killed by air inserted into his stomach via the NGT (not into his bloodstream). Prosecution opening note, par. 81.

36 In a 2017 report, Dr Evans wrote of Baby C: 'One may never know the cause of (his) collapse. He was at great risk of unexpected collapse.' PA court report of Lucy Letby trial, 1 November 2022

37 Dr Evans told Mr Myers: 'That was my opinion at the time. As a clinician, if I receive additional information that allows me to change or modify my opinion, that is what we do as clinicians.'

38 Asked repeatedly what evidence he relied on to show air was forced down an NGT, Dr Evans said there were 'three scenarios' – air through the NGT, air travelling intravenously or a combination of both. He agreed with Mr Myers that he had not previously suggested an intravenous injection in Child C's case. PA court report of Lucy Letby trial, 1 November 2022.

39 'You just came up with that now to support the allegation. You are not independent at all.' PA court report of Lucy Letby trial, 1 November 2022.

40 Lee and Tanswell, 508.

41 Supported by trial evidence

42 Lee and Tanswell, 508.

43 Bajanowski, West, and Brinkmann note: 'Venous air embolism is a rare cause of death. Entry of gas into the circulation is caused by trauma, mostly surgical or therapeutic, and sometimes resulting from criminal intervention. The detection of air embolisms requires special precautions

during autopsy. An aspirometer has to be used for the detection, measurement and storage of gas originating from the heart ventricles. The aspirometer has to be filled completely with distilled water containing two drops of Tween 80 to reduce the surface tension of the water and to prevent adherence of small air bubbles to the wall of the aspirometer. Subsequently the gas has to be analysed by gas chromatography. When the results correspond with the main criteria defined by Pierucci and Gherson [2] the diagnosis "air embolism" is justified. The technique for the detection of air embolism is simple but requires a careful procedure which is described in detail.' T. Bajanowski, A West, and B Brinkmann "Proof of fatal air embolism", nt J Legal Med. 1998;111(4):208-11. https://pubmed. ncbi.nlm.nih.gov/9646167/#:~:text=The%20detection%20of%20air%20 embolisms,originating%20from%20the%20heart%20ventricles.

44 'In 1980 in Swansea, the health board built a brand new children's department with a new neonatal unit that I had designed.' PA court report of Lucy Letby trial, 7 March 2023.

45 BBC court report of Lucy Letby trial, 9 February 2023.

46 Author's notes from Lucy Letby trial, 24 January 2023.

47 'Cyanosis is when your skin, lips and/or nails turn a bluish tone. It occurs when your blood lacks the oxygen it needs to reach the different tissues in your body. Cyanosis can be caused by many different conditions. Some may be serious medical conditions.' https://my.clevelandclinic.org/ health/diseases/24297-cyanosis

48 *Chester Standard* court report of Lucy Letby trial, Tuesday 25 October:

> Dr Evans said, just before Child A's collapse, he was 'in a stable condition'. In his report he had described his condition as 'perfectly satisfactory.' He added: 'He was as well as could be expected. All the markers of well-being were very satisfactory. He was in air, not need- ing additional oxygen, heart rate in normal limits, oxygen saturation normal – it had been in the 90s . . . respiratory rate slightly above normal rate but that was the only marker outside normal rate.'

49 In a 2017 report, Dr Evans wrote of Child C: 'One may never know the cause of (his) collapse. He was at great risk of unexpected collapse.' PA court report of Lucy Letby trial, 1 November 2022

50 https://www.dailymail.co.uk/debate/article-12552809/peter-hitchens-lucy-letby-not-guilty.html

Chapter 9

1 https://www.thesun.co.uk/news/24899872/fury-lucy-letby-cushy-private-jail-security/?utm_source=onesignal&utm_medium=web_push_notification&utm_campaign=web_push_2023-11-29
2 PA court report of Lucy Letby trial on, 24 October 2022.
3 Functional bowel issues can aff ect how bowel contents are moved through the system and are known as 'pseudo-obstruction'. Unlike physical obstructions, these functional 'pseudo-obstructions' may not be easily excluded at autopsy.
4 https://www.theguardian.com/uk-news/article/2024/jul/09/lucy-letbyevidence-experts-question
5 Prosecution opening note in Lucy Letby trial, par. 166.
6 Rachel Aviv, *The New Yorker*.
7 Rachel Aviv, *The New Yorker*.

Chapter 10

1 https://www.theguardian.com/uk/2011/jul/22/stepping-hill-nurse-rebecca-leighton-held-by-police
2 https://www.manchestereveningnews.co.uk/news/greater-manchester-news/rebecca-leighton-stepping-hill-murders-9361840
3 Lucy Letby evidence in court, 25 May 2023.
4 https://news.sky.com/story/healthcare-worker-arrested-on-suspicion-of-murdering-eight-babies-11424735
5 https://www.whatdotheyknow.com/request/neonatal_deaths_and_fois#incoming-1255362

Chapter 11

1 Rulings of Mr Justice Goss, 11 June 2024.
2 Mother's statement, as read to court on 13 June 2024.
3 Judge summing up, 2 July 2024
4 Prosecution closing speech, 1 July 2024
5 Evidence of Dr Ravi Jayaram 19/06/24
6 Letby police interview, 12/06/19

Chapter 12

1 *Panorama* interview
2 Allitt Inquiry report, chaired by Sir Cecil Clothier. Chapter 5.3.4
3 Allitt Inquiry report, chaired by Sir Cecil Clothier. Chapter 5.2.1
4 https://www.theguardian.com/uk/2007/dec/06/ukcrime.health
5 http://news.bbc.co.uk/1/hi/england/lincolnshire/7130211.stm
6 Detail on procedure for assessing mental fitness after arrest is contained within the Police and Criminal Evidence Act 'Code of Practice for the detention, treatment and questioning of persons by Police Officers' (via Home Office website).
7 Dame Janet Smith, Shipman Inquiry, First report, 'Death Disguised' (section 13.9), July 2002.
8 Evidence from Lucy Letby trial on 20 June 2023.
9 Evidence from Lucy Letby trial on 3 November 2022.
10 Evidence from Lucy Letby trial on 10 February 2023.
11 Shipman report, Vol 1.
12 Interview with mother of Babies E and F.
13 Lucy Letby evidence 18/5/23
14 Lucy Letby evidence 2/6/23
15 Cross-examination of Lucy Letby during her trial, 8 June 2023.
16 Source: International Classification of Diseases – World Health Organisation – ICD 11
17 Source: NHS – https://www.nhs.uk/mental-health/conditions/fabricated-or-induced-illness/overview/
18 BBC *Panorama* interview with Dawn.
19 Allitt Inquiry report, 5.7.4
20 Richard Henriques, Crime to Crime: Harold Shipman to Operation Midland – 17 cases that shocked the world (London: Hodder, 2020), p. 83.
21 Shipman Inquiry, Report One, 13.21.

Postcript

1 Statement given to the Daily Telegraph by Alison Kelly and reported on 18 August 2023. https://www.telegraph.co.uk/news/2023/08/18/hospital-bosses-countess-chester-lucy-letby-baby-ward/#:~:text=In%20a%20statement%20to%20The,that%20this%20happened%20to%20them.

Picture Credits

Acknowledgements

The Lucy Letby case is so emotive that the perils of speaking about it for those involved are considerable. Despite this, many people who either knew Lucy Letby or were involved in her case did agree to speak to us and we are immensely grateful to all of them. There are plenty for whom Letby's guilt is not in doubt. Others believe she is innocent. Some are not completely sure either way. Every one of those who spoke to us did so, we believe, out of a sincere concern for the truth.

In addition to those with direct involvement in the case, we would like to thank the many experts who helped us in our efforts to grapple with the science and other complexities of the story. These include Professor Joseph Wolfsdorf, Dr Alan Wayne Jones, Dr Simon Mitchell, Allison Mitchell, Dr Angus Jones, Professor Rousseau Gama, Professor Mark Freestone, Dr Michael Crawford, Sir Richard Henriques, Professor David Wilson, Pete Weatherby KC, Nazir Afzal, Elizabeth Cook and Julia Quenzler. Most of the medical and scientific experts we spoke to did not wish to be named, but gave up hours of their time to help us. We are indebted to them all.

We are also grateful to our editors and senior colleagues at the BBC who gave us moral support and the time and space to write this book.

Special thanks are due to our agent Natasha Fairweather, who first came to us with the idea for this project and has been a pillar of support and wisdom, and our editor at Orion, Vicky Eribo. We couldn't have hoped to work with better people.

Finally, we would like to thank our families for their love, support and patience during many months of intense writing. From Jonathan, love and thanks to Sinéad, Bill, Maggie and Amie. From Judith, to Nick, Dan, Orli and Eden - my love and gratitude always.